The Guest Beer Guide 1997

SCOTLAND
M9
M90
M8
M8
M74
A74(M)
NORTHUMBERLAND
TYNE AND WEAR
DURHAM
M6
CUMBRIA
A1(M)
YORKSHIRE
ISLE OF MAN
LANCS
M55
M65
M62
M1
M18
M80
M58
GRTR. MANCHESTER
MERSEYSIDE
M62
M56
CHESHIRE
DERBS.
NOTTS.
LINCOLNSHIRE
M6
M1
STAFFS.
M54
SHROPSHIRE
M42
LEICS.
NORFOLK
WEST MIDLANDS
M6
M45
NORTHANTS.
CAMBS.
WALES
M5
M42
WARWICKS.
SUFFOLK
HEREFORD & WORCS.
M1
BEDS.
M1
A1(M)
M11
M40
BUCKS
M50
GLOS.
OXON
HERTS
ESSEX
M5
M40
M25
M4
M4
GREATER LONDON
M4
BERKS
WILTS.
M3
M25
M20
M2
SURREY
KENT
M20
SOMERSET
HANTS.
M23
WEST SUSSEX
EAST SUSSEX
M27
M27
DEVON
M5
DORSET
I.O.W.
CORNWALL

The Guest Beer Guide 1997

by

GRAHAM TITCOMBE

and

NICOLAS ANDREWS

foulsham

LONDON • NEW • YORK • TORONTO • SYDNEY

foulsham

The Publishing House, Bennetts Close,
Cippenham, Berkshire SL1 5AP, England.

While every effort has been made to ensure the accuracy of all the information contained within this book, neither the authors nor the publisher can be liable for any errors. The publisher would welcome letters of correction and further information.

ISBN 0–572-02220-4

Typeset by Brains Typography, Reading.
Printed in Great Britain by St Edmundsbury Press, Bury St. Edmonds, Suffolk.

CONTENTS

INTRODUCTION

Cans, kegs and widgets, sparklers, gases – even a slice of lime. The multi-national conglomerates that still dictate much of the British beer-drinking market will stop at nothing in their determined drive to make their latest product appear new, exciting and the ultimate accessory for the sophisticated drinker. Presentation and image are all: huge sums are spent on advertising and packaging; film stars and stand-up comedians are employed to try and make you, the consumer, believe that whatever they finally force down your neck really is the final word in state-of-the-art British brewing. It ain't what you drink, it's who sees you drinking it.

As the trends move relentlessly on, from Third-World imports to ice beers to can-conditioned creamy confections that in one case, apparently, doubles up as moisturiser, the shallowness of all this image control becomes increasingly clear. Alcoholic lemonade is all very well, but will they be encouraging you to drink it in 12 months time? And if not, why not?

Fortunately, at the same time, there is an ever-increasing band of independent micro-brewers and discerning drinkers who have discovered that the best way to move forward is in fact to take a step back. Modern methods and the latest in brewing expertise can be successfully allied to a product that has served us well for centuries. The problems associated with producing *real* real ale, which the big drinks companies were so keen to exaggerate 30 years ago, can be and have been overcome. The best beers in Britain are now brewed, transported and then served to perfection. They need no advance advertising or heavy promotion for these are products that speak for themselves.

The exclusive world of truly traditional brewing is closer to that of the makers of fine wines than of fine television commercials. Once tasted, these beers will hook you forever and draw you in. All other ales will be exposed as the pale and unsophisticated imitations that they really are.

The Guest Beer Guide is a celebration of these brews and of the brewers for whom quality, not quantity, is all that matters. Other guides do an admirable job in listing those pubs with handpumps or by telling you about the impressive architecture, decor and food to be found at inns around the country. In this book, it is quite simply the beer that counts – and not just any old beer at that. Use this guide and lose yourself in an exhilarating world of exceptional craftsmen and exquisite tastes. Timeless techniques and sufficient attention to detail ensure that never again need you be disappointed by the product in your glass.

We tell you where to go to find beers of the finest character and complexity, served by enthusiasts who really care about what you are drinking. We explain why the way it is stored and served is as important as the contents of the barrel itself. And we invite you to help us to put the very best beers in Britain, and the brewers and barmen responsible for them, on the map so that, having travelled to the pubs we list, hopefully, that first sip from the first pint will tell you that you have truly arrived.

THE HISTORY OF BEER

Possibly discovered as a result of airborne wild yeast infecting open food, the art of brewing originated in Mesopotamia, between 8000 and 6000 BC. Slowly, the secret spread to Greece, Egypt and eventually to Rome. It was Caesar's invading army that brought beer to Britain in 55 AD.

Roman aristocracy still preferred to drink wine but, over the centuries, beer became an important source of nutrition for the native Britons and was often safer to drink than water. Beer continued to thrive long after the Romans had gone, and more than 40 breweries were listed in the Domesday Book of 1086.

Hops, which impart flavour, aroma and act as a preservative, were initially introduced from Scandinavia in the middle of the tenth century, but they were not widely used until the fifteenth century, when growing became widespread in Kent.

Brewing took place in monasteries and the monks improved brewing techniques and introduced better varieties of barley. But, during Henry VIII's break with Rome in the 1530s, the monasteries were abolished and their land and assets seized by the crown. The noble art passed into the hands of farmers and owners of landed estates, who installed private brewhouses which provided beer for farm workers and staff. These were the forerunners of the breweries we have today.

Commercial breweries began to set up in business during the latter part of the sixteenth century, growing steadily in number until around 30,000 breweries were registered in Great Britain in the 1870s, when beer drinking per head of the population was at its peak. Breweries were then found serving local communities throughout the British Isles. Even small towns could support such establishments. The Beer Act of 1830 permitted any householder to obtain a licence from the excise authorities allowing them to brew and sell beer on the premises. But, gradually, home-brewing went into decline. New taxes were levied on malt and hops which accelerated this demise until, by the end of the nineteenth century, the market was dominated by commercial brewers.

Many of these, too, have now gone, either bought up and closed down by large national breweries or, unable to survive in an increasingly competitive market, having simply faded away. A considerable number of excellent breweries have been lost with them and only 55 of the independent breweries that were in operation at the turn of the century still brew today.

Of these, Shepherd Neame Ltd at Faversham in Kent is believed to be the oldest. Beer has been produced on the same site without interruption since the brewery's official foundation in 1698. Britain's oldest surviving brew-pub is believed to be the Blue Anchor at Helston in Cornwall. It first became a pub around the middle of the sixteenth century, although it seems certain that monks were already brewing beer on the premises long before then.

The title of the oldest pub in Britain probably belongs to the Trip to Jerusalem in Nottingham, part of which is cut into the rock of the castle and dates from 1189. This was once the malthouse for the castle brewery.

Although brewing technology may have progressed over the centuries, the process and basic ingredients have changed very little. Today, real ales still arrive at the pub with live yeast and fermentable sugars present in the brew, allowing the final stages of fermentation to take place in the cellar. This produces a fresh, pert, rounded flavour and natural effervescence. This is beer at its very best, and part of the proud tradition which spans the centuries.

Happily, new breweries are again setting up across the land and total around 400, a considerable improvement on the situation of just 20 years ago. The real ale cause is a rare triumph for quality and tradition in an age of all-consuming commercialism.

What went wrong

Many pubs originally brewed their own beer in an outbuilding or similar adjacent place, often drawing water from a spring or well beneath. Frequently it was the lady of the house who did the brewing while her husband worked elsewhere.

But cask-conditioned beers tended to be unreliable and were too often not properly looked after in the cellar. To overcome this problem, the larger brewers turned to bottles and keg beers which, though bland and characterless by comparison, were consistent and had a much longer shelf life. They were easy to transport and easy to look after. Huge investments were made in kegs, equipment and advertising and, by the middle of the 1960s, real ale had all but disappeared from the British pub. Watneys Red Barrel, Worthington E and Double Diamond became the order of the day.

Just four of the once ubiquitous brewpubs remained and, as recently as 1985, there were fewer than 150 independent breweries in operation. Lager, too, although a poor imitation of some of the excellent continental brews, became increasingly successful in Britain, due largely to massive advertising campaigns which targeted the trend-conscious younger drinker. The national breweries had imposed their corporate will to increase profits at the expense of quality. Real ale sales continued to decline to the verge of extinction.

Though consistent, keg beer is a disappointing substitute for the natural product. It starts life as real ale but, prior to filling into containers, the beer is filtered, pasteurised and chilled. This process destroys and removes the yeast, preventing any further fermentation, and ensures that the beer is clear and bright in the keg.

But the beer is now dead. It produces no natural carbon dioxide and lacks the depth of character that cask-conditioned beers offer. In an effort to overcome this problem, they are now frequently served using a mixture of nitrogen and carbon dioxide, which gives the beer a tighter, creamy head in the glass while reducing the overall fizziness associated with carbon dioxide dispense. The result can be compared with drinking cappuccino, which often uses the cheapest coffee beans available but becomes acceptable when frothed.

Additionally, no work is required in the pub cellar to bring keg beer into condition. It can be dispensed upon receipt and will remain servable, under the layer of gas used to dispense it, for many weeks. Consequently, no skill is required of the cellarman and very few keg beers are unfit to be served, necessitating their return to the brewery.

Little wonder that the national brewers, and some publicans too, would prefer it if cask-conditioned beers quietly faded away.

The Real Ale Revival

Over the past 20 years, due to the dedication of a number of small brewery owners and the campaigning efforts of CAMRA (Campaign for Real Ale), the country's excellent real ales have gradually been rediscovered and Britain's great heritage of independent breweries is now thriving once more.

A change in the law known as The Beer Orders has helped, too, permitting pubs previously tied to one brewery for all beer supplies to take one guest beer from elsewhere. This has increased considerably the potential market for the smaller independent suppliers.

The European Commission is currently reviewing the block exemption, which permits Britain's brewers to retain the tied-pub system. Politicians in Brussels are arguing that British pubs should no longer be allowed to favour British brewers at the expense of their continental counterparts. The outcome of this will be known during 1997.

While some would argue that the tied pub system works against the smaller breweries which are unable to supply beer at sufficiently competitive prices, if at all, there is a strongly held view among larger independents and regional brewers that complete abolition of the system could result in the closure of some breweries which would no longer be able to rely on the necessary guaranteed outlets for their brews.

Meanwhile, new micro-breweries are springing up all over the country. These operate on a much smaller scale, so costs and overheads are much smaller. The micro-brewers concentrate, at least initially, on supplying a limited range of pubs. Some brewpubs produce beer on the premises that is not available anywhere else.

Not to be outdone, most existing brewers are adding new beers to their portfolios too. Today, there are approximately 400 independent breweries in Britain providing well over 1000 beers of widely varying styles and character, plus a plethora of one-off special or occasional brews. Wheat, tandoori, garlic, vanilla, melon, coriander, lemon, orange, strawberry and liquorice are just a few of the flavours on offer, in addition to the whole raft of more traditional beers.

Fortunately, more and more enterprising publicans are now offering these delightful brews and the revived interest in cask-conditioned beers has produced a new breed of drinker, the "Scooper" or "Ticker", who will often travel many miles just to find a new beer.

The market should easily be able to support the current crop of independents and those that produce good brews of consistent quality and possess sufficient marketing and distribution skills should continue to thrive. But, the national brewers have not gone to sleep. Keg beer, dispensed using mixed gases in an effort to mimic the character of real ale, is gaining ground on the back of multi-million pound marketing campaigns. But why drink a substitute when the real thing is available from the independent breweries in so many pubs throughout Britain?

If you take the trouble to search those pubs out, you will undoubtedly enjoy the best beer that Britain has to offer and help to prevent a return to the dark days of the 1960s and 70s.

THE BREWING PROCESS

The brewing process is a delicate one and most brewers inevitably experience occasional problems. The very nature of ale makes it impossible to produce a consistently uniform product, barrel after barrel, month after month. Also, brewers will be constantly striving to improve and refine the quality of the beer they produce.

Of course, this is part of the attraction for the real ale drinker. There is nothing like the experience of discovering new tastes and drinking sensations, and it places a premium on the skills and experience of both the brewer and the publican. But this inconsistency is something that the makers of bland, uniform keg beers are also keen to emphasise.

The slightest variation in established practice or, more commonly, yeast infections, equipment failures, change in water or ingredient sources can upset the brewing process and affect the resulting beer. Often, a combination of these elements causes problems. No matter how much care is taken, it is simply not feasible to expect every new brew to taste and behave just the same as it did the last time. But each one must be of a similar high standard and as consistent as possible.

It is not unknown for beers that are particularly popular to become inconsistent. One beer which won a prestigious award in 1994 became steadily less recognisable as the months went by, only returning to its former excellence a short time before judging was due for the CAMRA Great British Beer Festival in 1995. Almost certainly, increased demand had prompted short cuts to be taken and beer to be sent out "green" or too soon.

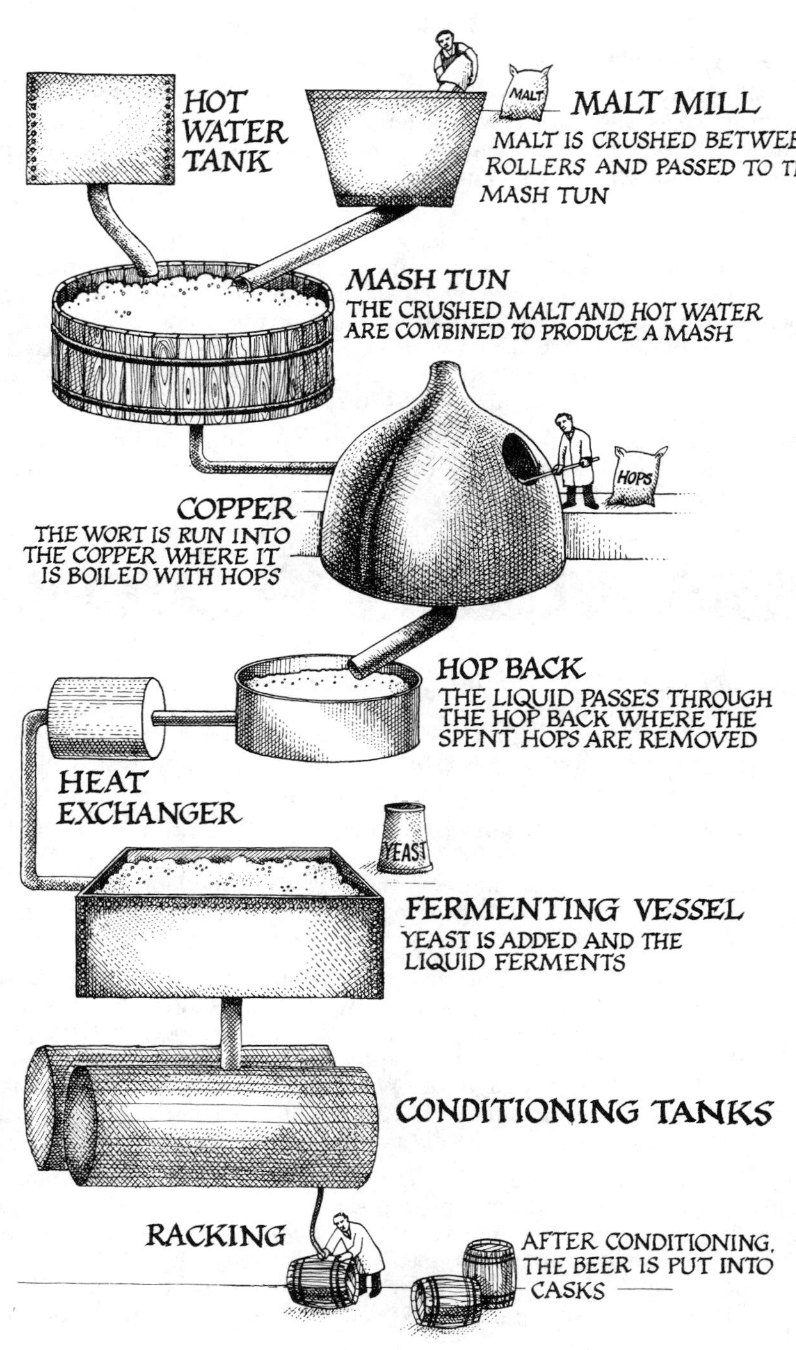
HOT WATER TANK
MALT
MALT MILL
MALT IS CRUSHED BETWEEN ROLLERS AND PASSED TO THE MASH TUN
MASH TUN
THE CRUSHED MALT AND HOT WATER ARE COMBINED TO PRODUCE A MASH
HOPS
COPPER
THE WORT IS RUN INTO THE COPPER WHERE IT IS BOILED WITH HOPS
HOP BACK
THE LIQUID PASSES THROUGH THE HOP BACK WHERE THE SPENT HOPS ARE REMOVED
HEAT EXCHANGER
YEAST
FERMENTING VESSEL
YEAST IS ADDED AND THE LIQUID FERMENTS
CONDITIONING TANKS
RACKING
AFTER CONDITIONING, THE BEER IS PUT INTO CASKS

Barley, which the Mesopotamians were lucky enough to have growing wild, is still an important ingredient for beer making today. It is soaked in water, then spread over the floor of the malthouse and gently heated to promote germination. This releases sugars, which are vital for fermentation. The barley is constantly raked to ensure even germination throughout. Once the grains start to produce rootlets, they are roasted to prevent further germination. The higher the temperature, the darker the malt will be, and the beer produced from it will be darker, with a more roasted flavour. Pale malt will impart a sweeter, more delicate flavour to the brew.

MALT MILL

At the brewery, the malt is passed through rollers in the malt mill, which crushes the grains releasing the soluble starch.

MASH TUN

The malt is passed from the malt mill into the mash tun where it is mixed with hot water or "liquor". This is known as "mashing" and converts the soluble starches into fermentable and non fermentable sugars. Depending on the type of beer required a mix of malts may be used.

Water used in the brewing process is usually treated in order to remove any unwanted characteristics, and to emulate water found in other areas, which is considered most suitable to the style of beer required.

The "mash" is thoroughly stirred then allowed to stand until it becomes clear, when it is known as "wort".

THE COPPER

The wort is then run into the copper, where it is boiled and hops are added. At this stage, various "adjuncts" may be added to the wort, such as invert sugar, to increase fermentability, but any additive is considered by many to be an insult to the brewer's art.

Depending on the variety used, hops impart bitterness of flavour or aroma and help to prevent infection in the wort. A mixture of hops may be used.

But, they were not always popular with everyone. Henry VIII objected to this foreign habit of putting hops into beer and suggested that it should be outlawed but, fortunately, the noble hop survived.

Of the many varieties available, those most commonly used in Britain are still the Golding and the Fuggle, although other types are rapidly finding favour.

Unfortunately, some brewers substitute hop oils but it is widely felt that this has a detrimental effect on the flavour of the finished brew. Perhaps we should learn from some of our continental friends where this practice would contravene purity laws.

The wort will remain in the copper for 1 to 2 hours.

HOP BACK

From the copper the wort is then passed through the hop back where the spent hops are removed.

HEAT EXCHANGER

On its way to the fermenting vessel, the wort is passed through a heat exchanger, where its temperature is reduced to 20°C. This is important to produce ideal conditions for the yeast. Extremes of temperature will either kill the yeast or result in a sluggish fermentation.

FERMENTING VESSEL

The wort is now "pitched" or has yeast added. It will remain here for around five days, the yeast feeding on the fermentable sugars, while excreting alcohol and producing carbon dioxide.

A thick creamy head of yeast builds up in the fermentation vessel, which is skimmed and retained for further use. But, as the yeast in the brew becomes tired and much of the sugar has been converted to alcohol, the process slows down. The primary fermentation is now over, and it is at this point that beer produced for the keg will go its separate way.

CONDITIONING TANKS

At this stage, beer is said to be "green" and the flavour is harsh. It is passed into conditioning tanks, where it will remain for several days, and much of the remaining sugar will ferment out to produce a more rounded flavour.

RACKING

At last, the beer is ready to be put into the cask, or "racked". By now, any harsh or undesirable flavours will have disappeared, but the brew will be crisp and fresh.

Finings, which draw the dying yeast cells to the bottom of the cask, are added allowing the beer to "drop bright" or clear down.

Some fermentable sugars and living yeast cells remain, so the beer continues to ferment in the cask. Sometimes, priming sugar will be added to assist this secondary fermentation. Hops may also be added to impart a hoppy aroma to the brew.

Once in the pub cellar, the beer will continue to ferment, producing carbon dioxide, which gives real ale its natural vitality.

The finings will clear the beer down until it is bright, and the cask will then be tapped, in preparation for use. This final stage, which is known as cask-conditioning, typically takes two or three days and brings the beer naturally to perfection. It should now be served as soon as possible.

TRAVELLING BEER

Assuming that a beer is in the proper condition when it leaves the brewery, plenty of damage can still be done during distribution. Most beers will "travel" providing that they are properly handled.

The brew within the cask is a living product that must be treated with respect if it is ultimately to be served at its best. Every time a cask is rolled, the finings, which draw all the solid matter to the bottom of the cask, are activated and these will work effectively for approximately five cask rollings.

Therefore, a cask from a brewer in Scotland arriving at a pub in Cornwall may well have been moved between wholesalers and rolled a number of times. It may also have been in transit too long, having been left in various stores en route, and so be nearing the end of its life even before it arrives. The result will almost certainly be a lifeless, dull brew lacking in any subtlety of flavour.

Extremes of temperature can also prevent a brew from getting into condition properly and dropping clear and bright. Casks may be left in very hot or cold conditions, in warehouses, garages or on the back of vehicles where there is no temperature control equipment. This, too, may result in a brew being damaged before it arrives at the pub and, unfortunately, the publican will not know about this until it is too late.

Co-operation is the answer. Regional and larger independent brewers have, for some time, also offered beers from other breweries and an increasing number of the smaller independents are now offering their product wholesale in an effort to improve turnover and distribution. Delivering beers to a brewery in another part of the country, while collecting that brewery's beer for sale with one's own, is obviously of great benefit to both parties. These beers are likely to be subjected to a minimum amount of movement and a shorter transit time, resulting in beer reaching the pub in a much better condition than if it had been shipped from wholesaler to wholesaler.

So, it is very much in a publican's interest to deal directly with the breweries wherever possible and to avoid brews from wholesalers which may arrive via a devious route. It is important, too, to boycott any source of supply if it proves necessary to return more than the occasional cask. Having said that, there are some excellent real ale wholesalers operating in Britain. The key is to find them and then deal with them only, even if this ultimately limits the range of beers on offer.

IN THE CELLAR

During the hot summer of 1995, pubs were on the receiving end of an unusually high proportion of brews that were sour or, more usually, which would not "drop bright". With limited cellar capacity, this can cause problems. Many publicans pursuing a more adventurous guest beer policy found it necessary to restrict the range of beers on offer in order to maintain quality and availability at the bar.

Unlike keg beer, cask-conditioned brews are alive and have not finished fermenting when they are delivered to the pub. The final stages of the conditioning process take place in the cellar before the beer is served. Temperature control and cleanliness are therefore vital if the beer is to drop clear and bright and without infection. Additionally, good stock control and rapid turnover combined with regular beer line cleaning are essential if each pint is to be served in peak condition.

A small amount of beer is inevitably lost when spilling and tapping each cask and, no matter how carefully it may be stooped, some beer will always be unservable. For this reason, many licensees prefer to buy larger casks in order to minimise wastage, but this often results in casks remaining on-line in the cellar for too long. Once a beer has worked into condition, it will remain at its best for a relatively short period of time. Every pint pulled draws more air into the cask, increasing the rate of oxidisation. If a beer remains on-line for four or five days, not unusual in some pubs, although still drinkable, it will be well past its best.

Controversially, in order to prevent air being taken into the cask, some cellarmen use a cask breather system, which maintains a blanket of carbon dioxide on top of the beer. The gas is at a much lower pressure than that used for the dispensing of keg beer, so there is relatively little absorbence, although it is often detectable as a pint is served.

Some drinkers also believe that the flavour of the beer is impaired by this, although blind tasting tests have not proved that this is so. While it is certainly better than serving a beer that is out of condition, this process inevitably offends the purist and so it is surely preferable to use smaller containers that allow the beer to be served naturally and at its best.

The method of dispensing beer has also become a very contentious issue and there are few hard and fast rules. Many people object to long "swan necks" or multi-holed sparklers on the end of a handpump, although some beers are brewed specifically to be served in this way. Some beer is at its best served through the conventional slit-type sparkler and short neck, although some brews lose much of their condition and hoppiness if served through any form of sparkler at all. In such cases, the beer should be served straight from the barrel if all its subtleties of flavour are to be enjoyed to the full.

Different beers are at their best served in different ways. To insist that all sparklers are an abomination or that all beer is at its best straight from the wood, is to misunderstand the nature of cask-conditioned beers.

SMALL IS BEAUTIFUL

So many things can go wrong between the start of the brewing process and the presentation of the pint at the bar and inconsistency, for whatever reason, inevitably plays right into the hands of the big, national brewers. They have the ability to undercut smaller breweries on price and to capitalise on first-class marketing and distribution expertise.

Recently, the introduction of nitro-keg products to the market has also proved a great success. Keg beer is served using a mixture of carbon dioxide and nitrogen to give it a tighter, creamier head. The beer itself may be bland, but such products are becoming increasingly popular. With all the investment tied up in kegs and plant, national and larger independent brewers will understandably continue to look for new ways to utilise existing equipment.

Most so-called freehouses still retain some type of trading agreement with a particular brewery and many emerging brewers have difficulty finding regular outlets for their beers. Frequently unable to raise money to buy a pub, a publican will borrow additional funds from a national brewer. Conditions will obviously be attached to such loans, usually in the form of stipulated barrelage figures. A pub will be required to serve a certain amount of a particular well-known beer.

Such a policy leaves the publican with little room for manoeuvre. A guest beer may prove more popular than the permanent offering and it will then be difficult to honour the commitment to the national brewer, resulting in stiff financial penalties. National brewers have also been know to offer financial inducements to a publican to drop a guest beer not supplied by them if it becomes too popular. Additionally, most trading agreements provide discounts, which may be substantial in certain cases.

A publican operating a true freehouse, free of all ties and agreements, and providing a constantly changing range of unusual guest beers, will probably not deal with any one source in sufficient volume to receive much, if any, discount. Even by reducing his profit margins to significantly below the accepted norm, he may struggle to sell his beers at a competitive rate. Only by then increasing the volume of beer sold can he hope to survive.

Little wonder then that most publicans are not prepared to take such risks and so stick to a regular range of guest beers upon which good discounts are available. In areas where beer is traditionally cheaper, or where there are high levels of unemployment, these discounts can be critical to a pub's survival and so few publicans are likely to risk their livelihood by pursuing an adventurous guest beer policy.

THE NEXT 1000 YEARS

One priceless commodity that the small, independent brewer can use in his favour is the British drinking public's insatiable curiosity. The pub remains an integral part of our way of life, just as it has done for several hundred years, and the national brewers know only too well that there will always be a market for something new and exciting.

So, the brewer who puts the quality of his product first will always find a market of potential pub-goers easy to try something different and something which represents good value for money. Seasonal ales and celebration brews are an excellent way to revive flagging interest.

Even for those drinkers who believe they already know what they like, a degree of variety remains the key. And once the pub-goer knows that he can trust a particular publican, whether he knows the beer in question or not, a bond is established that can be nurtured and strengthened.

When it comes to real ale, you cannot have too much of a good thing, so independent pub chains that can afford to are rapidly adding new sites to their estates. Many large towns and cities now boast a number of group-owned pubs offering a good range of brews from the independent breweries. Their purchasing power allows them to be very competitive, although they are usually still subject to some trading agreements which can limit the range of beers available.

One day, perhaps, everyone will get the message, but it can still prove frustratingly difficult to find good-quality beers from the smaller and new independent breweries even when visiting the area in which they are produced. Independent brewers today still supply less than 15 per cent of the beer found in Britain's pubs and clubs.

However, that 15 per cent can and is rising as pub-goers discover the delights of real ale in increasing numbers. And so there is a growing band of true freehouses, some with an interesting range of tried and tested beers and others serving a constantly changing range of guest beers from across the British Isles, including those from the smallest and newest breweries.

The pubs that you will find in the pages that follow vary in character from the basic back-street boozer to the idyllic country inn, but all offer beer well worth searching out. So, while we enjoy British beer at its best, let us spare a thought for brews unlucky enough to be sent to the keg. Cold, devoid of character and flavour and dependent on a gas cylinder for life ... a sad existence indeed.

Even today's commercial giants have been unable to substitute their lifeless, pale imitations for the real thing. Instinctively, one recognises the genuine article, regardless of hype and advertising. Britain's independent brewers have been producing traditional ales for 1000 years. They have withstood the test of time, even through adversity, with banners held high. Let us drink to them, and the next 1000 years.

THE TOP 100 BEERS IN BRITAIN

Most regular drinkers still appreciate a first-class pint that they may have tried before more than an indifferent brew, no matter how new or exotic. But fortunately, there are pubs where both of these needs can be satisfied. For an increasing number of publicans serving beer in peak condition, an interesting guest beer policy remains paramount, and so it is possible to find beers from Orkney in Cornwall, and brews from Jersey in Cumbria.

We all have our favourite real ales but, given the amazing variety of character and flavours that are produced from such a limited number of ingredients, these obviously vary from individual to individual.

Lighter, paler brews are generally more popular during the summer months, while porters and stouts come into their own when the weather is colder. There are, however, certain brews that, regardless of style and time of year, prove to be most popular.

Graham Titcombe, who currently owns the Bell Inn at Pensax, Worcestershire serves a constantly changing range of brews from the independent breweries. From records kept of almost 2000 different beers served there and at his previous pub, over a five year period, it has been possible to compile a list of drinkers' favourite 100 brews.

The picture is constantly changing, with many new beers and breweries appearing, so although many of the beers displayed here are familiar favourites, there are a number of welcome newcomers.

Those beers for which, despite all our efforts, we can find no pump label are represented by a slate, as shown right.

1 Hop Back:
Summer Lightning
Wiltshire

2 Exmoor: Gold
Somerset

3 Archers: Golden
Wiltshire

4 Enville: Ale
West Midlands

5 Bathams: Best Bitter
West Midlands

6 Otter: Bright
Devon

7 Timothy Taylor: Landlord
Yorkshire

8 Cheriton: Diggers Gold
Hampshire

9 Woodforde's: Wherry
Norfolk

10 Black Sheep: Special Strong
Yorkshire

11 Moorhouses: Pendle Witches Brew
Lancashire

12 Berrow: Topsy Turvy
Somerset

13 Hardys Hanson:
Kimberley Classic
Nottinghamshire

14 Sarah Hughes: Dark Ruby Mild
West Midlands

15 Hook Norton: Old Hooky
Oxfordshire

16 Kelham Island: Golden Eagle
Yorkshire

17 Bull's Head: Light
Warwickshire

18 Mauldons: White Adder
Suffolk

19 Mordue: Workie Ticket
Tyne & Wear

20 Ringwood: Old Thumper
Hampshire

21 Leatherbritches: Ashbourne
Derbyshire

22 Cartmel: Lakeland Gold
Cumbria

23 Rebellion: Mutiny
Buckinghamshire

24 Cotleigh: Tawny
Somerset

25 Holdens: Special
West Midlands

26 Oakham: JHB
Leicestershire

27 Hexhamshire: Whapweazel
Northumberland

28 Kelham Island: Pale Rider
Yorkshire

29 Ballards: Golden Bine
Hampshire

30 Goachers: Special
Kent

31 Mildmay: Colours Best
Devon

32 Titanic: Captain Smith's
Staffordshire

33 Bunces: Danish Dynamite
Wiltshire

34 Hogs Back: Hop Garden Gold
Surrey

35 Harviestoun: Schiehallion
Scotland

36 Exmoor: Ale
Somerset

37 Hopback: Thunderstorm
Wiltshire

38 Morrells: Varsity
Oxfordshire

39 Earl Soham: Albert Ale
Suffolk

40 Ushers: Founders
Wiltshire

41 Yates: Premium
Cumbria

42 Ridleys: Rumpus
Essex

43 West Berkshire: Long Dog
Berkshire

44 Enville: Gothic
West Midlands

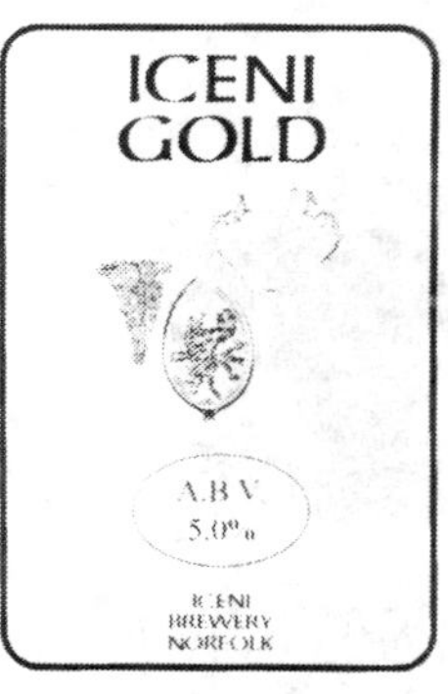

45 Iceni: Gold
Norfolk

46 Church End: GMT
West Midlands

47 Berkley: Lurcher
Gloucestershire

48 Ringwood: XXXX Porter
Hampshire

49 Shardlow: Alternative Lager
Leicestershire

50 Adnams: Bitter
Suffolk

51 Exmoor: Beast
Somerset

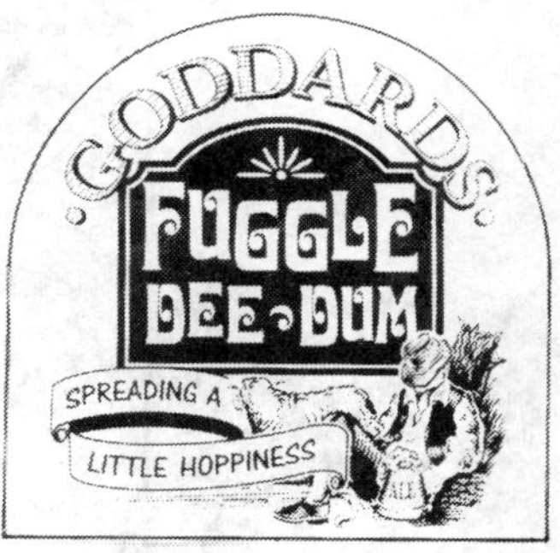

52 Goddards: Fuggle de dum
Isle of Wight

53 Frog Island: Best
Northamptonshire

54 Smiles: Mayfly
Avon

55 Barnsley Brewing: Barnsley Bitter
Yorkshire

56 Vale: Notley Ale
Buckinghamshire

57 Salopian: Minsterley
Shropshire

58 Bateman: Victory
Lincolnshire

59 Dark Star: Skinners Dunroamin
Sussex

60 Hesket Newmarket: Doris' 90th Birthday
Cumbria

61 Wadworth: Farmers Glory
Wiltshire

62 Old Mill: Traditional
Yorkshire

63 Townes: GMT
Derbyshire

64 Traquair: Bear Ale
Scotland

65 Hardington: Old Ale
Avon

66 Goffs: Jouster
Gloucestershire

67 Moorhouses: Owd Ale
Lancashire

69 Burtonwood: Bitter
Cheshire

68 Cannon Royal: Buckshot
Hereford & Worcester

70 Lloyds: VIP
Derbyshire

71 Dent: Aviator
Cumbria

72 Mitchells: Lancaster Bomber
Lancashire

73 Sharp's: Cornish Coaster
Cornwall

74 Wye Valley: Hereford Pale Ale
Hereford & Worcester

75 Arundel: Wheatsheaf
Sussex

76 Hampshire: Ironside
Hampshire

77 Hilden: Strong Irish Festival Ale
Northern Ireland

78 Gibbs Mew: Bishops Tipple
Wiltshire

79 Durham: Canny Lad
County Durham

80 Maypole: Celebration
Nottinghamshire

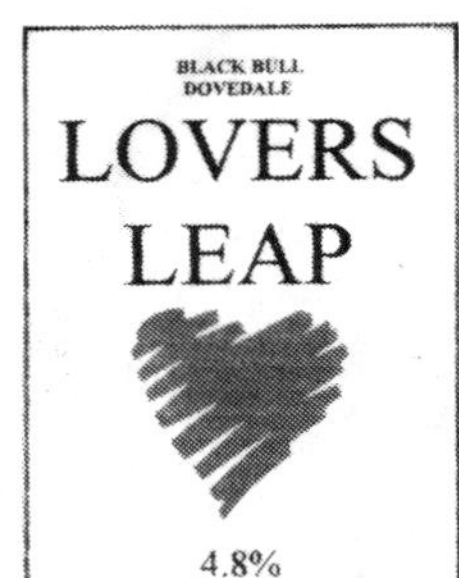

82 Black Bull: Lovers Leap
Derbyshire

81 Jollyboat: Plunder
Devon

83 Featherstone: Best
Leicestershire

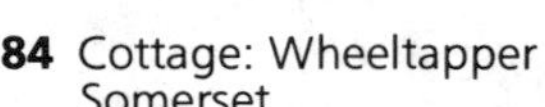

84 Cottage: Wheeltapper
Somerset

85 Harviestoun: Waverley 70/-
Scotland

87 Orkney: Skullsplitter
Scotland

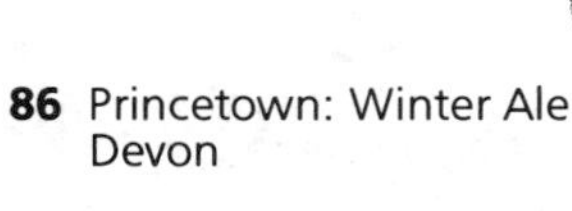

86 Princetown: Winter Ale
Devon

88 BlackMoor: Exhibitionism
Yorkshire

89 Border: Special
Northumberland

90 Wilds: Wild Oats
Yorkshire

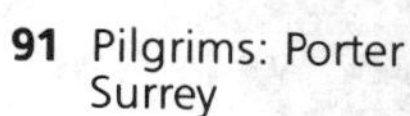

91 Pilgrims: Porter
Surrey

92 Wyre Piddle: Piddle in the Snow
Hereford & Worcester

93 Ash Vine: Stocking Filler
Somerset

94 Wickwar: Station Porter
Gloucestershire

95 Caledonian: Strong Ale
Scotland

96 Blewitts: Winter Ale
Devon

97 Hoskins & Oldfield: Old Navigation
Leicestershire

98 Crouch Vale: Willie Warmer
Essex

99 Rat & Ratchet: Cratchets Christmas Cracker
Yorkshire

100 Robinsons: Old Tom
Cheshire

HOW TO USE THIS BOOK

The Guest Beer Guide is a celebration of the rejuvenated art of brewing in Great Britain. Our concern, deliberately, is not with the often bland and certainly mass-produced market leaders, but simply with the smaller, independent makers of what we consider to be the *real* real ales. For this reason, we do not tell you about the big, multi-national brewers and their products, good or bad. Nor do we tell you about the pubs whose reputation owes more to their impressive location, their excellent cooking or their extensive range of malt whiskies. This is a book about beer and is aimed squarely at those who love drinking it, who want to know more about it and who want to know where to find it at its best. The entries within England are arranged alphabetically by county, taking into account the boundary changes that came into force on 1 April 1996. While plenty of people never got used to the last round of boundary changes and the new counties that resulted, this will inevitably cause some confusion.

For example, Avon, Cleveland and Humberside now no longer exist. Parts of these counties have been swallowed up by their recent neighbours and towns have returned to what many have always considered to be their spiritual homes. Elsewhere the situation is less simple and a large number of new unitary authorities have been established. Bristol, for example, is no longer at the heart of Avon, but nor has it returned to its Gloucestershire roots. Leicester has an authority of its own despite being located in the middle of the county of Leicestershire.

We have attempted to adopt a logical approach (incorporating Bristol within Gloucestershire and Leicester within Leicestershire etc) to minimise this confusion and to ensure that you have no trouble navigating your way around the book. Some border towns and villages may still surprise you, however. The postal address may be in one county whereas the actual pub or brewery is to be found over the boundary. We have tried to place all entries in the counties to which they actually belong (and not where the post office may indicate that they should be) so, be prepared for a bit of county-hopping when travelling along the borders.

Within each town, the brewery entries come first, followed by the brewpubs and then the pubs. We have attempted to give as full an address as possible and a telephone number in every case. Brief directions may also be found within the entry itself but, if you do get lost and there is no one available to ask, a call ahead should keep the inconvenience to a minimum.

Where possible, we have sought to include the licensee's name for we believe that the character and quality of a pub owes much to the person who runs it. Inevitably, these people move on and many enjoy the challenge of taking on a new pub and establishing its place on the map. While every acknowledgement should be made of the nation's finest innkeepers, this is more than just a chance for a publican to see his name in print. We hope that readers will recognise the people who run particularly successful pubs and, as they move, need no other recommendation to visit than the name of the man or woman whom they will find behind the bar.

Because we believe the beers are the most important thing to be found in a pub, we have sought to give an indication of the names and numbers of ales that you are likely to find when you walk through the door. Of course, there are few hard and fast rules. Availability varies and, on some days, the choice will probably be wider than on others. Nevertheless, a pub that says it has 12 beers on tap should come reasonably close to doing just that. If you discover this is simply not the case, then we want to know.

There is a short description of the type of pub to be found with each entry. We have not dwelt on the quality or selection of food served, but have simply indicated where it is or is not available. Equally, this is not a guide to bed and breakfast establishments but, where a pub has accommodation to offer, we have sought to say so.

Opening hours are another feature that will inevitably vary, particularly as the Government relaxes the licensing laws. An increasing number of pubs are opening for longer and later than was the case just a few years ago. However, we suggest that, if you are proposing to visit in the middle of the afternoon, for instance, a telephone call ahead will ensure that you are not disappointed.

At the back of the book you will find a chance to contribute to the success of next year's guide. We have already begun our research to ensure that it will be as accurate and comprehensive as possible, but we should be very grateful for your help. If an entry you visit fails to live up to expectations, then we want to know. Equally, there are many pubs that need to be considered for next year's guide that have not appeared this time around. Some parts of Britain are very poorly represented. *The Guest Beer Guide* has an important part to play in the nation's continued enjoyment of real ale at its best. The book's production is an ongoing and developing process and must rely in part on the good will of those who know about and love what they drink. So please give us the benefit of your experience and thank you, in advance, for your help.

Graham Titcombe and Nicolas Andrews

Bedford

Charles Wells

The Eagle Brewery,
Havelock Street,
Bedford MK40 4LU
☎ *(01234) 272766*
No visitors. Tied houses: 288

Charles Wells was born in Bedford in 1842. He left school at 14 and sailed to India and Australia, becoming a chief officer in 1868. His marriage plans were thwarted when his prospective father-in-law would not permit Josephine Grimbly to marry a sea captain, who would often be away for long periods at sea. Charles, determined to win her hand, embarked on a second career as a brewer. The Charles Wells Family Brewery was established in 1876 and is still owned and run by the family today. Each pint is brewed using water from a well that Charles sank himself. As the water from the well takes 70 years to reach its pure state, after filtering through numerous layers of rock, its availability is limited, and so demand for Charles Wells beers inevitably exceeds supply.

EAGLE 3.6% ABV
A notably dry, thirst-quenching IPA renowned for its full flavour and balance.

BOMBARDIER 4.3% ABV
A premium bitter with a distinctive rich copper colour and characteristic robust flavour derived from the finest barley malt and Challenger and Goldings hop.

FARGO 5.0% ABV
Charles Wells flagship ale, brewed to provide a uniquely smooth, fully matured flavour.

The Castle

17 Newnham Street,
Bedford MK40 3JR
☎ *(01234) 353295*
Michael Holmes

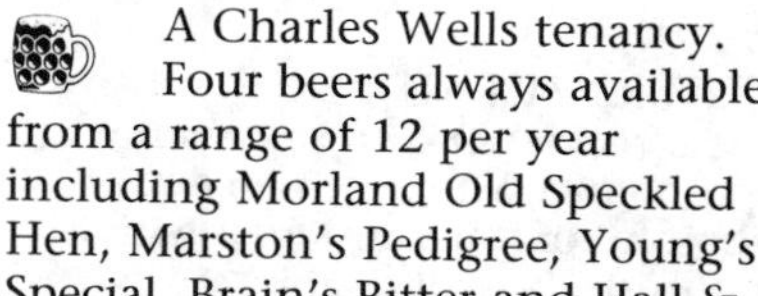

A Charles Wells tenancy. Four beers always available from a range of 12 per year including Morland Old Speckled Hen, Marston's Pedigree, Young's Special, Brain's Bitter and Hall & Woodhouse Tanglefoot.

Two-bar public house with good clientele and country pub atmosphere. Bar food available at lunchtime and evenings. Thai menu Monday to Thursday. Car park, accommodation. Children allowed at lunchtime only.

12–3pm and 5.30–11pm Mon–Thurs and Sun; all day Fri–Sat.

Shefford

B&T Brewery

The Brewery,
Shefford SG17 5DZ
☎ *(01462) 815080*
Visitors welcome. Tied houses: 1

Founded in 1981 in a small industrial unit, Banks & Taylor ran into financial difficulties in early 1994 and in April the receivers were called in. The following month, however, a new company led by Lewis Shepherd acquired all the trading rights and set up business with several of the old Banks & Taylor team.

Beers available at: The Two Brewers, 43 Dumfries Street, Luton, Bedfordshire *and* The Plough Inn, Tebworth Road, Wingfield, Bedfordshire.

SHEFFORD MILD 3.8% ABV
A mellow dark mild, dry

and hoppy, with a surprising richness.

SHEFFORD BITTER 3.8% ABV
A creamy-tasting, hoppy bitter, drinkable and refreshing with a warm light golden colour and a dry hop finish.

SHEFFORD PALE ALE 4.5% ABV
Warm reddish-brown in colour with a pronounced hoppy aroma. A mouthful of hops and malt with a dry finish, very drinkable.

DRAGONSLAYER 4.5% ABV
A refreshing sharp light golden beer with an excellent body.

EDWIN TAYLOR'S EXTRA STOUT 4.5% ABV
A creamy black stout.

SHEFFORD OLD STRONG 5.0% ABV
Paler than the name suggests, with a hoppy and fruity aroma. Bitter and malty on the tongue.

SHEFFORD OLD DARK 5.0% ABV
Deep rich red, with a pronounced caramel, fruit and hop aroma and a sweetish, malty flavour.

2XS 6.0% ABV
Golden in colour, with a rich aroma, slightly fruity undertones.

BLACK BAT 6.0% ABV
A powerful, sipping beer, ruby-black in colour, with a malty aroma.

OLD BAT 7.0 % ABV
A pale golden draught barley wine, dry and refreshing.

Plus various limited edition ales brewed and sold throughout the year.

STOTFOLD

ABEL BROWN'S BREWERY

The Stag Inn, Brook Street,
Stotfold SG5 4LA
☎ *(01462) 730261*
Ray Rudzki

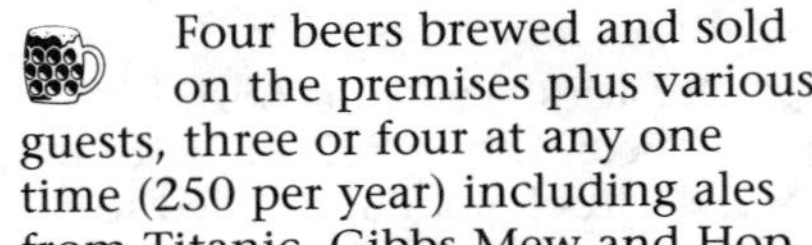

Four beers brewed and sold on the premises plus various guests, three or four at any one time (250 per year) including ales from Titanic, Gibbs Mew and Hop Back breweries.

Brewing only started here in Spring 1995. The brewery is named after the first publican of The Stag Inn. The beers are all named after traction engines. The pub, built in 1920, is set in a rural location. Thai and Indian restaurant food available in evenings. Car park, accommodation. Children allowed. One mile from A1 junction 10.

JACK OF HEARTS 4.0% ABV
A premium bitter with malty overtones and a dry finish.

LITTLE BILLY 4.0% ABV
A light-coloured pale ale.

POCOLOCO 5.0% ABV

PLOUGHMAN'S PICKLE 5.0% ABV
A strong brown ale.

12–2.30pm and 5–11pm Mon–Thurs; all day Fri–Sat; 12–10.30pm Sun.

WINGFIELD

The Plough Inn

Tebworth Road, Wingfield, Leighton Buzzard LU7 9QH
☎ *(01525) 873077*
Mr and Mrs Worsley

Seven beers permanently available including B&T Shefford Bitter and Black Bat. Also Fuller's London Pride. Also approx 140 guests per year including brews from Cotleigh, Morland, Wood and Eldridge Pope.

Thatched olde-English pub. CAMRA South Bedfordshire Pub of the Year 1993 and 1994. Bar food at lunchtime and evenings. Car park, garden, children's room and pool room. From M1 junction 12, follow the A5120 through Toddington to Houghton Regis. Turn off to Wingfield.

12–3pm and 6–11pm Mon–Sat; 12–3pm and 7–10.30pm Sun.

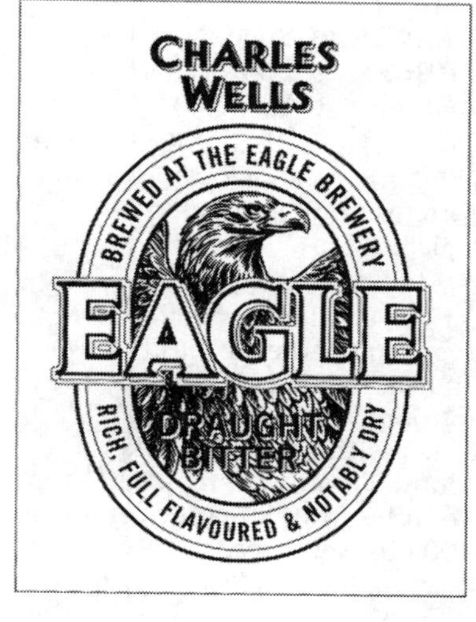

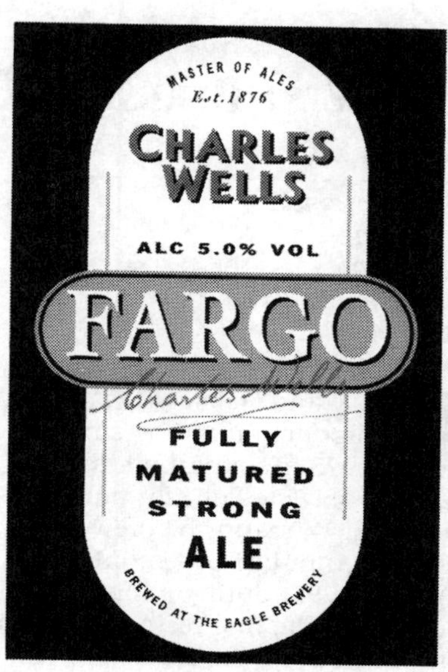

Aldworth

The Bell

Aldworth,
Nr Reading RG8 9SE
☎ *(01635) 578272*
Mr and Mrs IJ Macaulay

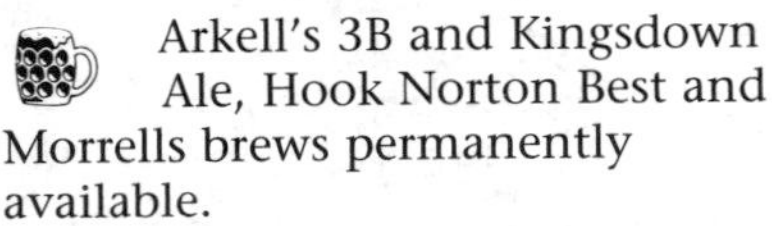

Arkell's 3B and Kingsdown Ale, Hook Norton Best and Morrells brews permanently available.

Small, unaltered inn dating from 1340. Bar food available at lunchtime and evenings. Well-behaved children allowed in the tap room. Car park and country garden with adjacent cricket ground. Good walking area. Approx two miles from Streatley on the B4009 to Newbury.

11am–3pm and 6–11pm Mon–Sat; 12–3pm and 7–10.30pm Sun.

Frilsham

The West Berkshire Brewery

Pot Kiln Lane,
Frilsham,
Yattendon,
Nr Newbury RG18 0XX
☎ *(01635) 202638*
Visitors by appointment

Dave and Helen Maggs started production in September 1995 in an outbuilding leased from The Pot Kiln pub at Frilsham. Work on the brewery was completed in just one month (August 1995) during a blistering heatwave. The first recipe was for a unique beer, Brick Kiln Bitter, and proved successful from the start. A second beer, Good Old Boy, was soon added to sell to other pubs and the novice brewers were delighted when this won an award in its first week of sale. This is now available in pubs near the brewery. Two winter beers are also available (Long Dog and Talon) and more seasonal beers are planned during 1996 based on recipes developed over years of home brewing, incorporating herbs and flowers appropriate to the time of year.

Beers available at: The Pot Kiln, Frilsham, Berkshire *and* The Bull Inn, Stamford Dingley, Berkshire.

BRICK KILN BITTER 4.0% ABV
A slightly sweet, fruity bitter. Sold only at The Pot Kiln.

GOOD OLD BOY 4.0% ABV
A darkish bitter with a full hop flavour suggesting a stronger brew.

Plus winter and seasonal brews.

Reading

The Hop Leaf

163–165 Southampton Street,
Reading RG1 2QZ
☎ *(01734) 314700*

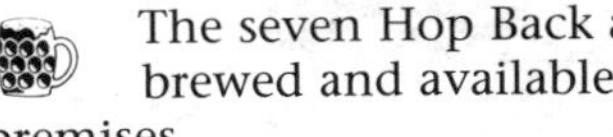

The seven Hop Back ales are brewed and available on the premises.

This formerly derelict pub was owned by Courage before being taken over and revitalised as a brewpub by the Hop Back Brewery. The five-barrel plant was brought in from the Wyndham Arms in Salisbury (Hop Back's original brewpub). The pub is a late Victorian building, recently refurbished. Parking can be difficult.

MILD 3.0% ABV

GFB 3.5% ABV

HOP LEAF 4.0% ABV

SUMMER LIGHTNING 5.0% ABV

RYE BEER 5.0% ABV

WHEAT BEER 5.0% ABV

EXTRA STOUT 4.0% ABV

12–11pm (10.30pm Sun).

The Hobgoblin

2 Broad Street,
Reading RG1 2BH
☎ *(01734) 508119*
Duncan Ward

Wychwood beers always available plus up to 700 guests per year exclusively from small independent brewers. No national products are stocked. Also real cider and perry and genuine German lager.

Small, friendly town-centre pub, full of locals. No jukebox but background blues, R&B etc. Occasional live music. Bare boards, traditional pub games. No pool table etc. Bar food available at lunchtime. Supervised children allowed in the rear of pub up to 7pm. Join CAMRA here.

All permitted hours.

WOKINGHAM

GREENWOOD'S BREWERY

Bell Farm, Bell Foundry Lane,
Wokingham RG11 5QF
☎ *(01734) 793516*
No visitors at present

Production began at this ten-barrel brew-length (full mash) brewery at the end of 1994 using ex-Trough Brewery equipment. The ales are brewed with floor-malted Maris Otter malt and whole hops with no other adjuncts employed. The range of beers varies throughout the year with seasonal and one-off brews produced to order. A porter or stout is planned. Beers are delivered direct locally and wholesalers are employed for further afield.

Beers available at: The Hobgoblin, 2 Broad Street, Reading, Berkshire *and* Watership Down Inn, Nr Overton, Hampshire.

MAHOGANY MILD 3.4% ABV
Malt, fruit jam and chocolate aromas. Smooth chewy malt in the mouth with nutty chocolate finish. A tasty mild full of dark malt character.

HOP POCKET BITTER 3.8% ABV
Citrus fruit and peppery Goldings hops aroma. Full-bodied malt and hops in the mouth; tart, quenching fruit and hop bitterness in the finish. A straw-coloured pale ale with tangy hop character.

TEMPERANCE RELIEF 4.3% ABV
Rich malt, orange fruit and resiny hops aroma. Complex malt and citrus fruit in the mouth; hoppy bitter finish with a hint of chocolate. A fruity amber ale.

PROHIBITION 4.8% ABV
Ripe citrus fruit and chocolate aroma. Spices, chocolate and grapefruit in the mouth; deep bittersweet finish. A complex copper-coloured ale.

AMBER GAMBLER 5.5% ABV
Rich malt and orange fruit aroma. Mouth-filling malt, marmalade fruit and hops with a deep, bittersweet finish and cobnuts from the crystal malt. An amber-coloured ale packed with fruit and hops.

Plus winter and seasonal brews including:
GOLD PROSPECTOR (4.6% ABV)
DRAUGHT EXCLUDER (6.0% ABV) and
WEISSE SQUAD (4.0% ABV).

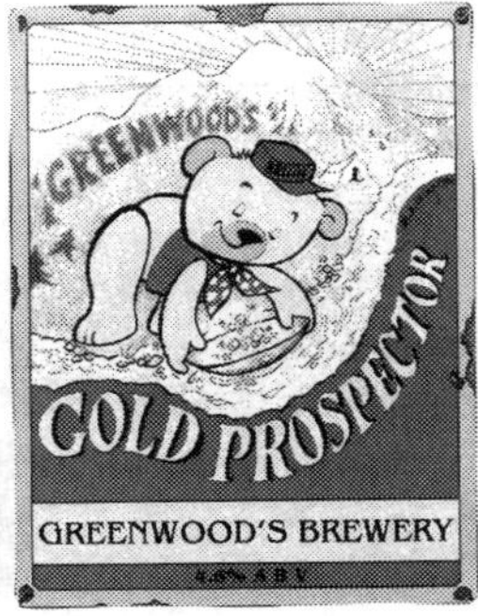

ASHENDEN

Gatehangers

Lower End, Ashenden HP18 OHE
☎ *(01296) 651296*

 Wadworth IPA and 6X, Adnams Bitter and Hall & Woodhouse Badger always available plus a guest beer (up to 30 per year) from breweries such as Mole's, Elgood's, Hook Norton, Felinfoel, Everard's, Bateman's, Smiles, or Marston's.

A 300-year-old country pub with traditional atmosphere. Beamed in part with open fires and large L-shaped bar. Bar food at lunchtime and evenings. Car park and garden. Children allowed. Twenty minutes to Oxford. Between the A41 and A418 west of Aylesbury, near the church.

 *12–2.30pm and 7–11pm.*

CUBLINGTON

The Unicorn

High Street, Cublington
☎ *(01296) 681261*
Mr and Mrs Ibbotson

 Five beers always available including brews from Morland plus Jennings Bitter and Shepherd Neame Spitfire Ale. Approx 100 guests per year including Vale Wychert Ale and Greene King Abbot.

Country pub dating from 1600 with open fires and low beams in the main bar. Bar and restaurant food served at lunchtime and evenings during the week. Car park and garden. Children allowed in the restaurant.

 *12–3pm and 5.30–11pm.*

HADDENHAM

VALE BREWERY CO.

Thame Road, Haddenham,
Nr Aylesbury HP17 8BY
☎ *(01844) 290008*
Visitors welcome if booked in advance.
Tied houses: None

Established in January 1995, this company is owned by brothers Mark and Phil Stevens, who first gained years of experience working elsewhere in the industry. They produce beers from only the finest malted barley and whole English hops, with no preservatives, conditioners, colouring agents or other additives.

Beers available at: The Grapes, 36 Market Street, Aylesbury, Buckinghamshire *and* Abingdon Arms, 21 Cornmarket, Thame, Oxfordshire.

NOTLEY ALE 3.3% ABV

WYCHERT ALE 3.9% ABV

GRUMPLING OLD ALE 4.6% ABV

Hambleden

Old Luxters Farm Brewery

Hambleden,
Henley-on-Thames RG9 6JW
☎ *(01491) 638330*
Visitors welcome. Tied houses: None

David Eland set up Chiltern Valley wines at Old Luxters Farm in 1984 and, since 1990, has broken into the real ale trade as well. Frank Bloss runs the brewery in a seventeenth-century barn and they now produce 100,000 bottles of their Barn Ale a year, and supply it in casks to a number of discerning local pubs. They also export to Sweden. Note that Hambleden is actually in Buckinghamshire, despite the postal address.

Beers available at: The Black Horse, Checkendon, Oxfordshire *and* The Stag and Huntsman, Hambleden, Buckinghamshire.

OLD LUXTERS BARN ALE 4.5% ABV
Also available bottle-conditioned at 5.4% ABV.

Hedgerley

The White Horse

Village Lane,
Hedgerley,
Nr Slough SL2 3UY
☎ *(01753) 643225*
Mr and Mrs Hobbs

Seven or eight beers permanently available and dispensed by gravity including brews from Charles Wells and Greene King. Also dozens of guest beers from small breweries only.

Beer festival held every year. No machines, no music, no straight glasses. Bar food at weekends. Car park, garden. Bird sanctuary nearby.

11am–2.30pm and 5.30–11pm Mon–Fri; 11am–3pm and 6–11pm Sat; usual Sun hours.

Little Missenden

The Unicorn

Little Missenden HP7 ORD
☎ *(01494) 862571*
Mr T How

Morrells Varsity, Hook Norton Best and Rebellion Mutiny always available plus up to 20 guest beers per year including Adnams Broadside, Hook Norton Old Hooky, Fuller's London Pride, Marston's Pedigree, Bateman XXXB and Greene King Abbot.

Old traditional village pub in the same family hands for 90 years. Simple bar food at lunchtimes. Car park and garden. Children not allowed.

11am–2.30pm and 6–11pm Mon–Sat; 12–2.30pm and 7–10.30pm Sun.

Littleworth Common

The Blackwood Arms

Common Lane,
Littleworth Common,
Nr Burnham SL1 8PP
☎ *(01753) 642169*
Colin Whale

Rebellion Mutiny always available plus five others from a considerable range that ran into four figures last year. Hop Back Summer Lightning, Archers Golden,

Exmoor Gold, Otter Bright, Enville Ale and Bathams Bitter are among the favourites.

Traditional country pub with open fires. Bar meals available at lunchtime and evenings. Car park and garden. Children allowed. Tucked away two miles from Burnham High Street. Turn into Common Lane after The Jolly Woodman.

11am–2.30pm and 5.30–11pm Mon–Thurs; 11am–11pm Fri–Sat; 12–10.30pm Sun.

LOUDWATER

Derehams Inn

5 Derehams Lane,
Loudwater HP14 3ND
☎ *(01494) 530965*
Ray and Val Kearney

Eight beers always available including Fuller's London Pride, Wadworth 6X, Young's Bitter, Timothy Taylor Landlord and Brakspear's brews. Vale Wychert Ale is among the guest beers.

Small and cosy local freehouse. Bar food on weekdays at lunchtime. Car park, garden. Children allowed in the restaurant area. Less than a mile from M40 junction 3.

11.30am–3pm and 5.30–11pm.

MARLOW

REBELLION BEER CO.

Unit J, Rose Industrial Estate,
Marlow Bottom Road,
Marlow SL7 3ND
☎ *(01628) 476594*
Visitors welcome. Tied houses: None

The Rebellion Beer Company was established in January 1993 by Tim Coombes and Mark Gloyens, who both grew up in Marlow at the height of the success of the old Wethered's Brewery. Extensive market research produced the recipe for Rebellion IPA, which was first brewed in March 1993. Rebellion ESB followed in December 1994 and this has since undergone more drastic change and is now known as Rebellion Mutiny. Both beers are available in more than 40 regular local outlets and approximately 10,000 pints are brewed each week. There are plans to relocate the brewery to a larger site within Marlow to increase capacity to 60,000 pints per week, and to double the range of beers. The old listed Wethered's buildings form one possible site.

Beers available at: The Blackwood Arms, Littleworth Common, Buckinghamshire *and* Jack o'Newbury, Binfield, Nr Bracknell, Berkshire.

REBELLION IPA 3.7% ABV
A blend of pale, crystal and chocolate malts and English hops. Its strength and balance is such as to make it a light easy drinking beer, while also having considerable depth and complexity.

REBELLION MUTINY 4.5% ABV
Formerly ESB. A rich, full-bodied real ale. The depth of colour, malty flavour and hop nose make it an excellent guest ale.

BUCKINGHAMSHIRE

PRESTWOOD

The King's Head

188 Wycombe Road,
Prestwood HP16 OHJ
☎ *(01494) 862392*
Dennis Winkworth

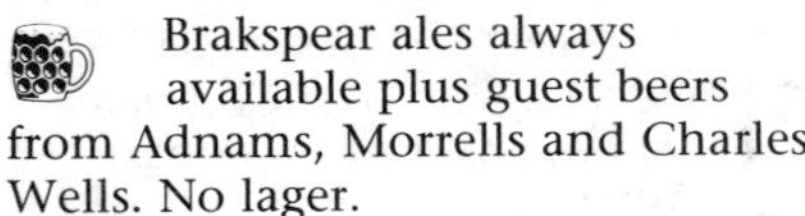

Brakspear ales always available plus guest beers from Adnams, Morrells and Charles Wells. No lager.

An old pub offering bar snacks at lunchtime and evenings. Car park. Children allowed in the garden. Take the A4128 from High Wycombe.

11am–11pm Mon–Sat; 12–3pm and 7–10.30pm Sun.

TERRICK

CHILTERN BREWERY

Nash Lee Road, Terrick,
Aylesbury HP17 0TQ
☎ *(01296) 613647*
Visitors welcome. There is a brewery shop and small museum.
Tied houses: None

The award-winning Chiltern Brewery was set up on an old farm in 1980 to reintroduce the concept of local beers for local people to this part of the world. It has also supplied beers for the House of Commons bars. The company also specialises in a range of beer-related products, such as beer mustards, chutneys, cheeses and marmalade.

Beers available at: The Black Boy, Windmill Street, Bushey Heath, Hertfordshire *and* The Olde Coach House, Ashby St Ledgers, Nr Rugby, Northamptonshire.

CHILTERN ALE 3.7% ABV
Relatively light in colour with a creamy smoothness. It has a definition on the palate and a refreshing, clean finish.

BEECHWOOD BITTER 4.3% ABV
A higher crystal malt content gives added depth of flavour and colour and enhances the beer's nutty character. Hearty and well rounded on the palate, with a long, satisfying finish.

THREE HUNDREDS OLD ALE 5.0% ABV
In the true tradition of old ales. Satisfyingly dark but not impenetrable; good body but not overpowering, with a long, pleasing finish. Also available in bottles.

Plus a range of occasional and bottled beers.

THORNBOROUGH

The Lone Tree

Buckingham Road,
Thornborough MK18 2DZ
☎ *(01280) 812334*
Martin Lister

Six beers available (500 served so far) produced by breweries stretching from Orkney to Cornwall, Norfolk to Wales. Plus one real cider.

Small roadside pub with award-winning food and large garden. Bar and restaurant food at lunchtime and evenings. Car park, garden and children's room. Children also allowed in the restaurant.

11.30am–2.30pm and 5–11pm Mon–Sat; 12–3pm and 7–10.30pm Sun.

Boxworth

The Golden Ball

High Street, Boxworth CB3 8LY
☎ *(01954) 267397*
Mr and Mrs Arliss

Beers available may include Hop Back Summer Lightning, Greene King IPA and Abbot, Everard's Tiger and Nethergate Old Growler.

Typical country pub in good walking area. Bar and restaurant food at lunchtime and evenings. Meeting room, car park, disabled entrance and toilets. Large garden with separate entrance. Children allowed. Ten miles from Cambridge, six miles from St Ives.

11.30am–2.30pm and 6.30–11pm.

Cambridge

Ancient Druids

Napier Street, Cambridge CB1 1HR
☎ *(01223) 576324*
Tours by arrangement

There are plans to expand the range of beers brewed here. They have recently begun producing a dark mild of about 3.3% ABV. Plus a range of guest beers.

There is a history of brewing on the premises. Charles Wells set up business here in 1984 and the present managers took over and restarted production in 1993. This big, bright pub enjoys a laid-back atmosphere, with a wide variety of customers including students and shoppers. Background music. Bar food available all day until 10pm. Children allowed.

ELLIES SB 6.0% ABV

11am–11pm.

Cambridge Blue

85–87 Gwydir Street, Cambridge CB1 2LG
☎ *(01223) 361382*
Mandy and Nick Winnington

Six beers at a time including Nethergate Bitter, IPA and Old Growler. Approx 140 guest beers per year with an avowed policy of trying as many new brews as possible.

Terraced side-street pub with large garden and two bars (one no-smoking). Healthy bar food at lunchtimes. Children allowed in conservatory area until 9pm. Off Mill Road on the city side of railway bridge.

12–2.30pm and 6–11pm Mon–Fri and Sun; 12–3.30pm and 6–11pm Sat.

Live and Let Live

40 Mawson Road, Cambridge CB1 2EA
☎ *(01223) 460261*
Margaret Holliday

Seven beers available. The landlord deals mainly with Everards but also Adnams and B&T. Guest list (20 per year) includes Exmoor Stag, Felinfoel Double Dragon, Morland Old Speckled Hen, Shepherd Neame Bishops Finger, Hall & Woodhouse

Tanglefoot, Bateman Lincolnshire Yellow Belly and Victory Ale.

Situated in central Cambridge, off Mill Road, popular with students and businessmen alike. Wooden furniture and walls plus real gas lighting. Bar food available at lunchtime and evenings. Street parking. Children allowed in restaurant section.

12–2.30pm and 6–11pm.

St Radegund

129 King Street,
Cambridge CB1 1LD
☎ *(01223) 311794*
Terry Kavanagh

Four beers available, but nothing stronger than 4.7% ABV. Fuller's London Pride and Nethergate Bitter plus a selection from (20 per year) Timothy Taylor Landlord, Bateman XB, Hall & Woodhouse Badger, Mauldon's Best, Shepherd Neame Spitfire, Iceni Deirdre of Sorrows etc.

The smallest pub in Cambridge. CAMRA Pub of the Year 1993–94. No jukebox, no games machines. Background jazz music. Filled rolls only. Children not allowed. Opposite the Wesley church in King Street.

12–2.30pm and 5.30–11pm Mon–Fri; 12–11pm Sat; 6.30–10.30pm Sun.

Tap & Spile

14 Mill Lane,
Cambridge CB2 1RX
☎ *(01223) 357026*
Peter Snellgrover

Approx 300 beers per year (nine at any one time) including brews from Adnams, Bateman, Black Sheep, Hadrian, Hardington, Thwaites, Ushers, Nethergate and many other independent breweries.

Traditional ale house with oak floors and exposed brickwork in picturesque setting right next to the river (perhaps the biggest beer garden in England?). Punting station nearby. Bar food at lunchtime.

11am–11pm Mon–Sat; 12–3pm and 7–10.30pm Sun.

DEEPING ST JAMES

The Goat

155 Spalding Road, Frognall,
Deeping St James,
Nr Peterborough PE6 8SA
☎ *(01778) 347629*
Peter Wilkins

Adnams Bitter plus up to six guest beers from micro-breweries and brewpubs including Dark Star and Iceni Deirdre of Sorrows, Shardlow Session, Freeminer Speculation, Tisbury Old Wardour, Blackmoor Batley Shampayne and many more.

A country pub dating from 1640. Bar and restaurant food at lunchtime and evenings. Functions catered for. Car park, large beer garden with play equipment and children's room. On the A16 between Market Deeping and Spalding.

11am–2.30pm and 6–11pm Mon–Fri; 11am–3pm and 6–11pm Sat; 12–10.30pm Sun.

LEIGHTON BROMSWOLD

The Green Man

37 The Avenue,
Leighton Bromswold,
Nr Huntingdon PE18 0SH
☎ *(01480) 890238*
Mr Hanagan

Timothy Taylor Landlord, Nethergate Bitter, Hall & Woodhouse Tanglefoot and Fuller's London Pride always available plus two guest beers (150 per year) perhaps from Wadworth, Adnams, Nene Valley, Mitchell's, Young's, Robinson's, Everards or Goddard's breweries.

Seventeenth-century, detached public house with a collection of water jugs and memorabilia. Bar food available at lunchtime and evenings. Car park, garden, children's room. One mile off the A14.

12–3pm and 7–11pm; closed Mon.

CAMBRIDGESHIRE

NEEDINGWORTH

The Queen's Head

30 High Street,
Needingworth,
Nr Huntingdon PE17 2SA
☎ *(01480) 463946*
Mr and Mrs Vann

Six beers always available including Smiles Best, Woodforde's Wherry Best and Hop Back Summer Lightning. Approximately 100 guests per year including Nene Valley Old Black Bob, the Reindeer range, Timothy Taylor Landlord, Parish Somerby Premium, Butterknowle Conciliation, Hook Norton Best, Chiltern Beechwood, Sarah Hughes Dark Ruby Mild and brews from Wild's brewery.

Friendly pub. Bar snacks served 12–8pm. Car park and garden. Children allowed in lounge bar. Close to St Ives.

12–11pm.

NEWTON

Queen's Head

Newton,
Nr Cambridge CB2 5PG
☎ *(01223) 870436*
Mr Davidshot

Has specialised in Adnams beers for the past 27 years. Bitter and Broadside always available plus Old Ale in winter and Tally Ho at Christmas.

A typical early eighteenth-century pub beside the village green. Bar food at lunchtime and evenings. Car park, children's room, various bar games. Three miles from M11 junction 10; less than two miles off the A10 at Harston.

11.30am–2.30pm and 6–11pm Mon–Sat; 12–2pm and 7–10.30pm Sun.

PETERBOROUGH

Bogart's Bar and Grill

17 North Street,
Peterborough PE1 2RA
☎ (01733) 349995

House beer brewed by Eldridge Pope plus six guest beers always available from a varied selection (300+ per year) usually ranging in strength from a mild at 3.0% to 5.5% ABV. The pub hosts a regional beer festival at the start of each month, featuring brewers from a specific part of the United Kingdom. Real cider also available.

Bogart's was built at the turn of the century and now has a wide-ranging clientele of all ages. The horseshoe-shaped bar is decorated with film posters and Humphrey Bogart features prominently. There is background music but no jukebox or pool table etc. Bar food available at lunchtime. Car park opposite and beer garden. Children not allowed. Located off the main Lincoln Road.

11am–11pm Mon–Sat; closed Sun.

Charters Cafe Bar

Town Bridge,
Peterborough PE1 1DG
☎ (01733) 315700
Lorraine Morley

Oakham JHB plus Fuller's London Pride, Adnams Broadside and Everards Tiger always available. Also up to five (400 per year) guest beers from every independent brewery possible.

A floating connected Dutch barge moored in the centre of town. CAMRA Pub of the Year 1994. Bar and restaurant food available at lunchtime and evenings. Parking and garden. Children allowed. Town Bridge crosses the River Nene in central Peterborough.

All day in summer; 12–3pm and 5–11pm at other times.

STOW CUM QUY

Prince Albert

Newmarket Road,
Stow cum Quy CB5 9AQ
☎ (01223) 811294
Mr and Mrs Henderson

Five beers always available including Greene King IPA. Guests might include Ash Vine Bitter, Stormforce Ten, Worzel Wallop and Shardlow Reverend Eaton's Ale.

Lively roadside pub built in 1830. Bar and restaurant food served at lunchtime and weekend evenings. Private functions catered for. Car park and garden. Children allowed. Just off A14 on the Newmarket road (A1303).

11am–3.30pm and 5–11pm Mon–Fri; all day Sat–Sun.

THRIPLOW

The Green Man

2 Lower Street,
Thriplow SG8 7RJ
☎ *(01763) 208855*
DS and RJ Ward

Adnams Bitter, Hook Norton Best and Timothy Taylor Landlord always available plus two or three guests beers (30 per year) from Felinfoel, Nethergate, Bateman, Black Sheep or Morland's breweries.

Open-plan, two-bar pub by the village green with small non-smoking dining area. Formerly Charles Wells. Bar and restaurant food available at lunchtime and evenings (not Sunday). Car park and garden. Children not allowed. Turn off the A505 near the Imperial War Museum, Duxford.

12–3pm Mon–Sat;
12–3pm and 7–10.30pm Sun.

WHITTLESEY

The Boat Inn

2 Ramsey Road, Whittlesey,
Nr Peterborough PE7 1DR
☎ *(01733) 202488*

Elgood's Cambridge Bitter and Pageant Ale always available plus Black Dog Mild in May. Guest beers (12 per year) have included Morrells Graduate, Crouch Vale Millenium Gold and Mitchell's Lancaster Bomber.

Seventeenth-century pub on a site mentioned in the Domesday Book. Large informal bar, plus small restaurant featuring the bow of a boat as the bar. Resident ghost! Bar and restaurant food at lunchtime and evenings. Car park and garden. Children allowed. Ask anyone for directions on reaching Whittlesey.

11.30am–2.30pm and
6.30–11pm.

WISBECH

ELGOOD & SONS

North Brink Brewery,
Wisbech PE13 1LN
☎ *(01945) 583160*
Visitors welcome. Tied houses: 47

North Brink Brewery was established in 1795, having been converted from a mill and granary ten years before. The brewery changed hands several times and by 1877 had acquired a tied estate of 70 pubs, 21 of which were in Wisbech. It was at this point that John Elgood and George Harrison paid £38,965 for the business and, on 11 October 1878, the first brew of Elgood's Ales was mashed. Harrison sold his share of the partnership the following year but Elgood continued until his death, in 1890. The brewery stayed in the family and, in 1905, Elgood and Sons Ltd was formed with Horace Elgood, John's third son, as chairman. When Nigel Elgood took over in 1968, he became the fourth generation of the family to run the brewery, and intends to hand over to his eldest daughter, Belinda, in due course. The brewery stands on the River Nene.

Beers available at: Hare and Hounds Hotel, North Brink, Wisbech, Cambridgeshire *and* Spread Eagle Hotel, Bridge Street, Wisbech, Cambridgeshire.

BLACK DOG MILD 3.6% ABV
A cask-conditioned traditional dark mild, well-balanced,

giving a pleasant aroma and taste with roasted bitter flavours. Available in May.

CAMBRIDGE BITTER 3.8% ABV
Malty and fruity with a delicate hop aroma, a dry finish to the palate and a moreish taste.

BICENTENARY PAGEANT ALE 4.3% ABV
Celebrating 200 years of brewing at North Brink Brewery, a robust ale, well hopped with a rich malt aroma.

BARLEYMEAD 4.7% ABV
Brewed each Autumn with the fresh harvest of hops and barley. A light golden-coloured brew, contrasting with a strong hoppy flavour.

NORTH BRINK PORTER 5.0% ABV
Available on draught in winter and throughout the year in bottles. A dry stout taste complemented by a fruity flavour and hoppy character.

GREYHOUND STRONG BITTER 5.2% ABV
A premium ale with a light hop aroma giving a bitter-sweet palate.

WENCESLAS WINTER WARMER 7.5% ABV
The king of winter ales. A very strong beer.

Plus other bottled brews.

The Rose Tavern

53 North Brink,
Wisbech PE13 1JX
☎ *(01945) 588335*

Butterknowle Conciliation Ale and Cains FA always available plus guest beers.

A 200-year-old listed building forming a cosy, one-roomed pub on the riverside. The closest pub to Elgood's Brewery. Outdoor area, wheelchair access, traditional pub games, accommodation.

12–3pm and 5.30–11pm.

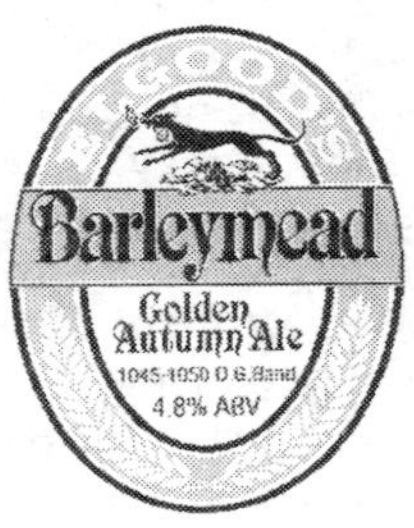

APPLETON THORN

Appleton Village Hall

Stretton Road,
Appleton Thorn,
Nr Warrington WA4 4RT
☎ *(01925) 261187*
Ian Hebenton

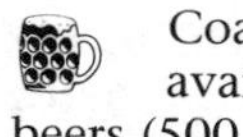
Coach House brews always available plus five guest beers (500 per year) and real cider.

A charitable village club operated voluntarily by local residents. 1994 CAMRA club of the year. Car park, garden and children's room. Boule, pool and darts. From M6 junction 2 or M56 junction, follow signs to Appleton Thorn.

8.30–11pm Thurs–Sun.

ASTON

Bhurtpore Inn

Wrenbury Road,
Aston, Nr Nantwich CW5 8DQ
☎ *(01270) 780917*
Simon and Nicki George

Hanby Drawwell always available plus up to nine guest beers (400 per year) which may include Crouch Vale SAS, Worth Neary's Stout, Nethergate Umbel Magna, Holt Mild, Oak Best, Bateman Strawberry Fields, Beartown Ambeardextrous and Wadworth Summersault. Also real cider and 130 bottled Belgian beers plus Belgian beer on draught.

The family has been connected with this comfortable traditional pub since 1849. Fresh bar and restaurant food at lunchtime and evenings. Car park, garden. Children allowed in pub at lunchtime and in early evening. CAMRA pub of the year 1993. Located just west of the A530, midway between Nantwich and Whitchurch.

12–2.30pm and 6.30–11pm Mon–Sat; 12–3pm and 7–10.30pm Sun.

BURTONWOOD

BURTONWOOD BREWERY

Bold Lane,
Burtonwood,
Warrington WA5 4PJ
☎ *(01925) 225131*
No visitors. Tied houses: 486

Burtonwood was founded by James Forshaw in 1867 and began with one 14-barrel open-fired copper and two 12-barrel fermenting vessels. Small 36-pint casks were filled and delivered by horse and cart to local freehouses, farms and private landlords. The business has grown and a £7 million investment programme on the original site is now underway. The family concern has always been to take the finest raw material (full-bodied malts, aromatic hops, high quality yeast and mineral-rich water) and to fashion beers of character and quality. For Burtonwood, excellence in brewing depends upon the exercise of time-honoured skills and judgment, combined with a continuous appraisal and investment in proven processes.

BURTONWOOD MILD 3.0% ABV
A dark, full-flavoured mild with a mellow, malty flavour, a smooth, creamy head and a delicate dry hop aroma.

BURTONWOOD PALE MILD 3.1% ABV

BURTONWOOD BITTER 3.7% ABV
One of the original beers brewed by Burtonwood. A rich, smooth, malty flavour complemented by a fragrant dry hop aroma and topped by a creamy head.

JAMES FORSHAW BITTER 4.0% ABV
A distinctly strong, full-bodied malty flavour, superb hop aroma, with a smooth, creamy palate.

TOP HAT PREMIUM BITTER 4.8% ABV
Drinkers like its style and unique, dry hop character. A top quality, richly flavoured bitter.

BUCCANEER QUALITY BITTER 5.2% ABV
A pale, golden ale, strong and complex in character. Carefully hand picked fuggle hops give it a distinctive aroma and gently kilned pale malt provides a smooth and satisying flavour.

Plus seasonal brews.

CHESTER

The Mill Hotel

Milton Street,
Chester CH1 3NF
☎ *(01244) 350035*

Mill Premium (house bitter brewed by Coach House), Weetwood Best Bitter and a mild always available plus up to five guests from 500+ per year including Morland Old Speckled Hen, Dyffryn Clwyd Castle Bitter and Sarah Hughes Ruby Mild.

Hotel bar and restaurant on the site of a working mill, which is visible behind glass walls. Bar and restaurant food available at lunchtime and evenings. Car park, canal-side garden, accommodation. Children allowed.

11am–11pm Mon–Sat; 12–10.30pm Sun.

CONGLETON

BEARTOWN BREWERY

Unit 9, Varey Road,
Eaton Bank Industrial Estate,
Congleton CW12 1VW
☎ *(01260) 299964*
No visitors. Tied houses: None

Opened in mid-March 1995, Beartown brewery is run on a part-time basis by two beer connoisseurs. It has a ten-barrel capacity and all brews feature a special mix of Maris Otter malt and, unusually, 10 per cent wheat. English hops and yeast from Robinson's brewery in Stockport.

Beers available at: Durham Ox, 54 West Street, Congleton, Cheshire *and* Wilbraham Arms, 58 Welsh Row, Nantwich, Cheshire.

AMBEARDEXTROUS 3.8% ABV
With added amber malt. A refreshing beer with a rich amber hue and good balance of body and flavour.

SB PREMIUM BITTER 4.2% ABV
A satisfying full-bodied bitter with a lingering hoppy aftertaste.

BRUIN'S RUIN 5.0% ABV
A well-hopped beer with a smooth distinctive flavour.

FRODSHAM

Rowland's Bar

31 Church Street,
Frodsham WA6 6PN
☎ *(01928) 733361*
Matt and Nick Rowland

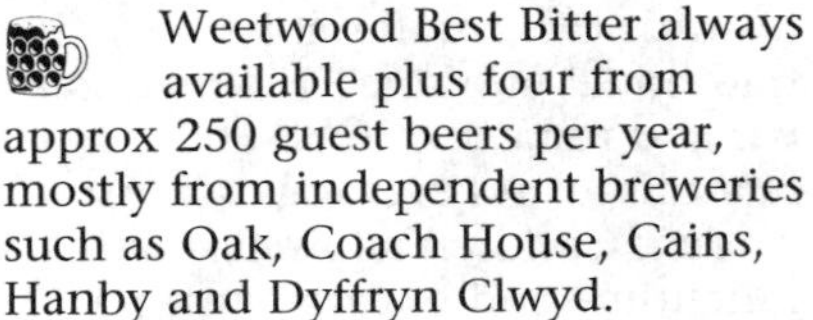

Weetwood Best Bitter always available plus four from approx 250 guest beers per year, mostly from independent breweries such as Oak, Coach House, Cains, Hanby and Dyffryn Clwyd.

One-room public bar with restaurant above. Bar and restaurant food at lunchtime and evenings. Restaurant closed all day Sunday and Saturday lunchtime. Parking. Children allowed in restaurant. In the main shopping area, close to British Rail station.

 *11am–11pm.*

LANGLEY

Leathers Smithy

Langley, Nr Macclesfield SK11 0NE
☎ *(01260) 252313*

 Banks's brews always available plus Marston's Pedigree and three guest beers which alternate slowly but could well include Morrells Varisty and Graduate.

Former smithy (originally run by William Leather), built in the early thirteenth century in beautiful surroundings on the edge of Macclesfield Forest overlooking Ridge Gate Reservoir (fishing possible). Food available lunchtime and evenings. Also 80 different whiskies. Car park, garden, family/function room.

 *12–3pm and 7–11pm Mon–Thurs and Sat; 12–3pm and 5.30–11pm Fri; 12–10.30pm Sun.*

NANTWICH

Wilbraham Arms

58 Welsh Row, Nantwich CW5 5EJ
☎ *(01270) 626419*

 Coach House Coachman's Bitter and Weetwood Best always available plus guests (50 per year) changed weekly from Beartown, Weetwood, Hanby and Holt's breweries.

Close to the town centre, near canal, with traditional Georgian frontage, bar and dining area. Bar food available at lunchtime and evenings. Small car park, accommodation. Children allowed in dining room.

 *11am–11pm Mon–Sat; 12–10.30pm Sun.*

STALYBRIDGE

The Buffet Bar

Stalybridge Station, Stalybridge SK15 1RF
☎ *(0345) 484950*

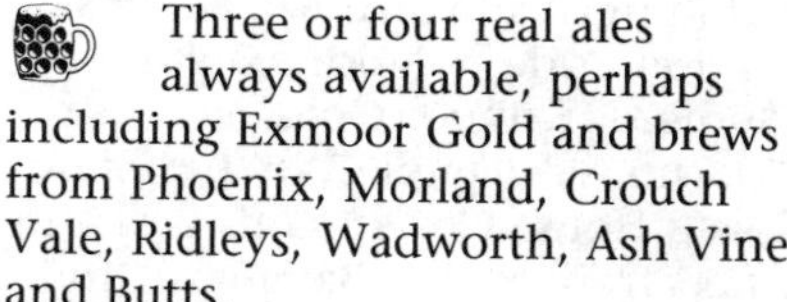 Three or four real ales always available, perhaps including Exmoor Gold and brews from Phoenix, Morland, Crouch Vale, Ridleys, Wadworth, Ash Vine and Butts.

A unique and authentic buffet bar built in 1885 with a real fire, real beer, and real people! Bar food available in the evenings. Parking. Children allowed. On platform one at Stalybridge railway station.

 *5–11pm Mon–Thurs; 12–3pm and 5–11pm Fri and Sat; 7–10.30pm Sun.*

Q Inn

3 Market Street, Stalybridge SK15 2AL
☎ *(0161) 303 9157*
David Conner

Beers from Marston and Thwaites always available. Guest beers (200 per year) from Gibbs Mew, Oak, Hull, Hart, Bateman, Fuller's, Wadworth, Exmoor and Morrells breweries.

The pub with the shortest name in Britain forms part of the Stalybridge Eight – eight pubs in the town offering 37 different beers. Brick walls and a flagstone floor. Quiz night on Monday, Cocktail bar on Friday. No food. Next to the railway station.

5–11pm Mon–Sat; 12–3pm and 7–10.30pm Sun.

The White House

Water Street, Stalybridge SK15 2AG
☎ *(0161) 303 2288*
Mr Conner

Marston ales and Bateman's Mild always available plus up to six guests (400 per year) including Wadworth 6X, Fuller's London Pride, Timothy Taylor Landlord, Exmoor Gold, Moorhouse's Pendle Witches Brew, Coach House Coachman's Best and others from Moles, Bateman's and Thwaites. Also many foreign beers.

There are four rooms in this traditional drinker's pub. Folk club meets on Thursday nights. More than 50 whiskies and 50 foreign beers. Bar snacks available at lunchtime. Parking. Children allowed. Opposite the bus station.

11am–11pm Mon–Sat; 12–4pm and 7–10.30pm Sun.

STOCKPORT

FREDERIC ROBINSON

Unicorn Brewery, Lower Hillgate, Stockport SK1 1JJ
☎ *(0161) 480 6571*
Visitors by appointment only.
Tied houses: 400

William Robinson bought the Unicorn Inn in Lower Hillgate, Stockport, in 1838 and, when his younger son Frederic joined him, they started brewing their own beer. In 1876, after William's death, Frederic bought The Railway at Marple Bridge, and the estate began to grow. When Frederic died in 1890, he owned 12 licensed houses. His widow, Emma, took over and, in 1920, the business became a limited company. It is now in the hands of a fifth generation of Robinsons. Several small breweries including Hartleys (Ulverston) Ltd, have now been acquired and a new packaging plant was commissioned in 1975.

Beers available at: The Royal Scot, Marple Bridge, Stockport, Cheshire *and* Church House, Buglawton, Congleton, Cheshire.

HATTERS MILD 3.3% ABV
A new name for Robinson's Best Mild, one of the few light-coloured milds available.

OLD STOCKPORT BITTER 3.5% ABV
A rich golden body with a refreshingly hoppy taste.

HARTLEYS XB BITTER 4.0% ABV
Famed for its rich body, a smooth bitter ale with a subtle tang of malt.

BEST BITTER 4.2% ABV
A full bitterness derived mainly from choice aroma hops. With its pale, bright colour and good head, this pint looks as good as it tastes.

FREDERICS 5.0% ABV
Brewed from all-British malt grist and only the finest, traditional aroma hop varieties. A light, golden colour but anything but light in character.

OLD TOM 8.5% ABV
Almost as old as the brewery itself. Brewed with meticulous care to produce a smooth, mellow ale with a dark winey colour.

The Crown Inn

154 Heaton Lane, Heaton Norris, Stockport SK4 1AR
☎ *(0161) 429 8646*
Steven James

JW Lees beers always available, plus a wide range of guest beers, hundreds each year and up to ten at any one time. Examples include Oak Thirsty Moon, Commercial Winter Blues, Kelham Island Bitter and Golden Eagle and Princetown Jail Ale.

Cosy five-roomed pub with small bar and cobbled beer garden. Cheap and cheerful bar food at lunchtime. Car park 50 yards away. No-smoking room. Children allowed. Underneath the viaduct.

12–11.30pm Mon–Sat; 12– 3.30pm and 7–10.30pm Sun.

STRINES

The Sportsman's Arms

105 Strines Road, Strines SK12 3AE
☎ *(0161) 427 2888*

Five real ales always available (150 per year) perhaps from Mitchells and Bateman's breweries. Also mild, cider and scrumpy.

An old, two-roomed pub with a lounge/dining room. Bar food is available at lunchtime and evenings. Car park, garden. On the B6101.

12–3pm and 5.30–11pm Mon–Sat; 12–3pm and 7–10.30pm Sun.

TARPORLEY

WEETWOOD ALES

The Brewery, Weetwood Grange, Weetwood, Tarporley CW6 0NQ
☎ *(01829) 752377*
No visitors. Tied houses: None

Weetwood Ales was developed in late 1992 by Adrian Slater and Roger Langford. Farm buildings in the heart of Cheshire were converted to house the brewery and the building work and installation of equipment took several months to complete. The first Weetwood brew appeared in March 1993.

Beers available at: Rowland's Bar, 31 Church Street, Frodsham, Cheshire *and* The Mill Hotel, Milton Street, Chester, Cheshire.

WEETWOOD BEST BITTER 3.8% ABV

Brewed in the traditional manner to produce the rounded flavour and sharp bitterness of a classic bitter, finishing with a full hoppy aftertaste.

OLD DOG PREMIUM BITTER 4.5% ABV

A premium bitter with a smooth, full-bodied flavour. Dark roasted malt produces a deep colour finish, and the use of whole hops provides extra flavour and aroma.

CHESHIRE

TUSHINGHAM

The Blue Bell Inn

Tushingham,
Nr Whitchurch
☎ *(01948) 662172*

Hanby Drawwell Bitter always available plus one or two others (20 per year), perhaps including beers from Plassey, Joules, Hadrian, Cains and Felinfoel breweries.

Dating from 1667, this claims to be Cheshire's oldest pub, with an American landlord and Russian landlady. Friendly and welcoming. No games machines or loud music. Sunday papers and comfortable settee. Bar and restaurant food available at lunchtime and evenings. Car park and garden. Four miles north of Whitchurch on the A41 Chester road.

12–3pm and
6–11pm Mon–Sat;
7–11pm Sun.

WARRINGTON

THE COACH HOUSE BREWING CO.

Wharf Street,
Howley,
Warrington WA1 2DQ
☎ *(01925) 232800*
No visitors. Tied houses: None

The Coach House Brewing Company was founded in 1991 and run mainly by former Greenall Whitley employees. The operation expanded in March 1995 to meet the growing demand for these beers. It serves at least 500 outlets across the country.

COACHMAN'S BEST BITTER 3.7% ABV
A smooth, stronger than average, cask-conditioned beer. Full bodied with a rich malty flavour and a touch of fruit.

GUNPOWDER STRONG MILD 3.8% ABV
A stronger than expected mild. Very dark and meaningful with a full flavour and slightly bitter aftertaste.

INNKEEPER'S SPECIAL RESERVE 4.5% ABV
A premium-strength beer with a ruby port colour. A full malty palate balanced by a crisp hop flavour and a lingering hoppy aftertaste.

POSTHORN PREMIUM ALE 5.0% ABV
A rich golden-coloured smooth ale. Brewed with a full malt mash. A robust palate and a well-balanced bitterness produce complex flavours.

Plus a substantial range of special occasion and seasonal brews.

ALTARNUM

The Rising Sun

Altarnum, Nr Launceston PL15 7SN
☎ *(01566) 86332*
Mr and Mrs Humphreys

Up to four guests available (70 per year) including brews from Robinson's, Elgood's, Hoskins & Oldfield, Butcombe, Otter and Exe Valley.

Sixteenth-century, single-bar pub with open fires and slate/hardwood floor. Bar food available at lunchtime and evenings. Parking. Children allowed. One mile off the A30, eight miles west of Launceston.

11am–3pm and 5.30–11pm.

FALMOUTH

The Quayside Inn

41 Arwenack Street,
Falmouth TR11 3JQ
☎ *(01326) 312113*
Mr and Mrs Keir

At least 15 beers always available including Sharp's Cornish Coaster and Ruddles County. More than 500 guest beers per year from Fuller's, Young's, Bateman's, Smiles, Exmoor, Cotleigh, Gibbs Mew, Shepherd Neame, Hook Norton, Hop Back, Summerskills etc.

Twice-yearly beer festivals at this waterside pub with two bars – comfy upstairs lounge and downstairs real ale bar with free peanuts. Bar food at lunchtime and evenings with local fresh fish. Also sells 200 whiskies including 179 single malts. Parking and garden. Children allowed. On Custom House Quay, overlooking Falmouth harbour.

Both bars all day in summer. Ale house all day in winter.

HELSTON

THE BLUE ANCHOR

50 Coinagehall Street,
Helston TR13 8EX
☎ *(01326) 562821*

One of only four pubs in Britain which has brewed continuously for centuries and still produces its famous Spingo ales, from a Victorian word for strong beer.

This thatched town pub was originally a monks' rest home in the fifteenth century. Brewing continued on the premises after the Reformation and the Blue Anchor is now believed to be the oldest brewpub in Britain. Bar snacks and meals are available at lunchtime. Garden, children's room, skittle alley, function room.

MIDDLE 4.9% ABV

BEST 4.9% ABV

SPECIAL 6.3% ABV

EXTRA SPECIAL 7.3% ABV

11am–11pm Mon–Sat; 12–10.30pm Sun.

LERRYN

The Ship

Lerryn, Nr Lostwithiel PL22 0PT
☎ *(01208) 872374*
Mr Packer

Four beers available including Sharp's brews and guests such as Exmoor Gold, Morland Old Speckled Hen, Fuller's

London Pride, Sharp's Cornish Coaster and Otter Ale.

A pub since the early 1600s, with a wood burner in the bar and slate floors. Bar and restaurant food available at lunchtime and evenings. Set in a quiet riverside village three miles south of Lostwithiel. Car park, garden, accommodation. Children allowed.

11.30am–3pm and 6–11pm Mon–Sat; 12–3pm and 7–10.30pm Sun.

LOSTWITHIEL

The Royal Oak Inn

Duke Street, Lostwithiel PL22 0AG
☎ *(01208) 872552*
Mr and Mrs Hine

Orkney Skullsplitter, Blue Anchor Spingos, St Austell Crippledick, Woodforde's Headcracker, Old Stoker, King's Head Golden Goose, Merrimans Old Fart, Exmoor Gold, Ash Vine Bitter, Hall & Woodhouse Tanglefoot and Badger Best are among the guest beers (50 per year). Marston's Pedigree, Sharp's Own and Fuller's London Pride always available.

A popular thirteenth-century inn catering for all tastes. Bar and restaurant food at lunchtime and evenings. Car park, garden, children's room. Spacious accommodation. Located just off the A390 going into Lostwithiel.

11am–11pm.

MORWENSTOW

The Bush Inn

Morwenstow, Nr Bude EX23 9SR
☎ *(01288) 331242*
BAJ Moore

St Austell HSD always available plus a seasonal brew in winter and guest beers such as Cotleigh Old Buzzard, Wadworth 6X and Farmer's Glory.

Parts of this pub apparently date back to 950 and it is very olde-worlde in character. Cliff walks and nature trails nearby. No piped music or games machines. Car park and tables in the yard. No children allowed. Three miles off the A39, north of Kilkhampton on the Devon and Cornwall border.

12–3pm and 7–11pm.

NANCENOY

Trengilly Wartha Inn

Nancenoy Constantine, Nr Falmouth TR11 5RP
☎ *(01326) 340332*
Nigel Logan and Michael McGuire

Sharp's Own, St Austell XXXX Mild and Dartmoor Best always available plus a couple of guests (up to 100 per year) including Exmoor Gold, Otter Ale and St Austell HSD.

A country freehouse and restaurant in six acres of valley gardens and meadows. Bar and restaurant food at lunchtime and evenings. Car park, garden and children's room. Six bedrooms. Just

south of Constantine – follow the signs.

11–2.30pm and 6.30–11pm.

POLPERRO

The Blue Peter Inn

The Quay, Polperro, Nr Looe PL13 2QZ
☎ *(01503) 272743*
Terry Bicknell

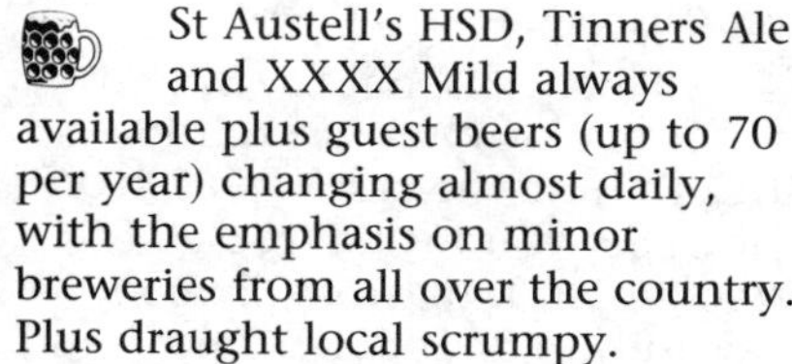

St Austell's HSD, Tinners Ale and XXXX Mild always available plus guest beers (up to 70 per year) changing almost daily, with the emphasis on minor breweries from all over the country. Plus draught local scrumpy.

Small, atmospheric, traditional pub with beamed ceilings and log fires. No games machines or juke box – the house plays the music; primarily blues and jazz. Live music on summer Saturdays. No food, so bring your own rolls and sandwiches. Family room. Children not allowed in the bar. At the end of the fish quay.

11am–11pm Mon–Sat; 12–10.30pm Sun.

QUINTRELL DOWNS

The Two Clomes

East Road, Quintrell Downs, Nr Newquay TR8 4PD
☎ *(01637) 871163*
Frank and Lynn Cheshire

Approx 100 guest beers per year, three or four at any one time. Beers from Exmoor, Otter, St Austell, Fuller's, Cains and Hadrian breweries all favoured.

A converted and extended old miner's cottage built from Cornish stone with a beer garden and games/children's room. Open log fires in winter. Bar food available at lunchtime and evenings. Car park. Take the A392 from Newquay to Quintrell Downs, straight on at the roundabout, then second right.

11.30am–2pm and 6.30–11pm Mon–Sat; 12–3pm and 7–10.30pm Sun.

ROCK

SHARP'S BREWERY

Rock, Wadebridge PL27 6NU
☎ *(01208) 862121*
Visitors welcome. Tied houses: None

This husband and wife partnership is just over one year old but already it supplies 200 outlets in Cornwall and the House of Commons.

Beers available at: Malsters Arms, Chapel Amble, Cornwall, *and* Mill House, Trebarwith Strand, Nr Tintagel, Cornwall.

CORNISH COASTER 3.6% ABV

DOOM BAR BITTER 4.0% ABV

SHARP'S OWN 4.4% ABV

ST AUSTELL

ST AUSTELL BREWERY

63 Trevarthian Road, St Austell PL25 4BY
☎ *(01726) 74444*
Visitors welcome (There is a visitors' centre). Tied houses: 141

In 1851, Walter Hicks mortgaged his farm for £1,500 and set up business as a brewer in St Austell. By 1869 he had moved to new premises and a steam brewery was built. A move in 1893 was to the present site, which has since been altered and improved. When fire broke out one night in June 1939, much damage was done, but the brewery has survived. The family connection survives as well and, today, nearly all of Walter Hicks's numerous descendants are involved as shareholders or, more actively, on the board.

Beers available at: The St Kew Inn, St Kew Church Tor, Nr Wadebridge, Cornwall *and* The Pandora Inn, Restronguet Creek, Mylor Bridge, Nr Falmouth, Cornwall.

BOSUN'S BITTER 3.4% ABV
A popular lunchtime pint, this well-balanced traditional bitter is light in flavour.

XXXX MILD 3.6% ABV

TINNERS ALE 3.7% ABV
The most popular of the traditional draught ales, a cask-conditioned bitter of character, dry-hopped and of medium strength.

HICKS SPECIAL DRAUGHT 5.0% ABV
A strong traditional draught bitter.

Plus a range of bottled beers.

TREBARWITH STRAND

Mill House

Trebarwith Strand,
Nr Tintagel, PL34 0HD
☎ *(01840) 770932*
Roy and Jenny Vickers

Seven beers available including Sharp's Cornish Coaster, Doom Bar Bitter and Own. Also St Austell Tinners Ale and HSD plus a guest beer changed each month.

Seventeenth-century mill with seven acres of woodland and a trout stream. Bar and restaurant food available at lunchtime and evenings. Car park, garden and patio, accommodation. Children welcome. Head for Trebarwith from Tintagel.

11am–11pm.

TRURO

The Old Ale House

7 Quay Street, Truro
☎ *(01872) 71122*
Ray Gascoigne

Sharp's Doom Bar Bitter is one of 11 beers available straight from the barrel, plus 250 guests per year including Hall & Woodhouse Tanglefoot, Exmoor Stag and Gold, Cotleigh Tawny and Old Buzzard, Fuller's London Pride, Shepherd Neame Spitfire, King's Head Golden Goose and King's Ransom etc.

Olde-worlde pub in the town centre with old furniture and free peanuts. Bar food available at lunchtime and evenings. Live music twice a week. Parking. Children allowed.

11am–11pm Mon–Sat;
12–3pm and 7–10.30pm Sun.

ALLONBY

Ship Hotel

Main Street, Allonby CA15 6PZ
☎ *(01900) 881017*
Roy Taylor

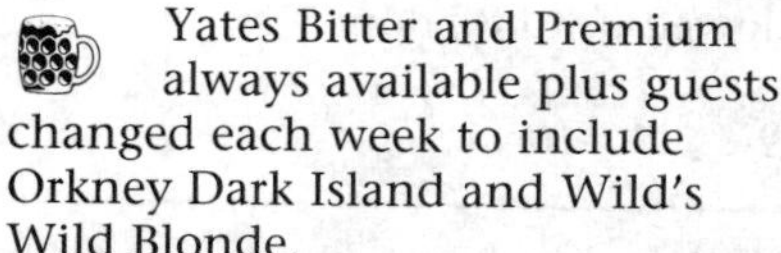

Yates Bitter and Premium always available plus guests changed each week to include Orkney Dark Island and Wild's Wild Blonde.

Overlooking Solway Firth, a 300-year-old hotel with considerable history. Bar and restaurant food served at lunchtime and evenings. Car park, accommodation. Children welcome.

12–11pm in summer;
12–3pm and 7–11pm in winter.

APPLEBY

The Royal Oak Inn

Bongate,
Appleby CA16 6UB
☎ *(017683) 51463*
Colin and Hilary Cheyne

Yates Bitter is among those beers permanently available plus up to seven guests (50 per year) including Holt's Bitter and ales from Maclay, Harviestoun, Wadworth, Hexhamshire, Hesket Newmarket, Timothy Taylor and Black Sheep breweries.

A long white-washed building, roughly 400 years old with lots of character. Bar and restaurant food available at lunchtime and evenings. Two dining rooms, one no-smoking. Parking and terrace. Children allowed. Accommodation. CAMRA Cumbria Pub of the Year 1993. On entering Appleby from Brough on the A66, the inn is at the foot of a hill, on the right.

11am–3pm and
6–11pm Mon–Sat;
12–3pm and 7–10.30pm Sun.

BROUGHTON IN FURNESS

The Manor Arms

The Square,
Broughton in Furness LA20 1XX
☎ *(01229) 716286*
David Varty

Six beers including Yates, Timothy Taylor and Butterknowle brews permanently available plus 160 guest beers per year from small breweries. New brews, winter warmers – you name it, they have served it!

Eighteenth-century traditional family-run freehouse with a welcoming atmosphere. Regular CAMRA pub of the year award-winner. Bar snacks available all day. Parking and outside seats overlooking a picturesque market square. Luxurious accommodation. Children allowed.

2–11pm in winter;
2–11pm Sun–Thurs;
2–midnight Fri–Sat in summer;

COCKERMOUTH

JENNINGS BROTHERS

The Castle Brewery,
Cockermouth CA13 9NE
☎ *(01900) 823214*
Visitors welcome, booking advised.
Tied houses: 105

John Jennings lived and farmed at Scales and it is thought his brewery first operated in buildings near to the present Lorton Village Hall around 1828. His son, John Jr, was also involved and they moved from Lorton to Cockermouth in 1874. In 1887, John Jr's three sons converted the concern of three maltings and 16 licensed outlets into a limited company and more small breweries and pubs were acquired. Today there is no longer a direct connection with the Jennings family and the company has 105 pubs in Cumbria. It retains strong connections with the local community and regards itself as a traditional brewer using the best traditional raw materials and methods.

JENNINGS DARK MILD 3.1% ABV
Very dark, malty and characteristically sweet.

JENNINGS BITER 3.5% ABV
The original. Distinctively dark bitter. Malty, nutty and mellow.

JENNINGS OATMEAL STOUT 3.8% ABV
Smooth, creamy and satisfying.

JENNINGS CUMBERLAND ALE 4.0% ABV
A golden-coloured bitter. Rich and smooth and satisfyingly hoppy.

JENNINGS COCKER HOOP 4.8% ABV
A well-hopped premium bitter.

JENNINGS SNECK-LIFTER 5.1% ABV
A very dark, strong bitter. Slightly sweet. Wonderfully warming.

CARTMEL

Cavendish Arms

Cavendish Street,
Cartmel LA11 6QA
☎ *(01539) 536240*
Tom Murray

Four beers always available from a range of 300+ per year. Favourites include all Cartmel brews, Timothy Taylor Landlord, Butterknowle Banner Bitter, Hop Back Summer Lightning, Fuller's ESB, Mitchells Lancaster Bomber and Shepherd Neame Spitfire.

Coaching inn, 500 years old, offering bar and restaurant food at lunchtime and evenings. Car park, dining room, no-smoking room, accommodation. Children allowed until 8.30pm.

11am–11pm Mon–Sat; 12–10pm Sun.

DENT

DENT BREWERY

Hollins, Cowgill, Dent LA10 5TQ
☎ *(01539) 625326*
Visitors welcome by appointment.
Tied houses: 2

Established in a converted barn within the Yorkshire Dales National Park in March 1990. The brewery uses its own spring water and runs both pubs in Dent. In 1993 it established its own cask ale distribution service, called Flying Firkin, with depots in Lancashire and west London.

Beers available at: The Sun Inn, Main Street, Dent, Cumbria, *and* The George and Dragon, Dent, Cumbria.

DENT BITTER 3.7% ABV
Lightly-hopped, session bitter with a slightly sweet palate.

AVIATOR 4.0% ABV
Medium-coloured with a full, rounded hop flavour. Popular session beer.

RAM'S BOTTOM 4.5% ABV
A medium-dark bitter with a rich caramel taste. Well-balanced hops.

KAMIKAZE 5.0% ABV
Very pale with plenty of hop flavour and a distinctive creamy maltiness.

T'OWD TUP 6.0% ABV
Traditional strong stout with lashings of roast barley giving the beer a nice bite with underlying softness.

Hayton

Stone Inn

Hayton,
Nr Carlisle CA4 9HR
☎ *(01228) 70498*
Mr and Mrs Tranter

Four beers from Jennings, Buchanans, Thwaites and Mitchells permanently available plus the occasional guest beer, perhaps from Maclays.

A traditional village pub serving bar food at lunchtime and evenings. Car park and garden. Children allowed in restaurant, but catering is for parties only (from six to 36). Seven minutes east of M6 junction 43, just off the A69.

11am–3pm and 5.30–11pm.

Hesket Newmarket

Hesket Newmarket Brewery

Old Crown Barn, Back Green,
Hesket Newmarket CA7 8JG
☎ *(01694) 78066*
Pre-booked visitors on Wednesday evenings or in groups.
Tied houses: None

Liz Blackwood and Jim Fearnley bought the Old Crown Inn at Hesket Newmarket in December 1986 and the following year converted the derelict barn at the back into a brewery. The first beer (Blencathra Bitter) was produced in March 1988 and a telex sent by Chris Bonington from Katmandu and delivered by his wife Wendy officially opened the brewery in April 1988. Six beers are now brewed, all but one named after local fells. The brewery supplies the licensed trade either directly or through beer agencies. Hesket Newmarket brews appear regularly at beer festivals nationwide.

Beers available at: The Old Crown Inn, Beck Green, Hesket Newmarket, Cumbria, *and* The Snooty Fox, Uldale, Nr Carlisle, Cumbria.

GREAT COCKUP PORTER 2.8% ABV
Black, with a dark malty flavour and a smooth bitterness.

BLENCATHRA BITTER 3.1% ABV
A ruby-coloured, hoppier, more bitter beer.

SKIDDAW SPECIAL BITTER 3.7% ABV
A golden, full-flavoured session beer.

DORIS'S 90TH BIRTHDAY ALE 4.3% ABV
A glorious, full-flavoured, fruity premium beer.

CATBELL'S PALE ALE 5.1% ABV
Refreshing, easy-to-drink pale ale.

OLD CARROCK STRONG ALE 5.6% ABV
A dark red strong ale, beguilingly smooth and definitely dangerous.

Ings

The Watermill Inn

Ings, Nr Staveley,
Kendal LA8 9PY
☎ *(01539) 821309*
AF and B Coulthwaite

JW Lees Moonraker is among those beers always available. Also perhaps a dozen guest beers (500 per year) which may come from the Hop Back, Cotleigh, Ridley's, Shepherd Neame, Exmoor, Ash Vine, Summerskills, Black Sheep, Coach House, Yates, Mitchell's and Wadworth breweries.

Formerly a wood mill, now a traditional, family-run pub full of character with log fires, brasses and beams. Two bars. No juke box or games machines. Relaxing atmosphere. Bar food at lunchtime and evenings. Car park, garden, seats and tables by the river. Disabled toilets. Children allowed. Accommodation. From the M6, junction 36, follow the A591 towards Windermere. One mile past the second turning for Staveley. Turn left after the garage, before the church.

12–2.30pm and 6–11pm Mon–Sat; 12–3pm and 7–10.30pm Sun.

KENDAL

CARTMEL BREWERY

Unit 7, Fell View Trading Park, Shap Road, Kendal
☎ *(01539) 724085*
Visitors welcome. Tied houses: None

The brewery was set up at the Cavendish Arms in Cartmel by Nick Murray in September 1994. Early in 1995 it moved to its present site as demand necessitated larger premises. The brewery is still looking to increase its production through serving freehouses on a full-time basis, as well as featuring as a guest beer in many other pubs.

Beers available at: Cavendish Arms, Cartmel, Cumbria, *and* Manor Arms, Broughton in Furness, Cumbria.

BUTTERMERE BITTER 3.8% ABV
A brownish, clean-tasting bitter with floral aroma.

LAKELAND GOLD 4.0% ABV
Very light coloured, fine tasting.

CARTMEL THOROUGHBRED 4.5% ABV
A dark, rich, full-bodied premium ale.

Ring o' Bells

39 Kirkland, Kendal LA9 5AF
☎ *(01539) 720326*
Tony Bibby

Vaux Samson and Ward's Best always available plus a guest beer (36 per year) such as Marston's Pedigree, Charles Wells Bombardier, Everard's Tiger, Fuller's London Pride, Adnams Broadside, Morland's Old Speckled Hen.

An unspoilt seventeeth-century pub situated in the grounds of the parish church. Bar food available at lunchtime and evenings. Parking. Children allowed. Accommodation. Take M6 junction 36, then follow the A590 and A591 to the A6 in Kendal.

12–3pm and 6–11pm Mon–Sat; usual hours Sun.

LANERCOST

Abbey Bridge Inn

Lanercost, Brampton CA8 2HG
☎ *(016977) 2224*
Phillip Sayers

Yates Bitter always available plus a couple of guests (100+ per year) including Wadworth 6X, Bateman XXXB, Shepherd Neame, Greene King, Fuller's, Burton Bridge, Black Sheep, Charles Wells, Jennings and Exmoor ales.

Family-run country hotel and bar in a converted seventeenth-century forge retaining original beams and character. Bar and restaurant food available at lunchtime and evenings. Car park, garden, children allowed. Accommodation. CAMRA Cumbria Pub of the Year 1992 plus merit award 1995. Situated close to Lanercost Priory on the riverbank.

12–2.30pm and 7–11pm.

WESTNEWTON

YATES BREWERY

Ghyll Farm, Westnewton, Aspatria, CA5 3NX
☎ *(016973) 21081*
No visitors. Tied houses: 1

Small, traditional brewery set up in 1986 by Peter and Carol Yates in a barn originally used to house the brewery's herd of pedigree goats. The farm was once a home-brew pub.

Beers available at: Ship Hotel, Main Street, Allonby, Cumbria *and* The Drunken Duck Inn, Barngates, Hawkshead, Nr Ambleside, Cumbria.

YATES BITTER 3.7% ABV
A light, straw-coloured session beer. Well hopped.

YATES PREMIUM 5.5% ABV
A very pale strong light ale. Malty with a good hoppy flavour.

YATES BEST CELLAR 5.5–6.2% ABV
A Christmas brew. A strong copper-coloured mild to be treated with respect.

CHESTERFIELD

TOWNES BREWERY

Bay 9, Suon Buildings, Lockoford Lane, Chesterfield S41 7JJ
☎ *(01246) 277994*
Visitors welcome. Tied houses: None

Townes Brewery is named after Townes Van Zandt, an American country music singer/songwriter and the favourite of a member of the partnership which began trading in May 1994, bringing brewing back to Chesterfield after a gap of almost 40 years. The brewery is located in a refurbished old bakery and features a five-barrel plant. Direct sales are confined to a 25-mile radius of the brewery and nationwide through various wholesalers. Current output is around ten barrels per week, but expansion may soon be necessary. All the beers are produced using 100 per cent all-malt recipes, as well as a variety of English, American and Slovakian whole-flower hops.

Beers available at: Royal Oak, 43 Chatsworth Road, Brampton, Chesterfield, Derbyshire *and* The Boat Inn, Scarthin, Cromford, Nr Matlock, Derbyshire.

MUFFIN ALE 3.5% ABV
A full-bodied brown ale with a smooth chocolatey flavour.

SUNSHINE 3.6% ABV
A pale and spicy summer beer with a deceptively full flavoured finish.

BEST LOCKOFORD BITTER 4.0% ABV
A golden, satisfying session bitter with an abundance of hop character.

IPA 4.5% ABV
A medium-bodied pale ale with a fine balance between hops and malt, and a clean satisfying finish.

PYNOT PORTER 4.5% ABV
A dark, rich but mellow beer with hints of roast malt, chocolate and fruit. A dry finish.

DOUBLE BAGGER 5.0% ABV
A full-bodied beer with a welcoming aroma of fruit and malt, leading to a well-balanced finish.

Plus occasional special and festival brews.

The Derby Tup

4 Sheffield Road, Wittington Moor, Chesterfield S41 8LS
☎ *(01246) 454316*
Mr Williams

Ten beers always available with Kelham Island Fat Cat and Marston's Pedigree among them. Guests come from Cotleigh, Robinsons, Timothy Taylor, Exmoor, Batemans etc.

Old and original, unspoilt, beamed with three rooms and open fires. Bar food available at lunchtime and evenings. Parking nearby, children allowed.

11.30am–3pm and 5–11pm Mon–Sat; 12–4pm and 7–10.30pm Sun.

Royal Oak

43 Chatsworth Road, Brampton, Chesterfield S40 2AH
☎ *(01246) 277854*
Mr Younger

Everards Tiger among the beers always available, with seven guests (500 per year) including at least two from Townes and one from Bathams. Also Elgood's Black Dog Mild, Charles Wells Bombardier, Leatherbritches Belt 'n' Braces, Morland Old Speckled Hen, Wadworth Old Timer.

A traditional local pub with timbers and open fire. Live music, table football and darts. Beer festivals. No food. Car park and patio. No children.

11am–11pm Mon–Sat; (10.30pm Sun.)

DERBY

THE BRUNSWICK INN AND BREWERY

1 Railway Terrace, Derby DE1 2RU
☎ *(01332) 290677*

Fourteen pumps serve beer from all around the country, notably Marston's Pedigree and Timothy Taylor Landlord, as well as five or six from the on-site brewery.

The Brunswick Inn was built in 1841–42 as the first purpose-built railwaymen's pub in the world. It was the birthplace of the Railway Institute, an educational establishment for railway workers. It fell into dereliction in the early 1970s and trading ceased in April 1974. As the building lay empty, a public outcry ensued and the Derbyshire Historic Buildings Trust started restoration work in 1981. The trust sold it to Trevor Harris, a local businessman, in May 1987. The pub reopened in October 1987 and the installation of the brewing plant followed in 1991. The first beer was produced on June 11 that year. Bar and restaurant food is available at lunchtime and on request in the evening. Parking, garden, children's room, no-smoking room, function room.

THE RECESSION ALE 3.3% ABV

FIRST BREW 3.6% ABV

RECESSION EXTRA 3.8% ABV

BRUNSWICK PROMISE 3.9% ABV

SECOND BREW 4.2% ABV

RAILWAY PORTER 4.3% ABV

FESTIVAL ALE 4.6% ABV

OLD ACCIDENTAL 4.9% ABV

OWD ABUSIVE 6.0% ABV

11am–11pm Mon–Sat; 12–10.30pm Sun.

The Alexandra Hotel

203 Siddals Road, Derby DE1 2QE
☎ *(01332) 293993*
Mark Robins

Bateman's Mild and XB and Marston's Pedigree always available plus six guest beers (600 per year) with the emphasis firmly on new and rare micro-breweries. Also traditional cider.

Built as a coffee and chop house in 1865. Now trading as a comfortable award-winning pub decorated with a railway and brewery theme. Bar food at lunchtime. Car park and garden. Located three minutes' walk from Derby Midland Railway Station.

11am–2.30pm and 4.30–11pm Mon–Fri and Sun; 11am–2.30pm and 6–11pm Sat.

The Crompton Tavern

46 Crompton Street,
Derby DE1 1NX
☎ *(01332) 733629*
Mr and Mrs Bailey

Marston's Pedigree and Timothy Taylor Landlord always available plus four guest beers (200 per year) perhaps from Fuller's, Coach House, Kelham Island, Banks & Taylor or Burton Bridge breweries. A porter or stout is normally available.

A small pub just outside the city centre. Popular with locals and students. Cobs and sandwiches available daily. Car park and garden. Children now allowed.

11am–11pm Mon–Sat;
12–10.30pm Sun.

The Flowerpot

25 King Street,
Derby DE1 3DZ
☎ *(012332) 204955*
John Evans

Marston's Pedigree and Timothy Taylor Landlord always available plus at least seven guest beers (500+ per year) from all over the United Kingdom.

A traditional friendly town pub with no music or games machines, but lots of regulars aged 18 to 95. Bar food is available at lunchtime and evenings. Car park 30 yards away. Garden and children's room. Function suite available for up to 250 people. Situated on the A6 just inside the inner ring road, 300 yards north of the cathedral.

11am–11pm Mon–Sat;
12–3pm and 7–10.30pm Sun.

Fenny Bentley

Black Bull Brewery

Ashes Farm, Ashes Lane, Fenny Bentley, Nr Ashbourne DE6 1LD
☎ *(01335) 350581*
Visitors by arrangement.
Tied houses: None

The Black Bull Brewery was founded in April 1994 by Michael Peach in his own farm buildings but is expanding to a larger plant during 1996 due to steadily increased demand, both locally and from further afield via wholesalers.

Beers available at: The Coach and Horses, Fenny Bentley, Derbyshire *and* The Flower Pot, 25 King Street, Derby.

DOVEDALE 3.6% ABV
Golden/straw.

BEST BITTER 4.0% ABV
Fruity and full bodied. Well hopped.

ANKLECRACKER 4.2% ABV

RAGING BULL 4.9% ABV
A stronger version of Best Bitter.

OWD SHROVETIDER 5.9% ABV
Winter warmer.

Leatherbritches Brewery

Bentley Brook, Brewery Yard, Fenny Bentley, Nr Ashbourne DE6 1LF
☎ *(01335) 350278*
Visitors welcome. Tied houses: 1

Leatherbritches has already expanded from an initial capacity of five barrels per week and supplies The Bentley Brook Inn and other local pubs and wholesalers. The brewery keeps its own pigs and produces beer sausages.

Beers available at: The Bentley Brook Inn, Fenny Bentley, Derbyshire.

BELT 'N' BRACES 3.8% ABV
Characterful session ale with good hoppy flavour. Mid-brown in colour.

BELTER 4.0% ABV
A light, golden beer with flowery hoppy aroma and bitter finish.

STOUT 4.0% ABV
Traditionally brewed with a dry finish.

ASHBOURNE ALE 4.5% ABV
Premium bitter with fruity hints and well balanced sweet finish. Mid-brown in colour.

HAIRY HELMET 4.7% ABV
Excellent light, hoppy ale with power to deliver.

BESPOKE 5.0% ABV
Ruby in colour, well balanced and smooth.

TAREBRANE 6.5% ABV
Full-bodied dark beer brewed for the Shrovetide football match in Ashbourne.

Hartington

Whim Ales

Whim Farm, Hartington, Buxton SK17 0AX
☎ *(01298) 84991*
No visitors. Tied houses: 1

Formed in December 1993 by Giles Witchfield in redundant farm outbuildings. Supplying a range of six beers to about 30 outlets, with further expansion planned as a result of a merger with the Broughton Brewery, in Scotland.

Beers available at: The Barley Mow, Bonsall, Derbyshire *and* The Charles Cotton, Hartington, Derbyshire.

MAGIC MUSHROOM MILD 3.8% ABV
Well-balanced mild with a complex mix of flavours. Ruby-black in colour.

HARTINGTON BITTER 4.0% ABV
Light coloured, well-hopped session beer.

HIGH PEAK PALE ALE 4.3% ABV
A smooth, pure single malt pale ale using high quality German lager hops.

SCHNEE WEISS (SNOW WHITE) WHEAT BEER 4.5% ABV
Bavarian-style beer brewed using a high proportion of wheat, giving an unusual texture. A thirst-quencher in summer.

OLD IZAAK 4.8–5.0% ABV
Traditional old ale named after Sir Izaak Walton. Full bodied and dark in colour with a mature, dry, rounded finish.

BLACK BEAR 6.2% ABV
A beer to sink the teeth into. Mature, full-bodied, black in colour with a strong, sweet, smooth flavour. Combines the qualities of a porter and barley wine.

Ingleby

Lloyds Country Beers

John Thompson Brewery, Ingleby DE7 1HW
☎ *(01332) 863426*
Visitors welcome. Tied houses: None

The brewery is set in the grounds of the John Thompson Inn but is run as a separate business. Beer was first brewed here in May 1977 by Colin Lloyd and is generally available in the West and East Midlands with occasional runs further afield.

However, the brewery prefers to deal directly with customers rather than using wholesalers.

Beers available at: John Thompson Inn, Ingleby, Derbyshire *and* The Fox Inn, Marston, Staffordshire.

COUNTRY GOLD 4.0% ABV
A straw colour and malty. Brewed in summer only.

VIXON VELVET 4.5% ABV
A porter, dark with lots of chocolate malt. Brewed in winter only.

DERBY BITTER OR JTSXXX 4.1% ABV
The main brew. Copper in colour and fruity.

VIP 4.8% ABV
A stronger version of the Derby Bitter.

Plus a range of one-off brews every few weeks, most with an ABV of 4.0–5.0%.

MAKENEY

The Holly Bush Inn

Holly Bush Lane,
Makeney, Milford
☎ *(01332 841729*
JJK Bilbie

Marston's Pedigree and Ruddles County always available plus four (200+ per year) guests beers that may include Morland's Old Speckled Hen, Exmoor Gold, Fuller's ESB, Marston's Owd Roger, Greene King Abbot, Timothy Taylor Landlord and brews from Bateman's and Mitchell's. Also scrumpy cider.

A Grade II-listed twelfth-century coaching inn with flagstone floors and open fires. Bar food available at lunchtime, barbecues in summer. Car park and children's room. Private parties welcome. Just off the main A6 at Milford, opposite the Makeney Hotel.

12–3pm and 6–11pm Mon–Fri; 12–11pm Sat–Sun.

SHARDLOW

The Old Crown

Candish Bridge,
Nr Shardlow DE72 2HL
☎ *(01332) 792392*
DM Morton and GR Horton Harrison

Marston's Pedigree permanently available plus three guest beers (400 per year) which may include Bateman's XXXB, Otter Ale, Wide Eye'd and Crownless, Shardlow Ale, Enville White, Eldridge Pope Royal Oak, Shepherd Neame Spitfire and Brewery on Sea Black Rock.

A small inn by the River Trent serving bar food at lunchtime. Car park and garden. Children allowed in the bar at lunchtime for food. Turn left on the A6 before the river bridge, before Shardlow from the M1.

11.30am–3pm and 5–11pm Mon–Sat; 12–3pm and 7–10.30pm Sun.

Ticknall

The Staff of Life

7 High Street, Ticknall DE73 1JH
☎ *(01332) 862479*
Bruce Petford

Marston's Pedigree, Everard's Tiger, Mill's Old Original, Timothy Taylor Landlord and Fuller's ESB available plus five guests (200 per year) which may include Exmoor Gold, Hook Norton Old Hooky, Hop Back Summer Lightning, Mauldon's Black Adder, Ringwood Old Thumper, Uley Old Spot and Temperance Relief.

A fifteenth-century heavily beamed former bakehouse. Bar and restaurant food at lunchtime and evenings. Car park, garden and children's room. At the south end of the village and the intersection between the Ashby-de-la-Zouch and Swadlincote roads.

11.30am–2.30pm and 6–11pm Mon–Sat; 12–2.30pm and 7–10.20pm Sun.

Wardlow Mires

Three Stags' Heads

Wardlow Mires, Tideswell SK17 8RW
☎ *(01298) 872268*
Mr and Mrs Fuller

Springhead Bitter, Kelham Island Fat Cat Pale Ale and Pale Rider plus Hoskins & Oldfield Old Navigation Ale always available. Also a guest (ten per year) such as Springhead Leveller, Uley Old Spot, H&O Ginger Tom, Christmas Noggin or Wheat Beer. Also farmhouse cider and a selection of bottled beers.

A small seventeenth-century Peak District farmhouse pub with stone-flagged bar and its own pottery workshop. Unspoilt, with no frills, no piped muzak, no games machines. Live folk/Irish music at weekends. Bar food at lunchtime and evenings. Car park. Children allowed. On the A623 at the junction with the B6465.

7–11pm Mon–Fri; 12–11pm Sat–Sun and bank holidays.

DEVON

Ashburton

Thompson's Brewery

11 West Street,
Ashburton TQ13 7JW
☎ *(01392) 467797*
Visitors welcome. Tied houses: 1

Mel Thompson began brewing Thompson's Aysheburton Bitter in what is now the function suite of The London Hotel in 1981. The brew was originally for the hotel only but demand soon grew to such an extent that Thompson's began supplying other pubs in the South West. New recipes were developed over the next few years and, by 1991, the present range had been created and perfected. In 1992, a new brewhouse was commissioned with a 5,000-barrel capacity. Today, Thompson's brews can be found all over the South West and South East England.

Beers available at: Lazy Landlord, 11 Bonhay Road, Exeter, Devon *and* Mary Tavy Inn, Lane Head, Mary Tavy, Nr Tavistock, Devon.

THOMPSON'S LUNCHTIME BITTER 3.4% ABV
A new ale to fill the session beer gap. Light and refreshing, but with a surprisingly full and strong flavour. It has a fruity palate, nutty aroma, clear appearance and bitter aftertaste.

THOMPSON'S BEST 4.1% ABV
A pleasant hoppy brew, pale brown in colour, with a hoppy aroma. It has a bitter, slightly yeasty taste and a strong bitter finish.

THOMPSON'S IPA 4.4% ABV
A fruity distinctive ale, yeasty with a hoppy aroma. Strong and fruity with a full bitter finish.

THOMPSON'S FIGUREHEAD 5.0% ABV
A very fruity copper-red beer, with roast hop flavours and a smooth but bitter finish. It has both hops and fruit in the aroma. Popular in winter.

THOMPSON'S MAN O' WAR 5.1% ABV
A light straw-coloured brew with a fruity aroma and a clean bitter finish. Particularly popular in the summer.

THOMPSON'S CELEBRATION PORTER 6.0% ABV
A rich porter, with a strong malt aroma. It has a luscious fruity malt flavour and a bitter finish.
Plus a keg stout.

Bideford

Jolly Boat Brewery

4 Buttgarden Street,
Bideford EX39 2AU
☎ *(01237) 424343*
Visitors welcome by prior arrangement.
Tied houses: None

The Jolly Boat Brewery was established in April 1995 and produces a range of four brews which are supplied to approximately 30 outlets and wholesalers.

Beers available at: The White Hart, Bideford, Devon *and* Half Moon Inn, Sheepwash, Devon.

BUCCANEERS BITTER 3.7% ABV
A buoyant best bitter, nut-brown in colour.

MAINBRACE 4.2% ABV
Light chestnut premium bitter, late-hopped for aroma.

PLUNDER 4.8% ABV
Stronger red-brown bitter with hints of chocolate and tropical flavours.

CONTRABAND PORTER 5.8% ABV
Available October to April, festive dark porter, rich and strong.

BRANSCOMBE

BRANSCOMBE VALE BREWERY

Great Seaside Farm, Branscombe, Seaton EX12 3DP
☎ *(01297) 680511*
Visitors by prior arrangement.
Tied houses: None

The Branscombe Vale Brewery was established in two National Trust cowsheds by former dairy workers Paul Dimond and Graham Luxton in 1992 as a small independent, offering high quality ales and an efficient, personal service to its customers. The ales are traditionally brewed from English malt and hops, using Branscombe village spring water. The process utilises modern, hygenic equipment yet never forgets the traditional methods.

Beers available at: The Fountain Head, Branscombe, Devon *and* The Bridge Inn, Bridge Hill, Topsham, Nr Exeter, Devon

BRANOC TRADITIONAL ALE 3.8% ABV
A light golden colour with a palate displaying maltiness in the mouth, with a light dry hop finish.

OWN LABEL 4.6% ABV
A mellow malty beer of tremendous character. Currently only available as a house beer in a few local outlets.

ANNIVERSARY ALE 4.6% ABV
A pale subtle ale full of fruit and hops. Available from the middle of January each year, only 15 barrels brewed.

OLDE STOKER 5.4% ABV
A dark ruby ale with a palate displaying massive maltiness in the mouth with a long full roast finish. *Plus* Christmas and summer brews in the pipe-line.

The Fountain Head

Branscombe EX12 3AG
☎ *(01297) 680359*
Mrs Luxton

Branscombe Vale Branoc, Jolly Jeff, Summer That and Olde Stocker available plus guests (60 per year) including Hook Norton Old Hooky, Crouch Vale Millennium Gold and Freeminer Speculation Ale.

A fourteenth-century pub at the top of the village with flagstone floors, log fires and wood panelling. The lounge bar was formerly the village blacksmith's. Food available at lunchtime and evenings. Car park, outside seating, no-smoking area and children's room. Self-catering accommodation.

11.30am–2.30pm and 6.30–11pm Mon–Sat; 12–2.30pm and 7–10.30pm Sun.

DODDISCOMBSLEIGH

The Nobody Inn

Doddiscombsleigh, Nr Exeter EX6 7DS
☎ *(01647) 252394*
Nick Borst-Smith

Nobody's House Ale permanently available plus two guest beers (40 per year) which may include Ballard's Wassail, Titanic Anniversary, Rebellion Mutiny, Exmoor Stag and Exe Valley Devon Glory.

A sixteenth-century inn with beams and inglenook fireplaces. Bar and restaurant food available lunchtime and evenings. Speciality cheeses. Car park and garden. Children allowed in the restaurant. Accommodation unsuitable for children under 14. Three miles southwest of Exeter racecourse.

12–2.30pm and 6–11pm.

EXETER

Double Locks Hotel

Canal Banks, Marsh Barton, Exeter EX2 6LT
☎ *(01392) 56947*
Tony Steerman

Smiles brews always available plus up to six guest beers (50 per year) including Gibbs Mew Bishop's Tipple, Hall & Woodhouse Tanglefoot, Bateman's XXXB and Ushers Founders Ale.

Recently acquired by Smiles, the pub is located in a 250-year-old building situated by twin locks on the oldest ship canal in the country. Bar food is available all the day. Car park, large garden, volleyball, barbecue in summer and children's room. Located on the south-west edge of the city, through the Marsh Barton Trading Estate.

*11am–11pm Mon–Sat;
12–10.30pm Sun.*

The Well House Tavern

Cathedral Yard, Exeter EX1 1HB
☎ *(01392) 495365*
Tracy Cherry and Ian Scanes

Five guest beers available which may include Cannonball, Norkies, Morland's Old Speckled Hen, Sunbeam Bitter and Oakhill Best.

There is live music and a quiz night at this popular pub with a Roman cellar on alternate Sundays. Bar food is available at lunchtime and evenings. Facing Exeter Cathedral.

*11am–11pm Mon–Sat;
7–11pm Sun.*

GEORGEHAM

The Rock Inn

Rock Hill, Georgeham EX33 1JW
☎ *(01271) 890322*
Mr and Mrs Scutts

Ruddles, Ushers and Wadworth brews always available plus Morland's Old Speckled Hen. Also a couple of guest beers perhaps including ales from Cotleigh, St Austell and Fuller's breweries.

A 400-year-old inn one mile from the sea. CAMRA North Devon Pub of the Year 1994–96. Bar food available at lunchtime and evenings. Car park, garden and children's room. Accommodation.

11am–3pm; all day Sat–Sun when possible.

HATHERLEIGH

TALLY HO COUNTRY INN AND BREWERY

14 Market Street, Hatherleigh EX20 3JN
☎ *(01837) 810306*

Offers a range of six popular brews which are produced in the micro-brewery on the premises.

Although the present brewery only started brewing in 1990, its history goes back over 200 years. Records show that it was producing ales in 1790, when it was known as The New Inn Brewery. It was destroyed by fire in 1806 but was brewing again in 1824. The brewery finally closed down in the early 1900s, when it could no longer compete with the larger breweries of the time. The new brewery is situated at the back of The Tally Ho Country Inn in what used to be the town bakery and can produce 260 gallons of real ale a week. All beer is brewed using the traditional full-mash method with English malt and hops and no sugars, extracts or preservatives. Bar and restaurant food available at lunchtime and evenings. Car park, garden, accommodation. Children allowed.

POTBOILER'S BREW 3.5% ABV

MASTER JACK'S MILD 3.5% ABV

TARKA'S TIPPLE 4.0% ABV

NUTTERS ALE 4.6% ABV

THURGIA 5.7% ABV

JANNAI JOLLOP 6.6% ABV

11am–2.30pm and 6–11pm.

HOLBETON

MILDMAY BREWERY

Holbeton, Nr Plymouth PL8 1NA
☎ *(01752) 830302*
Visitors welcome. Tied houses: 1

Situated on the Flete Estate in south Devon, the brewery is owned by the Mildmay White family. The late Lord Mildmay was famous in racing circles, hence the racing theme that runs through all the beers. Production began two years ago to brew Best Bitter for the adjacent Mildmay Colours Inn. The first year was then spent perfecting four different brews and, at Christmas 1994, the brewery was expended to a 60-barrel per week capacity. Initially local village brews, Mildmay beer can now be found in inns throughout Devon and the South West. Visitors are welcome at any time, but large parties or organised tours by prior arrangement.

Beers available at: Mildmay Colours Inn, Holbeton, Devon *and* New Inn, 1 Boringdon Road, Turnchapel, Plymstock, Devon.

COLOURS BEST 3.8% ABV
A light golden and hoppy bitter with a clean taste. The badge is in the Mildmay racing colours, light blue and white.

SP ALE 4.5% ABV
A slightly darker mid-brown beer with complex tastes both nutty and hoppy.

50/1 5.1% ABV
A stronger beer, dark with a strong bittersweet malty taste. It is of a rich and creamy appearance with excellent lacing.

OLD HORSE WHIP 5.7% ABV
A unique pale ale with a less aromatic nose than the other beers. It is light and easy to drink, although this belies its strong character.

TIPSTER 5.1% ABV
Smooth, dark, golden and strong.

JOCKEY WARMER 6.2% ABV
Dark brown, hoppy and warming.

Mildmay Colours Inn

Holbeton, Nr Plymouth PL8 1NA
☎ *(01752) 830248*
Mr A Patrick

Mildmay Colours Best, SP Ale, 50/1 and Old Horse Whip available plus guests (50 per year) such as Hop Back Summer Lightning, Bunces Danish Dynamite, RCH Pitchfork and Harviestoun Ptarmigan.

Large sixteenth-century Devonshire freehouse with two bars, pool, jukebox etc. Bar and restaurant food available at lunchtime and evenings. Car park, garden, terrace, children's room. Accommodation and tours arranged of the adjacent brewery.

11am–3pm and 6–11pm Mon–Sat; 12–10.30pm Sun.

HONITON

OTTER BREWERY

Mathayes Farm, Luppitt, Honiton EX14 0SA
☎ *(01404) 891285*
Visits welcome in organised parties.
Tied houses: None

Otter began brewing in November 1990 and has progressed steadily from a five-barrel plant to a 15-barrel plant currently producing 50 barrels a week. The brewery serves 60 pubs and nine wholesalers or agents. Using only malt and whole hops, spring water and having developed a very satisfactory yeast culture, the optimum production will be 60 barrels a week.

OTTER BITTER 3.6% ABV
A pale brown session bitter with a hoppy, fruity aroma and a bitter finish.

OTTER BRIGHT 4.3% ABV
A summer brew with a light, delicate flavour and long malty finish.

OTTER ALE 4.5% ABV
A well-balanced beer with malty, well-hopped aroma and taste.

OTTER DARK 4.8% ABV
A winter brew, dark in colour, with a chocolate malt aroma and taste and a well-rounded bitter finish.

OTTER HEAD 5.8% ABV
A smooth, strong malt aroma and taste.

HORNDON

The Elephant's Nest

Horndon, Nr Mary Tavy, PL19 9NQ
☎ *(01822) 810273*
Nick Camer

Palmer's IPA and St Austell HSD always available plus two guest beers (150 per year) including those from Exe Valley, Wye Valley, Cotleigh, Exmoor, Thompson's, Hook Norton, Summerskills and Ash Vine breweries. Also draught cider.

This sixteenth-century Dartmoor inn with a large garden and log fires has a collection of "Elephant's Nests" written in different languages on the beams in chalk. Bar food available at lunchtime and evenings. Car park and children's room. The garden is home to rabbits, ducks and chickens. Travel along the A386 into Mary Tavy. Take the road signposted Horndon for just under two miles.

11.30am–2.30pm and 6.30–11pm Mon–Sat; 12–2.30pm and 7–10.30pm Sun.

KINGSBRIDGE

BLEWITTS BREWERY

Ship and Plough,
The Promenade,
Kingsbridge TQ7 1JD
☎ *(01548) 852485*
Tied houses: None

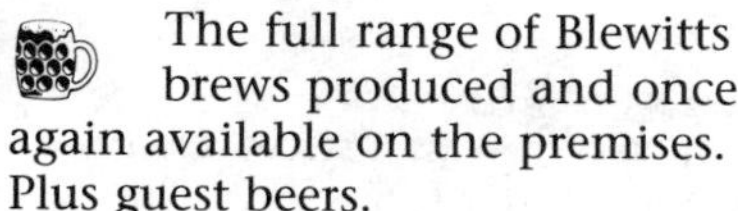
The full range of Blewitts brews produced and once again available on the premises. Plus guest beers.

Blewitts was originally set up as a brewpub at The Ship and Plough in 1990 but then moved to larger premises in Churchstow in February 1995. A problem with the water saw a return to The Ship and Plough in January 1996. The oak-beamed pub serves food at lunchtime and evenings (not Sunday evening). There is a family room.

BEST 3.8% ABV

WAGES 4.2% ABV

BRAINS OUT 6.0% ABV

11am–11pm.

LAPFORD

The Old Malt Scoop Inn

Lapford, Nr Crediton EX17 6PZ
☎ *(01363) 83330*
John and Pamela Berry

Wadworths 6X permanently available plus up to three guest beers (52 per year) to include Adnams Broadside, Shepherd Neame Spitfire, Charles Wells Bombadier, Crown Buckley Rev James Original, Marston's Pedigree and Bateman's XXXB. Also traditional cider.

This sixteenth-cenutry freehouse is open for morning coffee, bar snacks, meals and cream teas. There is an inglenook fireplace, beamed ceiling, skittle alley, beer garden and car park. Children allowed. Lapford is on the A377 between Crediton and Barnstaple. The pub is at the centre of the village, opposite the church.

10.30am–11pm May–Sept; 11.30am–3pm and 6–11pm Oct–end April.

NEWTON ABBOT

TEIGNWORTHY BREWERY

The Maltings, Teign Road,
Newton Abbot TQ12 4AA
☎ *(01626) 332066*
Visitors welcome April–October.
Tied houses: None

Teignworth Brewery was established in June 1994 by John and Rachel Lawton. John is a former Oakhill and Ringwood brewer. The operation is based at the historic Tuckers Maltings in Newton Abbot. Tours are operated at intervals during the day. Teignworthy Brewery produces cask ales which are sold in Devon, south Somerset and west Dorset. The present production rate is 18 barrels per week.

Beers available at: Bell Inn, 29 Fore Street, Kingsteignton, Nr Newton Abbot, Devon *and* Golden Lion, Newton Abbot, Devon.

REEL ALE 4.0% ABV
A hoppy, dry session beer.

BEACHCOMBER 4.5% ABV
A thirst-quenching lager-coloured brew.

SPRINGTIDE 4.7% ABV
A sweeter, darker brew with a hoppy character.

CHRISTMAS CRACKER 6.0% ABV
A mahogany-coloured strong winter ale.

Dartmouth Inn

63 East Street,
Newton Abbot TQ12 2JP
☎ *(01626) 53451*
Mr and Mrs Crovia

Guest beers (250 per year) may include Sticky Wicket, Jollyboat Plunder or Campaigna.

The pub is in a seventeenth-century building with oak beams. Bar food is available at lunchtime and evenings. Small garden and children's room. CAMRA south Devon pub of the year. Five minutes' walk from the railway station.

All day.

Newton St Cyres

The Beer Engine

Sweetham, Newton St Cyres,
Nr Exeter EX5 5AX
☎ *(01392) 851282*

Three beers brewed on the premises.

The brewery was established along with a cellar bar in the basement of a former station hotel in 1983. It has now expanded to produce three brews and 65 barrels per month, and supplies a couple of local pubs and wholesalers. Food available at lunchtime and evenings. Car park, garden, accommodation. Children allowed.

RAIL ALE 3.8% ABV
Amber-coloured beer with a malty aroma and a sweet fruity taste.

SISTON BITTER 4.3% ABV
Sweet-tasting beer with a bittersweet aftertaste.

SLEEPER HEAVY 5.4% ABV
Red in colour, with a sweet, fruity taste and a bitter finish.

11.30am–2.30pm and 6–11pm Mon–Fri (12pm Sat); 12–3pm and 7–10.30pm Sun.

Plymouth

Summerskills Brewery

Unit 15, Pomphlett Farm Ind Estate,
Broxton Drive, Billacombe PL9 7BG
☎ *(01752) 481283*
Visitors welcome. Tied houses: None

The brewery logo is taken from the ship's crest of *HMS Bigbury Bay*. It was founded by Adam Summerskill in 1983 in his vineyard at St Anne's Chapel near Bigbury-on-Sea, south Devon, with an initial capacity of two and a half barrels. In 1985 the brewery moved to its present location and the capacity was increased to ten barrels with the purchase of the redundant Penrhos Brewery, owned by Terry Jones of Monty Python fame. After two dormant years, Rick Wilson and Carl Beeson took over in October 1990. Brewing of Summerskills Best Bitter began, supplying outlets in Plymouth and also the House of Commons bars. Whistle Belly Vengeance was launched in 1991, followed by Ninjabeer in 1992 and Indiana's Bones in 1993. All the brews are produced by traditional methods using local malt and whole hops and are available nationally via carefully selected wholesalers.

Beers available at: Clifton Hotel, 35 Clifton Street, Greenbank, Plymouth, Devon *and* Prince Maurice,3 Church Hill, Eggbuckland, Plymouth, Devon.

BEST BITTER 4.3% ABV
A pale bitter with a fine crystal malt and hops character, a full malt flavour in the mouth and aromas of rich malt, nuts and hops, with a hint of honey.

WHISTLE BELLY VENGEANCE 4.7% ABV
A dark ruby beer full of dark malt character, with aromas of rich dark malt and hops. The mouth is dominated with hops, dark malt and liquorice.

NINJABEER 5.0% ABV
A dark golden beer, well balanced with malt and hops, a taste of soft malt, hops and toffee, light malt and hops aroma. Winter only.

INDIANA'S BONES 5.6% ABV
The latest addition, launched in November 1993. A rich dark winter warmer brewed all year, soft chocolate in the mouth with characteristic Goldings aromas.

King's Head Ale House and Brewery

21 Bretonside, Plymouth PL4 0BB
☎ (01752) 665619

The town's first brewpub sells Marston's Pedigree, Morland's Old Speckled Hen, Wadworth 6X and a range of own brews.

Neil Potts, licensee of Plymouth's oldest pub, decided to realise an ambition in 1993 by building a brewery at the King's Head. The business is now growing rapidly as the portfolio increases. Bar food available at lunchtime. Parking, garden. Children allowed.

KING'S RANSOM 4.08% ABV

BRETONSIDE'S BEST 4.2% ABV

GEZ'S ALE 5.0% ABV

GOLDEN GOOSE 5.0% ABV

MA HUSSON'S STRONG ALE 5.6% ABV

OLD HOPPY 5.6% ABV

10am–11pm.

Thistle Park Tavern

Sutton Brewing Company,
31 Commercial Road,
Plymouth PL4 0LE
☎ (01752) 667677

The five beers brewed by Sutton Brewing Company are sold in the tavern next door.

Brewing began in November 1993. The Thistle Park Tavern in central Plymouth features polished wooden floors, maritime relics and oil paintings by a local artist. Food served at lunchtime and evenings. Parking, patio. Children allowed. Polished wooden floors, maritime relics, oil paintings by local artist. Very good pub grub served lunchtimes and evenings. Parking, patio. Children allowed.

DARTMOOR PRIDE 3.8% ABV

XSB 4.2% ABV

HOPNOSIS 4.5% ABV

EDDYSTONE LIGHT 5.0% ABV

KNICKADRAGGA GLORY 5.5% ABV

11am–11pm Mon–Sat; 12–10.30pm Sun.

Prince Maurice

3 Church Hill, Eggbuckland, Plymouth PL6 5RJ
☎ *(01752) 771515*
Irene Green and Dave Fuzzard

Ten brews available, among them Hall & Woodhouse Tanglefoot and Summerskills brews always plus guests (100+ per year) including Blackbeard Stairway to Heaven, Eldridge Pope Royal Oak, Titanic Stout, Exmoor Stout and Everards Bitter.

Small, seventeenth-century beamed freehouse with two bars and log fires. CAMRA pub of the year. No food. Car park, patio. No children.

11am–3pm and 7–11pm Mon–Thurs (6–11pm Fri); all day Sat; 12–3 and 7–10.30pm Sun.

Plymstock

The Boringdon Arms

13 Boringdon Terrace, Turnchapel, Nr Plymstock PL9 9TQ
☎ *(01752) 402053*

Butcombe Bitter and Summerskills Best among the beers always available plus up to four guests beers (250 per year) from Orkney (north), Burts (south), Sharps (west), Scotts (east) and all points in between.

An ex-quarrymaster's house with a good atmosphere. No juke box. Live music on Saturday nights. CAMRA Plymouth pub of the year. Bar food available at lunchtime and evenings. Car park, children's room, conservatory and beer garden in the old quarry to the rear of the pub. Accommodation. Located at the centre of the village, four miles south-east of Plymouth. Signposted from the A379.

11am–11pm Mon–Sat; 12–3pm and 7–10.30pm Sun.

Princetown

Princetown Brewery

The Brewery, Tavistock Road, Princetown PL20 6QF
☎ *(01822) 890789*
Visitors welcome by appointment.
Tied houses: 5

Founded in October 1994 by Simon Loveless, the original Hop Back head brewer, and friends, this brewery, set in the middle of Dartmoor, claims to be the highest in England.

Beers available at: Prince of Wales, Tavistock Road, Princetown, Devon *and* Two Bridge Hotel, Two Bridges, Dartmoor, Devon.

DARTMOOR IPA 4.0% ABV
A light-coloured, refreshing, hoppy beer.

DARTMOOR ROYAL STOUT 4.5% ABV

WINTER ALE 4.7% ABV
A blend of Jail Ale and stout, available from December to February.

JAIL ALE 4.8% ABV
Mid-brown, full-flavoured bitter with a slightly sweet aftertaste.

DARTMOOR GOLD 5.0% ABV

RINGMORE

The Journey's End

Ringmore, Nr Kingsbridge TQ7 4HL
☎ *(01548) 810205*

Up to ten brews available including Exmoor and Otter Ale, Hall & Woodhouse Tanglefoot, Shepherd Neame Spitfire, Adnams Broadside and Crown Buckley Reverend James Original. Also guests (50 per year) changed weekly including Archers Golden, Greene King Abbot and brews from Palmers, Fuller's, Cains and Wadworth.

An eleventh-century thatched inn with flagstone floors and open fires. Bar and restaurant food served at lunchtime and evenings. Conservatory, car park, garden, non-smoking dining room. Accommodation. No children in the bar.

11am–3pm and 6–11pm Mon–Sat; 12–3pm and 7–10.30pm Sun.

SILVERTON

EXE VALLEY BREWERY

Land Farm, Silverton,
Nr Exeter EX5 4HF
☎ *(01392) 860406*
Visits for pre-arranged groups only.
Tied houses: None

Richard Barron established the Barron Brewery in 1984. Formerly the landlord of the Three Tuns in Silverton, he converted a redundant cow shed into the brewery. By 1991, the demand was too great for one person and so Guy Sheppard joined the operation and the name was changed to Exe Valley Brewery.

Guy had opted out of a career in accountancy after graduating from Exeter University. He set up the wholesale brewers' agents business of Sheppard and Nason in 1977, which was sold in 1991. In March 1994 a new plant was installed and officially opened by the local MP, Angela Browning, as part of the tenth anniversary celebrations. The brewery can now produce up to 60 barrels per week. The recipes use local spring water, Devon malt and hops with no additives. Local pubs are supplied direct within a 25-mile radius and the beers are also available nationally via wholesalers.

Beers available at: Silverton Inn, Fore Street, Silverton, Nr Exeter, Devon *and* Lamb Inn, 47 Fore Street, Silverton, Nr Exeter, Devon.

EXE VALLEY BITTER 3.7% ABV
A full-bodied bitter based on an old West Country recipe.

DEVON SUMMER 3.9% ABV
A pale summer beer, made from 100% pale Devon Malt and Fuggles and Goldings hops.

DOB'S BEST BITTER 4.1% ABV
A finely balanced fruity bitter with that extra touch of hops.

SPRING BEER 4.3% ABV
A light, well-hopped, refreshing beer brewed in spring to help forget the winter blues.

DEVON GLORY 4.7% ABV
A distinctive premium beer made from the finest Devon malt.

EXETER OLD BITTER 4.8% ABV
A smooth, well-hopped, strong beer.
Plus autumn and winter brews are planned.

DEVON

Silverton Inn

Fore Street, Silverton,
Nr Exeter EX5 4HP
☎ *(01392) 860196*

Exe Valley brews and Fuller's London Pride always available plus guests (60 per year) including Orkney Dark Island, Sutton Brewing Hypnosis and Knickerdroppa Glory, Blewitts Head Off, Wychwood Dr Thirsty's Draught, Hope Back Summer Lightning and Ringwood 49er.

Traditional, cosy wooden pub between Exeter and Tiverton with a separate upstairs restaurant. Food available at lunchtime and evenings. Nearby parking, beer garden. Children allowed in restaurant.

11.30am–3pm and 6–11pm.

SLAPTON

The Tower Inn

Slapton,
Nr Kingsbridge TQ7 2PN
☎ *(01548) 580216*
Mr and Mrs Dickman

Dartmoor Best, Exmoor Ale and Hall & Woodhouse Tanglefoot alwas available plus three or four guest beers (20+ per year) which may include Gibbs Mew Bishop's Tipple, Blackawton Headstrong, Palmer's IPA, Timothy Taylor Landlord and Eldridge Pope Royal Oak.

A fourteenth-century inn offering accommodation and a superb garden. Bar and restaurant food available at lunchtime and evenings. Car park and children's room. Hidden in the centre of the village at the foot of the old ruined tower.

12–3pm and 6–11pm.

TAVISTOCK

ROYAL INN AND HORSEBRIDGE BREWERY

Horsebridge,
Nr Tavistock PL19 8TJ
☎ *(01822) 870214*

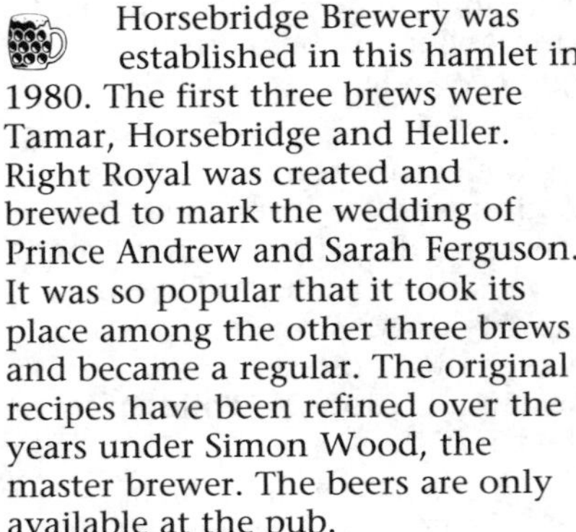

Horsebridge Brewery was established in this hamlet in 1980. The first three brews were Tamar, Horsebridge and Heller. Right Royal was created and brewed to mark the wedding of Prince Andrew and Sarah Ferguson. It was so popular that it took its place among the other three brews and became a regular. The original recipes have been refined over the years under Simon Wood, the master brewer. The beers are only available at the pub.

The Royal Inn is a fifteenth-century freehouse and former nunnery with log fires and quaint olde worlde charm. The seal of Charles I is set in the doorstep. Bar and restaurant food available at lunchtime and evenings. Car park, garden, accommodation. Children allowed in small room adjacent to the lounge bar under strict supervision only.

TAMAR 3.9% ABV
Light, malty beer.

HORSEBRIDGE BEST 4.5% ABV
Light bitter.

RIGHT ROYAL 5.0% ABV
Rich, full flavoured malty beer.

HELLER 6.0% ABV
Dark, rich and full bodied.

 *12–2.30pm and 7–11pm (10.30pm Sun) in winter. 11am–11pm in summer.*

Teignmouth

The Golden Lion

85 Bitton Park Road, Teignmouth TQ14 9BY
☎ *(01626) 776442*

At least two guest beers (approx 50 per year) usually available from regional brewers such as Blackawton, Teignworthy, Exe Valley and Oak Hill.

This is a locals' pub on the main road just out of the town with a public and lounge bar. Darts and pool are played. Bar food is available at lunchtime and evenings. Small car park. Children not allowed.

 *12–4pm and 6–11pm (10.30pm Sun).*

Topsham

Bridge Inn

Bridge Hill, Topsham, Nr Exeter EX3 0QQ
☎ *(01392) 873862*
Mr and Mrs Cheffers

Branscombe Vale Brnocand Olde Stoker, Adnams Broadside, Eldridge Pope Royal Oak, Hall & Woodhouse Tanglefoot, Exe Valley Devon Glory, Gibbs Mew Bishop's Tipple, Conquest, Devon Summer and Wadworth 6X always available.

This sixteenth-century pub overlooking the River Clyst has remained in the same family since 1897 through four generations. Simple bar food at lunchtime. Car park and children's room. Two miles from M5 junction 30. Topsham is signposted from the exit. In Topsham, follow the yellow signpost (A376) to Exmouth.

 *12–2pm and 6–10.30pm (11pm Fri–Sat).*

Totnes

Blackawton Brewery

Washbourne, Totnes TQ9 7UF
☎ *(01803) 732339*
No visitors. Tied houses: None

The brewery began in the village of Blackawton, near Dartmouth, in 1977 and moved to its present site, just outside a neighbouring village, in 1981 and claims now to be the county's oldest brewery. There was a change of ownership in 1988. All beers are produced without additives using only whole grain malted barley, whole hops, fresh yeast and water. Red seaweed is used as a fining agent.

Beers available at: Normandy Arms, Blackawton, Nr Totnes, Devon *and* Blue Anchor, Fore Street, Brixham, Devon.

BLACKAWTON BITTER 3.8% ABV
The brewery's original and best-known beer. A true best bitter, generously hopped and carefully matured. An ideal session brew.

DEVON GOLD 4.1% ABV
Summer brew matured in the European style with a light, fresh taste and smooth flavour of pale malted English barleys and fresh European hops.

44 SPECIAL 4.5% ABV
Premium, full-strength bitter, full bodied with a rich nut flavour.

HEADSTRONG 5.2% ABV
Strong, but deceptively smooth.

DARTMOOR GOLD 5.0% ABV

Blandford St Mary

Hall & Woodhouse

The Brewery, Blandford St Mary, Blandford Forum DT11 9LS
☎ *(01258) 452141*
Visitors welcome. Tied houses: 64

The brewery was founded in 1777 in Ansty, Dorset, by Charles Hall, whose son, Robert, went into partnership with Mr GEI Woodhouse in 1847. It was relocated to Blandford St Mary more than 100 years ago and remains in family hands. Hall & Woodhouse also owns the Gribble Inn brewpub in Oving, West Sussex.

BADGER BEST BITTER 4.0% ABV
A fine best bitter whose taste is strong in hop and bitterness, with underlying malt and fruit. A hoppy finish with a bitter edge.

HARD TACKLE 4.6% ABV
A well-balanced, tawny-coloured beer. The nose is fruity and hoppy with some malt, and the palate has similar characteristics. A mainly bitter aftertaste.

TANGLEFOOT ALE 5.0% ABV
A pale-coloured beer with a full fruit character throughout. Some malt and hop are also present in the palate, while the finish is bittersweet. Dangerously drinkable.

12–3pm and 7–10.30pm Sun.

Bridport

JC & RH Palmer

The Old Brewery, West Bay Road, Bridport DT6 4JA
☎ *(01308) 422396*
Visitors by appointment.
Tied houses: 64

The Old Brewery was first used to brew beer in 1794, making Palmers one of the few UK producers able to claim continuous production over 200 years on the original site. Part of the building is still thatched. The brewery was founded by the Gundry family, local rope and net makers, and was subsequently acquired, in the late nineteenth century, by the Palmer brothers, John Cleeves and Robert Henry. Since then, the business has been growing steadily and has been handed down from one generation to another. Today, two more Palmer brothers are in charge – John, is chairman and managing director; Cleeves is marketing and wine director. They are great grandsons of the original Palmers.

Beers available at: Boot Inn, 124 North Allington, Bridport, Dorset *and* Angel Inn, Mill Green, Monmouth Street, Lyme Regis, Dorset.

PALMERS BRIDPORT BITTER 3.9% ABV
A pleasant, light and refreshing bitter. It drinks fuller than the gravity suggests.

PALMERS IPA TRADITIONAL BEST BITTER 4.2% ABV
A full-drinking, well-balanced beer with a delicious hop character.

PALMERS TALLY HO! 4.7% ABV
A strong, nutty, full-strength dark beer that delivers a deep, distinctive and long-lasting taste.

PALMERS 200 PREMIUM ALE 5.0% ABV
Brewed for the first time in March

1994 to celebrate 200 years of brewing at Bridport. A distinctive full-flavoured beer, rich in colour imparting a smooth, balanced taste.

CATTISTOCK

The Fox and Hounds

Duck Street, Cattistock
☎ *(01300) 320444*
Anne Hinton

 Lots of guest beers, two at any one time. These may include Fuller's London Pride, Charles Wells Bombadier and ales from Oakhill, Devon and Somerset and Cottage breweries.

A fifteenth-century village inn with large fires, flagstones and a separate restaurant. Relaxing atmosphere. Bar and restaurant food available at lunchtime and evenings. Parking, garden and play area opposite. Campsite nearby. Accommodation. On the A37, look out for the sign for Cattistock, just past the Clay Pigeon Cafe from Yeovil or the sign on the road from Dorchester.

OPEN *12–2.30pm and 7–11pm.*

DORCHESTER

ELDRIDGE, POPE

Weymouth Avenue,
Dorchester DT1 1QT
☎ *(01305) 251251*
Visitors welcome. Tied houses: 200

Charles Eldridge and his wife, Sarah, took over the Antelope Hotel in Dorchester in 1833 and established the Green Dragon Brewery in 1837. Charles died in 1846 but his wife continued to run the business with Alfred Mason, who retired in 1870 and sold his share of the company to Edwin Pope. By 1874, Edwin and his brother, Alfred, had acquired complete control and Eldridge Pope was born. The business expanded rapidly and the present brewery was built in 1880 next to the main southern rail link. Licensed premises were acquired along the railway line through Poole, Bournemouth, Southampton and onto Winchester and Portsmouth. Although very considerable growth has taken place, the south coast remains the heart of Eldridge Pope country. Alfred Pope's descendants continue to maintain the traditions of quality and service that contributed to that growth. They have expanded the brewery and installed modern plant.

DORCHESTER BITTER 3.3% ABV
Pale amber colour with fresh hop and malt aroma. Light and refreshing with a clean finish. A more satisfying pint than its alcohol level would lead you to expect.

BLACKDOWN PORTER 4.0% ABV
Dark, winter beer with a roast malt aroma. Traces of coffee, chocolate and blackcurrant in the taste and a dry bitter finish.

THOMAS HARDY COUNTRY BITTER 4.2% ABV
A rich amber-coloured beer with a full well-balanced body. Delicious with the aroma of malt and fruit overlaid with a distinctive dry-hop fragrance and clean bitter finish.

ROYAL OAK 5.0% ABV
Deep red-amber colour with an abundance of rich malt and fruit aroma complimented by English hops. Immediately warming with a delicious balance of flavour and bitterness, giving way to a rich smooth finish.

Plus a range of bottle-conditioned brews.

North Wootton

The Three Elms

North Wootton,
Nr Sherborne DT9 5JW
☎ *(01935) 812881*
Mr and Mrs Manning

Fuller's London Pride, Shepherd Neame Spitfire Ale, Hop Back Summer Lightning, Smiles and Butcombe brews permanently available. Plus two or three guests (160 per year) to include Oakhill Somer Ale, Black Sheep Special, RCH Pitchfork, Smiles Mayfly and Bateman's Strawberry Fields.

A busy roadside pub with a large garden and car park. Contains a collection of 1000+ diecast model cars and lorries in display cabinets around the walls. Bar and restaurant food available at lunchtime and evenings. Children allowed. Accommodation. Situated on the A3030 Sherborne to Sturminster Newton road, two miles from Sherborne.

11–2.30pm Mon–Sat,
12–3pm Sun;
6.30–11pm Mon–Thurs,
6–11pm Fri–Sat,
7–10.30pm Sun.

Poole

The Bermuda Triangle Free House

Parr Street, Lower Parkstone,
Poole BH14 0JY
☎ *(01202) 748087*
Mrs G Crane

No permanent beers but three guests constantly changing. These may include Timothy Taylor Landlord, Fuller's ESB and London Pride, Adnams Broadside, Hop Back Summer Lightning, Greene King Abbot Ale, Ringwood Old Thumper and 49er. Also Youngs, Wychwood, Hampshire, Smiles and Shepherd Neame brews.

An interesting theme pub. German lagers on draught and at least 30 bottled beers from all around the world. Good music, great atmosphere. Bar food at lunchtime. Car park. Near Ashley Cross.

11.30am–3pm and
5.30–11pm.

Sherborne

The Digby Tap

Cooks Lane, Sherborne DT9 3NS
☎ *(01935) 813148*
Mrs Parker

Twenty different beers served each week from a range of 100 per year. Brews from the Smiles, Teignworthy, Ringwood, Ash Vine, Oakhill, Burtonwood and Cottage breweries, plus many other regional producers.

A traditional, local, one-bar drinking house with flagstone floors. Bar snacks available at lunchtime (not Sundays). Children allowed at lunchtime only. Just 100 yards from the abbey, towards the railway station.

11am–2.30pm and
5.30–11pm Mon–Sat;
12–2.30pm and
7–10.30pm Sun.

Tarrant Monkton

The Langton Arms

Tarrant Monkton,
Nr Blandford DT11 8RX
☎ *(01258) 830225*
Mr and Mrs Davidson

Approximately 100 guest beers per year, none permanent, four at any one time. These may include Ringwood 49er, Smiles Best, Tisbury Old Wardour, Shepherd Neame Spitfire, brews from Tally Ho! and many other micro-breweries.

An attractive seventeenth-century thatched inn with a separate restaurant (evenings only). Bar food available lunchtime and evenings. Car park, garden, children's room and play area. Accommodation. Less than two miles off the A354 Blandford to Salisbury road, five miles north of Blandford.

11.30am–2.30pm and 6–11pm; all day Sat.

Trent

The Rose and Crown

Trent, Nr Sherborne DT9 4SL
☎ (01935) 850776
Mr and Mrs Crawford

Butcombe Best and Shepherd Neame Spitfire always available plus two guest beers (24 per year) including Wadworth 6X, Charles Wells Bombardier, Otter Ale plus brews from Smiles, Hook Norton, Morland and Sam Smith.

A fifteenth-century part-thatched freehouse situated opposite Trent church. Bar and restaurant food available at lunchtime and evenings. Car park, garden, children's room and playground. Less than two miles north of the A30 between Sherborne and Yeovil.

12–2.30pm and 7–11pm Mon–Sat; 12–3pm and 7–10.30pm Sun.

Weymouth

The Weatherbury Hotel

7 Carlton Road North,
Weymouth DT4 7PX
☎ *(01305) 786040*
Mr and Mrs Cromack

Four guest beers (200 per year) which may include Townes IPA, Hall & Woodhouse Tanglefoot, Wild's Redhead and Fuller's London Pride.

A busy town local in a residential position. Bar and restaurant food available at lunchtime and evenings. Car park, patio and dining area (where children are allowed). Dart board and pool table. Accommmodation. Coming in to Weymouth, turn right off the Dorchester road.

11am–2.30pm and 5.30–11pm Mon–Thurs; all day Fri–Sun.

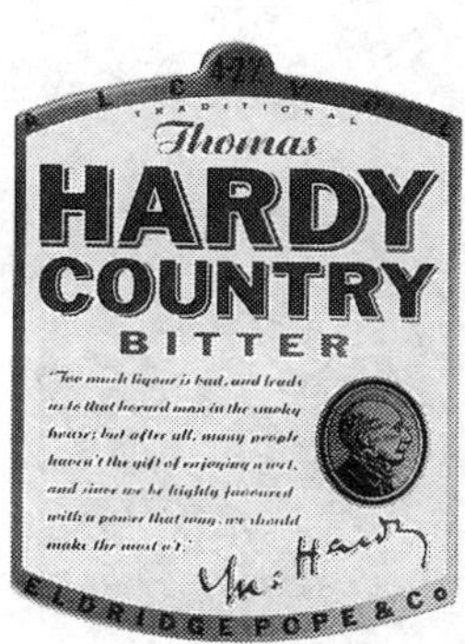

DORSET

Winkton

The Lamb Inn

Burley Road, Winkton BM23 7AN
☎ *(01425) 672427*
Mr and Mrs Plevey

Ringwood 49er and Best, plus Hall & Woodhouse Badger Best permanently available. Also a guest beer (five per year) likely to include H&W Tanglefoot or Fuller's London Pride.

Situated in the heart of the New Forest, this pub has a lounge and public bar. Bar and restaurant food available at lunchtime and evenings. Car park and garden. Children are allowed in the restaurant.

11am–3pm and 5–11pm Mon–Sat; 12–3pm and 7–10.30pm Sun.

Bowburn

Durham Brewery

Units 6D/E, Bowburn North Industrial Estate, Bowburn DH6 5PF
☎ *(0191) 377 1991*
No visitors. Tied houses: None

Launched at the Durham Beer Festival in 1994, the range of beers has been steadily updated ever since. The plant is now working to a capacity of 15 barrels per week and there are plans for an upgrade and a bottling operation.

Beers available at: Half Moon, Kirk Merrington, Durham *and* Miners Arms, Acomb, Durham.

SUNSTROKE 3.6% ABV
Light and slightly sweet, hugely aromatic with Saaz and Styrian Goldings hops. A popular summer ale.

MAGUS 3.8% ABV
Pale ale with lager qualities. Drier and more bitter than Sunstroke but still aromatic with citrus overtones.

CELTIC 4.2% ABV
Robust premium bitter using Fuggles hops.

OLD HUNDRED 4.4% ABV
Smooth maltiness balanced with good bitterness and fine hop aroma. Golden in colour.

CANNY LAD 4.2% ABV
Complex background with six different malts. Round and satisfying, fairly light in colour.

BLACK BISHOP 4.5% ABV
Truly black with roast malts, a smooth, drinkable stout.

PAGAN 4.8% ABV
Golden, mouthfilling strong bitter using Goldings hops.

SANCTUARY 6.0% ABV
Sweet, ruby-coloured old ale matured in the brewery.

Crook

Hodge's Brewhouse

Brewhouse Towers, Unit 5a, Castle Close, Crook DL15 8LU
☎ *(01388) 763200*
Visitors welcome. Tied houses: None

Ian Robinson and Stephen Brooke met in Sheffield and, real ale fans, they decided to set up a micro-brewery near Ian's home in Wear Valley, Co Durham, which he had left 25 years before. They opened for business in October 1994 and began by brewing Original. Best was added to the portfolio in June and Traditional arrived over the August bank holiday. A number of supportive local outlets, including Spennymoor United Football Club, have helped them to become firmly established.

Beers available at: Neville's Cross Hotel, Darlington Road, Durham City, Co Durham *and* The Commercial, Front Street, Tantobie, Nr Stanley, Co Durham.

TRADITIONAL 3.7% ABV
A clean, bittter session beer

ORIGINAL 4.0% ABV
A fruity, medium bitter.

BEST 4.5% ABV
A sharp, hoppy bitter.

DURHAM

Darlington

Number Twenty 2

Coniscliffe Road,
Darlington DL3 7RG
☎ *(01325) 354590*
Mr Wilkinson

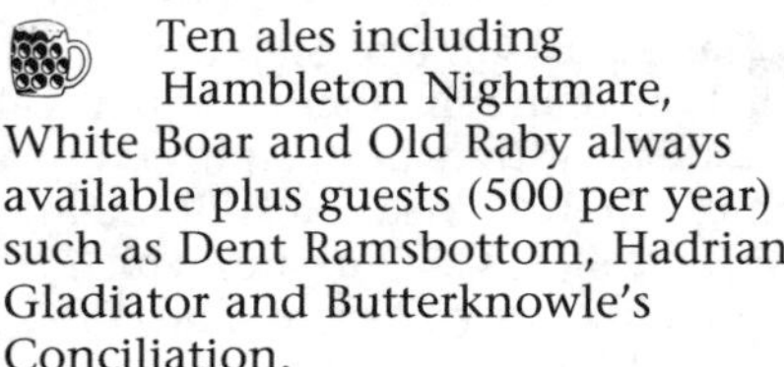

Ten ales including Hambleton Nightmare, White Boar and Old Raby always available plus guests (500 per year) such as Dent Ramsbottom, Hadrian Gladiator and Butterknowle's Conciliation.

Traditional town centre freehouse. Food available at lunchtime and evenings. Parking nearby, children allowed.

11am–11pm.

The Tap & Spile

99 Bondgate, Darlington DL3 7JY
☎ *(01325) 381679*
Stella Bowden

Eight guests (100 per year) at any one time continually changing with brews from Marstons, Greene King, Butterknowle, Durham, Hadrian, Hambleton, Lees, Robinsons, Adnams, Batemans, Burtonwood, Exmoor, Jennings, Hardington, Morland, Nethergate, Steam Packet, Ridleys, Titanic, Ushers, Oak, Belhaven and Harviestoun.

A traditional town centre ale house where the policy is to offer one beer a month at a discounted price (£1.19–£1.24), sponsored by the brewer. Food available at lunchtime. Parking, children's room and non-smoking room.

11.30am–11pm Mon–Sat; 12–10.30pm Sun.

Framwellgate Moor

The Tap & Spile

27 Front Street,
Framwellgate Moor, DH1 5EE
☎ *(0191) 386 5451*
Mr DE Robson

Village White Boar always available plus seven guests from a list of approximately 500, including Greene King, Batemans, Marstons and many small independent breweries.

Converted in 1988, recently refurbished, but unaltered. Bar food available until 10.30pm. Children's room. Less than two miles north of Durham city centre.

11.30am–3pm and 6–11pm.

Hartlepool

The Camerons Brewery Co.

Lion Brewery,
Hartlepool TS24 7QS
☎ *(01429) 266666*
Visitors welcome. Tied houses: 100

Brewing began on this site in 1852 and JW Cameron became involved after the death of its founder, William Waldon, in 1854. The brewery grew through the acquisition of JJ Hunt of York (1955), West Auckland Brewery (1959) and Russells and Wrangham (1961). Camerons remained a family brewery until 1975, when it was purchased by Ellerman Lines. In 1992 Wolverhampton & Dudley Breweries bought the business from Brent Walker, along with 52 pubs. Thus began a new era for The Lion Brewery, the Cameron pubs and Strongarm.

CAMERON'S BEST SCOTCH 3.5% ABV
A full-flavoured sweet beer with a nutty flavour and a rich dark colour.

CAMERON'S BITTER 3.6% ABV
A popular full-flavoured, smooth, well-balanced northern bitter.

STRONGARM RUBY RED BITTER 4.0% ABV
A distinctive, rose-red flavour bitter with a rich ruby-red colour and a smooth creamy head.

CROWN SPECIAL 4.6% ABV
Lightly hopped, light-coloured ale with a moreish reputation.

STANLEY

The Highlander

White-le-Head, Tantobie, Nr Stanley DH9 9SN
☎ *(01207) 232416*
Mr CD Wright

Up to 100 beers per year changed weekly including those from Thwaites, Timothy Taylor, Black Sheep and Marstons, plus beers from many other smaller breweries as available.

One bar has games and music (pool, darts, etc). Also a small lounge and dining area. Hot food available on weekday evenings and weekend afternoons. Car park, beer garden, children's room and function room. Occasional accommodation. Ring to check. One mile off the A692 between Tantobie and Flint Hill.

OPEN *7.30–11pm Mon–Fri; 12.30–3pm and 7.30–11pm Sat–Sun.*

Brightlingsea

Railway Tavern

58 Station Road,
Brightlingsea CO7 0DT
☎ *(01206) 302581*
David English

Mauldon's brews always available plus up to four guests including Tolly Cobbold Anniversary and IPA, Ridley's ESX, Crouch Vale Best Bitter, Golden Duck and Millennium Gold, Nethergate IPA, Brakspear Special and Morland's Old Masters.

A friendly, traditional pub with real fire and floorboards. No fruit machines or juke box. Parking, garden, children's room. Pool, shove ha'penny, darts, cribbage, dominoes. Campsite opposite, 12 pubs within walking distance.

5pm–11pm Mon–Thurs;
12–11pm Fri–Sat;
12–10.30pm summer Sun,
12–3pm and
7–10.30pm winter Sun.

Chelmsford

TD Ridley & Sons

Hartford End Brewery, Felsted,
Chelmsford CM3 1JZ
☎*(01371) 820316*
Visitors welcome by appointment.
Tied houses: 60

The Ridley family can be traced back to the tenth century. Bishop Nicholas Ridley was martyred during the reign of Mary, Queen of Scots, Sir Thomas Ridley was Master of Eton College and Marke Ridley was physician to the Czar of Russia in 1595. Thomas Dixon Ridley was born in 1814. In 1841 he married Lydia Wells, who came from a brewing family in Chelmsford, and, soon afterwards, he built a brewery on the banks of the River Chelmer. Business expanded rapidly and, by his death in 1882, a chain of inns had been established. In 1906, a limited company was formed. Today, it is still in the hands of the Ridley family and is run by Nicholas Ridley, the founder's great great grandson.

Beers available at: The Anchor, Runsell Green, Danbury, Nr Chelmsford, Essex *and* The Beehive, Baddow Road, Chelmsford, Essex.

RIDLEYS IPA BITTER 3.5% ABV
An award-winning, well-balanced hoppy bitter.

CHAMPION MILD 3.5% ABV
A real ale with a dark, full character.

ESX BEST BITTER 4.3% ABV
A stronger ale with a well-hopped flavour.

WITCHFINDER PORTER 4.3% ABV
A dark and full-flavoured brew, based on a traditional porter recipe. Available October to March.

RUMPUS 4.5% ABV
A new mid-strength ruby ale with a smooth nutty character. Available September to April.

SPECTACULAR 4.6% ABV
A strong, unusually pale bitter ale. Available April to September.

WINTER ALE 5.0% ABV
A seasonal beer, strong and warming.

Plus a range of bottled brews.

The White Horse

25 Townfield Road,
Chelmsford CM1 1QT
☎ *(01245) 269556*

Up to seven guests (600 per year) including Hambleton Stallion, Rooster's Yankee, Otter Bright, Bateman's Strawberry Fields,

Pilgrim Great Crusader, Freeminer Slaughter Porter and Hook Norton Haymaker.

Large comfortable one-bar pub with a plethora of traditional pub games. Bar food available at lunchtime and evenings. Specialises in gourmet sausages cooked over a griddle. Turn right from the rear of the railway station.

11am–3pm and 5.30–11pm.

COLCHESTER

Odd One Out

28 Mersea Road,
Colchester CO2 7ET
☎ (01206) 578140
John Parrick

Ridley's IPA, Archer's Best and a mild permanently available plus up to four guest beers which may include Maclays 80/–, Hull Mild, Jennings Bitter, Tolly Cobbold IPA, Mauldon's Porter, Crouch Vale SAS, Arkell's, Kinsgdown etc.

Friendly pub located about 100 yards up the Mersea Road from St Botolph's roundabout. A traditional drinker's alehouse with garden.

4.30–11pm only Mon–Thurs;
11am–11pm Fri–Sat;
usual hours Sun.

The Tap & Spile

123 Crouch Street,
Colchester CO3 3HA
☎ (01206) 573572
Mr and Mrs Mathieson

Adnams Bitter, Marston's Pedigree and Nethergate Bitter always available plus up to five others including Morland Old Speckled Hen, Greene King Abbot Ale, Charles Wells Bombardier, Shepherd Neame ales, Thwaite's Mild, Usher's Founders Ale, Everard's Tiger, Black Sheep Best and many more.

Traditional English alehouse with no carpets, video machines or jukebox. Soft background music. Bar food served at lunchtime. Outside patio. Children allowed. Just outside the town centre, opposite the Essex County Hospital, on Lexden Road.

11am–2.30pm and
5.30–11pm Mon–Fri;
all day Sat;
12–3pm and 7–10.30pm Sun.

FEERING

The Sun Inn

3 Feering Hill, Feering,
Nr Kelvedon CO5 9NH
☎ (01376) 570442
Mr and Mrs Scicluna

Wadworth 6X always available plus too many guest beers to list (four at any one time). The emphasis is firmly on the more unusual micro-breweries.

A heavily timbered former mansion, richly decorated with carved beams and featuring open fires. Bar and restaurant food is available at lunchtime and evenings. Car park and garden. Small functions (up to 28 persons) catered for. Turn off the Kelveden bypass when coming from the north or south.

11am–3pm and 6–11pm
Mon–Sat; 12–3pm and
7–10.30pm Sun.

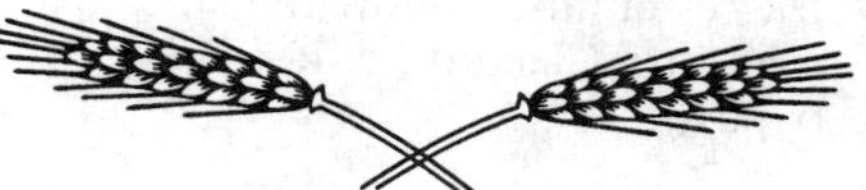

Gestingthorpe

The Pheasant

Audley End,
Gestingthorpe CO9 3AX
☎ *(01787) 461196*

Greene King IPA, Adnams Best and Broadside permanently available with a guest beer in summer.

This recently refurbished multi-roomed, 400-year-old freehouse has exposed timbers, open fires and a warm friendly atmosphere. There are three bars, including a dining area. Food is available at lunchtime and evenings, except Sunday and Monday. Car park, garden. Children allowed. Well signposted, the only pub in the village.

12–3pm and
6–11pm Mon–Sat;
7–10.30pm Sun.

Little Clacton

The Apple Tree

The Street, Little Clacton CO16 9LS
☎ *(01255) 861026*
Mrs Clarke

Charles Wells IPA always available plus three others (60+ per year) including Nethergate Old Growler, Morland's Old Speckled Hen, Wadworth 6X, Adnams Broadside, Hook Norton Old Hooky, Brakspear's Special, Everard's Tiger and Gale's HSB.

A well-run family pub with live entertainment every Saturday. Bar and restaurant food available at lunchtime and evenings. Car park and garden. Children allowed in the restaurant. Follow the "old" road into Clacton (ie. not the bypass).

11am–11pm Mon–Fri;
11am–midnight Sat;
12–3pm and 7–10.30pm Sun.

Littlebury

The Queen's Head

High Street, Littlebury
Nr Saffron Walden CB11 4TD
☎ *(01799) 522251*
Jeremy O'Gorman

Timothy Taylor Landlord among those beers always available plus four or five guests (140 per year) to include Border Rover, Burton Bridge Spring Ale, Fuller's London Pride, Marston's Pedigree, Mauldons Black Adder etc.

Sixteenth-century coaching inn with exposed beams, a snug and two open fires. Beer festival at Easter. Bar and restaurant food available at lunchtime and evenings. No-smoking area, car park, garden. Accommodation. Children allowed. On the B1383, between Newport and M11 junction nine.

12–11pm Mon–Sat;
12–10.30pm Sun.

Mill Green

The Viper

Mill Green Road, Mill Green,
Nr Ingatestone CM40 0PS
☎ *(01277) 352010*
Mr and Mrs Beard

All beers changed monthly, but three always available (36 per year). These may include Ridley's IPA, Wadworth 6X, Fuller's London Pride and beers from Mansfield, Thwaites, Jennings, Shepherd Neame, Marston's and Bateman breweries.

A small, traditional unspoilt country pub with award-winning garden. Bar food available at lunchtime and evenings. Car park. Children allowed. Take the Ivy Barn road off the A12. Turn off at Margaretting. Two miles north-west of Ingatestone.

11am–2.30pm Mon–Fri; 11am–3pm Sat–Sun.

NAVESTOCK HEATH

The Plough Inn

Sabines Road,
Navestock Heath RM4 1HD
☎ *(01277) 372296*

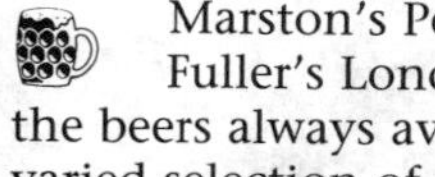
Marston's Pedigree and Fuller's London Pride among the beers always available in a varied selection of eight real ales (100+ per year) chosen from all across the land.

A one-bar public house with a small dining room and family room. Background music, no jukebox, machines or pool table. Bar snacks and meals are available at lunchtime and evenings (except Sunday and Monday). Car park, two gardens, children allowed. The pub is difficult to find, so ring for directions.

11am–11pm Mon–Sat; 12–10.30pm Sun.

PEBMARSH

The King's Head

The Street, Pebmarsh,
Nr Halstead CO9 2NH
☎ *(01787) 269306*
Ian Miller

Greene King IPA always available plus three guest beers including Timothy Taylor Landlord, Fuller's London Pride, Woodforde's, Mauldon's, Ridleys, Simpkiss and Roosters brews.

A freehouse built in 1740, with oak-beamed interior. Bar snacks and meals available at lunchtime and evenings. Barbecues in season. Car park, garden, barn with skittle alley, children's room. One mile off the Halstead to Sudbury road.

12–2pm and 7–11pm.

PLESHEY

The White Horse

Pleshey,
Nr Chelmsford CM3 1HA
☎ *(01245) 37281*

Beers from Crouch Vale and Nethergate always available plus a guest beer (25 per year), perhaps from Jennings, Archer's, Bateman's, Elgood's, Morland, Eichbaum, Gales, Malton, Mitchell's or Clarke's brewery.

A fifteenth-century village pub. Bar and restaurant food available at lunchtime and evenings. Large car park, garden and children's room.

11am–3pm and 7–11pm.

SOUTH WOODHAM FERRERS

CROUCH VALE BREWERY

12 Redhills Road,
South Woodham Ferrers,
Nr Chelmsford CM3 5UP
☎ *(01245) 322744*
Visitors welcome. Tied houses: 1

Crouch Vale Brewery was founded in 1981 by two enthusiasts who saw a need for a locally brewed beer of distinctive character. The initial Best Bitter was precisely this, full bodied and malty. Brewing was usually carried out on a Saturday, when plenty of interested onlookers were available to help and deliveries were carried out in a dilapidated Bedford van which spent more time with its bonnet up than down. The brewery adopted the Thames Barge as its logo as a link with the locality. These vessels have plied the coastal waters of Essex and Suffolk for hundreds of years. Nowadays, the brewery has six full-time employees, although the brewing process has not changed and only first-class ingredients are used. Beer is now delivered in a smart liveried dray throughout Essex, south Suffolk and London. The first tied house, the Cap and Feathers at Tillingham, was purchased in 1985.

Beers available: Cap and Feathers, 8 South Street, Tilllingham, Essex *and* The Windmill, The Tye, East Hanningfield, Nr Chelmsford, Essex.

WOODHAM IPA 3.6% ABV
An amber beer with a fresh, hoppy nose with slight fruitiness. A good session bitter with a well-balanced taste leading to a fruit and hop finish.

THE GOLDEN DUCK 3.8% ABV
A classic golden summer ale with a dry refreshing flavour and a pronounced Styrian Golding hop character.

BEST BITTER 4.0% ABV
The fruity aroma of this red/brown brew invites drinkers into a splendid taste of malt and fruit, with some hops, leading to a bitter finish.

MILLENNIUM GOLD 4.2% ABV
A golden beer featuring a strong, hoppy nose with maltiness. A mixture of hops and fruit combines with pale malt for a sharp, bitter flavour with malty undertones.

STRONG ANGLIAN SPECIAL OR SAS 4.8% ABV
A tawny-coloured beer with a fruity nose. Well-balanced, full-bodied and sharply bitter, with a dry aftertaste.

ESSEX PORTER 4.9% ABV
A dark brew with a complex aroma followed by a flavour that is fruit and slightly nutty on a sweet base. Balanced sweet finish.

SANTA'S REVENGE 5.7% ABV
A Christmas ale sold throught the year under house names.

WILLIE WARMER 6.4% ABV
A meal in a mug.
Plus a range of seasonal brews.

Southend on Sea

Cork & Cheese

10 Talza Way, Victoria Circus, Southend on Sea SS2 5BG
☎ *(01702) 616914*
John Murray

Cork & Cheese Best (from Tolly Cobbold) always available plus three guests (250 per year) including brews from Concertina, Butterknowle, Rooster's, Woodforde's, Titanic, Hop Back, Wild's, Clark's, Burt's and Foxley.

An ale house with a cosmopolitan trade. Separate dining area for bar and restaurant meals. Food available at lunchtime. Multistorey car park nearby. Patio in summer. Children allowed in the restaurant. Located on the basement floor of the Victoria Circus shopping centre in Southend.

11am–11pm Mon–Sat; closed Sun.

Southminister

The Station Arms

39 Station Road, Southminster CM0 7EW
☎ *(01621) 772225*
Martin Park

Crouch Vale Best always available plus three guest beers (150 per year) from Titanic, Hop Back, Concertina, Fuller's, Jennings, Mitchell's, Rooster's and Timothy Taylor breweries.

A friendly, single-bar, Essex weather-boarded pub with open fire and traditional pub furniture. Pub games played. Restaurant and courtyard to the rear. Bar and restaurant food served at lunchtime and evenings. Parking. Children allowed in the restaurant. Situated 200 yards from Southminster railway station.

12–3pm and 5.30–11pm Mon–Fri; 12–11pm Sat; 12–3pm and 7–10.30pm Sun.

Stock

The Hoop

21 High Street, Stock CM4 9BD
☎ *(01277) 841137*
Albert and David Kitchen

Up to ten beers available. Brews from Adnams, Crouch Vale, Wadworth and Charles Wells always. Guests from Bateman, Archer's, Ringwood, Hop Back, Jennings, Exmoor, Fuller's, Marston's, Nethergate, Rooster's, Shepherd Neame and Mitchells.

The pub has been adapted from some late fifteenth-century beamed cottages. There is an extensive beer garden to the rear. Bar food available all day. Barbecues at weekends in summer, weather permitting. Parking. Children not allowed. Take the B1007 from the A12 Chelmsford bypass, then take the Galleywood-Billericay turn off.

11am–11pm.

Stow Maries

The Prince of Wales

Woodham Road, Stow Maries CM3 6SA
☎ *(01621) 828971*
Robert Walster

Fuller's Chiswick always available plus any four

guests (too many to count) including a mild and a stout/porter from small independent and the better regional brewers.

A traditional Essex weatherboarded pub with real fires and working Victorian bakery. Bar food available at lunchtime and evenings. Car park, garden and family room. Under two miles from South Woodham Ferrers on the road to Cold Norton.

11am–11pm Mon–Sat; 12–10.30pm Sun.

TILLINGHAM

Cap and Feathers

8 South Street, Tillingham CM70 7TH
☎ (01621) 779212
John Moore

Crouch Vale Woodham IPA, Best Bitter, Dark Ale and Essex Porter always available plus a guest (400 per year) which might include Morland Old Speckled Hen, Titanic Best, Buffy's Polly's Folly and Clark's Burglar Bill.

Dates from 1427, an old weatherboard building. Unspoilt with a relaxed atmosphere. Bar food available at lunchtime and evenings. Car park, garden, no-smoking family room. Accommodation. Between Southminster and Bradwell.

11.30am–3pm and 6–11pm Mon–Sat; 12–3pm and 7–10.30pm Sun.

WENDENS AMBO

The Bell

Royston Road, Wendens Ambo CB11 4JU
☎ (01799) 540382
Jeff Bates

Adnams Bitter and Ansell's Dark Mild always available plus a couple of guests (50 per year) perhaps including Everards Tiger, Mitchell's Lancaster Bomber, Charles Wells Bombardier, Eldridge Pope Royal Oak, Adnams Broadside and Gales brews.

Built 1576, beamed with open fires in winter. Background music only. Bar food available at lunchtime and evenings (not Monday). Car park, garden, children's play area.

11.30am–3pm and 6–11pm Mon–Sat; 12–3pm and 7–10.30pm Sun.

Ashleworth

The Boat Inn

The Quay,
Ashleworth GL19 4HZ
☎ *(01452) 700272*
Mrs Nichols

Arkell's 3B, Smiles Best and Oakhill Yeoman 1767 always available plus two of many guest beers served straight from the cask including Exmoor Gold, Archer's Golden Bitter, Uley Pig's Ear and Old Spot, Wild's Blonde and Thing, Oakhill Somer Ale and Black Magic, Arkell's Summer Ale, Smiles Exhibition and various Christmas ales.

A fifteenth-century cottage pub on the bank of the River Severn. Small and friendly, has remained in the same family for 400 years. Bar food available at lunchtime. Car park and garden. Children allowed. Ashleworth is signposted off the A417 north of Gloucester. The Quay is signed from the village.

OPEN *11am–3pm and 6–11pm in summer; 11am–2.30pm and 7–11pm in winter; 12–3pm Sun.*

Berkeley

Berkeley Brewing Co.

The Brewery, Bucketts Hill Farm,
Berkeley GL13 9NL
☎ *(01453) 811895*
Visitors welcome by appointment.
Tied houses: None

Established in September 1994 as a part-time business. The brewery is in an old cider cellar within a listed farm building. Brewing is on demand and at least six local pubs are supplied.

OLD FRIEND 3.8% ABV
A hoppy aroma leads into this fruity, hoppy beer. Moderately hoppy, bitter finish.

BERKELEY VALE ALE 4.5% ABV
Winter ale.

Birdlip

The Golden Heart Inn

Nettleton Bottom,
Nr Birdlip GL4 8LA
☎ *(01242) 870261*
Mr D Morgan and Miss C Stevens

Marston's Pedigree, Hook Norton Best and Ruddles brews always available plus four guest beers (400 per year), perhaps from Greene King, Timothy Taylor and many local brewers.

A sixteenth-century pub with stone floors, beams and bric-a-brac. Bar food available at lunchtime and evenings. Car park, garden, children's room and function room. Situated on the A417 between Cheltenham, Gloucester and Cirencester, two miles from Birdlip.

OPEN *10.30am–3pm and 6–11pm Mon–Sat; 12–3pm and 7–10.30pm Sun.*

Bristol

Hardington Brewery

Albany Buildings, Dean Lane,
Bedminster, Bristol BS3 1BT
☎ *(0117) 963 6194*
No visitors. Tied houses: 3

No connection with the old Somerset brewery of the same name. Established in April 1991, demand for the brews has grown steadily. Some 200 outlets are now supplied.

Beers available at: The Swan with Two Necks, 12 Little Ann Street, St Judes, Bristol *and* White Horse, Lower Ashley Road, St Agnes, Bristol.

TRADITIONAL BITTER 3.6% ABV
Amber in colour, clean, refreshing bitter with a floral hop and citrus fruit aroma. Long, dry, bitter hop finish.

BEST BITTER 4.1% ABV
Crisp, refreshing pale brown best bitter with malt complexity and slight sweetness, becoming bitter with a dry finish. Floral hop and citrus fruit aroma.

JUBILEE 5.0% ABV
A mid-brown, strong bitter, rich in fruit and malt. Beautifully balanced, with a contrasting dry, bitter finish.

MOONSHINE 5.0% ABV
A yellow-gold beer with a wheaty malt and slightly citrus fruit aroma. Smooth, sweetish taste of pale malt with hints of fruit and spice. Dry, bitter finish.

OLD LUCIFER 5.5% ABV
Winter ale. Pale brown, smooth and powerful strong bitter. Sweet, fruity and warming with a complex biscuit and chocolate malt balance and a dry bitter finish.

OLD ALE 6.0% ABV
Winter ale. Rich copper-red, warming ale. Well balanced, fruity, hoppy roast malt aroma. Complex finish.

Plus a range of occasional and special brews.

SMILES BREWERY

Colston Yard, Colston Street, Bristol BS1 5BD
☎ *(0117) 929 7350*
Visitors welcome. Tied houses: 15

Originally set up to supply a local restaurant, Smiles started full-scale brewing in 1978. Demand in Bristol for natural beer with a local character and a rebirth of interest in traditional brewing methods helped to bring rapid success. The original Best Bitter was soon joined by Exhibition and, more recently, the Brewery Bitter. Built vertically on the classic tower principles, the brewery uses gravity to move malt and hops from the store at the top of the building to the brewing floors below before the finished brews are dropped to the bottom of the brewery to be casked and matured.

Beers available at: The Double Locks Hotel, Canal Banks, Marsh Barton, Exeter, Devon *and* Highbury Vaults, 64 St Michael's Hill, Cotham, Bristol.

SMILES BREWERY BITTER 3.7% ABV
A golden pale, well-balanced beer with a thirst-quenching and satisfying hoppy flavour.

SMILES BEST BITTER 4.1% ABV
A traditional well-rounded bitter with a rich colour, a slightly malty taste and faintly fruity finish.

SMILES BRISTOL STOUT 4.7% ABV
A seasonal brew only. A dark and fulfilling stout brewed from an old recipe and generously flavoured with roast barley.

SMILES EXHIBITION EXTRA STRONG BITTER 5.2% ABV
A full-bodied beer, dark and ruby in colour with a roast malt character and fruity aroma.

Plus various limited edition ales throughout the year.

The Highbury Vaults

164 St Michael's Hill, Cotham, Bristol BS2 8DE
☎ *(0117) 973 3203*
Brad Francis

Smiles Best, Brewery and Exhibition always available, also Brains SA and three guest beers (approximately 20 per year) to include Fuller's London Pride, Hall & Woodhouse Tanglefoot, Greene King Abbot, Adnams Broadside, Shepherd Neame Spitfire, Crown Buckley Rev James Original, Batemans XXXB and Ruddles County.

Very traditional pub set in the heart of university land with no music, fruit machines, pool tables etc. Lots of atmosphere for young and old, students and locals. Cheap bar food available lunchtime and evening (nothing fried). Children allowed in garden.

12–11pm Mon–Sat; normal hours Sun.

The Hope and Anchor

38 Jacobs Wells Road, Clifton, Bristol BS8 1DR
☎ *(0117) 929 2987*
Steven Simpsonwells

Own brews promised soon. Four beers permanently available, changed every few days. Up to 30 brews per year including Fuller's London Pride, Gale's HSB, Titanic Best, Felinfoel Double Dragon, Greene King Abbot, Palmer's IPA and Hall & Woodhouse Tanglefoot.

Friendly one-bar pub with relaxed atmosphere. No TV or games machines. Bar food available at lunchtime and evenings. Children allowed in beer garden. Near The Triangle in Clifton, north of Bristol city centre.

12–11pm Mon–Sat; 12–10.30pm Sun.

The Phoenix

15 Wellington Street, St Judes, Bristol BS2
☎ *(0117) 955 8327*
Jeffrey Fowler

Ten beers permanently available including those from Oakhill and Wickwar breweries plus Wadworth 6X. Also a selection from 100 guest beers per year. Brews from Youngs, Shepherd Neame, Cottage, Batemans, Ever-ards, Ash Vine, Uley, Burton Bridge, Burtonwood, Exmoor and many more.

Small, local one-bar freehouse in grade II listed building. Snacks available at lunchtime and evenings. Parking, garden, children's room, accommodation. On the edge of Broadmead shopping area.

11.30am–11pm Mon–Sat; 12–3pm and 7–10.30pm Sun.

The Swan with Two Necks

12 Little Ann Street, St Judes, Bristol BS2 9EB
☎ *(0117) 955 1893*
John Lansall

Six beers permanently available including beers from Hardington and 130+ guest beers per year. Emphasis on unusual first brews from new breweries and brewpubs.

Basic one-bar pub ten minutes from city centre and docks. No music or machines. Bar food available at lunchtime. Parking. Well-behaved children allowed. Tricky to find. Coming into Bristol on M32, left at first set of lights, then 3rd left.

11.30am–3pm and 5–11pm Mon–Thurs; 11.30am–11pm Fri; 12–11pm Sat; 12–3pm and 7–10.30pm Sun.

The Woolpack Inn

Shepherds Way, St Georges,
Nr Bristol BA3 6SP
☎ *(01934) 521670*
PW Sampson

Four beers permanently available, 30 per year to include Morrells Graduate, Charles Wells Bombardier and Oakhill Best.

Village freehouse in 200-year-old building. Bar and restaurant food at lunchtime and evenings. Car park, garden, conservatory planned. Children not allowed. Off M5, junction 21.

12–2.30pm and 6–11pm Mon–Sat; 12–3pm and 7–10.30pm Sun.

BROAD CAMPDEN

The Baker's Arms

Broad Campden,
Nr Chipping Campden GL55 6UR
☎ *(01386) 840515*
Mrs CW Perry

Stanway Stanney, Wickwar Brand Oak, Hook Norton Best and Donnington BB always available plus a constantly changing (300 per year) supply of up to four guest beers.

A small, friendly Cotswold country pub with open fires. Bar food available at lunchtime and evenings. Car park, garden, patio and children's play area. In a village between Chipping Campden and Blockley.

11.30am–2.30pm and 6–11pm.

BUTCOMBE

BUTCOMBE BREWERY

Butcombe, Nr Bristol BS18 6XQ
☎ *(01275) 472240*
Trade visits only. Tied houses: 4

Set up in 1978 by Simon Whitmore, formerly of Courage, the brewery had doubled in size by 1983, allowing for an 80-barrel brew. Real ale supplied mostly to outlets within a 50-mile radius.

BUTCOMBE BITTER 4.0% ABV
A dry, clean-tasting bitter with a strong hop flavour.

CHELTENHAM

The Golden Ball Inn

Lower Swell,
Nr Cheltenham GL54 1LF
☎ *(01451) 830247*
Steven Aldridge

The pub is tied to the nearby Donnington Brewery, so BB and SBA are always available. No guest beers.

A seventeenth-century, Cotswold stone, village local with log fires in winter. Accommodation available. Typical old pub games played (darts, dominoes, cribbage, Aunt Sally). Bar food served at lunchtime and evenings. Car park and garden. Children at lunchtime only. On the B4068, one mile from Stow-on-the-Wold.

11am–3pm and 6–11pm Mon–Sat; 12–3pm and 7–10.30pm Sun.

Churchill

The Crown Inn

The Batch, Skinners Lane,
Churchill, Nr Bristol.
☎ *(01934) 852995*

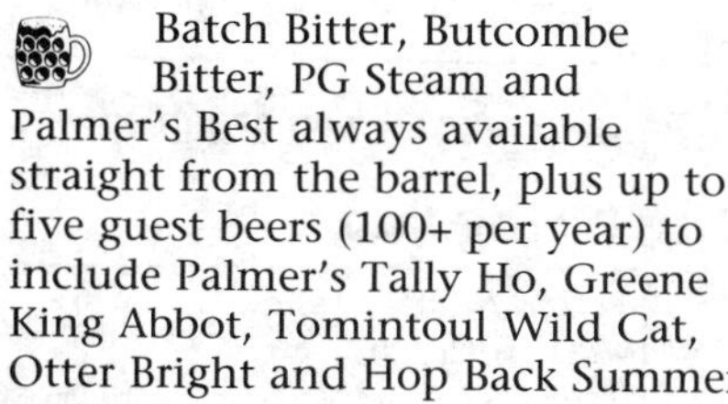

Batch Bitter, Butcombe Bitter, PG Steam and Palmer's Best always available straight from the barrel, plus up to five guest beers (100+ per year) to include Palmer's Tally Ho, Greene King Abbot, Tomintoul Wild Cat, Otter Bright and Hop Back Summer Lightning.

Old pub with small rooms and flagstone floors. Large fires in winter. Food made and prepared to order when practical. Parking, garden, children's room. Children not allowed in bar area. South of Bristol, just off the A38, not far from M5.

11.30am–3pm and 5.30–11pm.

GLOUCESTERSHIRE

Coleford

Freeminer Brewery

The Laurels, Sling,
Coleford GL16 8JJ
☎ *(01594) 810408*
Visitors welcome. Tied houses: 1

The ancient freeminers of the Royal Forest of Dean are believed to have held the rights to the coal and minerals under the forest since before the time of Edward I. The brewery was formed in November 1992 and production soon reached 25 barrels per week. All of the beers produced are named after local mines or landmarks and the brewery goes to great lengths to introduce this historic area to the interested drinker.

Beers available at: Brockweir Country Inn, Brockweir, Nr Chepstow, Gloucestershire *and* Fountain Inn, Parkend, Forest of Dean, Gloucestershire.

FREEMINER BITTER 4.0% ABV
A pale bitter with a very distinctive hop character, satisfyingly bitter.

SPECULATION ALE 4.8% ABV
A rich chestnut brown-coloured premium ale, surprisingly bitter with a pronounced hop character and a satisfying malt balance.

STAIRWAY TO HEAVEN 5.0.% ABV
A pale beer of superior character. Well hopped but light on the palate.

IRON BREW 4.2% ABV
A ruby-red bitter, rich in hops and malt character.

SHAKEMANTLE GINGER ALE 5.0% ABV
A summer special, cloudy and unfined in the tradition of this beer style.

Cowley

The Green Dragon

Cockleford, Cowley,
Nr Cheltenham GL53 9NW
☎ *(01242) 870271*
Pia-Maria Boast

Smiles Best, Brewery Bitter and Exhibition always available plus up to three guest beers (30 per year) which may include Fuller's ESB, Hall & Woodhouse Badger and Tanglefoot, Marston's Owd Roger, Hook Norton Best, Cotleigh Old Buzzard, Greene King Abbot, Bateman's Victory, Shepherd Neame Spitfire etc.

A traditional seventeenth-century pub with flagstones, open fires and candles. Bar food served at lunchtime and evenings. Car park and patio. Private function room and bar available for wedding receptions and parties.

11.30am–2.30pm and 6–11pm.

Dursley

Old Spot Inn

Hill Road, Dursley GL11 4JQ
☎ *(01453) 542870*

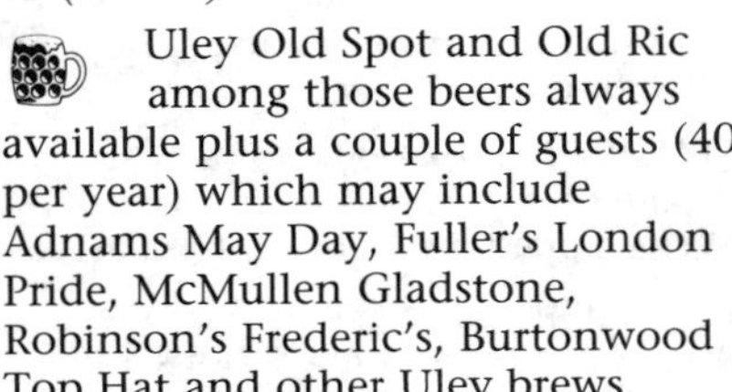
Uley Old Spot and Old Ric among those beers always available plus a couple of guests (40 per year) which may include Adnams May Day, Fuller's London Pride, McMullen Gladstone, Robinson's Frederic's, Burtonwood Top Hat and other Uley brews.

Originally a farm cottage, then a school, built in 1776 on the Cotswold Way, beamed with open fires. Bar snacks available at lunchtime. Live music. Parking, garden. No children.

11am–11pm Mon–Sat; 12–3pm and 7–10.30pm Sun.

Ebrington

The Ebrington Arms

Ebrington, Nr Chipping Campden GL55 6NH
☎ *(01386) 593223*
Gareth Richards

Hook Norton Best and Donnington SBA permanently available plus a guest beer (52 per year), perhaps from Wadworth, Fuller's, Wychwood, Goff's, Uley, or Greene King brewery.

An unspoilt traditional Cotswold village pub. No music or machines. Traditional games. Bar and restaurant food at lunchtime and evenings. Car park and garden. Children in the restaurant only. The owner has a pottery in the courtyard where he makes bowls, jugs and cruet sets used in the restaurant. Accommodation.

11am–2.30pm and 6–11pm Mon–Sat; 12–3pm and 7–10.30pm Sun.

Frampton Cotterell

The Rising Sun

43 Ryecroft Road, Frampton Cotterell, Nr Bristol BS17 2HN
☎ *(01454) 772330*
Roger Stone

Six beers permanently available with 25–30 featured per year. Examples include Smiles brews, Mayfly, Crown Buckley Rev James Original and Buchanan Original.

Small, friendly, single-bar local. CAMRA Pub of the Year for Avon in 1995. Bar food available at lunchtime. Large patio area.

11.30am–3pm and 7–11pm Mon–Sat; 12–3pm and 7–10.30pm Sun.

Gloucester

The Linden Tree

73-75 Bristol Road, Gloucester GL1 5SN
☎ *(01452) 527869*
Simon Cairns

Hook Norton Best, Smiles Exhibition, Wadworth 6X and IPA and Hall & Woodhouse Tanglefoot always available plus two guest beers (100+ per year) which may include Exmoor Stag, Mitchell's Lancaster Bomber, Crown Buckley Rev James Original and Wadworth Old Timer.

A true country pub in the heart of Gloucester, south of the city centre. Large Georgian grade II listed building. Bar food available at lunchtime and evenings. Parking, skittle alley, function room. Children allowed. Accommodation. Follow the Bristol road from the M5.

11am–2.30pm and 5–11pm Mon–Thurs; 11am–11pm Fri–Sat; 12–3pm and 7–10.30pm Sun.

Littleton upon Severn

The White Hart Inn

Littleton upon Severn, Nr Bristol BS12 1NR
☎ *(01454) 412275*
Mr and Mrs Berryman

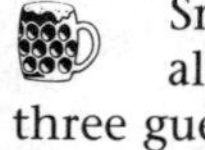

Smiles Best and Exhibition always available plus two or three guest beers to include Burton Bridge Bitter, Wadworth 6X, Bateman's XXB, Fuller's London Pride, Spitfire Ale and Greene King Abbot.

Near the Severn Bridges and Thornbury Castle. Bar food at lunchtime and evenings. Children not allowed. Leave the M4 at junction 21. Head towards Thornbury, then Elberton village. Signposted from there.

11.30am–3pm and 6–11pm weekdays; 11.30am–11pm Sat;

Lower Apperley

Mayhem's Brewery

The Farmer's Arms
Ledbury Road,
Lower Apperley GL19 4DR
☎ *(01452) 780307*

Mayhem's own brews plus six other guests, which may include Marton's Pedigree and Wadworth 6X.

Brewery opened in 1992 in the grounds of The Farmer's Arms, an eighteenth-century inn with oak beams and open fires. Bar and restaurant food available at lunchtime and evenings. Car park, garden, children's play area. B4213 Ledbury Road, four miles south of Tewkesbury.

ODDA'S LIGHT 3.8% ABV

SUNDOWNER'S HEAVY 4.5% ABV

11am–3pm and 6–11pm Mon–Sat; 12–3pm and 7–11pm Sun.

Newland

The Ostrich Inn

Newland, Nr Coleford GL16 8NP
☎ *(01594) 833260*
Mr and Mrs Dewe

Wadworth 6X, Shepherd Neame Spitfire Ale and RCH Old Slug Porter permanently available plus four guest beers (50 per year) which may include Otter Head, RCH Pitchfork, Moles Tap, Vale Ale, Durham's Pagan, Uley Pig's Ear, Ridley's Spectacular, Bull Mastiff Best, Marston's Pedigree, Black Sheep Bitter and Exmoor Gold. Real cider and German lager.

A thirteenth-century inn in the Forest of Dean with beams, log fire, settles and candles. Bar and restaurant food available at lunchtime and evenings. Garden and accommodation. In the village centre, opposite the church.

12–2.20pm and 6.30–11pm Mon–Fri; 12–3pm and 6.30–11pm Sat; 12–3pm and 7–10.30pm Sun.

PILL

The Star Inn

13 Bank Place, Pill,
Nr Bristol BS20 0AQ
☎ *(01275) 374926*
Mrs Fey

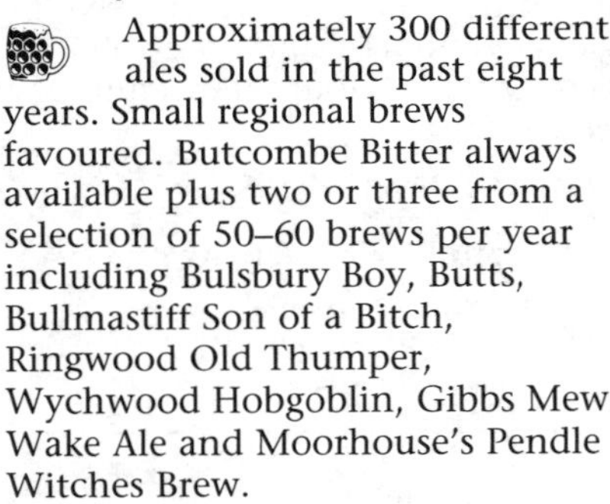
Approximately 300 different ales sold in the past eight years. Small regional brews favoured. Butcombe Bitter always available plus two or three from a selection of 50–60 brews per year including Bulsbury Boy, Butts, Bullmastiff Son of a Bitch, Ringwood Old Thumper, Wychwood Hobgoblin, Gibbs Mew Wake Ale and Moorhouse's Pendle Witches Brew.

Local village pub with a wide range of customers. Parking. Children allowed in bar. Junction 19 off the M5.

12–4pm and 7–11pm.

SAPPERTON

The Daneway

Sapperton,
Nr Cirencester GL7 6LN
☎ *(01285) 760297*

Five real ales always available including Wadworth 6X, Archer's Best and Daneway Bitter. Guests (30+ per year) might come from the West Berkshire Brewery or Greene King.

Built in 1784, this beamed pub is set in some wonderful Gloucestershire countryside. It features a lounge and public bar, plus small no-smoking family room. No music, machines or pool but traditional pub games. Bar food is available at lunchtime and meals in the evening. Car park, garden, children allowed in family room. Less than two miles off the A419 Stroud–Cirencester road.

11am–2.30pm and 6.30–11pm.

SOUTH WOODCHESTER

The Ram Inn

Station Road,
South Woodchester,
Nr Stroud GL5 5EL
☎ *(01453) 873329*
Mike McAsey

Uley Bitter and Old Spot, Archer's Best and Ruddles Best always available plus two guests (100 per year) including Hook Norton Best and Old Hooky, Buchanan brews, Fuller's London Pride, Exmoor Gold, Smiles brews, Morland Old Speckled Hen, Robinsons, Butcombe and Charles Wells brews, Hall & Woodhouse Badger, Cotleigh and Ash Vine.

A bustling sixteenth-century Cotswold inn with beautiful views. Open fires in winter, plenty of outside seating in summer. Bar and restaurant food available at lunchtime and evenings. Car park and garden. Children allowed. Off the A46 from Stroud. After

approximately two miles, turn right to South Woodchester village.

11am–3pm and 5.30–11pm Mon–Fri. All day Sat; normal hours Sun.

TEWKESBURY

The Berkeley Arms

8 Church Street, Tewkesbury GL20 5PA
☎ *(01684) 293034*
Mr and Mrs Thorn

Wadworth IPA, 6X and Farmer's Glory permanently available, plus two guests (15 per year) which may include Hall & Woodhouse Tanglefoot, Wadworth Old Timer, Morland Old Speckled Hen and Charles Wells Bombardier.

A small, homely fifteenth-century pub. Bar and restaurant food available. Street parking. The restaurant can be hired for functions. Children allowed in the restaurant.

All day except Sun.

ULEY

ULEY BREWERY

The Old Brewery, Uley, Nr Dursley GL11 5TB
☎ *(01453) 860120*
No visitors. Tied houses: None

Built in 1833 as Prices' Brewery and re–opened in 1985 after many years of dereliction, the Uley Brewey is a classic tower brewery with the original brewery spring water still in use. The beers are produced solely from malted barley, whole hops and spring water. No sugars or other adjuncts are employed.

Beers available at: Old Spot Inn, Hill Road, Dursley, Gloucestershire *and* The Old Crown, Uley, Gloucestershire.

HOGSHEAD BITTER 3.5% ABV
A session bitter.

ULEY BITTER 4.0% ABV
A dry best bitter.

OLD RIC 4.5% ABV
A rounded premium bitter.

PIGS EAR 5.0% ABV
A smooth IPA.

OLD SPOT ALE 5.0% ABV
Flagship strong ale.

PIGOR MORTIS 6.0% ABV
Brewed at Christmas only.

WATERLEY BOTTOM

The New Inn

Waterley Bottom, North Nibley, Nr Dursley GL11 6EF
☎ *(01453) 543659*
Ruby Sainty

Cotleigh Hobby Ale and Tawny, Greene King Abbot Ale, Smiles Best and Exhibition always available plus occasional guests (104 per year) to include B&T Dragonslayer and Adnams May Day.

A remote freehouse with two bars set in a beautiful valley. Bar food available at lunchtime and evenings. Car park, garden and accommodation. CAMRA Gloucestershire Pub of the Year 1992–93. From North Nibley, follow signs for Waterley Bottom.

12–2.30pm and 7–11pm 10.30pm Sun.

Westbury on Trym

The Post Office Tavern

17 Westbury Hill,
Westbury on Trym,
Nr Bristol BS9 3AH
☎ *(0117) 940 1233*
Steve Fitzgerald

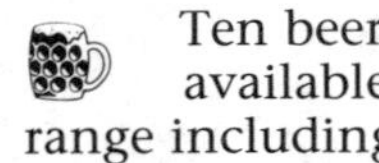

Ten beers permanently available from extensive range including Shepherd Neame Spitfire Ale, Fuller's London Pride and Smiles brews.

Early twentieth-century ale house full of post office memorabilia. Non-smoking lounge. Bar food lunchtime and evenings. Street parking, small patio. Children allowed with parents for food in early evenings only. On main road in Westbury village.

11.30am–11pm Mon–Sat;
12–3pm and 7–10.30pm Sun.

Wickwar

Wickwar Brewing

The Old Cider Mill, Station Road,
Wickwar GL12 8NB
☎ *(01454) 294168*
Visitors welcome. Tied houses: None

Ray Penny and Brian Rides originally ran Courage pubs in the Bristol area. When the government introduced the guest beer law in 1990, they considered the local possibilities and then decided to produce their own. They learnt their trade at the Jolly Roger brewpub in Worcester and then began work at an old cider mill near Chipping Sodbury. They stick closely to traditional methods and the popularity of their brews has forced a reorganisation at the brewery from its initial length of ten barrels per week. They can now produce up to 100 barrels per week but are adamant that this will remain the upper limit.

Beers available at: Cadbury House, Montpelier, Bristol *and* The Black Horse, Waterley Bottom, North Nibley, Nr Dursley, Gloucestershire.

COOPERS WPA 3.5% ABV
A refreshing pale ale, full of flavour.

BRAND OAK BITTER 4.0% ABV
A well-balanced bitter, full of character.

OLDE MERRYFORD ALE 5.1% ABV
A full-flavoured bitter with a hoppy fruity aroma.

STATION PORTER 6.1% ABV
A dark smooth beer, for the winter only.

Winchcombe

Goff's Brewery

9 Isbourne Way,
Winchcombe GL54 5NS
☎ *(01242) 603383*
Visitors welcome. Tied houese: None

Goff's Brewery has been in production since August 1994. It is a small family concern run by Marcus and Alison Goff and Marcus' father, Brian, a former Allied Breweries brewer. At present two ales are produced on a regular basis, with the possibility of a third in the near future.

Beers available at: The Plasterer's Arms, Winchcombe, Gloucestershire *and* The Hewlett Arms, Harp Hill, Battledown, Cheltenham, Gloucestershire.

JOUSTER ALE 4.0% ABV
A medium-tinted, fruity session bitter with a light hoppy aftertaste.

WHITE KNIGHT 4.7% ABV
A light-coloured, well-hopped, premium bitter.

ANDOVER

HAMPSHIRE BREWERY

5 Anton Trading Estate, Andover SP10 2NJ
☎ *(01264) 336699*
No visitors. Tied houses: None

Hampshire Brewery is a small independent brewery which began trading in Andover in 1992 with the objective of providing the rare combination of premium quality ales supported by original product presentation. The original King Alfred's brew took its name from Alfred the Great, who reigned in the ninth century and whose parliament resided in Andover. The latter brews continue the theme of noble kings of England (Lionheart, Ironside, Pendragon and 1066). The 25-barrel brewery supports more than 250 outlets across Hampshire as well as supplying wholesalers who distribute the products nationwide. 100 pubs supplied regularly.

Beers available at: Red Lion, Chalton, Nr Horndean, Hampshire *and* The Bull Inn, High Street, Sonning on Thames, Berkshire.

KING ALFRED'S 3.8% ABV
A refreshing, hoppy session bitter.

LIONHEART 4.2% ABV
A smooth golden best bitter.

IRONSIDE 4.2% ABV
A well-balanced, traditional best bitter.

PENDRAGON 4.8% ABV
A full-bodied and fruity premium ale.

1066 6.0% ABV
A classic strong English pale ale.

NEWALE BREWING CO

6 Viscount Court, Southway, Walworth Industrial Estate, Andover SP10 5NW
☎ *(01264) 336336*
Visitors welcome. Tied houses: None

This seven-barrel purpose-built plant was set up by Phil Newton in September 1993. It currently serves 25–30 freehouses and uses two national distributors. The beer names come from local village names and landmarks.

Beers available at: The Wyke Down Country Pub, Picket Peace, Nr Andover, Hampshire *and* Crook and Shears, Upper Clatford, Hampshire.

AMBER ALE 3.6% ABV
Brewed to celebrate the birth of the owners' baby daughter. A light amber colour, pleasantly hoppy. A full tasting session bitter.

ANNA VALLEY ALE 4.2% ABV
A light yet smooth, malty beer with a high hop content giving excellent aroma and pleasant aftertaste.

BALKSBURY BITTER 4.5% ABV
A dry, dark red-brown bitter, rich in taste and highly hopped.

CLATFORD CLOUT 5.0% ABV
A golden pale ale with a fruity hoppy flavour .

OLD HATCH ALE 6.0% ABV
Brewed from November to March, a dark, slightly sweeter, full-bodied ale.

BISHOPS WALTHAM

The Hampshire Bowman

Dunbridge Lane, Bishops Waltham, Nr Southampton SO32 1GD
☎ *(01489) 892940*

Archer's Village and Golden Bitter, Ringwood 49er and Best always available plus the occasional guest beer.

A Victorian brick-built pub on the Hampshire downs. Bar food available at lunchtime and evenings (except Sunday evening and all day Monday). Car park and garden. Nearby camp site. Children not allowed.

11am–2.30pm and 6–11pm Mon–Sat; 12–3pm and 7–10.30pm Sun.

Cheriton

Cheriton Brewhouse

The Flower Pots Inn, Cheriton, Alresford SO24 0QQ
☎ *(01962) 771318*
Paul Tucker and Jo Bartlett

Three brews and various specials supplied to The Flower Pots Inn next door plus a second pub, the Tally Ho! at Broughton, and various free trade outlets.

Paul Tucker and Jo Bartlett, owners of the Flower Pots Inn, built the brewery in the grounds of the pub in 1993, and took on Martin Roberts and Ray Page as partners in the brewery business only. Their beers have won many awards and production is close to capacity. The pub is an unspoilt village inn on the edge of the village. Bar food is available at lunchtime and evenings. Car park, garden, children's room, accommodation. Children not allowed in the pub. CAMRA regional pub of the year 1995.

POTS ALE 3.8% ABV
Golden in colour with a hoppy nose, well-balanced taste and bitter aftertaste.

BEST BITTER 4.2% ABV

DIGGERS GOLD 4.6% ABV

12–2.30pm and 6–11pm Mon–Sat; 12–3pm and 7–10.30pm Sun.

East Worldham

Worldham Brewery

Smith's Farm, East Worldham, Alton, GU34 3AT
☎ *(01420) 83383*
Visitors welcome. Tied houses: None

Hugo Sharpe converted a hop kiln into a ten-barrel brewery in 1991 using second-hand plant acquired from other breweries. The operation is now well established and the brewery serves 50 outlets.

Beers available at: The Dover Arms, Ash, Nr Aldershot, Hampshire *and* The Railway Arms, Alton, Hampshire.

SESSION BITTER 3.6% ABV

OLD DRAY 5.2% ABV
A unique hoppy bitter flavour, using 100 per cent malt.

BARBARIAN 5.2% ABV
Full-flavoured and well-hopped premium bitter. Golding hops and 100 per cent malt.

Farnborough

The Prince of Wales

184 Rectory Road, Farnborough GU14 8AL
☎ *(01252) 5545578*

Brakspear's Bitter, Hall & Woodhouse Badger and Tanglefoot, Fuller's London Pride, Hog's Back TEA and Ringwood 49er always available plus up to four guest beers at any one time, which may include Hop Back Summer Lightning, Cheriton Pots Ale and Gale's Festival.

An Edwardian freehouse with antique touches in three small connecting rooms. A busy, traditional pub serving food at lunchtime. Just around the corner from Farnborough North railway station. Children over 14 allowed.

11.30am–2.30pm and 5.30–11pm Mon–Sat; 12–3.30pm and 7–10.30pm Sun.

FREEFOLK PRIORS

The Watership Down Inn

Freefolk, Nr Whitchurch RG28 7NJ
☎ *(01256) 892254*
Mr and Mrs Lodge

Archer's Best, Brakspear IPA, Mild and Best always available plus guest beers (100+ per year) from Oakhill, Hop Back, Hog's Back, Ringwood, Ash Vine, Bunces, Lastingham, Juwards, Greenwoods, Shepherd Neame, Thwaites, New Ale and Smiles breweries.

Built in 1840, renamed after the Richard Adams novel, a one-bar pub with open fire and pretty garden with many outside tables. Bar and restaurant food available at lunchtime and evenings. Car park, children's play area. Children allowed in the restaurant. On the B3400 between Whitchurch and Overton.

11.30am–3pm and 6–11pm.

HORNDEAN

GEORGE GALE & CO

The Hampshire Brewery, Horndean PO8 0DA
☎ *(01705) 571212*
Visitors welcome. Tied houses: 135

The Gale family were contributing to Horndean's commercial life from the eighteenth century as grocers and bakers. Richard Gale, born in 1802, acquired the Ship and Bell Inn in 1847. It had its own brewery and his son, George Alexander, decided to expand in 1853. A substantial brewery was largely destroyed by fire in 1869. A new brewery was quickly built on the same site. George Alexander Gale continued to expand and acquired further inns. His business became a limited company in 1888. In 1896 he sold his major shareholding and Herbert Frederick Bowyer became chairman. Homewell Brewery, Havant, was purchased and, in 1923, the Angel Brewery in Midhurst. By World War Two, this was a substantial regional brewing enterprise. Further expansion followed and today the company owns 135 pubs throughout the south and southeast England.

Beers available at: The Red Lion, Chalton, Nr Horndean, Hampshire *and* The Bull Inn, High Street, Sonning-on-Thames, Berkshire.

BUTSER BREW BITTER 3.4% ABV
A thirst-quenching beer of average strength brewed with water drawn from the brewery well. A pleasantly hopped and malty flavoured bitter.

GALE'S BEST BITTER 3.8% ABV
Delicious hop flavour produced from a blend of English aroma hops with the rich maltiness of East Anglian

barleys to give a distinctive bitter beer.

WINTER BREW 4.2% ABV
A rich, warm and satisfying winter ale with a blend of fruity and hoppy flavours. Produced between October and March.

HORNDEAN SPECIAL BITTER 4.8% ABV
Sweet, distinctive quality beer brewed from hand-selected malt and hops.

LASHAM

The Royal Oak

Lasham, Nr Alton GU34 5SJ
☎ *(01256) 381213*
Andy Hore

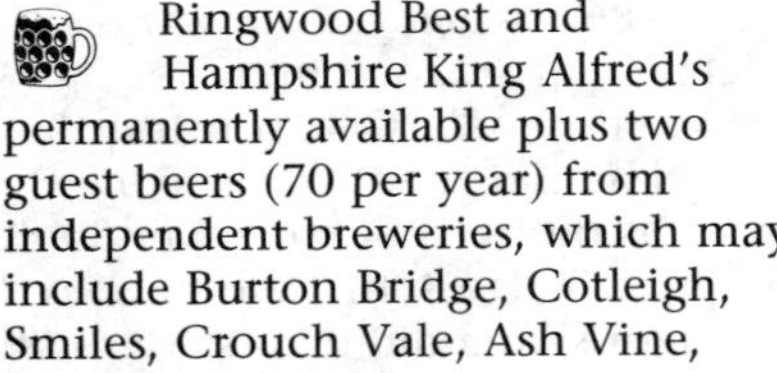
Ringwood Best and Hampshire King Alfred's permanently available plus two guest beers (70 per year) from independent breweries, which may include Burton Bridge, Cotleigh, Smiles, Crouch Vale, Ash Vine, Hogs Back, Hop Back and Mauldon's. Also traditional cider.

A cosy, two-bar pub with open fires, beams and brickwork. Beer garden. Pool table in the village bar. Bar food available at lunchtime and evenings. Car park. Just off the A339, four miles from Alton, six miles from Basingstoke.

11am–2.30pm and 6–11 Mon–Fri; 11am–3pm Sat; 12–3pm and 7–10.30pm Sun.

MICHELDEVER

The Dever Arms

Winchester Road, Micheldever SO21 3DG
☎ *(01962) 774339*
Mr and Mrs Penny

Cheriton Pots Ale and Hall & Woodhouse Badger always available plus up to four guest beers which may include Greenwood's Prohibition, Smiles Best, Fuller's London Pride and Timothy Taylor Landlord.

A popular country pub with restaurant and gardens. Bar and restaurant food served at lunchtime and evenings. Car park, garden and children's room. Less than a mile off the A33, six miles north of Winchester, 12 miles south of Basingstoke.

11.30am–3pm and 6–11pm.

PETERSFIELD

BALLARD'S BREWERY

Unit C, The Old Sawmill, Nyewood, Nr Petersfield GU31 5HA
☎ *(01730) 821362*
Visitors welcome. Tied houses: None

Established in 1980, from its beginnings in the cow-house behind Carol Brown's family home in Sussex, Ballard's Brewery has grown to produce an average of 1,300 gallons per week. It produces cask-conditioned ales using only malt, hops, yeast and water. No additives are used, making Ballard's beer absolutely pure. Orders are regularly delivered directly to pubs but are also available around the country through a network of specialist agents.

Beers available at: The Elsted Inn, Elsted Marsh, Nr Midhurst, Sussex *and* The Wyndham Arms, Rogate, Nr Petersfield, Hampshire.

MIDHURST MILD 3.5% ABV
A dark beer, lightly hopped and well malted without being too sweet.

BALLARD'S TROTTON BITTER 3.6% ABV
A well-flavoured and hoppy session bitter.

BALLARD'S BEST BITTER 4.2% ABV
A nutty, well-balanced beer of medium strength.

BALLARD'S GOLDEN BINE 4.2% ABV
A golden bitter, refreshingly hoppy.

BALLARD'S WILD 4.7% ABV
A dark bitter with a deceptively mild flavour and rich, malty aftertaste with a hint of chocolate malt.

BALLARD'S WASSAIL 6.0% ABV
Malty and full-bodied, without being oversweet.

Plus a range of bottled beers.

PORTSMOUTH

The Dolphin

41 High Street,
Portsmouth PO1 2LV
☎ *(01705) 823595*
Michael Parkes and Amanda Dewhurst

Fourteen beers on tap including Wadworth 6X and Ringwood Old Thumper plus several guest beers (100 per year) including Timothy Taylor Landlord, Rebellion Hobgoblin, Fuller's ESB, Hall & Woodhouse Tanglefoot, Adnam's Bitter, Gibbs Mew Bishops Tipple, Marston's Pedigree and Clarks, Bunces, Hop Back and Thwaites brews.

Sixteenth-century coaching inn with wood and flagstone floors. Bar food available at lunchtime and evenings. Skittle alley and small function room. Children allowed. Directly opposite the cathedral in old Portsmouth.

11am–11pm Mon–Sat; normal hours Sun.

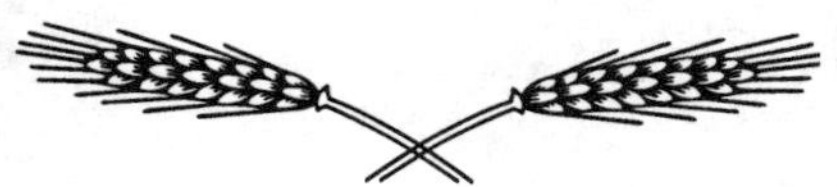

The Tap

17 London Road, North End,
Portsmouth PO2 0BQ
☎ *(01705) 614861*

Eleven beers always available including Ruddles Best and Ringwood Old Thumper. Guests (100 per year) will include Ringwood Best, Hall & Woodhouse Tanglefoot, Gale's HSB and brews from the Brewery on Sea. Micro-breweries particularly favoured.

A one-bar drinking pub in the town centre with no jukebox or fruit machines. Formerly the brewery tap for the now defunct Southsea Brewery. Bar meals available at lunchtime. Street parking opposite, small yard, disabled toilet. Children not allowed.

10.30am–11pm Mon–Sat; 12–10.30pm Sun.

PRIORS DEAN

The White Horse Inn

Priors Dean,
Nr Petersfield GU32 1DA
☎ *(01420) 588387*
Mr J Eddleston

Gales Festival Mild, HSB and Butser Brew Bitter, Ballard's Best plus Ringwood 49er always available and guest beers (ten per year) including Wadworth 6X, Morrells Graduate, Summer Breeze, Gales IPA and Porter, plus a range of one-off brews from Gales.

An olde-world pub untouched for years with log fires, rocking chairs, antique furniture and a grandfather clock. Bar food available at lunchtime. Car park and garden. Nearby caravan site. Tricky to find. Midway between

Petersfield and Alton, five miles from Petersfield, seven miles from Alton.

11am–2.30pm and 6–11pm Mon–Fri; 11am–3pm and 6–11pm Sat; 12–3pm and 7–10.30pm Sun.

RINGWOOD

RINGWOOD BREWERY

138 Christchurch Road, Ringwood BH24 3AP
☎ *(014205) 471177*
Visitors welcome.
Tied houses: 2

Founded in 1978 and housed in attractive eighteenth-century buildings. Formerly part of the old Tunks brewery. A new brewhouse was commissioned just before Christmas 1994. The business now serves about 350 outlets, including two tied houses. There is a brewery shop.

Beers available at: Inn on the Furlong, 12 Meeting House Lane, Ringwood, Hampshire, *and* The Porterhouse, 113 Poole Road, Westbourne, Bournemouth, Dorset.

BEST BITTER 3.8% ABV
Golden-brown, moreish beer. The aroma has a hint of hops and leads to malty sweetness, becoming dry with a hint of orange. Malty and bitter finish.

TRUE GLORY 4.3% ABV

XXXX PORTER 4.7% ABV
Available October to March. A rich, dark brew with a strong aroma of roasted malt, hops and fruit. Rich in flavour, with hints of coffee, vanilla, damsons, apples and molasses. Overall roast maltiness continues into a drying, hoppy bitter finish.

FORTYNINER 4.8% ABV
Premium beer with a good balance of malt and hops. Flavours slowly increase to a malty finish.

OLD THUMPER 5.8% ABV
Golden beer with a bitter aftertaste following a middle period of various fruits.

SOUTHSEA

SPIKES BREWERY

The Wine Vaults, 43–47 Albert Road, Southsea PO5 2SF
☎ *(01705) 864712*

In addition to the three own brews, some 100+ guests are served per year including Hop Back Summer Lightning, Hampshire King Alfred's and Ringwood Best.

Spikes Brewery has been in production since 1994 and was originally owned by Otley Brewery. It took four years to get going and there are plans for a new brewery capable of commercial brewing. The pub is wood-panelled, with three bars, pew seating and a wooden floor. No juke box or machine, background music only. Food available at lunchtime and evenings. Parking, small garden, function room, disabled toilets. Children welcome.

SPIKE'S IMPALED ALE 3.6% ABV
Hoppy session bitter.

SPIKE'S RUBY SPECIAL 4.0% ABV
Dark porter-like beer.

STINGER 4.8% ABV
Made with malt and honey.

11am–11pm.

WEYHILL

Weyhill Fair

Weyhill Road, Weyhill,
Nr Andover SP11 0PP
☎ *(01264) 773631*
Mr and Mrs Rayner

Morrells Bitter, Varsity and Graduate permanently available plus three guest beers (120 per year) including Timothy Taylor Landlord and Juwards, Shepherd Neame, Fuller's and Rebellion ales.

A friendly local freehouse offering bar food at lunchtime and evenings. Car park, garden and children's room. On the A342 west of Andover.

11am–3pm and 6–11pm Mon–Thurs; 11am–3pm and 5–11pm Fri; 11am–3pm and 6.30–11pm Sat; 12–3pm and 7–10.30pm Sun.

WHITSBURY

The Cartwheel

Whitsbury Road, Whitsbury,
Nr Fordingbridge SP6 3PQ
☎ *(01725) 518362*
Gini McGraghan

Up to six beers always available (120 per year) but brews continually changing. Breweries favoured include Adnams, Shepherd Neame, Bunce's, Hop Back, Ringwood and Moles. Seasonal beers and small breweries preferred.

A relaxed bar with exposed beams and open fire, in good walking country. Bar and restaurant food available at lunchtime and evenings. Car park and garden. Children allowed in the restaurant. Turn west of Salisbury onto the Fordingbridge road at Breamore. Signposted from the A338.

11am–2.30pm and 6–11pm; all day Sun in summer.

HEREFORD & WORCS

Aston Crews

The Ha'Penny

Aston Crews,
Nr Ross-on-Wye HR9 7LW
☎ *(01989) 750203*

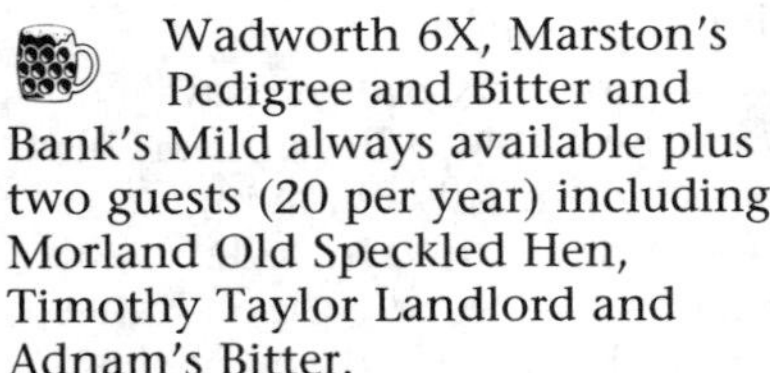

Wadworth 6X, Marston's Pedigree and Bitter and Bank's Mild always available plus two guests (20 per year) including Morland Old Speckled Hen, Timothy Taylor Landlord and Adnam's Bitter.

A beautifully restored old country pub in glorious countryside. Bar food available at lunchtime and evenings. Car park, garden and games room. Turn off the A40 Ross to Gloucester road at Lea, onto the B4222.

12–3pm and 6–11pm.

The Penny Farthing

Aston Crews,
Nr Ross-on-Wye HR9 7LW
☎ *(01989) 750366*
Mr and Mrs Brown

Marston's Pedigree and Bitter and Wadworth 6X always available plus a guest beer (ten per year) which may be from Robinsons, Hook Norton, Shepherd Neame Spitfire Ale or Morland Old Speckled Hen.

A country inn and restaurant. Bar and restaurant food available at lunchtime and evenings. Car park and garden. Children allowed in the restaurant. Turn off the A40 Ross-on-Wye to Gloucester road at Lea, on to the B4222 (signposted to Newent). The Penny Farthing is one mile down this road.

12–3pm and 7–11pm.

Bretforton

The Fleece Inn

The Cross, Bretforton WR11 5JE
☎ *(01386) 831173*
Linda Griffiths

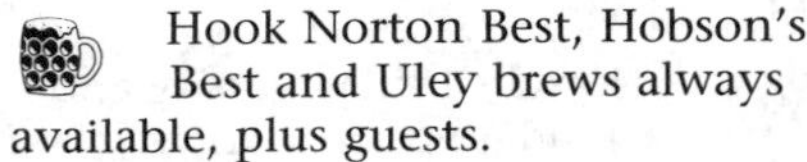

Hook Norton Best, Hobson's Best and Uley brews always available, plus guests.

This pub is 650 years old and has been used by the BBC as a film location. Owned by the National Trust, it is also a working museum. No-smoking family room. East of Evesham, in the middle of the village.

11am–2.30pm and 6–11pm.

Bromsgrove

Red Cross Brewery

Red Cross Farm, Perryfields Road,
Bromsgrove B61 8QW
☎ *(01527) 871409*
Visitors by arrangement only.
Tied houses: 1

After a two-year battle with planning problems, the brewery was opened in October 1993 by Ian Hughes, landlord of The Hop Pole Inn, in the old bull pen at Red Cross Farm, a seventeenth-century farmhouse. The first pint was pulled the following month. The name of the beer comes from the nineteenth-century "slave" nailmakers of Bromsgrove who, when they could afford ale, called it "Oh Be Joyful".

Beers available at: The Hop Pole Inn, 78 Birmingham Road, Bromsgrove, Worcestershire *and* The Greyhound, Eldersfield, Nr Tewkesbury, Gloucestershire.

NAILER'S OH BE JOYFUL 4.5% ABV
A light straw-coloured bitter with no added sugars.

The Hop Pole Inn

78 Birmingham Road,
Bromsgrove B60 0DG
☎ *(01527) 870200*

Red Cross Nailers OBJ brewed by the landlord and always available plus one other from a guest list of 30 per year including Brains SA, Fuller's London Pride, Stanway Stanney Bitter, Judges brews etc.

Small eighteenth-century cottage-style inn with antique furnishings. Headquarters of the Bromsgrove folk club. Bar food available at lunchtime. Street parking, garden, function room. No children allowed. On the A38.

12–2.30pm and 5.30–11pm.

Cleobury Mortimer

Hobsons Brewery

The Brewery, Cleobury Industrial Estate, Cleobury Mortimer, Nr Kidderminster DY14 8DP
☎ *(01299) 270837*
Visitors welcome. Tied houses: None

Established at Easter 1993 in a former sawmill and serving public houses in the locality, Hobsons Brewery is run by Nick Davies and his parents and will be moving premises to a converted granary, pushing production up to 70 barrels a week.

Beers available at: The Kings Arms, Cleobury Mortimer, Worcestershire *and* The Boot Inn, Orleton, Nr Ludlow, Shropshire.

HOBSONS BEST BITTER 3.8% ABV
Hoppy, bitter, nutty.

HOBSONS TOWN CRIER 4.5% ABV
Straw-coloured, full aroma.

HOBSONS OLD HENRY 5.2% ABV
Strong, full, hops and malt.

EVESHAM

EVESHAM BREWERY

Behind The Green Dragon,
17 Oat Street, Evesham WR11 4PJ
☎ *(01386) 443462*

Two Asum brews produced and sold, "Asum" being the local pronunciation of "Evesham". Other guest ales also sold.

The brewery has been set up in the old bottle store of The Green Dragon Inn, a grade II listed pub with a cosy lounge. Bar and restaurant food is served at lunchtime and evenings. Car park, garden, large function room. Children allowed.

ASUM ALE 3.8% ABV
Malty session ale.

ASUM GOLD 5.2% ABV
Fruity, malty and sweet strong ale.

11am–3pm and 7–11pm; midnight Fri.

FLADBURY

WYRE PIDDLE BREWERY

Unit 21, Craycombe Farm,
Fladbury, Nr Evesham WR10 2QS
☎ *(01386) 861383*
Visitors welcome. Tied houses: None

Founded in October 1994, Wyre Piddle Brewery has proved an enormous success. Upgraded in mid-1995 and reorganised in November 1995, the brewery is running to full capacity and producing all three beers. Great things are expected for 1996. Watch out for the "Piddlesner".

Beers available at: The Three Tuns, Lacester, Worcestershire *and* The Fleece, Bretforton, Worcestershire.

PIDDLE IN THE HOLE 3.9% ABV
A malty session ale.

PIDDLE IN THE WIND 4.5% ABV

PIDDLE IN THE SNOW 5.2% ABV
A thick, rich winter brew.

HANLEY CASTLE

The Three Kings

Church End,
Hanley Castle WR8 0BL
☎ *(01684) 592686*
Mrs Sheila Roberts

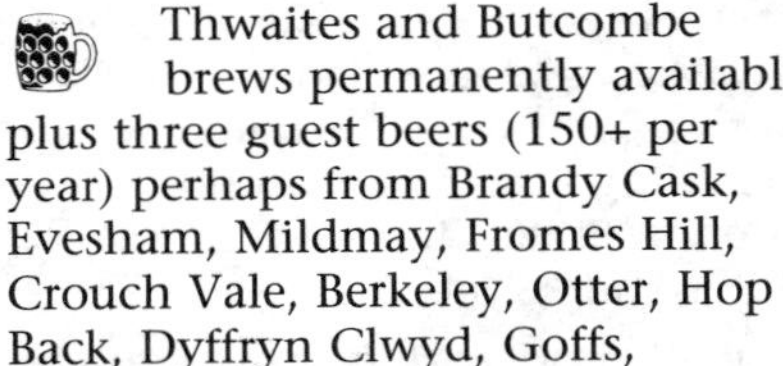

Thwaites and Butcombe brews permanently available plus three guest beers (150+ per year) perhaps from Brandy Cask, Evesham, Mildmay, Fromes Hill, Crouch Vale, Berkeley, Otter, Hop Back, Dyffryn Clwyd, Goffs, Stanway Woods, Hardington and Belhaven breweries.

A traditional fifteenth-century freehouse that has been in the same family for 84 years. Bar food available at lunchtime and evenings. Parking, garden and children's room. CAMRA pub of the Year 1993. Just off the B4211, Upton-upon-Severn to Malvern road. Take the third turn on the left from Upton.

11am–3pm and 7–11pm Mon–Sat; 12–3pm and 7–10.30pm Sun.

HEREFORD

WYE VALLEY BREWERY

69 St Owen Street,
Hereford HR1 2JQ
☎ *(01432) 342546*
Visitors welcome. Tied houses: 1

Wye Valley Brewery was established in 1985 at Canon Pyon,

Herefordshire, and moved in October 1986 to its present address at The Barrels pub in St Owen Street, Hereford. The brewery produces four different ales under the Wye Valley Brewery banner and a portfolio of seasonal ales from the Dorothy Goodbody selection. Using only the finest Golden Promise malt, Herefordshire hops, local water and yeast, the ales are brewed using traditional methods. The scale is large enough to be consistent but small enough to receive the personal attention of the brewer.

HEREFORD BITTER 3.5% ABV
A light, hoppy, standard bitter.

HPA 4.0% ABV
Pale, smooth, medium-strength ale.

HEREFORD SUPREME 4.3% ABV
Malty, darker premium bitter.

BREW 69 5.6% ABV
A light, well-hopped strong ale.

Plus **DOROTHY GOODBODY** seasonal ales.

KIDDERMINSTER

LEDBURY BREWERY

The Royal Oak, The Southend, Ledbury HR8 2ND
☎ *(01531) 632110*

The range of five Ledbury brews produced and served on the premises.

Built in 1420, with the main building added in 1645, this was the original Ledbury inn. Bar and restaurant food served at lunchtime and evenings. Car park and accommodation. Children allowed.

DOGHILL BITTS 3.6% ABV

LEDBURY SB 3.8% ABV

LEDBURY BEST 4.2% ABV

EXHIBITION 5.1% ABV

XB 7.5% ABV

11am–11pm

Jolly Roger (Market Tavern)

Comberton Place, Kidderminster
☎ *(01562) 825868*
Tom Hudson

Quaff Old Kidder, Shipwrecked, Severn Bore and Flagship from the Jolly Roger Brewing Group always available.

The pub is attached to the market. Live music on Friday and Saturday nights. Bar food available at lunchtime. Car park and garden. Children allowed. Near the Severn Valley railway station.

Phone for details.

King and Castle

Severn Valley Railway Station, Comberton Hill, Kidderminster
☎ *(01562) 747505*
Peter Williamson

Batham Best is among the brews always available plus guest beers (250 per year) including Enville Simpkiss and Hobson's, Hanby's, Three Tuns, Timothy Taylor, Holt's, Holden's, Berrow, Wood's, Burton Bridge and Wye Valley ales.

The pub is a copy of the Victorian railway refreshment rooms, decorated in the 1930s, GWR-style. Bar food available. Car park and garden. Children allowed until 9pm. Located next to Kidderminster railway station.

11am–4pm and 5–11pm.

LEOMINSTER

MARCHES ALES

Unit 6, Western Close,
Southern Avenue Industrial Estate.
Leominster HR6 0QD
☎ *(01568) 610063*
Visitors welcome

Marches Ales was set up in December 1994 by Paul and Georgina Harris on an industrial estate in Leominster. It currently supplies at least six outlets.

MARCHES BEST BITTER 3.8% ABV
A distinctly hoppy beer.

AUTUMN ALE 4.2% ABV

PRIORY ALE 4.8% ABV
Darker, premium ale.

JENNY PIPES SUMMER ALE 5.2% ABV

EARL LEOFRICS WINTER ALE 7.2% ABV

UPHAMPTON

CANNON ROYALL BREWERY

The Fruiterer's Arms,
Uphampton, Ombersley WR9 0JW
☎ *(01905) 621161*

Cannon Royall brews produced and served plus a guest beer.

Brewing began in this converted cider house in July 1993 and the maximum output is now 16 barrels per week and there are plans for expansion. The pub has two bars and a log fire in winter. Bar food is served at lunchtime. Car park. Children allowed.

KPA 3.4% ABV
A new summer beer.

MILD 3.7% ABV
Replaces Millward's Musket Mild.

ARROWHEAD 3.9% ABV
Beer with a strong hoppy finish.

BUCKSHOT 4.5% ABV
Rich and malty, leaving a round and hoppy aftertaste.

HEART OF OAK 5.4% ABV

OLDE MERRIE 6.0% ABV
Strong, malty winter brew.

12.30–2.30pm and 7–11pm
12–3pm Sat and Sun

PENSAX

The Bell

Pensax, Abberley WR6 6AE
☎ *(01299) 896677*
Graham Titcombe

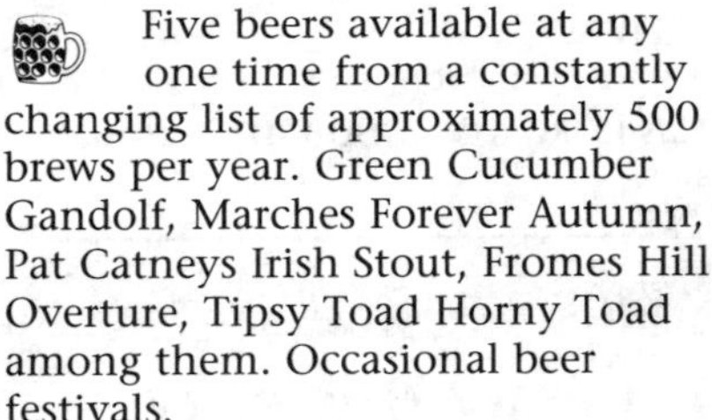
Five beers available at any one time from a constantly changing list of approximately 500 brews per year. Green Cucumber Gandolf, Marches Forever Autumn, Pat Catneys Irish Stout, Fromes Hill Overture, Tipsy Toad Horny Toad among them. Occasional beer festivals.

Attractive, rural Tudor-style pub with various traditional drinking areas and dining room. Large garden, superb views, three real fires in winter. Bar and restaurant food served at lunchtime and evenings. Located on the B4202 Great Witley to Cleobury Mortimer road, between Abberley and Clows Top.

12–2.30pm and
5–11pm Mon–Fri;
11am–11pm Sat;
12–10.30pm Sun.

PERSHORE

BRANDY CASK

25 Bridge Street,
Pershore WR10 1AJ
☎ *(01386) 552602*

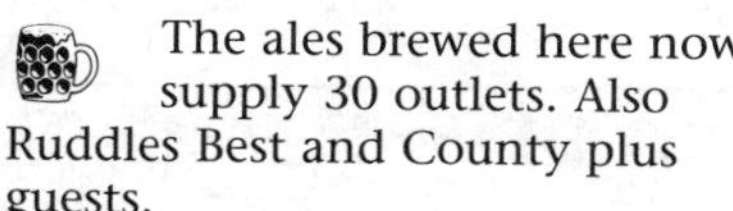

The ales brewed here now supply 30 outlets. Also Ruddles Best and County plus guests.

Town-centre freehouse. Bar and restaurant food is served at lunchtime and evenings. Large riverside garden. Children allowed.

BRANDY SNAPPER 4.0% ABV

JOHN BAKER ORIGINAL 4.8% ABV

11.30am–2.30pm and 7–11pm.

WORCESTER

The Brewery Tap

50 Lowesmoor,
Worcester WR1 2SE
☎ *(01905) 21540*
Jo Vukasovic

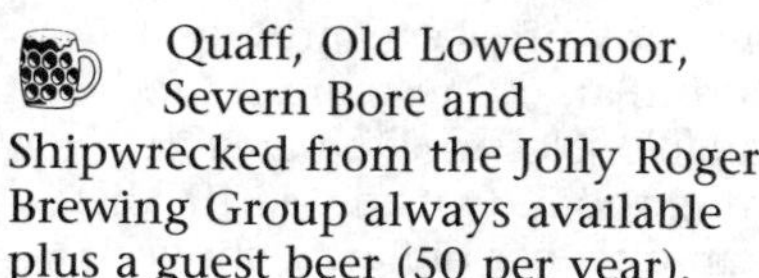

Quaff, Old Lowesmoor, Severn Bore and Shipwrecked from the Jolly Roger Brewing Group always available plus a guest beer (50 per year).

The original home of Jolly Roger beers, brewed just up the road. Live music three nights a week and Sunday afternoons. Bar and restaurant food available at lunchtime. Parking. Children allowed.

11.30am–11pm Mon-Sat; 12–10.30pm Sun.

The Toad and Tulip

53 Lowesmoor,
Worcester WR1 2RS
☎ *(01905) 26876*
Mrs Cordelia Knight

Jolly Roger A6, Shipwrecked and Flagship are always available plus a guest beer from a range of 50 per year.

Rough and ready pub with an impressive selection of rock music on the jukebox. No food. Parking and garden. Children not allowed.

11am–3pm and 5–11pm Mon–Thurs; 11am–11pm Fri–Sat; 12–10.30pm Sun.

AMWELL

Elephant and Castle

Amwell Lane, Amwell, Wheathampstead AL4 8EA

☎ *(01582) 832175*

Amwell Ale brewed specially for the pub is always available plus seven other real ales (80 per year) selected from anywhere and everywhere. Strengths generally vary from 3.7 per cent to 5.2 per cent ABV.

This pub is 475 years old, with three bars on different levels. There is a 200ft well in the middle of the bar. No music or machines, with the emphasis on good beer and good conversation. Bar meals available at lunchtime and evenings. Car park, two gardens (one for adults only), dining area. Children not allowed in bar. The pub is difficult to find. Ask in Wheathampstead or ring for directions.

11am–3pm and 5.30–11pm Mon–Fri; all day Sat–Sun.

AYOT ST LAWRENCE

The Brocket Arms

Ayot St Lawrence AL6 9RT

☎ *(01438) 820250*

Tony Wingfield-Digby

Greene King IPA and Abbot Ale, Wadworth 6X and Dark Horse Ale permanently available plus two guest beers (150 per year) perhaps including Gibbs Mew Bishop's Tipple, Adnam's Broadside and Old Icknield Ale from the Tring Brewery.

A traditional, oak-beamed pub with a walled garden and accommodation. Bar and restaurant food served at lunchtime and evenings (except Sunday and Monday nights). Parking. For access from the A1 or M1, head for Wheathampstead (B653 and A6129). Then take directions to Shaw's Corner at Ayot St Lawrence.

11am–11pm.

BARLEY

THE FOX AND HOUNDS

Barley Brewery, The Fox and Hounds, Barley SG8 8HU

☎ *(01763) 848459*

The pub brews and serves its own Nathaniel's Special, Flame Thrower and Old Dragon as well as a range of guest beers, perhaps ten in all, from brewers all around the country.

A brewery has been in production here for 13 years using a nineteenth-century brewhouse which is visible from the bar. Parts of the heavily beamed pub date back to 1450. Formerly known as The Waggon and Horses, there is an inglenook fireplace and original beams. Bar and restaurant food is available. No-smoking area in dining room. Outside skittle alley, petan-que, bar billiards, shove ha'penny, games tables, darts etc. Car park, garden, children's room (occas-ionally used for other functions), disabled toilets, baby-changing facilities. Well-behaved children welcome.

NATHANIEL'S SPECIAL 3.5% ABV

FLAME THROWER 4.5% ABV

OLD DRAGON 5.3% ABV

12–2.30pm and 6–11pm Mon–Sat; 12–3pm and 7.30–10.30pm Sun.

BENINGTON

The Lordship Arms

42 Whempstead Road, Benington
☎ *(01438) 869665*

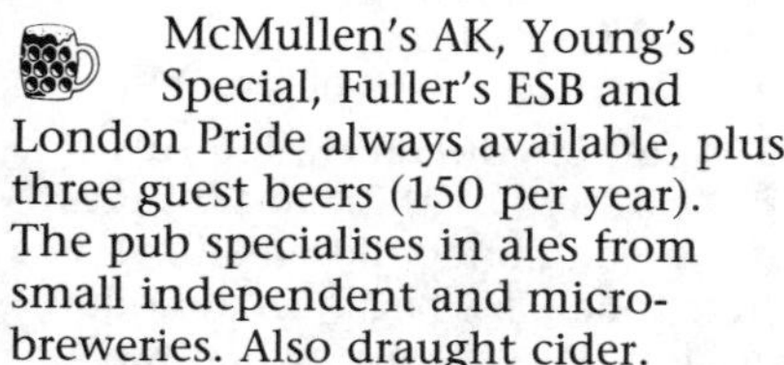

McMullen's AK, Young's Special, Fuller's ESB and London Pride always available, plus three guest beers (150 per year). The pub specialises in ales from small independent and micro-breweries. Also draught cider.

A 300-year-old village local, recently refurbished, with a display of telephone memorabilia. Bar food available at lunchtime. Book on Sunday. Car park and garden. Children not allowed. Take the A602 exit off the A1(M), follow the A602 then turn left. Signposted Aston, Benington.

12–3pm and 6–11pm Mon–Sat; 12–3pm and 7–10.30pm Sun.

BISHOPS STORTFORD

The Cock Inn

High Street, Huttfield Broadoak Bishops Stortford BM22 7HF
☎ *(01279) 718273*
Miss Holcroft

Adnams Best, Greene King IPA and Fuller's London Pride always available plus three guests (up to 150 per year) including Everards Tiger and brews from Robinsons, Oakhill, Marstons and Wadworths.

A sixteenth-century coaching inn, beamed with log fires. Bar and restaurant food available at lunchtime and evenings. No-smoking room, car park, function room. Children allowed. Easy to find.

12–3pm and 5–11pm Mon–Sat; 12–10.30pm Sun.

BRICKET WOOD

Moor Mill

Smug Oak Lane, Bricket Wood, Nr St Albans AL2 3TY
☎ *(01727) 875557*
Mr and Mrs Muir

A selection of ten real ales permanently available from breweries including Brakspears, Wadworths, Greene King and Gales. Seasonal and popular guests also available (50 per year).

An eighteenth-century converted corn mill sitting astride the River Ver. Bar and restaurant food available at lunchtime and evenings. Occasional pig roasts and barbecues. Car park, garden and meeting room. Children allowed.

11am–11pm Mon–Sat; 12–3pm and 7.30–10.30pm Sun.

DATCHWORTH

Tilbury (The Inn off the Green)

1 Watton Road, Datchworth SG3 6TB
☎ *(01438) 812496*
Ian Miller

Palmer's IPA is among the beers permanently available plus up to seven guests (250 per year) which may include Woodforde's Nelson's Revenge, Otter Ale, Brandy Cask, John Baker, Ryburn Mild, Featherstone Stage Ale, Kelham Island Bitter, Rocket Best Bitter, Buchanan's Best and others from micro and small independent breweries.

A seventeenth-century two-bar village pub. Bar and restaurant food available. Large garden and car park. Well-behaved children allowed. On the Datchworth crossroads, on the road from Woolmer Green to Watton.

11am–3pm and 5–11pm Mon–Wed; all day Thurs–Sun.

HARPENDEN

HARPENDEN BREWERY

The Red Cow,
171 Westfield Road,
Harpenden AL5 4ND
☎ *(01582) 460156*
VR Davies

Perhaps the smallest pub brewery in the country, producing and serving Harpenden Special plus Marston's Pedigree and Ruddles brews.

The Harpenden brewery has been in production since August 1994. It has a two-barrel brewlength. The Red Cow is a picturesque, grade II listed sixteenth-century hostelry with a friendly atmosphere. Bar food is available at lunchtime and evenings. Car park, garden. Children allowed.

HARPENDEN SPECIAL ALE 3.8% ABV

All day every day.

HERTFORD

MCMULLEN AND SONS

The Hertford Brewery,
26 Old Cross, Hertford SG14 1RD
☎ *(01992) 584911*
Visitors welcome. Tied houses: 146

Peter McMullen started this brewery in 1827 and his great-great grandchildren still work there today. He began in a modest building in what is now Railway Street, Hertford, and the first McMullen pub opened in 1836, in Bengeo, near Hertford. The original brewery soon outgrew itself and moved to Mill Bridge, where The Woolpack pub now stands. It moved again in 1891, when the original buildings of the present brewery were constructed on the site of three wells which still provide thousands of gallons of pure water today. In 1904 there were 35 different breweries in Hertfordshire. By 1949, only eight remained. McMullens remains an independent family business proud of its traditions.

ORIGINAL AK 3.7% ABV
A light bitter with a hoppy aroma

GLADSTONE 4.3% ABV
A beautifully smooth ale with a finely rounded bitterness.

COUNTRY BEST BITTER 4.3% ABV
A beer with a hoppy, fruity aroma

STRONGHART 7.0% ABV
A sweet, rich, dark beer, a single brew for the winter months

Old Knebworth

The Lytton Arms

Park Lane, Old Knebworth SG3 6QB
☎ *(01438) 812312*
Steven Nye

Fuller's London Pride, Woodforde's Wherry and Young's Special are among those ales permanently available plus up to six guest beers (200 per year) from Adnams, Nethergate, Cotleigh, Exmoor, B&T, Brewery on Sea, Morland and Elgood's etc. Note also the Belgian beers and malt whiskies.

A traditional freehouse on the edge of Knebworth Park, built in 1837. Beamed with open fires. Bar food available at lunchtime and evenings. Car park, garden and children's room. Located halfway between Knebworth and Codicote.

11am–3pm and 5–11pm Mon–Thurs; 11am–11pm Fri–Sat; 12–10.30pm Sun.

St Albans

The Lower Red Lion

34–36 Fishpond Street, St Albans AL3 4RX
☎ *(01727) 855669*
Mrs Turner

Fuller's London Pride, Adnams, Greene King Abbot Ale and a house ale permanently available plus four guests (500 per year) from far and wide. Two beer festivals held each year.

A seventeenth-century, two-bar, traditional public house on the edge of the town centre. with a wide ranging clientele. No music or games machines. Bar food is available at lunchtime and evenings (not Sun). Car park and garden.

12–2.30pm Mon–Fri; 12–3pm Sat–Sun; 5.30–11pm Mon–Sat; 7–10.30pm Sun.

Tring

The Tring Brewery

81–82 Akeman Street, Tring HP23 6AF
☎ *(01442) 890721*
Visitors welcome. Tied houses: None

Tring had two breweries during the last century but there was a 50-year gap before The Tring Brewery Company revived the tradition in December 1992, when brewer Richard Shardlow and soldier-turned-salesman Kerr Hill set up business. The original Ridgeway Bitter and the Old Icknield Ale take their names from prehistoric trackways which pass through the town. Situated in Akeman Street, there is now a staff of four and between them they produce 1,050 gallons per week sold primarily to about 60 outlets within a 15-mile radius.

Beers available at: The Black Horse, Frogmore Street, Tring, Hertfordshire *and* The Greyhound, Docks Road, Aldbury, Nr Tring, Hertfordshire.

FINEST SUMMER ALE 3.7% ABV
Only brewed in the summer, this ale is much lighter with a proportion of wheat malt in the grist.

RIDGEWAY BITTER 4.0% ABV
A session ale slightly dark in colour but full-flavoured and with a pronounced hop.

OLD CANTANKEROUS 4.8% ABV
Available during the autumn months, a dark porter beer making use of a grist comprising white, brown and chocolate malts.

OLD ICKNIELD ALE 5.0% ABV
A premium ale, even darker than the Ridgeway, well-balanced and with a good malty character.

DEATH OR GLORY 7.2% ABV
A special brew, produced annually on 25 October to commemorate the Charge of the Light Brigade in 1854. A small amount of this beer is hand-bottled.

Plus other seasonal and commemorative ales.

TYTTENHANGER GREEN

The Plough

Tyttenhanger Green,
Nr St Albans AL4 ORW
☎ *(01727) 857777*
Mike Barrowman

Marston's Pedigree, Morland's Old Speckled Hen, Wadworth 6X, Summer and Winter Ales, Fuller's London Pride and ESB, Greene King IPA and Abbot Ale, Tring Ridgeway and Timothy Taylor Landlord always available, plus numerous unusual and interesting guest beers.

These purveyors to the multitude of murky beers and watery spirits specialise in incompetent staff, greasy food and exhorbitant prices in a terrible atmosphere. Ideal for discreet liaisons. Not recommended by CAMRA or anyone else. Bar food available at lunchtime. Car park and garden.

Various and flexible without notice.

NEWPORT

BURTS BREWERY

16 Manners View,
Dodnor Industrial Estate,
Newport PO30 5FA
Visitors welcome. Tied houses: 4

Burts Ales, brewed in Ventnor in the traditional way for well over 150 years, are now being produced at Newport, where a new brewery has recently been established by brewer David Yates. There are now six ales, available throughout the island and which have now spread across to the mainland. Small groups of beer lovers may visit the brewery by appointment and so may professional brewers, who are welcome to lend a hand with mashing in! Burts' first pub, the Cask and Crispin, opened in Newport last year. Three others have already followed.

Beers available at: Cask and Crispin, 8–10 Carrisbrook Road, Newport, IoW *and* The Hole in the Wall, St Johns Road, Ryde, IoW.

NIPPER BITTER 3.8% ABV
A smooth and light quaffing bitter, well-balanced with a good hop note and finish.

PARKHURST PORTER 3.8% ABV

VENTNOR PREMIUM ALE 4.2% ABV
A toffee flavoured distinctive bitter with a good hop aroma and strong aftertaste.

NEWPORT NOBBLER 4.4% ABV
A bronze-coloured bitter with a golden glow. Brewed using pale ale malt to give a crisp dry taste, a good hoppy aroma and finish.

TANNER BITTER 4.8% ABV
A delightful chestnut-coloured malty brew with a fulsome character.

VECTIS VENOM 5.0% ABV
A strong light bitter. Amber coloured and deceptively strong with a dry well-hopped taste.

NITON

The Buddle

St Catherine's Road,
Niton PO38 2N3
☎ *(01983) 730243*
John Bourne

Six beers always available from a constantly changing range (150 per year). Hampshire Pendragon and 1066, Adnams Best, Morland Old Speckled Hen and Burts brews among them.

Sixteenth-century, stone-built pub with oak beams, flagstone floors and open fires. Food available at lunchtime and evenings. Car park, dining room and garden. Children allowed. Near St Catherine's Lighthouse.

11am–11pm Mon–Sat;
12–10.30pm Sun.

Northwood

Traveller's Joy

85 Pallance Road,
Northwood, Cowes PO31 8LS
☎ *(01983) 298024*
Mr and Mrs Smith

Goddards Special and Ringwood Old Thumper among those brews always available plus a wide range of guests from every brewery and at every strength.

A real ale pub situated on the outskirts of the village. CAMRA pub of the year. Bar food available at lunchtime. Children's room, play area and large garden with petanque. Car park. On the main Cowes to Yarmouth road.

11am–2.30pm and 5–11pm Mon–Thurs; 11am–11pm Fri–Sat; usual hours Sun.

Ryde

Goddard's Brewery

Barnsley Farm, Bullen Road,
Ryde PO33 1QF
☎ *(01983) 295024*
No visitors. Tied houses: None

A small, independent brewery based on a farm and opened in 1993.

Beers available at: Travellers Joy, 85 Pallance Road, Northwood, IoW *and* Fleming Arms, Binstead, Ryde, IoW.

GODDARD'S SPECIAL BITTER 4.0% ABV
Well balanced malty (Maris Otter) bitter with a hoppy nose.

FUGGLE-DEE-DUM 4.8% ABV
A golden, full-bodied, spicily aromatic award-winning bitter.

Wroxall

The Star Inn

Clarence Road, Wroxall,
Nr Ventnor PO38 3BY
☎ *(01983) 854701*
Mr and Mrs Boocock

Burts Nipper and VPA always available plus six guest beers (15 per year) including Eldridge Pope Royal Oak, Mansfield Old Baily, Wadworth 6X, Freetraders Twelve-Bore and Burts Vectis Venom and Parkhurst Porter.

The Star Inn offers the weary traveller hot and wholesome food and seven real ales. Destroyed by fire in 1980 but happily rebuilt. Food available at lunchtime and evenings. Car park and garden. Children allowed. Wroxhall lies in the south of the island, two miles north of Ventnor on the B3327.

11am–3pm and 7–11pm.

ASHFORD

Hooden Horse on the Hill

Silver Hill Road, Ashford TN24 0NY
☎ *(01233) 662226*

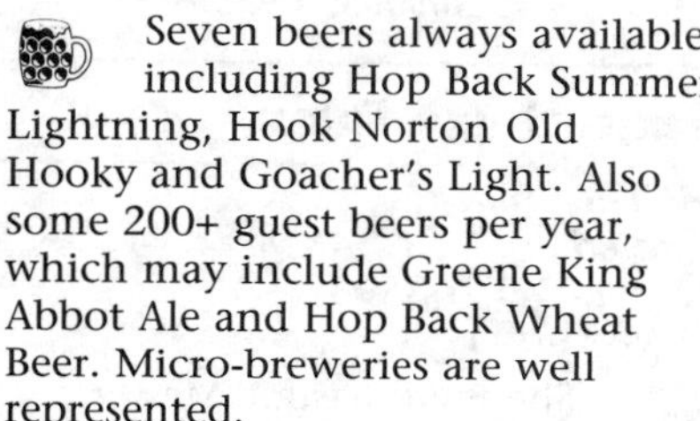

Seven beers always available including Hop Back Summer Lightning, Hook Norton Old Hooky and Goacher's Light. Also some 200+ guest beers per year, which may include Greene King Abbot Ale and Hop Back Wheat Beer. Micro-breweries are well represented.

The oldest and busiest pub in Ashford, beamed and candlelit with hops in the ceiling. One bar, friendly staff, background music only. Food available at lunchtime and evenings. Car park and garden. Children allowed. Situated off the Hythe Road, near the ambulance station.

12–10.30pm.

AYLESFORD

The Little Gem

19 High Street,
Aylesford ME20 7AX
☎ *(01622) 717510*
Sandra Brenchley

Fuller's London Pride and ESB, Shepherd Neame Spitfire Ale and Harveys Best permanently available plus a guest beer (30 per year) which may include Charles Wells Bombardier, Gale's HSB or Morland Old Speckled Hen.

Reputedly the smallest pub in Kent. A former bakery, the building dates back to 1106 in the reign on Henry I. The pub also has a small gallery which seats 12 people. Bar food available at lunchtime. Next door to the post office.

11am–3pm and 6–11pm; all day Sat.

BARFRESTON

Yew Tree Inn

Barfreston, Nr Dover CT15 7JH
☎ *(01304) 831619*
Mrs McSadyen

Greene King Mild and IPA, Otter Ale, Black Sheep Best, Timothy Taylor Landlord, Mauldon's Black Adder and Thatcher's cider always available plus at least one guest (40 per year) including Adnams Broadside, Mansfield Bitter and Old Baily, Wadworth 6X, Brewery on Sea Winter Widget, Greene King Sorcerer, Fuller's ESB and Hop Back Summer Lightning.

An unspoilt traditional village freehouse, with three bars. The main bar has a wooden floor and pine scrubbed tables. Bar food available at lunchtime and evenings. Car park, children's room and terrace at the back overlooking open countryside. Approximately eight miles south of Canterbury, two miles off the main A2 towards Dover, signposted Barfreston.

11am–3pm and 6–11pm Mon–Sat;
12–3pm and 7–10.30pm Sun.

Boughton Monchelsea

The Red House

Hermitage Lane,
Boughton Monchelsea ME17 4DA
☎ *(01622) 743986*
Mr and Mrs Richardson

Six beers available at any one time (150 per year) including Fuller's London Pride, Hop Back Summer Lightning, Otter Ale, Hampshire Lionheart, Greene King Abbot Ale, Arundel Old Knucker, Oak Wobbly Bob etc.

A country freehouse with pool room and two other bars, one with an open log fire, Also a conservatory/children's room, a large garden and camp site. Bar food available at lunchtime and evenings. Beer festival in May. South off the B2163 at Marlpit, take the Wierton Road, then left down East Hall Hill. OS783488.

12–3pm and 7–11pm Mon–Fri; 12–11pm Sat; 12–10.30pm Sun. Closed Tues lunch.

Canterbury

Minnis Brewery

The Rose and Crown,
The Minnis, Canterbury CT4 6AS
☎ *(01227) 709265*

The three beers available in The Rose and Crown are produced on the premises.

The brewery has been established in this village location for just over a year, run by Mr Withey. The pub dates back to 1739 and features open fires. Bar and restaurant food served at lunchtime and evenings. Car park, garden, children's play area, camp site. Children allowed.

LEGIONS BITTER 3.7% ABV

MINNIS ALE 4.5% ABV

SEASONAL SPECIAL 6.0% ABV

11am–2.30pm and 7–11pm Mon–Sat; 12–3pm and 7–10.30pm Sun.

Canterbury Tales

12 The Friars,
Canterbury CT1 2AS
☎ *(01227) 768594*
Steve Turner

Shepherd Neame Master Brew and Goacher's Light always available plus guest beers from all local micro-breweries. Three mini beer festivals and one big one every year.

A lively city centre pub used by locals and actors. Food available all day. Children allowed. Opposite the Marlowe Theatre.

11am–11pm Mon–Sat; 12–10.30pm Sun.

Chatham

Flagship Brewery

Unit 2, Building 64, The Dockyard,
Chatham ME4 4TE
☎ *(01634) 832828*
Visitors welcome. Tied houses: None

The brewery was started in February 1995 by Andrew Purcell and his father-in-law, Tony Smith, after Andrew was made redundant. Andrew, being a keen home brewer for ten years, took a natural step into micro-brewing. He decided to locate the brewery in the historic dockyard at Chatham, a preserved Georgian dockyard and visitor attraction. A display area has been formed in the brewery for visitors to discover how beer is made and learn something about beer and the Navy. The brewery's logo incorporates the Victory, Nelson's flagship, which was built at the dockyard.

Beers available at: Britannia, 376 High Street, Rochester, Kent *and* Canterbury Tales, 12 The Friars, Canterbury, Kent.

HOUSE SPECIAL ALE 3.5% ABV
known by various names in various places

CAPSTAN ALE 3.8% ABV

ENSIGN ALE 4.2% ABV

CROW'S NEST ALE 4.8% ABV

FUTTOCK ALE 5.2% ABV

GANGPLANK ALE 5.8% ABV
Winter only.

CHIDDINGSTONE

LARKINS BREWERY

Larkins Farm, Chiddingstone,
Nr Edenbridge TN8 7BB
☎ *(01892) 870328*
Visitors welcome on Saturday and Sunday mornings in winter.
Tied houses: None

The brewery moved to Larkins Farm in 1989, although the business originated three years before when the Dockerty family bought Kentish Ales in Tunbridge Wells, comprising Ashford and Royal Tunbridge Wells breweries. Another copper was added to the ten-barrel equipment and a 20-barrel fermenter. The capacity is now for 40-50 barrels per week using whole mash (no sugar or additives) and whole hops, preferably from Kent.

Beers available at: Castle Inn, Chiddingstone, Nr Edenbridge, Kent *and* The Rock, Chiddingstone Hoath, Kent.

TRADITIONAL BITTER 3.4% ABV
A full-bodied session bitter.

ROYAL SOVEREIGN 4.0% ABV
A fruity bitter.

BEST BITTER 4.4% ABV
Well balanced and very drinkable.

PORTER 5.2% ABV
A winter beer.

CHIDDINGSTONE CAUSEWAY

The Little Brown Jug

Chiddingstone Causeway,
Nr Tonbridge TN11 8JJ
☎ *(01892) 870318*
Mr and Mrs CR Cannon

Harveys Best permanently available plus three guest beers (130 per year) including Timothy Taylor Landlord, Brakspear's, Hop Back Summer Lightning, Ringwood Old Thumper, Fuller's London Pride, Larkin's, Adnams, Morland Old Speckled Hen, Exmoor Gold and Gales HSB.

A friendly, family-owned country pub with no games machines or music. Bar and restaurant food available at lunchtime and evenings. Car park, garden, conference facilities and accommodation. Children allowed.

11.30am–3pm and 6–11pm.

FAIRSEAT

The Vigo Inn

Gravesend Road, Fairseat,
Nr Sevenoaks TN15 7JL
☎ *(01732) 822547*
Mrs PJ Ashwell

Young's, Harvey's and Goacher's brews

permanently available plus a varied guest list which may include Ridley's ESX and Rumpus, Flagship Ensign etc.

Situated on the North Downs, partly no-smoking. No music or games machines. Bar food is available. Car park. Children allowed in the garden only.

12–3pm and 6–11pm Mon–Sat; 12–3pm and 7–10.30pm Sun. Closed Mon lunchtime.

Faversham

Shepherd Neame

17 Court Street,
Faversham ME13 7AX
☎ *(01795) 532206*
Visitors welcome by appointment.
Tied houses: 374

No other brewery can claim continuous production on the same site using the same water and on the same scale as Shepherd Neame. Founded by Richard Marsh in about 1698, the business was acquired by Samuel Shepherd in 1742 and the family connection was to last 136 years. In 1865, Henry Shepherd was joined by Percy Beale Neame. The latter developed the business considerably until his death in 1913, by which time the company had 85 tied houses. Percy's sons took over and Harry Neame handed over to his son, Jasper, who became managing director in 1943. His brother, Laurence, took over when he died unexpectedly in 1961 and expansion continued. Robert Neame is chairman today and his cousin, Colin Neame, is joint managing director. Colin's brother, Stuart, is vice-chairman. Considerable investment has followed with purchases from many major brewers to create the thriving business of today.

MASTER BREW BITTER 3.7% ABV
A traditional ale brewed with Kent's finest hops.

BEST BITTER 4.1% ABV
A Kentish ale, mid brown in colour with a rich malt and hop flavour.

SPITFIRE ALE 4.7% ABV
A premium bitter, first brewed in 1990 to commemorate the 50th anniversary of the Battle of Britain.

BISHOPS FINGER 5.2% ABV
A powerful premium ale brewed to a traditional Kentish recipe.

ORIGINAL PORTER 5.2% ABV
A strong, traditional winter warmer, dark in colour with heaps of flavours and added liquorice root. Available from October to March.

Plus a range of bottled beers.

The Elephant Inn

31 The Mall, Faversham ME13 8JN
☎(01795) 590157
Mr and Mrs Searle

Up to 20 beers at any one time, approx 600 per year. All sorts from all places.

A family-orientated fun pub with bar food available at lunchtime and evenings. Barbecues on summer Sundays. Parking, garden, children's room and eating area. Marquee available. Take the first exit for Faversham off the M2.

All day.

Gillingham

Roseneath

79 Arden Street, Gillingham ME7 1HS
☎ (01634) 852553
Mr T Robinson and Mrs H Dobson

Snakehound Bitter permanently available plus six guest beers that may include Greene King Abbot Ale, Bateman's Bitter, Cotleigh Barn Owl Bitter, Belcher's Best Bitter, Charles Wells Bombardier, Adnams Broadside, B&T Dragonslayer, Coach House Gunpowder Strong Mild, Ward's Waggle Dance and many more.

A friendly pub with perhaps the most adventurous selection of beers in north Kent. Doorstep sandwiches. Crazy bar billiards. Located just five minutes from the railway station.

11am–11.30pm Mon–Sat; 12–10.30pm Sun.

Gravesend

Somerset Arms

10 Darnley Road, Gravesend DA11 0RU
☎ (01474) 533837
Mr and Mrs Cerr

Six beers always available with hundreds of guests per year. These may include Exmoor Gold, Timothy Taylor Landlord, Kelham Island Pale Rider, Maclay's Broadsword, Ash Vine Hop and Glory and brews from Harviestoun, Hoskins & Oldfield, Youngs and Fullers.

A country-style pub. The Best Town Pub in Kent 1993. Bar food available. Garden. Children allowed. Opposite Gravesend railway station.

11am–3.30pm and 5pm–12am.

Ringlestone

Ringlestone Inn

Nr Harrietsham, Maidstone ME17 1NX
☎ (01622) 859900
Michael Millington-Buck

Five beers always available including Shepherd Neame Best and guests (40 per year) such as Brewery on Sea Summer Solstice, Timothy Taylor Landlord, Felinfoel Double Dragon, Harveys Best and Shepherd Neame Bishop's Finger.

Built as a hospice for monks, a sixteenth-century inn, beamed with open fires and two bars. Bar and restaurant food. Car parks, garden. Children allowed. Take the B2163 towards Sittingbourne. At the water tower above Hollingbourne turn right and straight over at next crossroads.

11.30am–3pm and 6–11pm.

Luddesdown

The Cock Inn

Henley Street,
Luddesdown DA13 0XB
☎ *(01474) 814208*
Mr A Turner

Adnams Bitter and Flagship Bitter always available plus six guest beers (two new ones per day). If it is brewed, it has probably been sold here.

A sixteenth-century traditional two-bar public house set in idyllic countryside. Bar food available at lunchtime and until 8pm. Seafood specialities. Car park, garden and children's room.

12–2.30pm and 5–11pm Mon–Thurs; 12–11pm Fri–Sun.

Maidstone

P and DJ Goacher

Unit 8, Tovil Green Business Park, Tovil, Maidstone ME15 6TA
☎ *(01622) 682112*
Visitors welcome. Tied houses: 1

Maidstone has had a long tradition of commercial brewing dating back to before 1650. Four breweries survived at the turn of the century, but the last ceased production in 1972. In 1983, Phil and Debbie Goacher opened their own brewery in the Loose Valley. The modern plant was purpose-built on site and constructed along classical lines, All Goacher's ales are produced from 100 per cent malted barley and whole Kentish hops without the addition of sugars or colouring.

Beers available at: The Royal Paper Mill, Tovil Hill, Tovil, Nr Maidstone, Kent *and* The Victory, East Farleigh, Maidstone, Kent.

REAL MILD ALE 3.4% ABV
A full-flavoured malty ale with a background bitterness.

FINE LIGHT ALE 3.7% ABV
A pale, golden-brown bitter ale with a strong hoppy aroma and aftertaste. A very hoppy and moderately malty session beer.

BEST DARK ALE 4.1% ABV
An intensely bitter beer, balanced by a moderate maltiness, with a complex aftertaste. Lighter in colour than it once was, but still darker than most bitters.

GOLD STAR 5.1% ABV
A summer pale ale.

MAIDSTONE PORTER 5.1% ABV
A dark ruby winter beer with a roast malt flavour.

OLD 1066 ALE 6.7% ABV
Black, potent old ale, produced in winter only.

RAMSGATE

VIKING BREWERY

PO Box 148,
Ramsgate CT11 9GJ
☎ *(01843) 865211*
Visitors welcome. Tied houses: None

Two years ago, Dick Parkin, a former publican, and Alan Kirkham, a keen amateur brewer, approached Leyland Ridings, a friend of Alan's, and started looking for financial backing to help them start a brewery. Funds, loans and finance were put together in May 1995 and brewing commenced in early July. Viking Ale and Thor's Thunder came first and were exhibited at the Canterbury Beer Festival in mid-July. Longship and Berserker followed soon afterwards.

VIKING ALE 3.9% ABV
A strong blend of fruit and hops on the nose, followed by a hoppy bitterness at all stages, ending with a sharp, dry aftertaste.

LONGSHIP 4.2% ABV

THOR'S THUNDER 4.4% ABV
Dark and full bodied, rich and pungent this is a strongly hopped ruby bitter, with a lingering, dry satisfying aftertaste.

BERSERKER 6.5% ABV
Christmas special.

ROCHESTER

The Man of Kent

6-8 John Street, Rochester ME1 1YN
☎ *(01634) 818771*
Mr and Mrs Sandmann

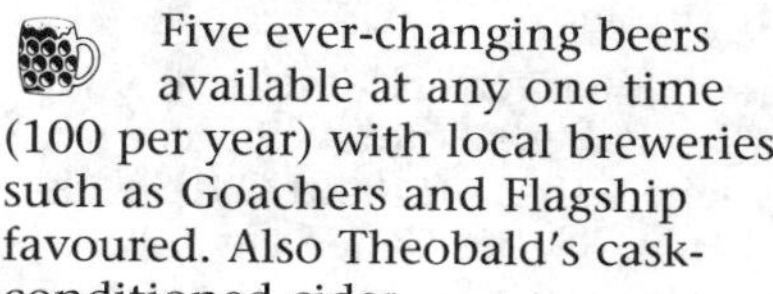

Five ever-changing beers available at any one time (100 per year) with local breweries such as Goachers and Flagship favoured. Also Theobald's cask-conditioned cider.

A friendly old-style pub with one L-shaped bar. Games include chess, bar billiards, darts, carpet bowls and shove ha'penny. Bar food is available at lunchtime and evenings. Parking and garden. Off Victoria Street, near the Main Star Hill junction. Near the school.

12–11pm.

Who'd Ha Thot It?

9 Baker Street, Rochester ME1 3DN
☎ *(01634) 830144*

Six beers always available including Butchers Brew (brewed specially for the pub), Greene King Abbot, Eldridge Pope Royal Oak and Thomas Hardy, Fuller's London Pride. Guests include Goachers brews and vary in strength from 3.5 per cent to 5.2 per cent. The landlord tries to favour smaller breweries.

A nineteenth-century pub off the main Maidstone Road, refurbished and with an open fire. There is a games bar and lounge bar, no jukebox. Bar food is available.. Street parking, beer garden. Well-behaved children only.

12–11pm Mon–Sat;
12–10.30pm Sun.

SMARDEN

The Bell Inn

Bell Lane, Smarden,
Nr Ashford TN27 8PW
☎ *(01233) 770283*
Ian Turner

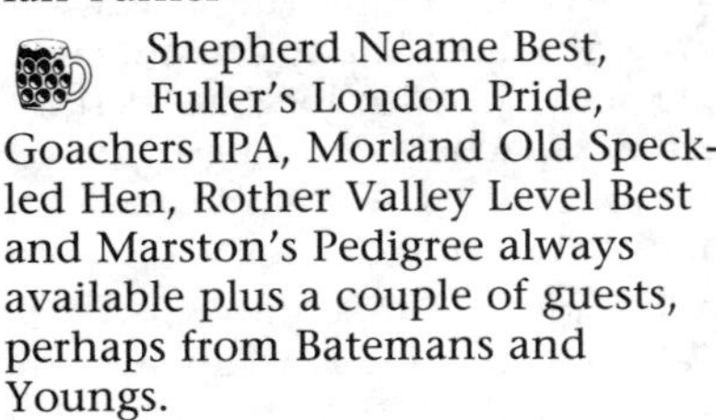

Shepherd Neame Best, Fuller's London Pride, Goachers IPA, Morland Old Speckled Hen, Rother Valley Level Best and Marston's Pedigree always available plus a couple of guests, perhaps from Batemans and Youngs.

Fifteenth-century inn, beamed with stone floors and inglenook fireplace. Three bars (one no-smoking). Bar food available. Car park, garden, children's room, accommodation.

11.30am–2.30pm and 6–11pm Mon–Sat; 12–3pm and 7–10.30pm Sun.

STONE STREET

The Padwell Arms

Stone Street TN15 0L
☎ *(01732) 761532*

Seven beers always available including Hall & Woodhouse Badger, Hook Norton Old Hooky and Harvey's Best. Some 300+ guest beers per year mainly from micro-breweries. Definitely no nationals.

Country pub one mile off the A25 between Seal and Borough Green. Features include two real fires and views overlooking apple and pear orchards. Bar food is available at lunchtime. Car park, garden and outside terrace with barbecues in summer. Children allowed under sufferance. Live Blues music on the last Saturday of every month.

12–3pm and 6–11pm Mon–Sat; 12–3pm and 7–10.30pm Sun.

TONBRIDGE

The Royal Oak

Lower Haysden Lane,
Tonbridge TN11 9BD
☎ *(01732) 350208*
Mr and Mrs Bird

Adnams Bitter always available plus two or three guest beers (100+ per year), perhaps from Bateman's, Wychwood, Ash Vine, Butterknowle, Crouch Vale or Harviestoun breweries.

Olde-world country pub and restaurant. Bar and restaurant food available at lunchtime. Car park and garden. Children allowed. Follow the signs to Haysden Country Park, south of Tonbridge.

11am–11pm Mon–Sat; 12–10.30pm Sun.

ACCRINGTON

The George Hotel

185 Blackburn Road,
Accrington BB5 0AF
☎ *(01254) 383441*

Four beers always available from an ever-changing list that might include Titanic Stout, Cains FA, Passageway St Arnold, Goose Eye Bitter and Steam Packet ales.

A friendly freehouse with an open-plan bar area and separate restaurant in converted stables. Bar and restaurant food available at lunchtime and evenings. Street parking, garden/patio area. Children allowed. Accommodation. Close to the railway and bus stations in a main road location.

12–11pm Mon–Sat;
12–10.30pm Sun.

BLACKBURN

DANIEL THWAITES BREWERY

Star Brewery, PO Box 50,
Blackburn BB1 5BU
☎ *(01254) 54431*
Visitors welcome. Tied houses: 414

Thwaites Brewery is a successful family-controlled company founded in 1807 on the site of a natural well. Daniel Thwaites was an excise officer whose job involved visiting breweries in the area. He got on so well with the two owners of one of them that he resigned his job and became a junior partner. The business flourished and, in due course, he became the sole owner. Today's company chairman is JohnYerburgh, great-great grandson of the founder. Thwaites still deliver to pubs in the area using their famous shire horses, which have been honoured by the local council as "great ambassadors for Blackburn". Thwaites launched the Connoisseur Collection in April 1995, introducing a new beer every month.

THWAITES BEST MILD 3.3% ABV

THWAITES BITTER 3.6% ABV

WHITE OAK 3.8% ABV
A clean-drinking amber beer with a sharp, lightly hopped palate.

SNIGBROOK ALE 4.0% ABV
Brewed to a long-lost recipe from Snigbrook Brewery, medium in colour, dry to the palate, it has a nutty flavour and a subtle bitterness.

CRAFTSMAN PREMIUM ALE 4.5% ABV

TOWN CRIER 4.5% ABV
Full-bodied, deep golden in colour with a touch of sweetness.

SCALLYWAG 4.5% ABV
Golden premium beer with an excellent blend of malt and hops to give a well–balanced flavour and hop aroma.

THUNDERBOLT 4.5% ABV
A clean, dry beer, light in colour with a malty taste.

FAWKES FOLLY 4.8% ABV
A dark porter ale with a hint of roasted malt and a dry palate.

BIG BEN 5.0% ABV
Strong ale, ruby in colour, with a sweet malty flavour.

DANIEL'S HAMMER 5.2% ABV
A strong beer, pale golden in colour, with a distinctly malty palate. It has a well balanced hop character with a slightly dry finish.

OLD DAN 6.5% ABV
Popular, dark winter warmer, with a mixture of malt and fruit flavour.

Burnley

Moorhouse's Brewery

4 Moorhouse Street,
Burnley BB11 5EN
☎ *(01282) 422864*
Visitors welcome. Tied houses: 6

Established in 1865, production on the present site began in 1870, making non-intoxicating hop bitters and mineral waters. The Moorhouse family sold their interest in 1978, when the company first commenced brewing cask-conditioned beer. A succession of owners followed up to 1985, when Bill Parkinson took over. The brewery has since grown from an output of 25 barrels per week to a maximum capacity of 270 barrels per week.

BLACK CAT MILD 3.2% ABV
A dark, nutty mild.

PREMIER BITTER 3.7% ABV
A light–coloured, hoppy session biter.

PENDLE WITCHES BREW 5.1% ABV
Fruity-flavoured strong bitter.

OWD ALE 6.0% ABV
A strong dark winter ale available from November to February.

Chorley

Malt 'n' Hops

50–52 Friday Street, Chorley
☎ *(01257) 260967*

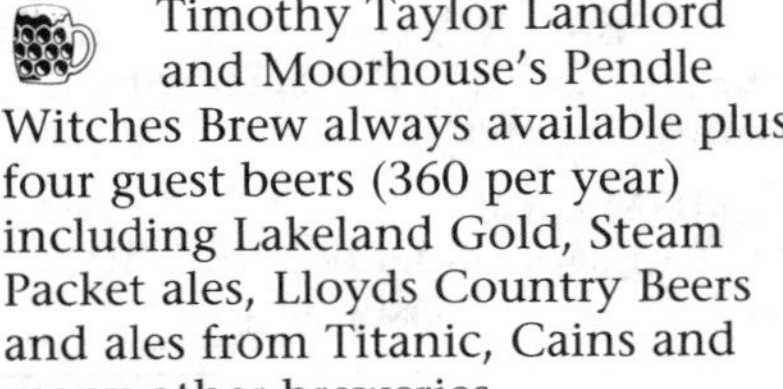

Timothy Taylor Landlord and Moorhouse's Pendle Witches Brew always available plus four guest beers (360 per year) including Lakeland Gold, Steam Packet ales, Lloyds Country Beers and ales from Titanic, Cains and many other breweries.

A single-bar Victorian-style pub ideal for trainspotters. Bar food available at lunchtime. Parking. Children allowed. Just 200 yards behind the Manchester to Preston railway station.

All day.

Croston

The Black Horse

Westhead Road, Croston,
Nr Chorley PR5 7RQ
☎ *(01772) 600338*
Mr S Welsh

Permanent ales plus four guest beers (650 per year) from breweries such as Cains, Hydes, Mansfield, Hanby, Lloyds, Cartmel, Tom Wood, Banks's and Timothy Taylor, Steam Packet, Coach House, Sutton and Bushys. Emphasis on micro-breweries and unusual brews.

A family-run traditional village freehouse. Bar and restaurant food is served at lunchtime and evenings. Car park, garden, children's play area, bowling green, French boules pitch. Children allowed in the restaurant. In the village of Croston, close to Chorley and midway between Preston and Southport.

All day.

Fleetwood

Wyre Lounge Bar

Marine Hall, The Esplanade,
Fleetwood FY7 6HF
☎ *(01253) 771141*

Eight beers always available including Moorhouse's

brews. Also 200+ guest beers per year which may come from Youngs, Charles Wells, Banks's and Timothy Taylor.

Part of the Marine Hall Sports Complex in Fleetwood. Food available at lunchtime. CAMRA pub of the year. Car park, garden, function room. No children.

11am–4.30pm and 7–11pm Mon–Sat; 12–4pm and 7–10.30pm Sun.

Haslingden

Porter Brewing Co.

Rossendale Brewery, The Griffin Inn, 86 Hud Rake, Haslingden BB4 5AF
☎ *(01706) 214021*
David Porter

A range of five Porter brews produced in the cellar and served on the premises.

The Porter Brewing Company, led by David Porter, bought The Griffin Inn in January 1994. It hopes to expand and serve other outlets. The pub is located on the edge of town and runs a policy of offering free soft drinks to drivers in a party of four or more during the week. Bar food is served at lunchtime. Parking. Children are not allowed.

Beers also available at: The Farmers Arms, Holmfirth, West Yorkshire.

DARK MILD 3.3% ABV

BITTER 3.8% ABV

PORTER 5.0% ABV

SUNSHINE 5.3% ABV

STOUT 5.5% ABV

Plus occasional and seasonal brews.

12–11pm Mon–Sat; 12–4pm and 7–10.30pm Sun.

Hawkshaw

The Red Lion

91 Ramsbottom Road, Hawkshaw BL7 0HT
☎ *(01204) 852539*

Seven beers always available from a list that changes every week. Favourites include Shepherd Neame Spitfire Ale, Charles Wells Bombardier and Morland's Old Speckled Hen.

In a picturesque setting, a Swiss-style cottage, originally built in 1805 and rebuilt to a high standard with a separate restaurant. Bar and restaurant food available.. Car park and accommodation. Children aged 14 and over are allowed in the bar.

12–3pm and 6–11pm.

Lancaster

Mitchell's

11 Moor Lane, Lancaster LA1 1QB
☎ *(01524) 63773*
Visitors welcome. Tied houses: 53

Mitchells was established in 1880 and moved to its present site in 1985, where a private bore hole supplies all the brewery water. The range of beers has changed considerably recently, with just two brews permanently available. Approximately one guest beer per month is also brewed in order to provide a choice in Mitchell's pubs and to satisfy a free trade hungry for something different in both gravity and taste.

WILLIAM MITCHELL'S ORIGINAL BITTER 3.8% ABV
Pale in colour and lightly hopped in both aroma and taste, this robust session bitter is very moreish.

Brewed with Maris Otter barley to give it a smooth malty flavour. A classic Northern bitter.

LANCASTER BOMBER 4.4% ABV
A deliciously light golden colour, brewed with three different hops, using Maris Otter barley and pure spring water, it has a hoppy nose and the initial taste is a well-balanced mixture of fruitiness and bitterness. A smooth and creamy aftertaste.

Also: **GOLDEN GLORY** (3.6% ABV)
BREWERS PRIDE (4.0% ABV)
JUST WILLIAM (4.0% ABV)
STOUT (4.1% ABV)
IPA (4.6% ABV)
FATAL ATTRACTION (4.8% ABV)
MIDSUMMER ALE (5.0% ABV),
RESOLUTION ALE (5.0% ABV)
CHRISTMAS CRACKER (5.5% ABV)
GUY FAWKES BITTER (5.7% ABV) and
SINGLE MALT (7.5% ABV).

LITTLE ECCLESTON

CARTFORD COUNTRY INN AND HOTEL

Cartford Lane, Little Eccleston,
Nr Preston PR3 0YP
☎ *(01995) 670166*

The Hart Brewery produces a range of eight beers for sale in the hotel and also some local freehouses.

The brewery was founded in 1994 in a small private garage and moved to premises at the rear of the Cartford Hotel during 1995. The hotel is an award-winning seventeenth-century riverside pub beside a toll bridge. Bar and restaurant food served at lunchtime and evenings. Car park, games room, outdoor children's play area. Functions and parties catered for. Accomodation.

SUN RAYS 3.5% ABV
LIBERATOR 3.8% ABV
MAYSON PREMIER 4.0% ABV
CRIMINALE PORTER 4.0% ABV
NEMESIS 4.5% ABV
OLD RAM 5.0% ABV
AMADEUS 5.5% ABV
NEMESIS SPECIAL 5.5% ABV

12–3pm and 6.30–11pm (7pm in winter) Mon–Sat; 12–4pm and 5–10.30pm Sun.

ROCHDALE

THOMAS MCGUINNESS BREWING CO.

Cask and Feather, 1 Oldham Road, Rochdale OL16 1UA
☎ *(01706) 711476*
Eric Hoare

The company produces a range of six real ales which are on sale in the Cask and Feather.

A small brewery founded in 1991 by Thomas McGuinness, who died in early 1993, and Eric Hoare. Expansion plans are in hand and the beers are now available in the House of Commons bars. The Cask and Feather is an old-style castle-fronted pub close to the town centre. Bar and restaurant food is available at lunchtime. Parking. Children allowed.

FEATHER PLUCKER MILD 3.4% ABV
A dark brown beer with roast malt dominant.

BEST BITTER 3.8% ABV
Golden, with a hoppy aroma. Clean and refreshing with hop and fruit tastes.

SPECIAL RESERVE BITTER 4.0% ABV
Tawny beer, sweet and malty with underlying fruit and bitterness.

STOUT 4.0% ABV

JUNCTION BITTER 4.2% ABV
Maltiness predominates.

TOMMY TODD PORTER 5.0% ABV
Winter warmer.

11am–11pm Mon–Sat; 12–10.30pm Sun.

ENDERBY

FEATHERSTONE BREWERY

Unit 3, King Street Buildings,
King Street, Enderby LE9 5NT
☎ *(0116) 275 0952*
Visitors welcome.
Tied houses: None

Brewing began in 1990 in a converted summer house behind The Saddle Inn in Twyford, Melton Mowbray. The operation moved to Enderby in 1992 and has since expanded to seven times the original capacity. Featherstone supplies wholesalers, agencies and a number of local outlets.

Beers available at: Fleckney WMC, Orchard Street, Fleckney, Leicestershire *and* British Shoe Corporation Sports and Social Club, Sunnydale Road, Braunstone, Leicestershire.

BEST BITTER 4.2% ABV

HOWES HOWLER 3.6% ABV

STAGE ALE 4.8% ABV

VULCAN BITTER 5.1% ABV

KINGSTONE STRONG 7.2% ABV

CAVENDISH BRIDGE

SHARDLOW BREWERY

British Waterways Yard,
Cavendish Bridge DE72 2HL
☎ *(01332) 799188*
Visitors welcome.
Tied houses: None

Production began in October 1993 on the site of the old Cavendish Bridge Brewery on the River Trent, which closed in the 1920s. The five-barrel plant supplies wholesalers and local outlets.

Beers available at: Old Crown, Cavendish Bridge, Shardlow, Leicestershire *and* Brunswick Inn, Railway Terrace, Derby.

CHANCELLOR'S REVENGE 3.6% ABV
Light-coloured, fruity beer.

KILN HOUSE ALE 4.1% ABV
Standard bitter.

ABU DERBY 4.1% ABV
Dark, spiced beer.

WIDE EYED AND CROWNLESS 4.4% ABV
Light-coloured beer brewed exclusively for The Old Crown, Cavendish Bridge.

REVEREND EATON'S ALE 4.5% ABV
Premium ale.

ALTERNATIVE LAGER 5.0% ABV
Summer brew. Lager produced in the traditional manner and cask-conditioned.

WHISTLESTOP 5.0% ABV
Pale ale.

BEER TODAY GONE TOMORROW 5.2% ABV
Strong bitter brewed exclusively for The Old Crown, Cavendish Bridge.

SLEIGHED 5.8% ABV
Dark, heavy ale brewed from October to March.

HOSE

The Rose and Crown

43 Bolton Lane,
Hose LE14 4JE
☎ *(01949) 860424*

Eight beers including a mild always available from a list that changes every week. Selected ales may vary in strength from 3.8 to 7 per cent.

Not easy to find at the back of the village, this modernised open-plan bar has a pool table and juke box. Bar and restaurant food is available at lunchtime and evenings. Car park, garden. Children allowed in the dining area.

12–2.30pm and 7–11pm.

GLOOSTON

The Old Barn Inn

Andrews Lane, Glooston, Nr Market Harborough LE16 7ST
☎ *(01858) 545215*
Charles Edmondson-Jones

Four beers (30 per year) always available from brewers such as Adnams, Hook Norton, Fuller's, Wadworth, Oakhill, Nene Valley, Ridley, Bateman, Thwaite, Leatherbritches, Mauldon, Cotleigh, Greene King and Tolly Cobbold.

A sixteenth-century village pub in rural location with a log fire, no juke box or games machines. Bar and restaurant food available in evenings and Sunday lunchtime. Car park and garden. Catering for parties, receptions and meetings. Well-behaved children and dogs welcome. Accommodation. Situated on an old Roman road between Hallaton and Tur Langton.

12–2.30pm Tues–Sun; 7–11pm, Mon–Sat.

LEICESTER

HOSKINS & OLDFIELD

North Mills, Frog Island, Leicester LE3 5DH
☎ *(0116) 2510532*
Visitors welcome by appointment.
Tied houses: None

Set up in 1984 by Steven and Philip Hoskins, members of Leicester's famous brewing family, after the sale of the old Hoskins Brewery. Their partner, Mr Oldfield, has since left the company. Brews solely for the free trade.

Beers available at: Cow & Plough, Stoughton Farm Park, Gartree Road, Leicester *and* Black Horse, Main Street, Walcote, Nr Lutterworth, Leicestershire.

HOB BEST MILD 3.5% ABV
Dark and chocolatey.

HOB BEST BITTER 4.0% ABV
Pale bitter with malty flavour.

LITTLE MATTY 4.0% ABV
Darker version of Hob Best.

WHITE DOLPHIN 4.0% ABV
Refreshing citrus-flavoured wheat beer.

TOM KELLY'S STOUT 4.2% ABV

SUPREME 4.4% ABV
Light gold best bitter.

EXS BITTER 5.0% ABV
Tawny-coloured premium bitter.

TOM KELLY'S CHRISTMAS PUDDING PORTER 5.0% ABV

GINGER TOM 5.2% ABV
A ginger beer.

OLD NAVIGATION 7.0% ABV
Ruby-black old ale.

Plus other occasional or seasonal brews.

Loughborough

The Swan in the Rushes

21 The Rushes, Loughborough
☎ *(01509) 217014*
Andrew Hambleton

Springhead Roaring Meg, Leatherbritches Belter, Archer's Golden and Marston's Pedigree always available plus six guest beers (300 per year) at any one time, to include absolutely anything.

A cosmopolitan town centre ale house, smart yet down to earth, with a friendly atmosphere. Bar and restaurant food is available at lunchtime and evenings. Car park and accommodation. Children allowed. On the A6, behind Sainsbury's.

12–2.30pm and 5–11pm; all day Fri–Sat.

Narborough

Everards Brewery

Castle Acres, Narborough LE9 5BY
☎ *(0116) 281 4110*
No visitors. Tied houses: 152

Everards was founded in 1849 in Southgate Street, Leicester, by William and Thomas Everard, who joined forces with a maltster named Thomas Hull. William was the force behind a flourishing business and a number of pubs were added to the portfolio as well as the Bridge Brewery and then the Tiger Brewery, where the ales were brewed until the late 1970s. Castle Acres was purchased in 1979 and a new brewery was built and opened in 1985, when the company finally moved out of Leicester. Capacity was doubled in 1990. Richard Everard, great-great grandson of William Everard, is the company chairman today.

Beers available at: The New Inn, High Street, Enderby, Leicestershire *and* The Railway Inn, Station Road, Ratby, Leicestershire.

MILD 3.3% ABV

BEACON BITTER 3.8% ABV
An award-winning fresh clean taste.

TIGER BEST BITTER 4.2% ABV
A true best bitter with plenty of body and flavour. The character is enhanced by the traditional technique of dry hopping. A fine balance of English malt and hops. The finish is long, dry and extremely satisfying.

OLD ORIGINAL ALE 5.2% ABV
A well balanced, smooth, distinctive flavour belies its true strength. The finish is malty and sweetish, the colour a copper brown.

DAREDEVIL WINTER WARMER 7.1% ABV

Oadby

The Cow and Plough

Stoughton Farm Park,
Gartree Road, Oadby LE2 2FB
☎ *(0116) 272 0852*

Hoskins & Oldfield Hob Bitter, Fuller's London Pride, Bateman Mild, Parish Farm Gold and Steamin' Billy always available plus a rotating guest beer (50 per year), mainly from small independents or micro-breweries such as Oakham Ales, Woodfordes, Leatherbritches, Hoskins & Oldfield.

A converted barn on a leisure park open as part of the park during the day and as a pub from 5pm daily. The vaults are full of breweriana with a Victorian bar. Adjoining cafe, car park, garden, children's room. CAMRA East Midlands Pub of the Year 1995. Signposted on the A6 as Farm Park.

5–9pm.

Oakham

Oakham Ales

12–13 Midland Court, Station Approach, Oakham, Rutland LE15 6QW
☎ *(01572) 755333*
Visitors welcome. Tied houses: None

The brewery was started in October 1993 in industrial units in Oakham, Rutland, by a keen, experienced home brewer. It is still essentially a one-man operation, although trade and the distribution area have now substantially increased. The small size of the premises restricts the range of beers available.

Beers available at: Finch's Arms, Hambleton, Oakham, Leicestershire *and* Charter's Cafe Bar, Peterborough, Cambridgeshire.

JEFFREY HUDSON BITTER 3.8% ABV
A honey-coloured, light, refreshing bitter with fruit and flowers in the aroma, malt and wheat taste and very hoppy finish.

HUNKY-DORY PREMIUM BITTER 4.5% ABV
Amber-coloured with full malt taste, a strong hint of coffee and a long, dry, bitter finish.

OLD TOSSPOT STRONG ALE 5.2% ABV
Deep copper colour, fruity nose, complex taste of fruit, toffee and chocolate, lingering hoppy, bitter aftertaste.

Old Dalby

The Crown Inn

Debdale Hill, Old Dalby, Nr Melton Mowbray LE14 3LF
☎ *(01664) 823134*
Miss Lynn Bryan

Marston's Best and Pedigree, Hardy's & Hanson Black Sheep, Timothy Taylor Landlord and Bateman XB and XXB always available plus eight guests including Greene King Abbot, Wadworth 6X, Woodforde's Wherry Best and Baldric, JW Lees Moonraker, Fuller's London Pride, Exmoor Gold, Marston's Owd Rodger, Mauldon Black Adder and Brains, Smiles, Thwaites and Adnams ales.

Built in 1590, a pub with six small rooms, oak beams, open fires, antique furniture, fresh flowers and prints. Large patio and terrace with orchard at bottom of the garden. Beer served from cellar near back door. Bar and restaurant food served at lunchtime and evenings. Car park, children's room, petanque pitch, ballooning and riding arranged. Take the A46 Nottingham to Leicester road. Turn off at Willougby Hotel, left for Upper Broughton, right for Old Dalby.

12–3pm and 6–11pm.

SOMERBY

PARISH BREWERY

The Old Brewery Inn,
High Street, Somerby,
Nr Melton Mowbray LE14 2PZ
☎ *(01664) 454781*
Barrie Parish

Eight Parish beers brewed and sold on the premises.

The brewery is to be found in the courtyard of the 400-year-old Old Brewery Inn, which serves eight real ales. The brewery lays claim to the stongest beer in the world. Bar and restaurant food is served at lunchtime and evenings. Car park, garden, children's room, function room. Accommodation.

PARISH MILD 3.5% ABV
Smooth, dark brew with caramel flavour.

SPECIAL BITTER 3.8% ABV
Refreshing bitter dominated by hops but with a tangy fruitiness.

FARM GOLD 4.0% ABV

SOMERBY PREMIUM 3.9% ABV
Tawny, medium-bodied beer with a malty, hoppy fragrance and a bitter, fruity taste.

PORTER 4.8% ABV
Winter brew.

POACHER'S ALE 6.0% ABV
Complex, ruby-coloured, full-flavoured ale. Caramel and marmalade flavours.

BAZ'S BONCE BLOWER 11.08% ABV
Robust and vigorous.

BAZ'S SUPER BREW 23.0% ABV

11 30am–3pm and 6–11pm.

WALCOTE

The Black Horse

Littleworld Road, Walcote LE17 4JU
☎ *(01455) 552684*
Mrs Tinker

Hoskins & Oldfield Hob Bitter, Timothy Taylor Landlord and Hook Norton Old Hooky permanently available plus two guest beers (75 per year) always from independent breweries.

A single-bar village pub. Bar and restaurant food available at lunchtime and evenings. Authentic Thai cooking. Car park, garden and children's room. One mile east of M1 junction 20.

12–2pm and 7–11pm. Closed Mon and Tues lunchtime.

AUBOURN

The Royal Oak

Royal Oak Lane,
Aubourn LN5 9DT
☎ *(01522) 788291*

Bateman XB and XXXB, and Samuel Smith OBB always available plus three guest beers from breweries stretching from the Orkneys to Cornwall.

A traditional village pub with character. Bar food available at lunchtime and evenings. Car park and garden. Children welcome at lunchtime and evenings in the function room until 8.30pm. South of Lincoln, off the A46.

12–2.30pm and 7–11pm (10.30pm Sun).

BARNETBY

HIGHWOOD BREWERY

Melton Highwood,
Barnetby DN38 6AA
☎ *(01652) 680020*
Visitors welcome. Tied houses: None

Highwood Brewery stands peacefully in a fold of the Lincolnshire Wolds, surrounded by rich farming land that has for centuries provided the highest quality malting barley for use in the brewing of fine beers. It was in this proud local tradition that Highwood was founded in 1995, converted from an old brick-built grain store. By restricting capacity to 50 barrels per week, the brewery produces beers of a consistently high quality, while not erring from the age-old methods.

Beers available at: The Sun Inn, Saxilby, Nr Lincoln, Lincolnshire *and* The New Inn, Limber, Nr Grimsby, Lincolnshire.

TOM WOOD BEST BITTER 3.5% ABV
A fresh, dry, hoppy flavour combined with a fruity aftertaste and heady aroma.

TOM WOOD OLD TIMBER 4.5% ABV
Premium bitter, a smooth dark-bodied bitter, with a well balanced malty flavour and sweet lingering aroma.

FOUR SEASONS SPECIALS 4.0–5.5% ABV
Spring – Brimming with freshness; a dry, light hoppy flavour, subtle colour and fruity aroma.
Summer – Refreshingly cool, sharp, fruity flavours combine with a bright colour and fragrant aroma.
Autumn – Brewed with a wealth and depth of colour, a balance of fruit, malty undertones and soft aroma.
Winter – A smooth, dark ale with a soft round maltiness and warm aroma.

GOOLE

OLD MILL BREWERY

Mill Street, Snaith,
Nr Goole DN14 9HS
☎ *(01405) 861813*
Visits for regular trade accounts only.
Tied houses: 12

Old Mill Brewery is a small independent concern founded in Snaith in 1983 with the object of producing beers using only the finest malt and hops. The original quality standards set than have been maintained and have resulted in the company winning several awards for its beers. The company now has 12 pubs and supplies an ever-growing number of freehouses.

Beers available at: The Mission, Posterngate, Hull. Brewers Arms, Snaith, Nr Goole.

TRADITIONAL BITTER 3.9% ABV
Fresh hoppy beer with good aroma, distinctly hoppy, clean flavour and a dry finish.

BULLION BITTER 4.7% ABV
A fine traditional premium bitter.

TRADITIONAL MILD 3.4% ABV
Chocolate and malt burst through dark roast characteristics.

GRANTHAM

The Blue Bull

64 Westgate,
Grantham NG31 6LA
☎ *(01476) 70929*

Bateman XB and Wadworth 6X permanently available plus three guest beers (100 per year) perhaps from Enville, Hampshire, Greene King, Clark's, Rooster's and Kelham Island.

CAMRA Lincolnshire Pub of the Year 1995. Dates from the 1850s. Bar and restaurant food available at lunchtime and evenings. Car park. Children allowed in the restaurant. Three minutes from the main line BR railway station.

11am–3pm and 7–11pm.

GRIMSBY

LEAKING BOOT BREWERY

Unit 3, 400 Cromwell Road,
Grimsby
☎ *(01472) 243303*
Visitors by arrangement.
Tied houses: None

Founded in April 1995, the brewery's name owes as much to the fell-walking experiences of two of the partners as anything else, although there is a famous statue of a boy with a leaking boot in Cleethorpes. Only one beer is in production at the moment, but the brewer is working on other recipes.

Beers available at: Kings Royal, Cleethorpes, Lincolnshire *and* The Kingsway Club, Cleethorpes, Lincolnshire.

LEAKING BOOT BITTER 3.9% ABV
A light bitter with a slightly sweet taste.

LINCOLN

The Golden Eagle

21 High Street, Lincoln LN5 8BD
☎ *(01522) 521058*
Mr and Mrs Fairclough

Seven beers always available at this on-going ever-changing beer festival. Regulars include Fuller's London Pride, Hop Back Summer Lightning, Bateman XB, Gale's Best, Everard's Beacon Bitter.

A locals' pub with two bars, one with no music or games machines, half a mile from the city centre. Food available at lunchtime. Car park and garden. Children not allowed in the pub.

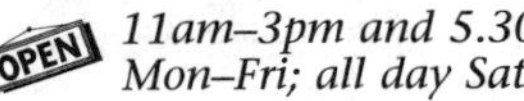

11am–3pm and 5.30–11pm Mon–Fri; all day Sat–Sun.

The Tap & Spile

21 Hungate, Lincoln LN1 1ES
☎ *(01522) 534015*
Mr and Mrs Cay

Eight beers always available but the range changes daily. Approx 150 brews per year including Mitchell's Lancaster Bomber, Charles Wells Fargo, Thwaites Craftsman and Greene King IPA, etc.

Formerly the White Horse, a city centre pub with stone and wood floors, bare brick and plaster walls. Bar food available at lunchtimes. Pay and display car park opposite. Children not allowed. At the top of the High Street turn left, then 200 yards on the left near the police station.

11am–11pm Mon–Sat; 12–3pm and 7–10.30pm Sun.

The Victoria

6 Union Road, Lincoln LN1 3BJ
☎ *(01522) 536048*

Ten beers always available including Everards Tiger and Old Original, Timothy Taylor Landlord and Bateman XB. Up to 200 guests per year including Orkney Raven Ale, Jersey Anne's Treat, Brains Bitter and Adnams brews.

A traditional old Victorian terraced pub in the city by the west gate of the castle. Bar food available at lunchtime. Regular beer festivals and brewery feature nights.

11am–11pm Mon–Sat; 12–10.30pm Sun.

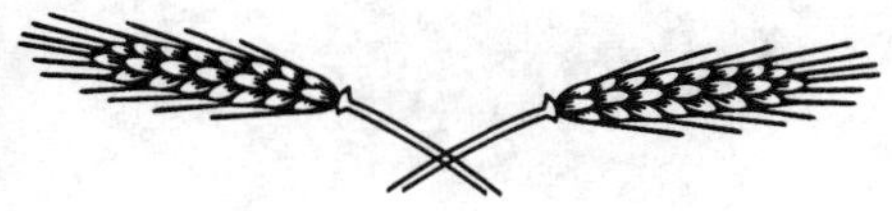

ROTHWELL

The Nickerson Arms

Hillrise, Rothwell LN7 6AZ
☎ *(01472) 371300*
Peter Wright

Bateman XB, Timothy Taylor Landlord and Fuller's London Pride permanently available plus approx eight guests (400 per year) including beers from Shepherd Neame, Bunces, Big Lamp, Rudgate, Adnams, Longstone and Hop Back breweries.

A 400-year-old haunted pub, formerly a blacksmiths, with oak beams, real fires and candles. Bar and restaurant food available at lunchtime and evenings. Car park, garden, children's room and function room. Live jazz on Sundays. Three miles off the A46 between Grimsby and Caistor.

12–2pm and 7–11pm Mon–Sat; 12–3pm and 7–10.30pm Sun.

WAINFLEET

GEORGE BATEMAN & SON

Salem Bridge Brewery, Wainfleet PE24 4JE
☎ *(01754) 880317*
Visitors by arrangement.
Tied houses: 60

In 1874, George and Suzanna Bateman, the present chairman's grandparents, gave up their farm in a small village ten miles east of Boston and moved to Wainfleet to rent a brewery. They paid £505 10s for the plant and machinery; then, a year later, purchased the brewery lease for £800. Beer was delivered by horse and dray to quench the thirst of local farmers and farmworkers. The farmers would then come to the brewery twice a year to pay for whatever their workers had consumed in the previous six months. Payments were commonly in kind and a massive feast usually ensued. A far cry from the operation today. In 1986, after resolving a disagreement between shareholders, George Bateman, the founder's grandson, took over the company and began to expand. The company now boasts 150 employees. Until this time, Bateman's brews could only be found in Lincolnshire; they are now distributed nationwide. Six award-winning ales are now produced on a regular basis, plus numerous occasional brews. Bateman's remains a family business; George's wife, son and daughter are all executive directors.

DARK MILD 3.0% ABV
A creamy mild with a fruity palate, some roast character and a hoppy finish.

XB 3.7% ABV
Distinctive, well-balanced bitter with a refreshing dry bitterness on the palate and a pleasing hoppy finish.

VALIANT 4.3% ABV
Golden beer with a delicate hop aroma, but a complex character giving an interesting well-balanced palate and a clean finish.

XXXB 4.8% ABV
Superb strong bitter with a complex palate consisting of a delicate aroma of hops balanced by a prominent malty character.

SALEM PORTER 4.7% ABV
Dry roast nutty palate with a rich malt finish and splendid hop flavour.

VICTORY ALE 5.7% ABV
Full-flavoured pale ale, predominantly fruity palate with malty overtones. Moderate hop character giving this strong ale a delicate overall palate.

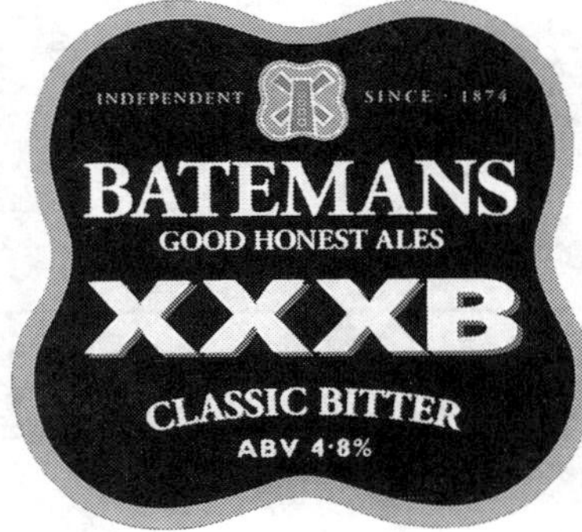

Borough

Bishops Brewery

2 Park Street, Borough Market, London SE1 9AB
☎ (0171) 357 8343
Visitors welcome. Tied houses: None

Bishops Brewery has been established for just over three years near the Borough fruit and vegetable market. It now supplies beers far beyond its south London base, to Scotland and Wales and all around England. It switched from malt extract to full mash brewing in April 1996 and has recently added a further two ales to its growing list.

Beers available at: The Wheatsheaf, 6 Stoney Street, Borough Market, London SE1 *and* The George, 77 Borough High Street, London SE1.

CATHEDRAL BITTER 3.7% ABV
A best-selling hoppy and distinctive ale.

THIRSTY WILLIE'S BITTER 3.7% ABV
Straw-coloured, session ale.

MITRE BEST BITTER 4.2% ABV
A soft bitterness allows the malt character to dominate.

WILLIE'S REVENGE 4.5% ABV
Once tasted, never forgotten.

CARDINAL ALE 4.7% ABV
Traditional ruby-coloured full-bodied strong ale.

The Market Porter

9 Stoney Street, London SE1 9AA
☎ (0171) 407 2495
Steve Turner

Harveys Best, Fuller's London Pride, Young's Bitter, Wadworth 6X and Spinnaker Buzz always available plus three guests which may include Timothy Taylor Landlord, Morland Old Speckled Hen, Otter Bright and Gibbs Mew Bishop's Tipple.

An old, traditional workers' pub within the fruit and vegetable market. Bar and restaurant food available at lunchtime. Function room. No children.

11am–11pm Mon–Fri; 11am–3pm and 7–11pm Sat; 12–3pm and 7–10.30pm Sun

Camberwell

Hermit's Cave

28 Camberwell Church Street, Camberwell, London SE5 8QU
☎ (0171) 703 3188

Twelve beers available on hand pump including Morland's Old Speckled Hen, Marston's Pedigree, Gale's HSB, Fuller's London Pride and Adnams Bitter. Microbrews feature as guest beers.

Built in 1902, this beamed pub serves bar food at lunchtime and evenings. Street parking. Children not allowed.

11am–11pm Mon–Sat; 12–10.30pm Sun.

Chelsea

The Anglesea Arms

15 Selwood Terrace, Chelsea, London SW7 3GG
☎ (0171) 373 7960

Seven beers always available including Adnams Bitter, Marston's Pedigree, Greene King Abbot, Fuller's London Pride and Young's Special. Guest beers are rotated monthly.

A lively, easy-to-find, 200-year-old pub with bar food available at lunchtime. Patio garden. Children over 14 allowed. Just off the Fulham Road.

11am–11pm Mon–Sat; 12–4pm and 7–10.30pm Sun.

CHISWICK

FULLER, SMITH & TURNER

Griffin Brewery,
Chiswick Lane South,
Chiswick, London W4 2QB
☎ *(0181) 996 2000*
Visitors welcome, by appointment.
Tied houses: 200

Beer has been brewed on Fuller's site at Chiswick for more than 325 years. The original brewery was in the gardens of Bedford House, on Chiswick Mall. Difficulties arose during the early part of the nineteenth century, when the owners, Douglas and Henry Thompson and Philip Wood, approached John Fuller, of Neston Park, Wiltshire, to see if he would inject funds needed for expansion. Fuller joined the enterprise in 1829 but the partnership was not a happy one and, when Douglas Thompson fled to France in 1841, it was dissolved. It was clear that one man could not run the business on his own, so John Bird Fuller, John Fuller's son, was joined in 1845 by Henry Smith, from the Romford brewers Ind and Smith, and his brother-in-law, John Turner, their head brewer. Descendants of the three are still heavily involved in the running of the company today and the Griffin Brewery has since gone from strength to strength.

HOCK 3.2% ABV
Available in spring, a reddish-brown malty mild.

CHISWICK BITTER 3.5% ABV
A distinctively hoppy, refreshing beer, with a moderate maltiness and a faint fruity character. Finishes with a lasting bitterness.

SUMMER ALE 3.9% ABV
Crisp, golden summer brew.

LONDON PRIDE 4.1% ABV
A strong, malty base and a rich balance of well-developed hop flavours.

INDIA PALE ALE 4.8% ABV

OLD WINTER ALE 4.8% ABV

ESB 5.5% ABV
Strong and aromatic. A full-bodied maltiness and a rich hoppiness are immediately evident and develop into a deep fruitiness.

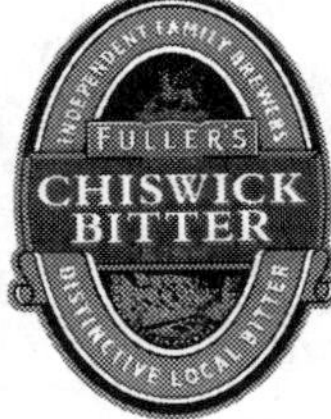

DEPTFORD

The Dog and Bell

116 Prince Street, Deptford,
London SE8 3JD
☎ *(0181) 692 5664*

Five beers always available. Guests include Fuller's London Pride and ESB, Shepherd Neame Spitfire Ale, Nethergate Bitter and brews from Larkins, Butterknowle, Archers and Hardingtons.

Built in 1850 and recently extended. Bar food available. Street parking, garden. Children aged 14 and over allowed. Tucked away, not far from the railway station.

11am–11pm Mon–Sat; 12–5pm and 7–10.30pm Sun.

EAST FINCHLEY

Welch's Ale House

130 High Road, East Finchley, London N2 7ED

Greene King Abbot, Wadworth 6X, Fuller's London Pride and Adnams Broadside permanently available plus up to eight guest beers (300 per year) including Ridleys Witchfinder Porter, Burts Old Vectis Venom, Wards Waggle Dance, Gibbs Mew The Bishops Tipple, Ringwood Old Thumper and 49er etc. Also country wines.

A converted shop on the High Road, not far from East Finchley tube. Bar food available at lunchtime. Children allowed.

11am–11pm Mon–Fri; 12–10.30pm Sun.

FULHAM

The White Horse

1 Parson's Green, Fulham, London SW6 44L
☎ *(0171) 736 2115*
Mark Dorber and Rupert Reeves

Harveys Sussex and Adnams Extra permanently available plus two guests (160 per year) including Adnams Tally-Ho, Barley Mow, Old and Summer Ale, Archer's Golden Bitter, Bateman Strawberry Fields and Salem Porter, Butterknowle Black Diamond, Cains Traditional, Formidable, Stout and Mild, also Jennings, Lees, Mitchell's, Robinson's, Shepherd Neame and Young's.

A large, comfortable Victorian pub overlooking Parsons Green with a big reputation for good cask and bottled beers, flavoursome wines and food served at lunchtime and evenings. Regular beer festivals. Parking, terrace/garden. Children allowed. Just 100 yards from Parsons Green tube station.

11am–11pm Mon–Sat; 11.30am–3pm and 7–10.30pm Sun.

HAMPTON

The White Hart

70 High Street, Hampton TW12 2SW
☎ *(0181) 979 5352*
Mrs Macintosh

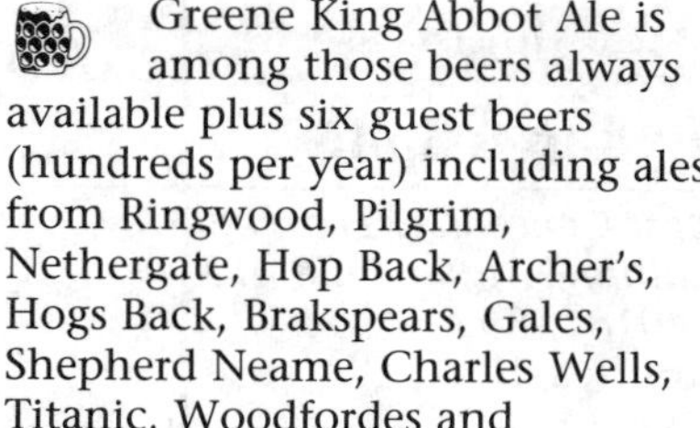
Greene King Abbot Ale is among those beers always available plus six guest beers (hundreds per year) including ales from Ringwood, Pilgrim, Nethergate, Hop Back, Archer's, Hogs Back, Brakspears, Gales, Shepherd Neame, Charles Wells, Titanic, Woodfordes and Harviestoun breweries.

Mock-Tudor pub in an historical area with log fire in winter and patio area. No music, darts or pool. Bar food served at lunchtime. Car park, garden and function room with bar. Close to Hampton BR station, one mile from Hampton Court BR station. Easy access from the M3 and A316. On main bus routes from Richmond, Heathrow and Wimbledon.

11am–3pm and 5–11pm Mon–Thurs; 11am–11pm Fri–Sat; 12–3pm and 7–10.30pm Sun.

LONDON

HAREFIELD

The Plough

Hill End Road,
Harefield UB9 6LQ
☎ (01895) 822129
Mr and Mrs Knight

Ruddles Best, Fuller's London Pride and Brakspear ales always available plus up to six guest beers including Beechwood and Black Sheep Bitter. Half a mile past the main entrance to Harefield Hospital.

A country-style family pub. Bar food available at lunchtime. Car park and garden. Children allowed.

11am–3pm and
5.30–11pm Mon–Sat;
12–3pm and 7–10.30pm Sun.

HEATHROW

The Tap & Spile

Upper Concourse, Terminal One,
Heathrow Airport UB5 4PX
☎ (0181) 897 8418
John Heaphy

Marston's Pedigree always available plus up to nine guest beers (50 per year) including Rooster's Bitter, Charles Wells Eagle, Brains SA, Nethergate IPA and Adnam's Best.

Cosy and relaxing refuge with a 1930s feel overlooking the anarchy of the check-in area. Bar food available at lunchtime and evenings. Car park and children's room. On the catering balcony at departure level in terminal one.

9–11am for breakfast,
then 11am–11pm.

SOHO

The Argyll Arms

18 Argyll Street,
London W1 1AA
☎ (0171) 734 6117
Mike Tayara

Seven beers always available including Wadworth 6X and an ever-changing selection that might feature Everards Daredevil, Hop Back Summer Lightning, Felinfoel Double Dragon, Charles Wells Bombardier and brews from Jennings, Ringwood, Tomintoul etc.

A 300-year-old pub just off Oxford Circus owned by the Duke of Argyll. Air-conditioned. Bar and restaurant food available at lunchtime and evenings. Function room, no-smoking area. Children allowed in play area.

11am–11pm Mon–Sat;
12–10.30pm Sun.

STOCKWELL

The Priory Arms

83 Lansdowne Way,
Stockwell, London SW8 2PB
☎ (0171) 622 1884
Gary Morris

Young's Bitter and Special always available plus four guests (350 per year) from breweries such as Woodforde's, Hop Back, Hog Back, Jennings and Goddard's.

The pub is being refurbished in early 1996. Bar food available at lunchtime. CAMRA pub of the year. Near Stockwell tube station.

11am–11pm Mon–Fri;
12–3pm and 7–10.30pm Sun.

WANDSWORTH

YOUNG AND CO.

The Ram Brewery,
High Street, Wandsworth,
London SW18 4JD
☎ *0181 (870 0141*
Visitors welcome, but restricted to customers from pubs.
Tied houses: 169

Records show that a brewery existed on the banks of the River Wandle at Wandsworth in 1675, owned by a family called Draper. In 1763, the family sold the brewery to Thomas Tritton, whose son, George, took over in 1786. The partnership of Charles Allen Young and Anthony Fothergill Bainbridge bought the Ram Brewery from the Trittons in 1831 and, despite serious fires in 1832 and 1882, the company flourished. The partnership dissolved in 1883 and Charles Florance Young, son of the founder, took over the running of Young and Co. It became a plc in 1890. Queen Elizabeth II visited Wandsworth in 1981 at the start of Young's 150th anniversary celebrations. The building of a new £5 million brewhouse was completed two years later. The company's own purpose-built hotel (The Bridge, at Greenford) opened in 1991 and further pubs, restaurants and wine bars have since been added to the expanding portfolio.

Beers available at: The Ship, 41 Jews Row, Wandsworth, London SW18 *and* The Orange Tree, 45 Kew Road, Richmond, Surrey.

YOUNG'S BITTER 3.7% ABV
Popular and award-winning standard gravity bitter.

YOUNG'S SPECIAL 4.6% ABV
The flagship bitter.

WINTER WARMER 5.0% ABV
A strong, dark winter brew. Available from October to March.

YOUNG'S RAM ROD 5.0% ABV
A new premium ale.

YOUNG'S OATMEAL STOUT 5.0% ABV
Plus a range of bottled beers.

MANCHESTER (GREATER)

CHEETHAM

The Queens Arms

Honey Street, Cheetham M8 8RG
☎ *(0161) 834 4239*

Twelve beers always available, perhaps including Bateman Dark Mild and XXXB, Exmoor Gold, Cotleigh Old Buzzard and Black Beth.

A traditional town pub built in the 1800s, subsequently extended. Bar food available at lunchtime and until 8pm. Street parking, children's play area and garden.

12–11pm Mon–Sat;
10–10.30pm Sun.

MANCHESTER

JW LEES & CO.

Greengate Brewery, PO Box 2, Middleton Junction M24 2AX
☎ *(0161) 643 2487*
Visitors welcome. Tied houses: 175

The brewery was founded in1828 by John Lees, a retired cotton manufacturer. It is still owned and run by his direct descendants today. The present brewhouse was built by the founder's grandson, John Willie Lees, in 1876 and has recently undergone significant modernisation and expansion.

GB MILD 3.5% ABV
Malty and fruity in aroma and taste. Rich, rounded and smooth finish. Dry, malty aftertaste.

GOLDEN ORIGINAL LAGER 4.0% ABV
A sweet, spicy aroma with floral hop notes. Sweet, fruity and citrus taste with tangy aftertaste.

JW LEES BITTER 4.0% ABV
A pale beer with a malty, fruity aroma and distinctive clean, malty dry finish.

MOONRAKER 7.3% ABV
Ruby-coloured, strong and with a rich fruity aroma. Dry, fruity finish.

Plus seasonal and occasional brews.

The Beerhouse

Angel Street, Manchester
☎ *(0161) 839 7019*

Moorhouse Pendle Witches Brew and Burtonwood Bitter always available plus ten other real ales (up to 300 per year) which might come from Burtonwood or Brains breweries.

A popular, recently refurbished traditional ale house off the Rochdale Road, just beyond Mill Street. Bar food is available at lunchtime and Wednesday to Friday evenings. Garden, bar billiards, family room, function room. Children over 14 years allowed before 7pm.

11am–11pm Mon–Sat;
12–10.30pm Sun.

The Lass o'Gowrie

36 Charles Street, Manchester M1 7DB
☎ *(0161) 273 6932*
Joe Fylan

Two house brews always available plus three guests from a range of 150 per year to include Morland Old Speckled Hen, Timothy Taylor Landlord and Marstons Pedigree.

A Victorian tiled pub with open view to cellar and gas lighting. Bar food available at lunchtime. Close to BBC North. Parking nearby. Children allowed.

11am–11pm Mon–Sat;
12–10.30pm Sun.

Marble Arch

*73 Rochdale Road,
Manchester M4 4HY*
☎ *(0161) 832 5914*
Vance Debchel

Marston's Pedigree and Bitter, Bateman's Mild, Oak Phoenix and Wobbly Bob permanently available plus a couple of guest beers (100+ per year) including Rooster's Bitter and RCH Pitchfork. Also draught continental beers.

A Victorian freehouse with ornate barrelled ceiling, glazed walls and mosaic floor. Bar food available at lunchtime. Children allowed.

*12–11pm Mon–Sat;
7–10.30pm Sun.*

HINDLEY

The Edington Arms

186 Ladies Lane, Hindley
☎ *(01942) 259229*

Holt Mild and Bitter and Savage's Head always available plus up to nine guest beers (200 per year).

An old coaching house with two large, comfortable rooms. No food. Parking and garden. Children allowed. A CAMRA Pub of the Year. Function room upstairs. Next to Hindley railway station.

12–11pm.

WIGAN

The Beer Engine

69 Poolstock, Wigan WN3 5DF
☎ *(01942) 321820*
John Moran

Marston's Pedigree and Ruddles brews permanently available plus up to five guest beers (186 per year) with the emphasis on supporting the smaller brewer.

Food available. Function room, pool, darts, dominoes, pigeon club and golf society. Car park, bowling green and garden. Children allowed. Well known in Wigan, five minutes' walk from the railway station.

OPEN *11am–11pm Mon–Sat;
12–10.30pm Sun.*

SALFORD

The Crescent

20 The Crescent, Salford M5 4PF
☎ *(0161) 736 5600*
Mrs J Davies

Crescent Bitter permanently available plus up to ten real ales (150 per year) primarily from local breweries, including Oak, Moorhouse, Titanic and Marstons. Other guests from all around the county. Occasional beer festivals.

A sprawling pub with a comfortable atmosphere popular with students and locals alike. Bar food available at lunchtime. Car park. Traditional pub games. Opposite Salford University. The nearest station is Salford Crescent, on the main A6.

*12–11pm Mon–Fri;
7.30–11pm Sat; 12–3pm and
7.30–10.30pm Sun.*

STOCKPORT

RICHARD COBDENS

Wellington Street,
Stockport SK1 1JE
☎ *(0161) 477 6994*
Visitors welcome by appointment.
Tied houses: None

This brewery began operating in January 1995, is owned by Mr Perkins and employs two people. The brewery name commemorates the fact that Richard Cobden and John Bright repealed the Corn Laws in the building. The company will brew for anyone, a minimum of five barrels to any recipe.

Beers available at: Old Vic, King Street, Stockport, Gtr Manchester *and* Cheadle Sports and Social Club, Councillor Lane, Cheadle, Gtr Manchester.

COBDEN'S STANDARD BITTER 3.4% ABV
Mildly hoppy flavour. Not so much a bitter taste, light coloured.

PREMIUM 3.8% ABV
A rich colour, hoppier than Standard.

FESTIVAL 4.4% ABV
A rich ruby-coloured fruity beer. Also developing a traditional lager from an old Bavarian recipe.

Stanley Arms

40 Newbridge Lane,
Stockport SK1 2NA
☎ *(0161) 480 5713*
Mike Belsham

Up to 16 different beers (hundreds per year, too many to name) available on tap at any one time. Commercial and Steam Packet brews permanently available.

Drinkers tend to be 25 and upwards. Pool area, darts area, small stage for occasional entertainment. Disco on Saturdays. Barbecues in summer. Bar food available at lunchtime and evenings. Car park, garden and children's play area. M63 junction 13, then follow Marple sign on to St Mary's Way. Turn right at the first traffic lights. The pub is on the left, after 300 yards.

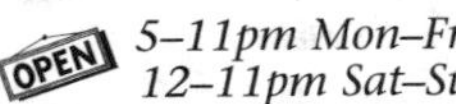

5–11pm Mon–Fri;
12–11pm Sat–Sun.

Birkenhead

The Crown Hotel

128 Conway Street,
Birkenhead L41 6JE
☎ *(0151) 647 9108*
Steve Eldon

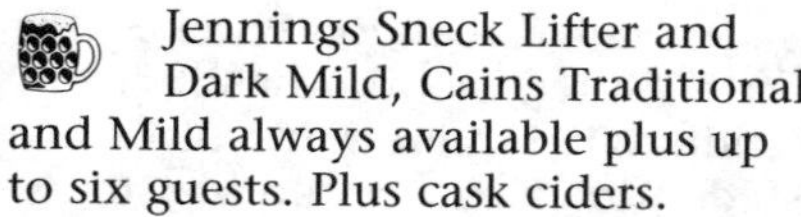

Jennings Sneck Lifter and Dark Mild, Cains Traditional and Mild always available plus up to six guests. Plus cask ciders.

A typical old ale house under new management. Bar food available. Parking, darts/meeting room. Children allowed. Head for Birkenhead town centre, not far from the Birkenhead tunnel (Europa Park).

11.30am–11pm Mon–Sat;
12–3pm and 7–10.30pm Sun.

Liverpool

Passageway Brewery

Unit G8,
Queens Dock Commercial Centre,
Norfolk Street, Liverpool L1 0BG
☎ *(0151) 708 0730*
Visitors welcome, by arrangement only.
Tied houses: None

Commercial brewing of St Arnold began in March 1994. The yeast comes from a monastic brewery in Begium and each brew contains 150ml of water from a "miraculous" well beside the Chapel of St Arnold in Tiegan, Belgium, a country where St Arnold is the patron saint of brewers. Redemption is named after the Redemptorist Fathers who maintain the Chapel of St Arnold. Phil Burke and Steve Dugmore, a chemistry teacher and lab technician respectively, are the force behind this micro-brewery. They brew once a week, producing five barrels at a time.

Beers available at: Cains Brewery Tap, 35 Stanhope Street, Liverpool, Merseyside and Ship and Mitre, 133 Dale Street, Liverpool, Merseyside.

DOCKERS HOOK BITTER 3.6% ABV
A full-bodied, fruity, hoppy, session beer.

REDEMPTION RYE BEER 4.0% ABV
Pale, amber, naturally cloudy beer. An assertive, thirst-quenching ale with a distinctive rye flavour.

ST ARNOLD 5.0% ABV
A dark, rich, fruity, full-bodied ale with a flowery-hoppy aroma.

Robert Cain & Co.

The Robert Cain Brewery,
Stanhope Street, Liverpool L8 5XJ
☎ *(0151) 709 8734*
Visitors welcome. Tied houses: 2

Robert Cain and Company was established in 1990 and, using one of the most modern brewhouses in Europe, produces the full range of Cains cask-conditioned ales alongside beers and lagers for the can. Named after a nineteenth-century brewer, the brewery was bought out by Higsons in the 1920s and then Boddingtons in 1985 before the present company was formed. It maintains a commitment to quality and tradition, using only the finest ingredients.

DARK MILD 3.2% ABV

TRADITIONAL BITTER 4.0% ABV

FORMIDABLE ALE 5.0% ABV

The Liverpool Brewing Co.

The Black Horse and Rainbow,
21–23 Berry Street,
Liverpool L1 9DF
☎ *(0151) 709 5055*

Beers brewed at this five-barrel plant solely for sale in the pub, although there are plans for a second outlet.

The Black Horse and Rainbow was reputedly Liverpool's first brewpub, founded in July 1990 as part of the conversion of an existing public house into a student-based real ale venue. Bar food is available at lunchtime and evenings. Parking, garden. Children not allowed.

BLACK HORSE BITTER 4.3% ABV

WINTER ALE 4.3% ABV

CELEBRATION BITTER 4.80% ABV

12pm–2am.

The Ship and Mitre

133 Dale Street,
Liverpool L2 2JH
☎ *(0151) 236 0859*
David R Stevenson

Holt's Bitter and Cains Mild and Bitter permanently available plus eight guest beers of all shapes and sizes. Two ciders.

A town-centre CAMRA pub of the year popular with students and council staff. Good value food served at lunchtime. Pay and display car park opposite. Children not allowed. Near the Mersey tunnel entrance, five minutes' walk from Lime Street station and Moorfields station.

11.30am–11pm Mon–Fri;
12.30–11pm Sat.
Closed Sun.

Southport

The Berkeley Hotel

19 Queens Road,
Southport PR9 9HN
☎ *(01704) 530163*
Mr and Mrs Ball

Fuller's London Pride, Holt's Bitter, Moorhouse Bitter, Pendle Witches Brew and Black Cat Mild, Adnams Bitter and Marston's Bitter permanently available plus several guest beers (200 per year) such as Timothy Taylor Landlord and ales from Thomas McGuinness, Hop Back, Exmoor, Marston's and Eldridge Pope breweries.

A family-run freehouse just outside the town centre, anxious to promote the real ale cause, with an extended bar. Bar food served at lunchtime and evenings. Car park and accommodation. Look behind the fire station.

12–11pm Mon–Sat;
12–10.30pm Sun.

CANTLEY

The Cock Tavern

Manor Road,
Cantley NR13 3JQ
☎ *(01493) 700895*
Mr and Mrs Johnson

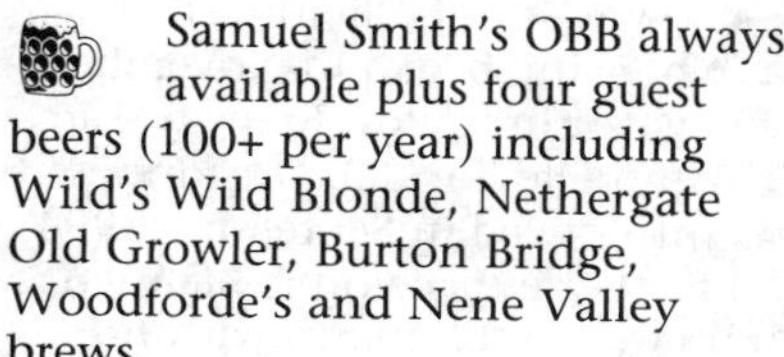

Samuel Smith's OBB always available plus four guest beers (100+ per year) including Wild's Wild Blonde, Nethergate Old Growler, Burton Bridge, Woodforde's and Nene Valley brews.

A traditional country pub not far from Norwich with many separate areas, a beamed ceiling and two open fires. Bar food is available at lunchtime and evenings. Car park, garden and children's room. Caravan Club campsite nearby. Turn right off the A47 (Norwich to Yarmouth road) near Acle, then signposted Cantley. Approx four miles from the turn.

11am–3.30pm and 6–11pm Mon–Fri; 7–11pm Sat; 12–10.30pm Sun.

MUNDFORD

THE ICENI BREWERY

3 Foulden Road,
Ickburgh, Mundford IP26 5BJ
☎ *(01842) 878922*
Visitors welcome by arrangement.
Tied houses: None

The idea of starting the Iceni Brewery came to Brendan Moore in a dream. He woke his wife, Judith, to tell her and production began less than 18 months later, in February 1995, with a grant from the Rural Development Commission. The brewery uses second-hand dairy equipment and has a brew-length of ten barrels with production at ten barrels per week. The beers are named after Celtic queens.

Beers available at: The Crown Hotel, Crown Street, Mundford, Norfolk *and* The Fat Cat, 49 West End Street, Norwich, Norfolk.

BOADICEA CHARIOT ALE 3.8% ABV
A session bitter.

DEIRDRE OF THE SORROWS 4.4% ABV
Summer ale.

ROISIN DUBH 4.4% ABV
Meaning Dark Rose.

QUEEN MAEVE STOUT 4.9% ABV

ICENI GOLD 5.0% ABV

The Crown Hotel

Crown Street, Mundford,
Nr Thetford IP26 5HQ
☎ *(01362) 637647*
Barry Walker

Seven beers always available including Samuel Smith OBB, Woodforde's Norfolk Wherry and Marston's Pedigree plus more than 100 guests per year including all Iceni brews, Morland Old Speckled Hen, Woodforde's Nelson's Revenge and Mauldons brews.

Sixteenth-century old beamed pub with open fires in winter. Bar and restaurant food available at lunchtime and evenings. Pool and darts, car park, garden, function room, accommodation. Children allowed.

11am–11pm Mon–Sat; 12–10.30pm Sun.

Norwich

Buffy's Brewery

Mardle Hall, Rectory Road, Tivetshall St Mary, Norwich NR15 2DD
☎ *(01379) 676523*
Visitors welcome

Buffy's Brewery was set up in November 1993 by Roger Abraham and Julie Savory in the garage of their listed fourteenth-century home. Buffy was the name of the house's previous owner. The business began on a shoestring budget and a lot of essential equipment was homemade. Initial production was of just 12 casks although there are now plans to expand by rebuilding the brewhouse and putting in a cellar underneath for cold storage. A 3.6 per cent-ish quaffing bitter should soon be available, and a mild is in the pipeline.

Beers available at: The Greyhound, The Street, Brockdish, Nr Diss, Norfolk *and* The King's Head, Pulham St Mary, Norfolk.

BUFFY'S BITTER 4.0% ABV
Dry, hoppy, refreshing session beer.

POLLY'S FOLLY 4.3% ABV
Brewed especially for the local university (UEA). A pale straw colour with a hoppy, clean aftertaste. A good thirst-quencher.

BUFFY'S BEST 4.9% ABV
Well-balanced, full-bodied, with a hint of sweetness.

BUFFY'S ALE 5.5% ABV
Full-bodied and smooth with a fruity, moreish taste.

BUFFY'S STRONG ALE 6.5% ABV
Complex, little sweetness despite its strength.

Chalk Hill Brewery

Rosary Road, Thorpe Hamlet, Norwich NR1 4DA
☎ *(01603) 620703*
Visitors welcome, by arrangement.
Tied houses: None

Run by Bill Thomas, a former owner of The Reindeer, brewing began in November 1993 with three ales (Brewery Tap, CHB and Old Tackle). Dreadnought was introduced in September 1994 and further expansion is planned. All brews are full mash, with no additives.

Beers available at: The Coach and Horses, 82 Thorpe Road, Norwich, Norfolk *and* The Alexandra Tavern, 16 Stafford Street, Norwich, Norfolk.

BREWERY TAP 3.6% ABV
A light session bitter.

CHALK HILL BEST 4.2% ABV
A well-balanced premium bitter.

DREADNOUGHT 4.9% ABV
Strong and fruity amber ale.

OLD TACKLE 5.6% ABV
A dark, dry, strong ale.

Woodforde's Norfolk Ales

Broadland Brewery, Woodbastwick, Norwich NR13 6SW
☎ *(01603) 720353*
Visitors welcome by arrangement.
Visitors' centre and shop.
Tied houses: 2

Woodforde's was started by Ray Ashworth in 1981. Named after Parson Woodforde, a noted eighteenth-century bon viveur, the company's initial industrial unit premises proved uninspiring. In 1983, Ashworth moved to a converted stable block behind The Spread Eagle at Erpingham. Disaster struck when a fire gutted the premises after the brewery had been open barely a month. Production resumed three months' later, an occasion celebrated with the introduction of Phoenix XXX. Eventually, demand forced further expansion and a new brewery was built in 1988 around a group of traditional farm buildings in the village of Woodbastwick. The brewery's water is taken from its own spring.

Beers available at: The Fur and Feather, Slab Lane, Woodbastwick, Nr Norwich, Norfolk *and* The Billy Bluelight, 27 Hall Road, Norwich, Norfolk.

BROADSMAN BITTER 3.5% ABV
A full-flavoured session pint with a hoppy character.

MARDLER'S MILD 3.5% ABV
Traditional Norfolk dark mild, smooth with a hint of sweetness.

WHERRY BEST BITTER 3.8% ABV
A best bitter with a full malty palate.

NORFOLK STOUT 4.2% ABV
Dark and flavoursome with a dry Irish style palate.

GREAT EASTERN ALE 4.3% ABV
A golden bitter brewed to commemorate 150 years of the Great Eastern Railway in Norfolk.

NELSON'S REVENGE 4.5% ABV
A full-flavoured premium best bitter, typically Norfolk in style.

NORFOLK NOG 4.6% ABV
Award-winning, traditional, strong "old ale".

PHOENIX XXX 4.8%

BALDRIC BITTER 5.6% ABV
"An evil brew with the pungent essence of old socks."

HEAD CRACKER 7.0% ABV
For he who dares! Deceptively strong pale ale.

Coach and Horses

82 Thorpe Road,
Norwich NR1 1BA
☎ *(01603) 477077*
Bob Cameron

Up to nine beers available at any one time including Chalk Hill Brewery Tap, CHB, Dreadnought and Old Tackle plus Timothy Taylor Landlord. Guests include Hop Back Summer Lightning, Cheriton Digger's Gold, Otter Bright and Coach House Gunpowder Mild.

Busy old-style pub with open fires. Bar food available at lunchtime and evenings. Children allowed.

11am–11pm Mon–Sat;
12–10.30pm Sun.

The Fat Cat

49 West End Street,
Norwich NR2 4NA
☎ *(01603) 624364*

Up to 25 beers available at any one time. Regulars include Adnams' Bitter, Woodforde's Nelson's Revenge, Kelham Island Pale Rider, Greene King Abbot and a guest list that now runs into thousands.

A traditional Victorian pub decorated with breweriana and pub signs. Bar food available at lunchtime. Street parking. Children not allowed.

11am–11pm Mon–Sat;
12–10.30pm Sun.

Rosary Tavern

95 Rosary Road, Norwich
☎ *(01603) 666287*

Up to ten beers available at any one time including brews from Adnams, Batemans, Iceni and Woodforde. The 300 guests per year might include Shepherd Neame Spitfire and Bishops Finger, B&T Dragonslayer, SOS etc.

A small town pub with one bar and a friendly atmosphere. Bar and restaurant food available at lunchtime and evenings. Car park, garden, dining room, function room, bar billiards. Children allowed under strict supervision. Easy to find, near the yacht station.

11.30am–11.30pm Mon–Sat;
12–5pm and 7.30–10.30pm Sun.

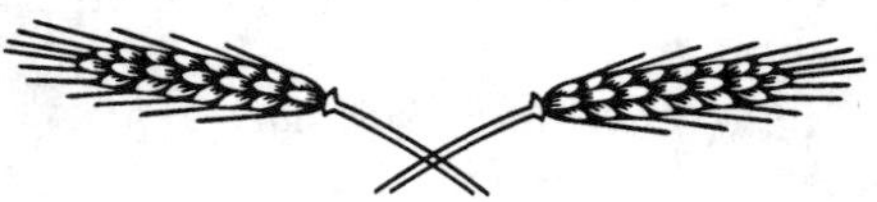

St Andrew's Tavern

4 St Andrews Street,
Norwich NR2 4AT
☎ *(01603) 614858*
John Croft

Adnam's Bitter and Broadside plus Charles Wells Bombardier permanently available. Eight guest beers (400 per year) may include K&B Festive, Arkell's Kingsdown, Wadworth Farmer's Glory, Mansfield Old Baily and Hop Back Summer Lightning.

A friendly city-centre pub with two bars. Bar food available at lunchtime and all day Saturday. Garden and cellar bar. Children not allowed. At the junction of Duke Street and St John Madmarket opposite St Andrews car park.

11am–11pm Mon–Sat;
closed Sun.

The Tap & Spile

73 Oak Street,
Norwich NR3 3AR
☎ *(01603) 620630*
Mr and Mrs Royle

Usher's Founder's Ale and Bateman's beers always available plus approx 12 guest beers (300+ per year) including Rooster's Yankee and B&T Dragonslayer.

A 450-year-old pub with old beams, slate floors, loads of wood, brass and pot plants. Candles every evening. Live music three times a week. Bar food available at lunchtime and evenings. Parking and children's room. On the inner ring road going anti-clockwise, first left before the river on the east side.

11am–3.30pm and
5.30–11pm Mon–Thurs;
11am–11pm Fri–Sat;
12–3pm and 7–10.30pm Sun.

PULHAM ST MARY

The King's Head

The Street,
Pulham St Mary IP21 4RD
☎ *(01379) 676318*
Graham Scott

Adnams Best always available plus three guests (150 per year) including Marston's Pedigree, Wadworth 6X, Shepherd Neame Spitfire, Woodforde's Wherry Best, Burts Newport Nobbler and brews from Buffys, Brains, Robinsons, Vaux and Scott's.

Built 1600s, old oak timber frame with exposed beams. Bar and restaurant food available at lunchtime and evenings. No-smoking dining area, bowling green, paddock, car park, garden, children's area, accommodation. Off the A140 to Harlesdon, on the B1134.

11.30am–3pm and 5.30–11pm Mon–Fri; all day Sat–Sun.

REEDHAM

The Railway Tavern

17 The Havaker,
Reedham NR13 3HG
☎ *(01493) 700340*
Mrs Cathy Swan and
Mr Ivor Cuders

Woodforde's and Adnams ales permanently available plus many guest beers including those from Scott's, Chalk Hill and Elgood's breweries. Four beer festivals held so far.

A listed Victorian railway hotel freehouse. CAMRA award. No fruit machines. Bar and restaurant food is available at lunchtime and evenings. Car park, garden and children's room. Take the A47 south of Acle, then six miles on the B1140. By rail from Norwich, Gt Yarmouth or Lowestoft.

12–3pm and 6.30–11pm Mon–Thurs; all day Fri–Sat; normal Sun hours.

SWANTON MORLEY

Darby's Freehouse

1 Elsing Road,
Swanton Morley,
Dereham NR20 4JU
☎ *(01362) 637647*
John Carrick

Adnams Bitter and Broadside, Woodforde's Wherry Best, Mardler's Mild and Hall & Woodhouse Tanglefoot permanently available plus a couple of guest beers (100 per year) from just about everywhere.

A genuine, family-owned and run freehouse converted from two derelict farm cottages. Good food available at lunchtimes and evenings. Accommodation. Fishing and farm trails. Car park, garden and children's room. Take the B1147 from Dereham to Bawdeswell, turn right on to Elsing Road at Swanton Morley.

11am–11pm Mon–Sat; 12–3pm and 7–10.30pm Sun.

Thornham

The Lifeboat Inn

Ship Lane, Thornham,
Hunstanton PE36 6LT
☎ *(01485) 512236*
Mr and Mrs Coach

Adnams, Greene King and Woodforde's ales permanently available plus a couple of guest beers, mainly from the small independents including Tolly Cobbold etc.

A sixteenth-century smugglers' ale house with wood beams, hanging paraffin lamps and open fires overlooking salt marshes. Bar and restaurant food available at lunchtime and evenings. Car park, garden and accommodation. Children allowed. Turn first left when entering the village from Hunstanton.

All day.

Warham

The Three Horseshoes

Bridge Street, Warham,
Wells next the Sea NR23 1NL
☎ *(01328) 710547*
Mr Salmon

Woodforde's Wherry Best, Greene King IPA and Abbot always available plus a guest (changed each week) such as Morland Old Speckled Hen, Woodforde's Nelson's Revenge and Wadworth 6X.

Traditional cottage pub in the centre of the village with gas lighting and open fires. Bar food available at lunchtime and evenings. Car park, garden, function room, no-smoking room, accommodation. Children allowed.

11.30am–3pm and 5.30–11pm Mon–Fri; all day Sat–Sun.

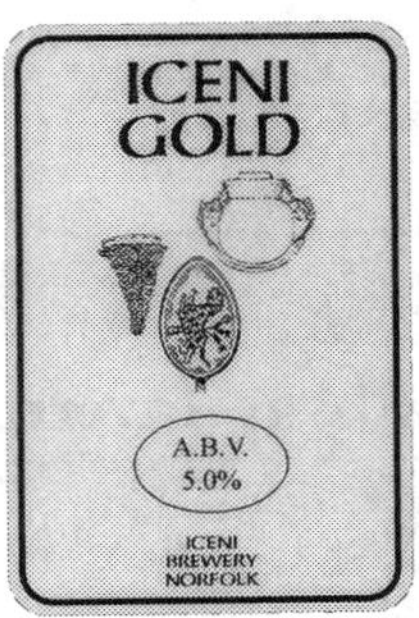

Ashby St Ledgers

The Olde Coach House Inn

Ashby St Ledgers,
Nr Rugby CV23 8UN
☎ *(01788) 890349*
Mr and Mrs McCabe

St Ledger Ale and Everard's Old Original always available plus five guest ales (200 per year) including Jennings' Cumberland, Mansfield Red Admiral, Hop Back Summer Lightning, Hook Norton Haymaker, Frog Island Natterjack, Burts Chucklehead and Adnams Broadside.

An olde-English converted farmhouse in the middle of an historic village. Lots of family tables and small intimate nooks and crannies. Large secure garden for children and plenty of parking space. Bar and restaurant food available at lunchtime and evenings. Car park. Accommodation. Three miles from M1 junction 18, close to M6 and M40 and adjacent to A5. Daventry three miles to the south, Rugby four miles to the north.

12–2.30pm and 6–11pm Mon–Fri; 12–11pm Sat; 12–2.30pm and 7–10.30pm Sun.

Great Brington

The Fox and Hounds

Althorpe Coaching Inn,
Great Brington NN7 4JA
☎ *(01604) 770651*
Paul Burchill and Zoe Cushie

Eight guest beers (hundreds per year) always available with the emphasis on independent breweries, avoiding the national brands other than Theakstons.

A sixteenth-century coaching inn with log fires, original beams and stone/wood floors. Bar and restaurant food available at lunchtime and evenings. Car park, garden, children's room and accommodation. Take the A428 from Northampton past Althorpe House, then first left turn before railway bridge.

12–3pm and 5.30–11pm Mon–Fri; 11am–11pm Sat; 12–3pm and 7–10.30pm Sun.

Northampton

Frog Island Brewery

The Maltings, Westbridge St James Road, Northampton NN5 5HS
☎ *(01604) 587772*
Visitors welcome. Tied houses: None

Bruce Littler and Graham Cherry established Frog Island Brewery in August 1994 in a former Thomas Manning Brewery's malthouse, which was closed in 1933 by Phipps and Co. They run a five-barrel plant, built by Bruce himself. An additional brew should now be available.

Beers available at: Ye Olde Saracens Head, High Street, Little Brington, Northamptonshire *and* The Griffin's Head, Wilby Road, Mears Ashby, Northamptonshire.

BEST BITTER 3.8% ABV
A full-flavoured session bitter.

NATTERJACK 4.8% ABV
Light, golden easy-drinking premium ale.

NORTHAMPTON

ORLINGBURY

The Queen's Arms

11 Isham Road,
Orlingbury NN14 1JD
☎ *(01933) 678258*
Mr P Stanbrook

Hook Norton Best, Fuller's London Pride, Morland Old Speckled Hen and Marston's Pedigree permanently available plus six guest beers (300 per year) – far too many to mention.

Recently refurbished country pub with no music, games machines or pool tables. CAMRA pub of the year 1994. Bar food is served at lunchtime. Car park and garden. Children not allowed.

11.30am–2.30pm and 5.30–11pm.

SUDBOROUGH

The Vane Arms

Main Street, Sudborough NN14 3BX
☎ *(01832) 733223*
Tom Tookey

Nine different beers changed regularly (150 per year) including Hoskins & Oldfield Ginger Tom, Hop Back Summer Lightning, Woodforde's Headcracker, Adnams Broadside and Oakham Old Tosspot.

A centuries-old listed thatched village inn. Bar and restaurant food available at lunchtime and evenings. Mexican specials. Car park, garden, games room. Children allowed. Accommodation. Just off the A6116 between Thrapston and Corby.

11.30am–3pm and 5.30–11pm.

WELLINGBOROUGH

PARKER & SONS (CANNON BREWERY)

The Cannon Public House,
Cannon Street,
Wellingborough NN8 4DJ
☎ *(01933) 279629*

The four Cannon Brewery brews plus a selection of up to five guest beers available at any one time.

This father, son and wife business opened for brewing in an old barn behind the pub in January 1993. The original beer brewed was Cannon Pride followed by Cannon Fodder, Light Brigade and Florries. It is now distributed all over the north of England, Scotland and the Midlands. The Cannon is a busy pub on the outskirts of the town, selling nine real ales. Filled rolls only. Car park, garden.

LIGHT BRIGADE 3.6% ABV

PRIDE 4.2% ABV

FLORRIE NIGHT-IN-ALE 4.8% ABV

FODDER 5.5% ABV

All day except Sundays.

Berwick-upon-Tweed

Border Brewery

The Old Kiln, Brewery Lane,
Tweedmouth,
Berwick-upon-Tweed TD15 2AH
☎ *(01289) 303303*
Visitors welcome. Tied houses: None

The original Border Brewery was formed in 1744, but it was bought by Vaux and closed in 1937. It re-opened in 1992 using old plant from the Hadrian Brewery. In June 1994 it changed hands as the present owners took over. The output is steadily increasing.

Beers available at: Angel Inn, Tweedmouth, Berwick-upon-Tweed, Northumberland *and* St Abbs Haven Hotel, Coldingham, Borders, Scotland.

SPECIAL BITTER 3.8% ABV
Pale golden bitter with delicate hoppy aroma.

OLD KILN BITTER 3.8% ABV
Amber-coloured, dry hoppy bitter with malty aftertaste.

OLD KILN ALE 4.0% ABV
Amber-coloured malty ale with a lasting sweetness.

NOGGINS NOG 4.2% ABV
Dark mild ale with a roast malt aroma.

S.O.B. 5.6% ABV
Red-brown strong ale with a distinct aftertaste.

RUDOLPH'S RUIN 7.1% ABV
Christmas special. Very strong, with complex flavours.

Hexham

Hexhamshire Brewery

Leafields, Ordley,
Hexham NE46 1SX
☎ *(01434) 673031*
Visitors welcome. Tied houses: 1

Established in December 1992 by Geoff Brown, owner of the Dipton Mill Inn, and two partners in a converted cattle shed.

Beers available at: Dipton Mill Inn, Dipton Mill Road, Dipton, Northumberland.

SHIRE BITTER 3.8% ABV
Bitter with malty overtones.

DEVIL'S WATER 4.1% ABV
Malt dominates with gradually declining bitterness to give a strong, sweet finish.

STOUT 4.3% ABV

WHAPWEASEL 4.8% ABV
Smooth malty bitter with a lasting hoppiness.

OLD HUMBUG 5.5% ABV

SHOTLEY BRIDGE

The Manor House

Carterway Heads, Shotley Bridge,
Nr Consett DH8 9LX
☎ *(01207) 258268*
Mr Pelley

Four beers at any one time. Brews from Big Lamp and Butterknowle breweries always available plus 100 guests per year.

Converted farmhouse, beamed with open fires. Bar and restaurant food available at lunchtime and evenings. Car park, garden, accommodation. Children allowed.

OPEN *11am–3pm and 6–11pm Mon–Sat; 12–3pm and 7–10.30pm Sun.*

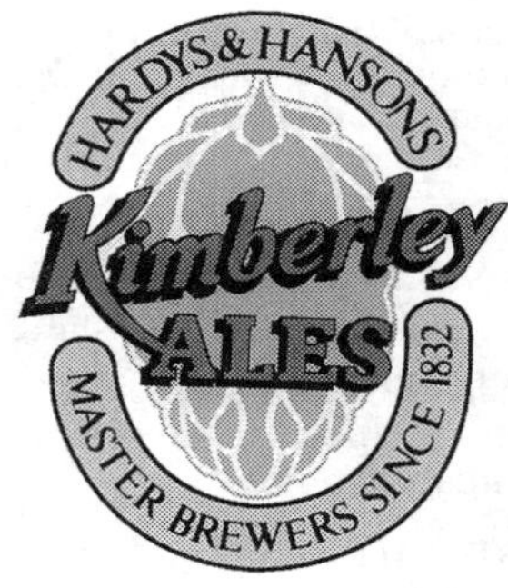

Beeston

The Victoria Hotel

85 Dovecote Lane, Beeston,
Nr Nottingham NG9 1JG
☎ *(0115) 925 4049*

A constantly changing range of ten beers always available from a list of 500 per year including Morland Old Speckled Hen, Woodforde's Wherry, Whim Hartington Bitter, Sam Smith's Old Brewery Bitter, Hop Back, Yates and Enville ales. Also 120 whiskies and extensive wine list.

Refurbished and redecorated Victorian railway pub with high ceilings. Bar and restaurant food is available at lunchtime and evenings. Car park, garden, conference room. Accompanied children allowed in the restaurant and outside. Off Queens Road, behind Beeston railway station.

11am–11pm Mon–Sat;
11am–10.30pm Sun.

Colston Bassett

The Martins Arms Inn

School Lane,
Colston Bassett NG12 3FN
☎ *(01949) 81361*
Miss L Bryan

Seven beers always available (200 per year), among them Bateman XB and XXXB, Marston's Best and Pedigree, Morland Old Speckled Hen, Greene King Abbot, Timothy Taylor Landlord, Wadworth 6X, Adnams Broadside, Robinsons etc.

This village freehouse was built in 1700 as a farmhouse set in 100 acres owned by the local squire. Now set in one acre with original stables surrounded by National Trust parkland. Antique furniture, prints, old beams, Jacobean fireplace and bar. Bar and restaurant food available at lunchtime and most evenings. Car park, large garden with croquet, children's room. Accommodation. On the A46 Newark to Leicester road.

12–3pm and 6–11pm.

Eakring

Maypole Brewery

North Laithes Farm, Wellow Road,
Eakring, NG22 0AN
☎ *(01636) 821000*
Visitors welcome. Tied houses: None

Maypole was established in March 1995 in a converted eighteenth-century farm building using equipment purchased from Springhead Brewery. This is a 2.25-barrel brewlength operation supplying approximately ten pubs per week.

CELEBRATION 4.0% ABV

MAYDAY 4.6% ABV

OLD HOME WRECKER 4.6% ABV

MAYWEST 4.6% ABV

POLEAXED 4.8% ABV

Kimberley

Hardys & Hansons

Kimberley Brewery,
Kimberley, Nottingham NG16 2NS
☎ *(01159) 383611*
Visitors welcome. Tied houses: 256

The Kimberley Brewery, in the heart of this small Nottinghamshire town, has been in production since 1832. William and Thomas Hardy bought the original brewhouse in 1857 and developed a larger brewery on the present premises. Meanwhile, on the other side of town, Stephen Hanson established a separate brewery in 1847. Both companies thrived, with fierce but friendly rivalry, until 1930, when increasing competition from larger brewers led the two to join forces. By 1993, the company was generating a turnover of £31 million. A strong family influence remains today. Richard Hanson, great-great grandson of the founder, is chairman and managing director and members of both families sit on the board.

Beers available at: Ye Olde Trip to Jerusalem, 1 Brewhouse Yard, Castle Road, Nottingham *and* The Corn Mill, Swiney Way, Chilwell, Nottinghamshire.

KIMBERLEY BEST MILD 3.1% ABV

KIMBEREY BEST BITTER 3.9% ABV

KIMBERLEY CLASSIC 4.8% ABV

The Nelson and Railway

Station Road, Kimberley NG16 2NR
☎ *(0115) 938 2177*
Harvey Burton

Four beers always available including Hardys & Hansons Kimberley Mild, Best and Classic. Also an interesting guest from a range of six per year.

Opposite the Hardys & Hansons brewery. A Victorian, family-run village pub with dining area. Originally two separate inns. Bar food available at lunchtime and evenings. Car park, garden, skittle alley and games. Accommodation. Children allowed in dining area for meals. One mile north of M1 junction 26.

11am–11pm Mon–Sat; 12–10.30pm Sun.

MANSFIELD

MANSFIELD BREWERY

Littleworth, Mansfield NG18 1AB
☎ *(01623) 25691*
Visitors welcome. Tied houses: 502

Mansfield Brewery was founded as a partnership in 1855 to take advantage of the water and good malt and hop producing farmland nearby. In 1925 the brewery was incorporated as a limited company and in 1933 shares were listed on the London Stock Exchange. Traditional production methods are still used today, including Yorkshire squares in the fermenting room. The brewery resumed production of cask ales in 1982 and has expanded and been redeveloped since 1983. There is now a new brewhouse, cylindro-conical fermenters and a new cask-racking facility.

MANSFIELD BITTER 3.9% ABV
English fuggle hops provide full flavour. Fermented in traditional Yorkshire squares.

MANSFIELD DARK MILD 3.5% ABV
A rich dark brewery-conditioned malt.

RIDING BITTER 3.6% ABV
English fuggle hops provide flavour and Styrian hops for aroma.

RIDING MILD 3.5% ABV
A rich mild. The dry roast flavour is complemented by traces of butterscotch and bittersweet fruit.

OLD BAILY STRONG BITTER 4.8% ABV
A full-bodied bitter. Dark copper red in colour with an aroma of malt and fruit.

NOTTINGHAM

Limelight

Wellington Circus,
Nottingham NG1 5AF
☎ *(0115) 941 8467*
Geoff Donahue

Bateman XB, Marston's Pedigree and Adnams Bitter among those beers permanently available plus five wide-ranging guest beers (385 per year).

Bar and restaurant food is available at lunchtime and evenings. Parking and garden. Children allowed in the restaurant and outside. Adjacent to Nottingham Playhouse and Nottingham Albert Hall. Featured brewery weeks.

All day, every day.

Lincolnshire Poacher

161–163 Mansfield Road,
Nottingham NG1 3FR
☎ *(0115) 941 1584*
Paul Montgomery

Bateman XB, XXXB and Victory plus Marston's Pedigree at all times. Also up to five guest beers, mostly from small independent brewers such as Kelham Island, Springhead, Shardlow, Highwood etc.

A traditional ale house. No juke box, no games machines, lots of conversation. Bar food available at lunchtimes and evenings. Parking and garden. Children allowed at the management's discretion. Just north of the city centre on the left-hand side. On the A612 Newark to Southwell road.

11am–3pm and 5–11pm Mon–Thurs; 11am–11pm Fri–Sat; 12–10.30pm Sun.

RADCLIFFE ON TRENT

The Royal Oak

Main Road,
Radcliffe on Trent NG12 2FD
☎ *(0115) 933 3798*

Up to 14 brews always available including Marston's Pedigree, Timothy Taylor Landlord, Morland Old Speckled Hen and Fuller's London Pride. Also guests (200 per year) including Exmoor Gold and Black Sheep Bitter.

An Austrian-style pub with a cosy lounge. Bar food available at lunchtime. Car park. Children not allowed.

11am–11pm Mon–Sat; 12–3.30pm and 7–10.30pm Sun.

RETFORD

Market Hotel

West Carr Road, Ordsall,
Nr Retford DN22 7SN
☎ *(01777) 703278*
Ray Brunt

Marston's Pedigree, Shepherd Neame Spitfire and Morland Old Speckled Hen among those beers permanently available plus up to six guest beers (200+ per year) including the Thwaites and Adnams ranges, also local brews.

Family-run traditionally decorated pub. Bar food is available at lunchtime and evenings. Car park, conservatory restaurant, large banqueting suite. Children allowed. Located two minutes through the subway from the railway station.

11am–3pm Mon–Fri; all day Sat; 12–4pm and 7–10.30pm Sun.

Sutton on Trent

Springhead Brewery

Unit 3, Sutton on Trent Workshops, Old Great North Road, Sutton on Trent, NG23 6QS
☎ *(01636) 821000*
Visitors welcome. Tied houses: None

Alan Gill started brewing on his father's allotment as a child, using nettles and water. By 1990 he had graduated to white plastic containers and pipework in the spare room. Cash was invested and the brewery established, named after a nearby bend in the River Trent. In 1993 Alan took voluntary redundancy from British Telecom and invested in a bigger brewery plant. Soon he was supplying 20 pubs and the range of brews increased. Most of the names have a connection with the English Civil War. Today, with 100 pubs and wholesalers to satisfy, a move to bigger premises was inevitable and so the brewery recently moved to a nearby industrial unit.

Beers available at: Three Stags Heads, Wardlow Mires, Nottinghamshire *and* Lord Nelson, Main Street, Sutton on Trent, Newark, Nottinghamshire.

HERSBRUCKER WEIZENBIER 3.6% ABV
Wheat beer with gentle lemony aroma. Light and refreshing with dry finish.

SPRINGHEAD BITTER 4.0% ABV
Clean-tasting, hoppy session beer.

THE LEVELLER 4.8% ABV
Dark, smokey, intense flavour with a toffee finish.

ROARING MEG 5.5% ABV
Citrus, honey aroma. Smooth and sweet with a dry finish.

CROMWELL'S HAT 6.0% ABV
Smooth as silk, robust with a hint of juniper and cinnamon.

Upton

Cross Keys

Main Street, Upton,
Nr Newark NG23 5SY
☎ *(01636) 813269*
Mr and Mrs Kirrage

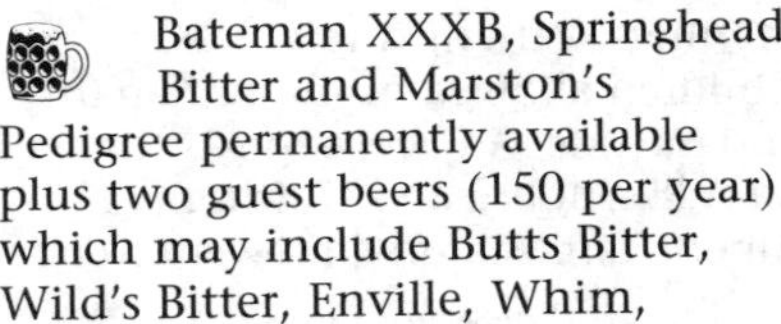

Bateman XXXB, Springhead Bitter and Marston's Pedigree permanently available plus two guest beers (150 per year) which may include Butts Bitter, Wild's Bitter, Enville, Whim, Oakham and Batham's brews.

A seventeenth-century listed freehouse and restaurant. Open fires, beams, brasses etc. The former dovecote has been converted into a restaurant, the tap room has carved pews from Newark parish church. Bar food available at lunchtime and evenings. Restaurant open Friday and Saturday evenings and Sunday lunch. Car park, garden, children's area.

11.30am–2.30pm and 5.30–11pm Mon–Sat; 12–2.30pm and 7–10.30pm Sun.

Worksop

Manor Lodge Hotel

Manor Lodge, off Mansfield Road, Worksop S80 3DL
☎ *(01909) 474177*
Mr AE Ranshaw

Mansfield, Adnams and Charles Wells beers plus six guest beers (60 per year) from Hardington, Brains, Stones, Ridleys, Woodforde and Burton Bridge breweries etc.

Totally independent unusual five-storey Elizabethan manor pub/restaurant. Open fires. Bar and restaurant food available at lunchtime and evenings. Car park, garden and children's room. Accommodation. Follow the brown tourist signs down the lane off Mansfield Road.

12–3pm and 5–11pm Mon–Fri; all day Sat–Sun.

ABINGDON

MORLAND & CO.

PO Box 5, The Brewery,
Ock Street, Abingdon OX14 5DD
☎ *(01235) 553377*
Visitors' reception centre. Brewery tours by appointment. Tied houses: 279

In 1711, John Morland, a farmer, bought a property in West Ilsey, south of Abingdon, from Benjamin Smith, a maltster. John and his son, Benjamin, got to work and a brewery was soon flourishing. In 1861, Edward Morland bought the Eagle Brewery in Abingdon from William Belcher, and this became the site of the present business. Thomas Skurray joined the company towards the end of the nineteenth century and much of Morland's growth and success is down to him. He was company chairman from 1923 to 1938. Investment in plant and buildings has been maintained and, in July 1991, the company acquired 101 pubs from Courage. A takeover bid by Greene King was rejected the following year. Old Speckled Hen is now being exported to Europe and North America. The brewery sign honours George Morland, a noted painter of rustic scenes, who died in 1804.

Beers available at: The Brewery Tap, 40/42 Ock Street, Abingdon, Oxfordshire *and* Castle Inn, Church Lane, Hurst, Reading, Berkshire.

INDEPENDENT IPA 3.4% ABV
A light malty fruity aroma. Full clean smooth bitter taste. Brewed to be served with a creamy head.

ORIGINAL BITTER 4.0% ABV
Fresh floral hop aroma. Distinctively dry and thirst-quenching with a light hoppy finish. Strong Goldings character makes this a refreshing session beer.

THE TANNERS JACK 4.4% ABV
Light citrus notes combined with malt. Good full malty flavour with hints of wholemeal toast and chocolate with a smooth dry finish. Well balanced.

OLD MASTERS 4.6% ABV
Ripe malt and hops aroma. Full malt body in mouth with bitter undertones, long dry finish with fruit notes. Rounded ale with good fruit character.

OLD SPECKLED HEN 5.2% ABV
Superb floral Goldings hop aroma. Full, complex flavour of malt and hops in the mouth, dry finish surprising for its strength. Richly-coloured strong pale ale.

BAMPTON

The Romany Inn

Bridge Street, Bampton OX18 2HA
☎ *(01993) 850237*
Mrs Booth

Archers Village, Hook Norton Best and Mild, Donnington SBA permanently available plus two guest beers (100+ per year) which might include brews from Fuller's, Timothy Taylor, Adnams, Batemans, Black Sheep, Brakspears, Cotleigh, Greene King, Hop Back, Marston's Morland, Ringwood, Robinson's, Titanic and Youngs.

A seventeenth-century grade II listed pub with Saxon arches in the cellar. Bar and restaurant food is available at lunchtime and evenings. Car park, garden, picnic tables and children's play area. Accommodation. Bampton is situated on the A4095 Witney to Faringdon road. The pub is in the centre of the village.

11am–11pm.

Bledington

The King's Head Inn

The Green, Bledington OX7 6HD
☎ (01608) 658365
Mr RM Royce

Hook Norton Best and Wadworth 6X always available plus guest beers (30 per year) including Uley Old Spot, Stanway Lords a Leaping, Shepherd Neame Spitfire and Wychwood Hobgoblin etc.

A traditional fifteenth-century Cotswold village inn retaining all its olde-worlde charm with pews, trestles, inglenook fireplace etc. Bar and restaurant food is available at lunchtime and evenings. Fresh fish and game. Two car parks, garden, children's room. Accommodation. Children not allowed in the lounge bar. Bledington is on the B4450, six miles from Chipping Norton, four miles from Stow-on-the- Wold.

11am–2.30pm and 6–11pm Mon–Sat; 12–2pm and 7–10.30pm Sun.

Bodicote

Bodicote Brewery

Plough Inn, Plough Lane, Bodicote, Nr Banbury OX15 4BZ
☎ (01295) 262327

Bodicote Bitter, No.9 and Porter brewed and sold in the Plough Inn.

The brewery was established in 1982. All beers are full mash. The Plough is a well-beamed two-bar pub below street level. The original building dates from the sixteenth century. Bar and restaurant food is available at lunchtime and evenings. Parking, garden, accommodation. Children allowed.

BITTER 3.2% ABV

NO.9 4.4% ABV

OLD ENGLISH PORTER 4.5% ABV

TRIPLEX 5.0% ABV

11am–3pm and 6–11pm.

Chadlington

The Tite Inn

Mill End, Chadlington OX7 3NY
☎ (01608) 676475
Michael Willis

Archers Village always available plus three guest beers (50 per year) which may include Titanic White Star, Wychwood Dr Thirstys and Nix Wincott That. The emphasis is on the smaller breweries.

A sixteenth-century Cotswold stone pub with superb country views. Bar and restaurant food is available at lunchtime and evenings. Car park, garden and garden room. Children allowed. Chadlington is just over two miles south of Chipping Norton off the A361.

12–3pm and 6.30–11pm (winter 7–11pm); closed Mon (except bank holidays).

CHARLBURY

The Rose and Crown

Market Street, Charlbury,
Chipping Norton OX7 3PL
☎ *(01608) 810103*
Mr T Page

Archers Best and Fuller's London Pride permanently available plus three guest beers (100 per year) with brews from such as Lichfield, Coach House, Smiles, Butcombe, Marston's, Timothy Taylor, Robinson's, Hall & Woodhouse and Hook Norton etc.

A popular, one-room Victorian pub with a courtyard. No food. Parking, garden and children's room. Located in the town centre.

OPEN *12–3pm and 5.30–11pm Mon–Thurs and Sun; all day Fri–Sat.*

CLIFTON

The Duke of Cumberland's Head

Clifton OX15 0PE
☎ *(01869) 338534*

Four beers always available including Hook Norton Best, Adnams Bitter and Wadworth 6X. Guests may include Hampshire King Alfred.

Built in the late 1600s, this thatched Oxfordshire village pub serves bar and restaurant food. Car park, attractive gardens, accommodation. Children allowed.

12–3pm and 6.30–11pm.

EDGCOTE

MERIVALES ALES (EDGCOTE BREWERY)

3 Snobs Row, Edgcote,
Banbury OX17 1AG
☎ *(01295) 660335*
Visitors welcome, by appointment.
Tied houses: None

The brewery was registered in June 1994. It remains a tiny one-barrel operation using local well water, supplying about 12 local freehouses and three wholesalers in Devon, Yorkshire and Banbury. The brews are 100 per cent all malt-grain beers using Challenger hops plus Goldings for dry hopping and no other additives. Plans are afoot to increase production to five barrels in the near future.

Beers available at: Olde House at Home, Moreton Pinkney, Daventry, Northamptonshire *and* Watling Well, Watling Street, Towcester, Northamptonshire.

ORDINARY BITTER 3.9% ABV
A session beer.

EDGECUTTER BITTER 4.0% ABV
Light and fruity.

BEST BITTER 4.8% ABV
Copper-coloured and well-hopped.

HURDLER BITTER 5.0% ABV
Full-bodied, with Goldings hops for aroma.

FARINGDON

The Bell

Market Place,
Faringdon SN7 7HP
☎ *(01367) 240534*
Darren Rawlings

 Wadworth 6X and IPA plus Hall & Woodhouse Tanglefoot permanently available. Also a guest beer (26 per year) which might be one of Wadworth Somersault, Everard's Tiger and Adnams Broadside.

A thirteenth-century coaching inn with cobbled courtyard. Bar and restaurant food is available at lunchtime and evenings. Specialities include kangaroo and crocodile. Car park and garden. Accommodation. Children allowed.

9.30am–11pm Mon–Sat; 10.30am–3pm and 7–10.30pm Sun.

GREAT TEW

The Falkland Arms

Great Tew OX7 4DB
☎ *(01608) 683653*
John and Hazel Milligan and Darren Rawlings

Eight beers available at any one time from a range of about 350 per year. Donington BB, Hall & Woodhouse Tanglefoot, Hook Norton Best and Wadworth 6X all favoured. Small brewers and some regionals preferred. Also country wines and draught cider.

A traditional seventeenth-century Oxfordshire village inn with a vast inglenook fireplace and smooth flagstones. High-backed settles, oak panelling and beams and sparkling brasses. Bar food at lunchtime (not Sunday and Monday). Parking and garden. Live folk music on Sundays. Accommodation. Filled clay pipes and snuff for sale. Off the B4022, five miles east of Chipping Norton.

11.30am–2.30pm Tues–Sat; 6–11pm Mon–Sat; 12–2pm and 7–10.30pm Sun.

HENLEY ON THAMES

WH BRAKSPEAR & SONS

The Brewery, New Street,
Henley on Thames RG9 2BU
☎ *(01491) 573636*
No visitors. Tied houses: 106

Although a brewery can be traced back to before 1700 on the present site, the history of Brakspear's really began in 1779, when Robert Brakspear, originally from Faringdon, set up a partnership with Richard Hayward. Robert's second son, William Henry, took over and expanded the business greatly and, by 1847, they were supplying 87 tied houses and many other outlets. Archibald Brakspear took over from his father and bought Greys Brewery in 1896, thus increasing the portfolio. The business became a limited company in 1896 and the present brewery buildings date from this time. Other breweries at Wokingham and Goring were also acquired and the business is now in the hands of a sixth generation. Paul William Brakspear is now trade director.

John Edward Chalcraft became a highly influential chairman in 1969 and his son, Michael, has since replaced him. A major redevelopment programme took place in 1985.

XXX MILD ALE 3.0% ABV
A light-bodied real ale with a red-brown colour and a sweet malty, fruity aroma. The well-balanced taste of malt, hops and toffee has a faint bitterness, complemented by a sweet fruity flavour with a hint of black cherries.

BITTER 3.4% ABV
Amber in colour with a good fruit, hop and malt nose. The initial taste of malt and the well-hopped bitterness quickly dissolve into a predominantly bitter-sweet and fruity finish.

KPA 3.4% ABV

SPECIAL BITTER ALE 4.3% ABV
Golden-red in colour, a well-balanced aroma with a hint of sweetness. The initial taste is moderately sweet and very malty, but this is quickly overpowered by the dry hop bitterness, before a slightly sweet fruity finish.

OLD ALE 4.3% ABV
A distinctively full-bodied real ale with a red-brown colour and a strong fruity nose. Its pronounced taste of malt, hops and roast caramel gives way to fruitiness. The aftertaste is of bitter-sweet chocolate.

OH BE JOYFUL 5.0% ABV
A seasonal brew. Rich and full-bodied with a tawny red colour and a fruity sweet aroma. A balanced full-bodied grapefruit-citrus and hoppy flavour with a lingering finish of peppery bitter-sweetness.

HOOK NORTON

HOOK NORTON BREWERY CO.

Hook Norton,
Banbury OX15 5NY
☎ *(01608) 737210*
Trade visits only, on request.
Tied houses: 34

John Harris moved into a farmhouse at Scotland End, Hook Norton, in 1849 with his mother. He set up business as a maltster, supplying brewhouses in the area. A year later he started brewing himself and sales were so encouraging that he enlarged the malthouse in 1865 and built a small three-storey tower brewery in 1872. His son, John Henry, and nephew, Alban Clark, took over on his death in 1887. They added several more pubs to the three John Harris had acquired and business boomed. A substantial programme of rebuilding and expansion was completed in 1900, the year in which the brewery became a limited company. The brewery suffered during the recession of the 1920s but, by 1939, 34 pubs had been acquired and 93 freehold outlets established. David Clark maintains the family connection today. He was head brewer under his father, Bill, and became managing director on his death in 1982.

Beers available at: The Pear Tree, Scotland End, Hook Norton, Oxfordshire *and* The Great Western Arms, Station Road, Blockley, Gloucestershire.

HOOK NORTON MILD 3.0% ABV

HOOKY BEST BITTER 3.4% ABV

OLD HOOKY 4.5% ABV

Also a range of bottled beers.

North Leigh

The Woodman Inn

New Yatt Road, North Leigh,
Nr Witney OX8 6TT
☎ *(01993) 881790*
Colin Dickenson

Wadworth 6X, Hook Norton Bitter and Wychwood Shires permanently available plus two guest beers (150 per year) from breweries such as Adnams, Shepherd Neame, Timothy Taylor, Cotleigh and Charles Wells. The Oxfordshire beer festival takes place here twice a year.

A local village pub on the edge of town, overlooking the Windrush valley. Bar food served at lunchtime and evenings. Car park and garden. Children allowed. Accommodation. Located off the A4095 Witney to Woodstock road.

12–2.30pm and 6–11pm Mon–Fri; 12–3pm and 6–11pm Sat; 12–10.30pm Sun.

Oxford

Morrells Brewery

The Lion Brewery,
St Thomas' Street, Oxford OX1 1LA
☎ *(01865) 792013*
Visitors welcome. Tied houses: 127

In 1454 the monks of Osney Abbey built a brewhouse beside the city wall to be leased to a commercial brewer. After the dissolution of the monasteries in 1542, the lands were given to Christ Church as part of the endowment of the new college founded by King Henry VIII. In 1570, Thomas Linke, a chorister at the cathedral, built a second brewhouse on the site which now forms the nucleus of the present brewery. The brewhouse was leased to a number of different brewers over the next 150 years. William Kenton took over in 1718 and Richard Tawney, a boatmaster on the Thames, in 1742. He was succeeded by his son, Sir Richard Tawney, who was Lord Mayor of Oxford on three occasions. His younger brother, Edward, later went into partnership with Mark and James Morrell, and they had bought out his interest by his death in 1800. Charles Eld, the present managing director, is the sixth member of the Morrell family to run the business.

OXFORD BITTER 3.7% ABV

OXFORD MILD 3.7% ABV

VARSITY 4.3% ABV

GRADUATE 5.2% ABV

COLLEGE 7.4% ABV

Plus **STRONGS COUNTRY BITTER** 3.9% ABV brewed under licence and a range of bottled beers.

Ramsden

The Royal Oak

High Street, Ramsden OX7 3AW
☎ *(01993) 868213*
John Oldham

Hook Norton Bitter, and Archers Golden permanently available plus a guest (40 per year) such as Brakspear's Special, Banks's Bitter, Caledonian 80/– and Titanic Premium.

A sixteenth-century former coaching inn situated in a small village. Bar and restaurant food available. Car park and garden. Ramsden is halfway between Witney and Charlbury off the B4022.

11.30am–2.30pm and 6.30–11pm Mon–Sat; 12–3pm and 7–10.30pm Sun.

SOUTH MORETON

The Crown Inn

High Street, South Moreton,
Nr Didcot OX11 9AG
☎ *(01235) 812262*
Mr and Mrs Cook

Wadworth IPA and 6X, Hall & Woodhouse Tanglefoot and Adnams Bitter permanently available plus a guest beer (26 per year) with brews from all over the British Isles, Wales and Scotland.

An attractive village pub. Bar and restaurant food available. Car park and garden. Children allowed. The village is signposted both from Didcot and Wallingford.

11am–3pm and 5.30–11pm.

WANTAGE

The Royal Oak Inn

Newbury Street,
Wantage OX12 8DF
☎ *(01234) 763129*
Paul Hexter

Wadworth 6X, Hall & Woodhouse Badger and Tanglefoot plus up to eight guest beers (200 per year) from breweries such as Archers, Arkell's, Brakspear, Butts, Foxley, Gibbs Mew, Hampshire, Hook Norton, Hop Back, Titanic, Wadworth and Wychwood.

Fair deals and no frills at this freehouse. Navy paraphenalia decorates the bar. Bar food only available Friday and Saturday lunchtime. Accommodation.

5.30–11pm Mon–Thurs; 12–2.30pm Fri–Sat; 5.30–11pm Fri; 7–11pm Sat; 12–3pm and 7–10.30pm Sun.

WITNEY

THE WYCHWOOD BREWERY

The Eagle Maltings, The Crofts,
Witney OX8 7AZ
☎ *(01993) 702574*
Visitors welcome. Tied houses: 30

The Wychwood Brewery was founded in 1983 with a seven-barrel plant at Eagle Maltings. It was upgraded to a 20-barrel plant in 1986 and moved to the Two Rivers Brewery in 1987, before returning to Eagle Maltings in 1994, where a 115-barrel plant is now in operation. Hobgoblinns Ltd was formed in 1992 and now runs 30 pubs located between Bristol, London and Brighton.

SHIRES BITTER 3.4% ABV

FIDDLER'S ELBOW 4.0% ABV
Available from May to September.

WYCHWOOD BEST 4.2% ABV

BLACK WYCH STOUT 5.0% ABV
Winter beer.

DR THIRSTY'S DRAUGHT 5.2% ABV
Winter beer.

HOBGOBLIN 6.0% ABV
Winter beer.

THE DOG'S BOLLOCKS 6.5% ABV

House of Windsor

31 West End,
Witney OX8 6NQ
☎ *(01993) 704277*
Maureen Mcintyre

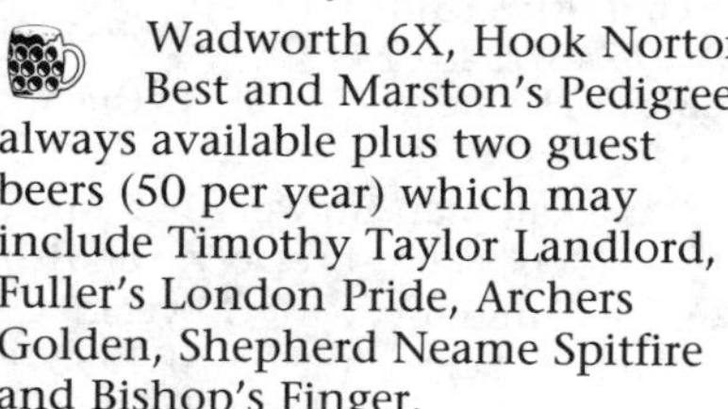

Wadworth 6X, Hook Norton Best and Marston's Pedigree always available plus two guest beers (50 per year) which may include Timothy Taylor Landlord, Fuller's London Pride, Archers Golden, Shepherd Neame Spitfire and Bishop's Finger.

No machines, no pool or darts in this friendly pub. Coal fire in winter. Bar and restaurant food is available at lunchtime and evenings. Large beer garden. Children allowed. Off the A40 and straight across two mini-roundabouts.

12–3.30pm Tues–Sun;
Evenings from 6pm (Sun 7pm).

WOODCOTE

The Highwayman

Exlade Street, Woodcote,
Nr Reading RG8 0UE
☎ *(01491) 682020*

Fuller's London Pride, Wadworth 6X and Gibbs Mew Bishop's Tipple among those brews permanently available plus a couple of guests (30 per year) to include Adnams Broadside, Timothy Taylor Landlord, Hook Norton Old Hooky, Shepherd Neame Spitfire and Rebellion ales.

Rambling seventeenth-century country inn with two-roomed bar, beams and open fire. Bar and restaurant food available at lunchtime and evenings. Car park, garden, accommodation. Children allowed in restaurant. Signposted from the A4074 Reading to Wallingford Road.

11am–3pm and
6–11pm Mon–Sat;
12–3pm and 7–10.30pm Sun.

EDGELEY

Olde Vic

1 Chatham Street,
Edgeley

Timothy Taylor Landlord permanently available plus five guest beers (700 per year), all from micro-breweries and independents – no big brewers. Names include Wyre Piddle, Bullmastiff, Wye Valley, Richard Cobdens, Goose Eye, Cotleigh, Ryburn and Hardington.

Small and cosy pub with beer garden for barbecues. Quiz nights. A CAMRA pub of the year. Bar food served at lunchtime and evenings. Car park. Children welcome. Situated near Stockport railway station.

12–3pm and 5.30–11pm Mon–Thurs; all day Fri–Sun.

SHREWSBURY

SALOPIAN BREWING CO.

The Brewery, 67 Mytton Oak Road, Shrewsbury SY3 8UQ
☎ *(01743) 248414*
Visitors welcome by prior arrangement.
Tied houses: None

The Salopian Brewery is a small independent brewery, the first in Shrewsbury for 30 years. Production began in August 1995 in a former purpose-built dairy in Copthorne, on the outskirts of town. It is owned by Mandy Evans, who formerly worked for British Rail. The head brewer originally trained as a chef but has been working in the trade since he was 16. Future plans involve expansion to cope with ever-increasing demand. There is a brewery shop open at weekends.

Beers available at: Coach and Horses, Swan Hill, Shrewsbury, Shropshire *and* Last Inn, Hengoed, Shropshire.

SALOPIAN BITTER 3.5% ABV
Hoppy, fruity bitter, strong flavoured with a creamy head.

MONKMOOR BITTER 4.0% ABV
Dark and malty with enhanced bitterness and fruity tones from four hops.

MANCHESTER FESTIVAL BEER (REMEMBER TOMMY DUCKS) 4.3% ABV
Dark, dry, full-bodied and fruity.

MINSTERLEY ALE 4.5% ABV
Premium bitter with a complex hop flavour, using three kinds of hop.

CHOIR PORTER 4.5% ABV
Prize-winning old-style porter with a very smooth taste.

PARSONS PROGRESS 4.5% ABV
Light-coloured, malty brew with balanced hoppiness.

LEMON BITTER 4.5% ABV
Proper bitter brewed with real lemons. Pale and opaque with balanced bitterness from hops against the acidity of the lemons.

WHITE WHEAT BEER 4.7% ABV
White, fruity, opaque beer with German hops.

IRONBRIDGE STOUT 5.0% ABV
Rich, complex taste using several malts and special hops.

SHROPSHIRE SPIRES STRONG BITTER 5.0% ABV
Red, very malty, strong ale.

HOLLYBUSH WINTER ALE 6.0% ABV
Winter warmer with a deep malty taste, liquorice tones, sweet bitterness and a floral finish.

Plus a range of bottle-conditioned beers and beers brewed exclusively for several local pubs including:
DARK WHEAT BEER (3.7% ABV),
ELROND (4.5% ABV),
GOODALLS GOLD (4.7% ABV),
BRAND X (4.8% ABV) and
PALE WHITE (5.0% ABV).

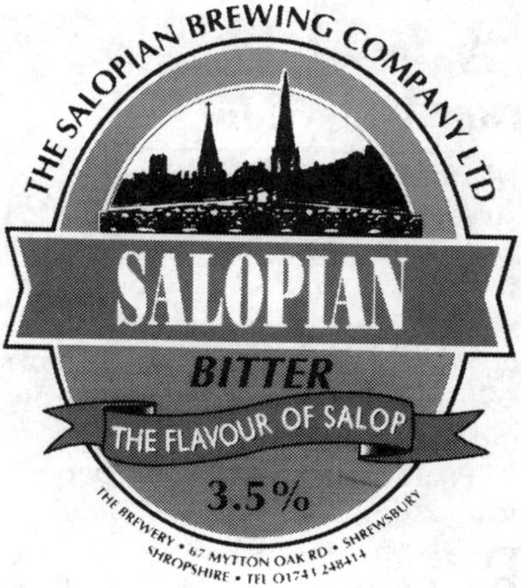
THE SALOPIAN BREWING COMPANY LTD
SALOPIAN
BITTER
THE FLAVOUR OF SALOP
3.5%
THE BREWERY • 67 MYTTON OAK RD • SHREWSBURY
SHROPSHIRE • TEL 01743 248414

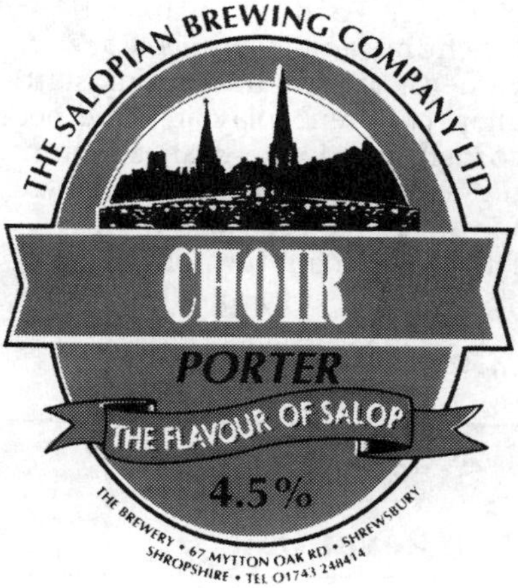
THE SALOPIAN BREWING COMPANY LTD
CHOIR
PORTER
THE FLAVOUR OF SALOP
4.5%
THE BREWERY • 67 MYTTON OAK RD • SHREWSBURY
SHROPSHIRE • TEL 01743 248414

THE SALOPIAN BREWING COMPANY LTD
SHROPSHIRE SPIRES
STRONG BITTER
THE FLAVOUR OF SALOP
5%
THE BREWERY • 67 MYTTON OAK RD • SHREWSBURY
SHROPSHIRE • TEL 01743 248414

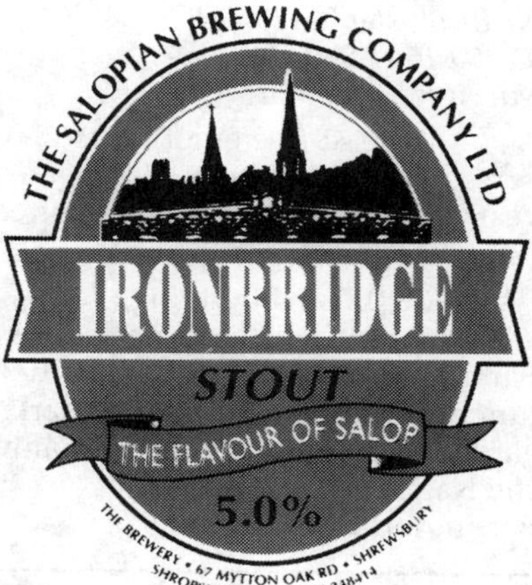
THE SALOPIAN BREWING COMPANY LTD
IRONBRIDGE
STOUT
THE FLAVOUR OF SALOP
5.0%
THE BREWERY • 67 MYTTON OAK RD • SHREWSBURY
SHROPSHIRE • TEL 01743 248414

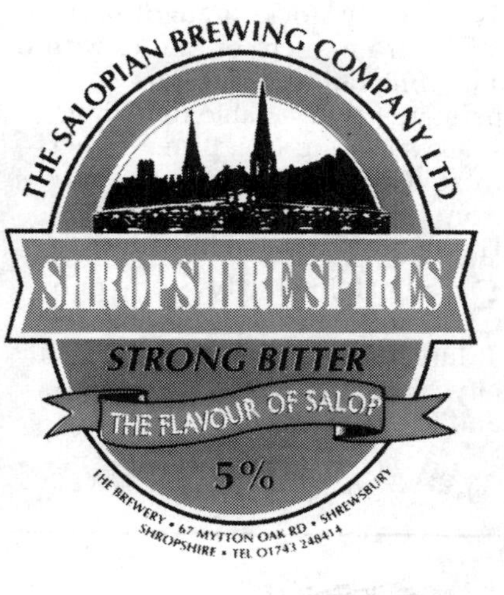

ALLERFORD CROSSING

The Victory Inn

Allerford Crossing,
Norton Fitzwarren,
Nr Taunton TA4 1AL
☎ *(01823) 461282*
NR Pike

Church End What the Fox's Hat, Cottage Golden Arrow and many many more. Twelve beers always available, 150 per year.

Recently refurbished to enhance the olde-worlde charm and character. Food is available at lunchtime and evenings. Car park, gardens, patio, family room, skittle alley, children's play area and pet's corner with donkeys, sheep, guinea pigs etc. A well room is available for hire. Take the Norton Fitzwarren road, turn off after Taunton Cider to Allerford.

11am–3pm and 6–11pm.

BARRINGTON

The Royal Oak

Barrington,
Nr Illminster TA19 0JB
☎ *(01460) 53455*
Mr Jarvis

At least five guest beers always available (300 per year) from all corners of the United Kingdom.

A grade II listed building, sixteenth-century cyder house. Bar and restaurant food served at lunchtime and evenings. Car park, garden and children's room. Follow the National Trust signs for Barrington Court.

BATH

Hatchett's

6-7 Queen Street, Bath BA1 1HE
☎ *(01225) 425045*
Mr and Mrs Cruxton

Up to five beers permanently available including a house bitter. The three or four guest beers may include Smiles Exhibition, Shepherd Neame Spitfire Ale, Hall & Woodhouse Hard Tackle and Exmoor Gold.

Nineteenth-century pub in Bath city centre with bars upstairs and down. House bitter available at £1.05. All beers at reasonable prices. Bar food available at lunchtimes. Side street in city centre.

11am–11pm Mon–Sat;
12–10.30pm Sun.

The Old Green Tree

12 Green Street, Bath BA1 2JZ
☎ *(01225) 448259*
Nick Luke

Only stocks draught beer from micro-breweries within a 60-mile radius. Five beers permanently available including Wickwar Brand Oak Bitter. Others rotated slowly including brews from Bridgwater, Uley, Cottage, Hardington and Oakhill etc.

Small oak-lined city centre pub. No music or machines. Bar food at lunchtime. On a small street in city centre between Milsom Street and the post office.

11am–11pm Mon–Sat;
7.30–10.30pm Sun.

The Pig and Fiddle

2 Saracen Street, Bath BA1 5BR
☎ *(01225) 460868*
Gregory Duckworth

Ash Vine Bitter, Challenger and Hop and Glory among six beers permanently available. Approximately 100 guest beers per year including Crouch Vale Golden Duck, Fuller's London Pride, Exmoor Stag and Butcombe Bitter.

Very busy town centre pub but with very relaxed atmosphere. Large outside area including garden. Bar food available at lunchtimes. Children not allowed in the pub. Opposite Hilton Hotel.

11.30am–11pm summer; 11.30am–3pm and 5–11pm winter.

Bleadon

The Queen's Arms

Celtic Way, Bleadon,
Nr Weston super Mare BS24 ONF
☎ *(01934) 812080*
Mr and Mrs Roads

Smiles brews always available straight from the barrel plus guests including Wadworth 6X, Hall & Woodhouse Tanglefoot, Crown Buckley Reverend James Original, Bateman XXXB, Greene King Abbot, Fuller's London Pride, Shepherd Neame Spitfire Ale and Adnams Broadside.

Typical village pub. Bar food available at lunchtime and evenings. Car park. Children allowed. The only pub in Bleadon.

11am–2.30pm and 5.30–11pm.

Burnham on Sea

Berrow Brewery

Coast Road, Berrow,
Burnham on Sea TA8 2QU
☎ *(01278) 751345*
Visitors welcome. Tied houses: None

The Berrow Brewery was founded in June 1982 and supplies pubs and clubs locally and further afield.

Beers available at: The Pack Horse Inn, Church Street, Mark, Nr Highbridge, Somerset *and* Cooper's Arms, Market Street, Highbridge, Somerset.

BERROW BREWERY BEST BITTER (BBBB) 4.0% ABV
A rich full-tasting malty beer.

BERROW PORTER 4.0% ABV

TOPSY TURVY STRONG ALE 6.0% ABV
A pale-coloured beer with a distinct hop character.

The Royal Clarence Hotel

31 The Esplanade,
Burnham on Sea TA8 1BQ
☎ *(01278) 783138*
Paul Davey

RCH Pitchfork, PG Steam, East Street Cream and Old Slug Porter permanently available plus four guest beers (200 per year) such as Wadworth 6X and brews from Hop Back, Morrells, Cotleigh, Exmoor, Otter, Summerskills, Beer Engine, Harviestoun, Orkney, Shardlow and Wyre Piddle and Dent.

An old coaching hotel and the RCH brewery tap. Hosts two beer festivals per year. Bar food available all day, restaurant food in the evenings. Parking, accommodation. Children allowed. Take M5 junction 22, then make for the sea front. The hotel is by the pier.

11am–11pm Mon–Sat; 12–10.30pm Sun.

GOATHURST

BRIDGWATER BREWING

Unit 1, Lovedere Farm, Goathurst, Bridgwater TA5 2DD
☎ *(01278) 663996*
Visitors welcome. Tied houses: None

Before becoming a successful brewer, Jeff Lucas was an horologist (watchmaker). Squeezed by the recession, he decided to develop what had initially been a cherished hobby. In April 1993, BBC went into production brewing and selling real ale. Jeff's plan was to sell four barrels in the first month, ten barels a month after six months, and 20 barrels a month within one year. But sales exceeded all expectations, and he now produces an average of 15 barrels per week. The BBC was soon winning awards for its brews and has now expanded to a ten-barrel brew plant. An enthusiastic and efficient team produce nine different ales, which are available in nine-gallon casks, 18-gallon casks and also 4.5-gallon polypins.

Beers available at: Halfway House, Pitney, Nr Langport, Somerset *and* Rose and Crown, Nether Stowey, Somerset.

BLAKE'S BITTER 3.4% ABV
A full-bodied, well-hopped session biter, light-brown in colour. It has a pleasing malty taste with a hint of chocolate in the after-taste.

CARNIVAL SPECIAL BREW 3.5% ABV
A straw-coloured, light quaffing ale. Brewed in autumn, refreshing and aromatic.

AMBER ALE 3.8% ABV
A medium-strength, well-hopped, malty session ale.

BOSUN'S TICKLE 4.1% ABV

CANNONBALL 4.2% ABV

COPPERNOB 4.4% ABV
A copper-coloured ale, with a slight ruby tinge. Well-hopped, malty and with a good body.

KRIMBLEALE 4.8% ABV

SUNBEAM 5.4% ABV
A deceptively strong golden, straw-coloured ale with a pleasing lager-style aroma, but still retaining its traditional pedigree. It has a well-balanced taste of slight hoppy bitterness, but with an underlying malty sweetness in the after-taste.

BLUTO'S REVENGE 6.0% ABV
A strong, dark porter/stout type of ale. An occasional brew, packed with hops and various malts, resulting in a smooth, dark and moreish ale.

Kelston

The Old Crown

Bath Road,
Kelston, Nr Bath
☎ *(01225) 423371*

Butcombe Bitter, Smiles Best, and Wadworth 6X permanently available plus Wadworth Old Timer in winter only.

Traditional olde-English pub and restaurant with open fire, original flagstones, candle-light and good atmosphere. Bar food at lunchtime (not Sunday), restaurant Thurs–Sat evenings only. Car park and garden. On A43 Bitton to Bath road, three miles outside Bath.

11.30am–2.30pm and 5–11pm Mon–Fri; 11.30am–3pm and 5–11pm Sat; 12–3pm and 7–10.30pm Sun.

Langley Marsh

The Three Horseshoes

Langley Marsh,
Wiveliscombe,
Nr Taunton TA4 2UL
☎ *(01984) 623763*
John Hopkins

Palmers IPA and Ringwood Best permanently available plus up to three guest beers including Wadworth 6X, Youngs Bitter, Dartmoor Best and brews form Butcombe, Shepherd Neame, Harveys and Morland.

An old, unspoilt, no-nonsense traditional pub. No juke box or games machines. Bar and restaurant food is available at lunchtime and evenings. Car park, garden and children's room. Children allowed in the restaurant. Follow the B3227 to Wiveliscombe, then follow signs to Langley Marsh.

12–3pm and 7–11pm (10.30pm Sun).

Luxborough

Royal Oak of Luxborough

Exmoor National Park, Luxborough,
Nr Dunster TA23 0SH
☎ *(01984) 640319*
Mr K Draper

Cotleigh Tawny, Exmoor Gold and Bateman XXXB permanently available plus up to four guest beers (150 per year) such as Cottage Norman Conquest, Hop Back Summer Lightning and brews from Summerskills, Caledonian, Jennings, Freeminers, Black Sheep and Woodfordes.

An unspoilt rural pub with loads of beams, flagstones etc. Farmhouse tables. Bar and restaurant food is available at lunchtime and evenings. Car park and garden. Children allowed in the restaurant. Accommodation. Off the A396, four miles south of Dunster.

11am–2.30pm and 6–11pm.

Oakhill

Oakhill Brewery

High Street, Oakhill,
Nr Bath BA3 5AS
☎ *(01749) 840134*
Visitors welcome. Tied houes: 3

Oakhill Brewery was originally founded in 1767 to produce its famous Invalid Stout, brewed using water which came down from the Mendip Hills and thought to have magical healing properties. The brewery continued to thrive until 1924, when it was destroyed by a fire. In 1984, it was reopened by Reg Keevil, a local farmer, and since then it has expanded steadily as the popularity of its traditional real ales grows. New premises have recently been acquired to cope with the ever-increasing demand.

Beers available at: Nettlebridge Inn, Nettlebridge, Oakhill, Nr Bath, Somerset *and* The White Hart, Corsley, Warminster, Wiltshire.

SOMER ALE 3.5% ABV
Smooth refreshing ale.

OAKHILL BEST BITTER 4.0% ABV
A light and flavoursome beer.

MENDIP GOLD 4.5% ABV

BLACK MAGIC STOUT 4.5% ABV
A traditional cask-conditioned bitter stout.

YEOMAN 1767 STRONG ALE 5.0% ABV
For the connoisseur.

MENDIP TICKLER 6.3% ABV

PITMINSTER

The Queen's Arms

Pitminster,
Nr Taunton TA3 7AZ
☎ *(01823) 421529*
Chris and Fay Handscombe

Cotleigh Tawny permanently available plus up to five guests including Everard Tiger and brews from Ballards, Teignworthy, Cottage Brewery etc.

A traditional stone-built pub with a dining room in an attached fourteenth-century restaurant. No background music or games machines. Bar and restaurant food is available at lunchtime and evenings. Fish and shellfish specialities. Car park and garden. Children allowed in the bar until 8pm. Follow the signs for Corfe from Taunton and turn right in Corfe.

11am–3pm and 5–11pm.

PITNEY

Halfway House

Pitney, Nr Langport, TA10 9AB
☎ *(01458) 252513*

Beers from Teignworthy, Oakhill, Cotleigh, Butcombe and Bridgwater permanently available plus guests (100 per year) such as Ringwood Old Thumper, Timothy Taylor Landlord, Hop Back Summer Lightning and Wheat Beer.

A real ale pub wth flagstone floors and log fires. No music or games machines. Bar food is available at lunchtime and evenings. Car park and garden. Well-behaved children allowed. CAMRA Somerset pub of the year. On the main road between Somerton and Langport (B3151).

11.30am–2.30pm and 5.30–11pm.

TRUDOXHILL

ASH VINE BREWERY

The White Hart,
Trudoxhill, Frome BA11 5DP
☎ *(01373) 836344*

Ash Vine Bitter, Challenger, Black Bess Porter and Hop and Glory plus a guest beer available at The White Hart.

They have been brewing for eight years at the Ash Vine brewery, behind the White Hart. The beer is now available nationally via a network of wholesalers in both draught and bottled form. Every month, a new beer is brewed to a new recipe, and is only available during that one month. The White Hart is a seventeenth-century village coaching inn. Bar and restaurant food is served at lunchtime and evenings. Car park and garden. Located off the A361 between Frome and Wells.

ASH VINE BITTER 3.5% ABV
Straw-coloured beer brewed with pale malt. Hops predominate, with a floral aroma followed by a smooth dryness. The aftertaste is dry and fades gently.

CHALLENGER 4.1% ABV
Classic well-balanced beer. Deep red-brown colour. Smooth flavour with a full mouth feel and a delicate hoppy aroma, leading to a clean finish.

BLACK BESS 4.2% ABV
Brewed from October to March, a very dark brown porter. Improves for at least two months when stored correctly, as a chocolate flavour emerges enhanced by a tight creamy head. Smooth malty flavour, although a hop taste and delicate hop aroma survive. The finish is smooth and dry.

HOP AND GLORY 5.0% ABV
Brewed using pale malt only producing a golden straw colour and a smoothness enhanced by the absence of astringent roast malt flavours. Strong, with a clean hoppy flavour.

12–2.30pm and 7–11pm.

Wellington

Juwards Brewery

c/o Fox Brothers and Co Ltd
Wellington TA21 0AW
☎ *(01823) 667909*
No visitors. Tied houses: None

Ted Bishop, a former Cotleigh and Ash Vine brewer runs this small, one-man operation which began production in June 1994 in an old wool mill.

Beers available at: The White Hart, Corfe, Nr Taunton, Somerset *and* The Cottage Inn, 31 Champford Lane, Wellington, Somerset.

BITTER 3.9% ABV

PREMIUM 4.9% ABV

GOLDEN 4.4% ABV

Plus a range of brews produced exclusively for certain outlets.

West Lydford

Cottage Brewing Co.

High Street,
West Lydford TA11 7DQ
☎ *(01963) 240551*
Visitors welcome. Tied houses: None

Chris and Helen Norman set up the Cottage Brewing Company in the heart of rural Somerset. Brewing commenced in 1993 and, since then, the company has trebled in size to keep pace with demand for its brews. The plant is custom-built to traditional principles.

Beers available at: The Volunteer Inn, Seavington St Michael, Nr Ilminster, Somerset *and* The Piper's Inn, Ashcott, Nr Bridgwater, Somerset.

SOUTHERN BITTER 3.7% ABV
Light in colour with a hoppy aroma. A mellow session bitter.

WHEELTAPPERS 4.0% ABV

SOMERSET AND DORSET ALE 4.4% ABV
Well-hopped, malty brew with a deep red colour.

GOLDEN ARROW 4.5% ABV

OLD FRECKLED KEN 4.5% ABV

GREAT WESTERN REAL ALE 5.4% ABV
Prize-winning dark ale.

NORMAN'S CONQUEST 7.0% ABV
Dark fruity ale. Champion Beer of Britain 1995.

WIVELISCOMBE

COTLEIGH BREWERY

Ford Road,
Wiveliscombe TA4 2RE
☎ *(01984) 624086*
No visitors. Tied houses: None

Run by John and Jennifer Aries, Cotleigh Brewery was established in 1979 and is now one of the most successful small breweries in the West Country. Situated in purpose-built premises in Wiveliscombe, the brewery supplies 150 pubs and clubs in Devon and Somerset. Their beers are also available nationwide through selected wholesalers.

Beers available at: The Butterleigh Inn, Butterleigh, Nr Cullompton, Devon *and* The White Horse, Stogumber, Nr Taunton, Somerset.

HARRIER SPA 3.6% ABV
Clean-tasting pale bitter. Very hoppy aroma and finish.

TAWNY BITTER 3.8% ABV
Smooth malty best bitter with a well-hopped finish.

BARN OWL BITTER 4.5% ABV
Premium bitter with an Abundance of malt and hop flavours.

ALDERCOTE ALE (4.2%) and **ALDERCOTE EXTRA** (4.7%) are brewed specifically for the Kent-based wholesalers, East West Ales.

Plus an additional guest beer is produced every month.

EXMOOR ALES

Golden Hill Brewery,
Wiveliscombe TA4 2NY
☎ *(01984) 623798*
Visitors welcome by arrangement only.
Tied houses: None

Founded in 1980 in the old Hancock's Brewery, which had been closed since 1959. Brewing capacity has been steadily increased to satisfy demand from more than 200 pubs and wholesalers.

EXMOOR ALE 3.8% ABV
Pale brown beer with a malty aroma and malty, dry taste with a bitter and malty finish.

EXMOOR GOLD 4.5% ABV
Golden in colour with a malty aroma and flavour. Slight sweetness and hoppiness with a sweet, malty finish.

EXMOOR STAG 5.2% ABV
Pale brown with a malty taste and aroma and a bitter finish. Slightly sweet.

Plus occasional brews including:
DARK (4.1% ABV),
STOAT (4.2% ABV),
EXMAS (6.0% ABV) and
EXMOOR BEAST (6.6% ABV).

Bignall End

The Plough

Ravens Lane, Bignall End
☎ *(01782) 720469*
Mr Gillespie

Broughton Merlin's Ale, Butterknowle Bitter, Fuller's London Pride, Morland Old Speckled Hen and Young's brews always available plus various guest beers supplied through the Caledonian Brewery.

A traditional Victorian working men's pub. Cold food available at lunchtime. Car park, garden, children's room. No children in bar. Easy to find.

11am–11.30pm Mon–Wed;
11am–11pm Thurs–Fri;
11–midnight Sat;
12.30–11pm Sun.

Burton upon Trent

Marston, Thompson and Evershed

Shobnall Road,
Burton upon Trent DE14 2BW
☎ *(01283) 531131*
Visitors welcome. Tied houses: 650

John Marston established J Marston and Son at the Horninglow Brewery, Burton upon Trent, in 1834. In 1898, the company joined forces with John Thompson and Son and moved to the Albion Brewery, where it still operates today. Sydney Evershed joined the company in 1905. The brewery is situated on the western edge of the Trent valley, drawing the special Burton brewing water from the surrounding hills. Marston's is the only company still using the Burton Union system, where the beer is fermented in oak casks.

MARSTON'S BITTER 3.8% ABV
Brewed with yeast from the Burton Union sets, a full-flavoured standard bitter.

MARSTON'S PEDIGREE 4.5% ABV
With its unique fruity flavour, Pedigree is the only beer still brewed in oak casks, the Burton Union way. A premium bitter with a unique, crisp flavour.

OWD RODGER 7.6% ABV
A rich fruity strong ale, also fermented in the Burton Unions. Provides a fine compliment to strong cheese.

Plus a range of limited edition brews under the label **MARSTON'S HEAD BREWER'S CHOICE** and bottled beers.

Eccleshall

The Eccleshall Brewery

The George Hotel, Castle Street,
Eccleshall ST21 6DF
☎ *(01785) 850300*

The Slaters Ales range of four beers brewed and available here plus a selection of guest beers.

Opened in March 1995 by Gerard and Moyra Slater. The beer is brewed by their son, Andrew. The brewery is a ten-barrel plant. The George is a sixteenth-century coaching inn with olde worlde beams, log fires, real ales, malt whisky. Bar and restaurant food available. Car park, garden, children's room, accommodation.

OLD FASHIONED BITTER 3.6% ABV
Golden amber coloured, hoppy beer with a hint of bitterness. Brewed the traditional way.

SLATER'S ORIGINAL 4.0% ABV
Distinctive amber beer, smooth and creamy.

SLATER'S PREMIUM 4.4% ABV
Strong light and creamy, slightly darker in appearance with a dry texture.

ALLMIGHTY 5.3% ABV
Light and hoppy.

All day every day.

LICHFIELD

LICHFIELD BREWERY

3 Europa Way, Boley Park, Lichfield WS14 9TZ
☎ *(01543) 415919*
No visitors. Tied houses: None

The Lichfield Brewery was started by two CAMRA members in 1992 bringing production back to the city after a 60-year absence. The brewery now has a dozen regular outlets. Its beers are available as guest beers throughout the Midlands.

Beers available at: The Scales Inn, 24 Market Street, Lichfield, Staffordshire *and* Royal Oak, Pelsall, Staffordshire.

STEEPLECHASE 3.7% ABV
A summer ale.

INSPIRED 4.0% ABV
Light and sharp.

SHERIFF'S RIDE 4.2% ABV
Creamy and smooth.

STEEPLEJACK 4.5% ABV
With a bitter aftertaste.

XPIRED 4.8% ABV
Dark and fruity.

GARGOYLE 5.0% ABV
Uncompromisingly bitter.

XMAS MINCESPIRED 5.8% ABV
Dark and distinctive occasional brew.

MARSTON

The Fox Inn

Marston, Nr Church Eaton ST20 0AS
☎ *(01785) 84072*

Eight beers available including Lloyds, Wood, Joule Old Priory, Mansfield Old Baily and Charles Wells Eagle. Loads of guests from Wychwood, John Joules, Mansfield, Charles Wells, Timothy Taylor etc.

An unadulterated ale house in the middle of nowhere. Bar and restaurant food is available at lunchtime and evenings. Car parking and children's room. Field for tents and caravans. Accommodation.

OPEN *12–3 pm and 6–11pm.*

OUTWOODS

Village Tavern

Outwoods
☎ *(01952) 691216*
Mr J Wildman

Wildman's Best (house beer brewed by Enville) and Hobson's brews always available plus 200 guests per year including Wadworth 6X, Morland Old Speckled Hen and brews from Hoskins & Oldfield and Wild's.

A quaint traditional pub on the Shropshire border. Bar food available lunchtime and evenings. Car park, garden. Children allowed. Signposted from the A518. OS788182.

12–3pm and 7.30–11pm in winter; 12–3pm and 6–11pm in summer.

Stafford

The Stafford Arms

43 Railway Street, Stafford
☎ *(01785) 253313*
Mike Watkins

Six Titanic beers permanently available plus four guests (400 per year) including brews from Orkney, Burt's, Caledonian, Sutton and many other small independent breweries.

A traditional pub with bar food available at lunchtime and evenings. CAMRA pub of the year 1994. Car park, garden, bar billiards, skittle alley and brewery trips. Children allowed. Just by the railway station.

12–11pm Mon–Sat.

Stoke on Trent

Titanic Brewery

Unit G, Harvey Works,
Lingard Street, Burslem,
Stoke on Trent ST6 1ED
☎ *(01782) 823447*
Visitors welcome. Tied houses: 2

The award-winning Titanic Brewery was founded in 1985 and moved to larger premises in 1992. It is based in Burslem, one of the five towns that join together to form Stoke on Trent. The brewery was named in honour of Captain Smith, captain of the Titanic, who hailed from the Potteries. Titanic Brewery is an honorary member of the Titanic Society and regularly makes contributions to the RNLI.

Beers available at: The Bull's Head, 14 St John's Square, Burslem, Stoke on Trent, Staffordshire *and* The Stafford Arms, Railway Street, Stafford, Staffordshire.

BEST BITTER 3.5% ABV
A refreshing clean-drinking, hoppy, amber/gold bitter. Fruit malt and predominantly hops carry through to the aftertaste.

LIFEBOAT ALE 3.9% ABV
A fruity and malty, red/brown, bittersweet beer, with a slight caramel character. The finish is dry and fruity.

PREMIUM BITTER 4.1% ABV
An impressive pale brown golden beer with a strong fruit and hops aroma. The taste is bitter and very hoppy.

STOUT 4.5% ABV
A true old-fashioned stout. A dark combination of malt and roast with some hops. Strongly flavoured and well balanced.

CAPTAIN SMITH'S STRONG ALE 4.8% ABV
A red/brown, full-bodied beer, hoppy and bitter with a malty sweetness and roast malt flavour and a good strong finish.

WHITE STAR 4.8% ABV
A light refreshing distinctively hoppy beer with a freshness which belies its strength.

WRECKAGE 7.8% ABV
A dark, full-flavoured winter brew.

The Rising Sun

Knowle Bank Road, Shraley Brook, Audley, Stoke on Trent ST7 8DS
☎ *(01782) 720600*

Eight beers brewed and available on the premises plus guest beers which might include brews from Adnams, Ash Vine, Hall & Woodhouse, Bateman, Charles Wells etc. etc.

The brewery began production in June 1989. The Rising Sun is an old beer-drinker's pub with a large bar and tap room. Bar and restaurant food served at lunchtime and evenings. Car park, garden. Children allowed. Three miles from M6 junction 16.

SUNLIGHT 3.5% ABV
Brewed in summer only.

RISING 3.3% ABV

SETTING 4.6% ABV
Popular hoppy beer.

PORTER 4.6% ABV
Rich-tasting, full-bodied dark brew.

DUSK 4.7% ABV
Fruity tasting, darker brew.

SUNSTROKE 5.0% ABV

TOTAL ECLIPSE 6.3% ABV
Heavy beer, popular with women.

SOLAR FLARE 11.0% ABV
Brewed in winter only.

12–3.30pm Mon–Thurs; all day from 12pm Fri–Sun.

The Bull's Head

14 St John's Square, Burslem, Stoke on Trent SR6 3AJ
☎ *(01782) 834153*
Keith Bott

Titanic Best, Lifeboat, Premium, Stout, Captain Smith's and White Star always available plus four guests (400 per year) which may include Crouch Vale Millennium Gold, Fuller's London Pride, Burton Bridge Summer Ale, Sarah Hughes Ruby Mild and many more.

A sixteenth-century pub with two rooms and open fires. No food. Nearby parking, garden. Children allowed. Easy to find in the town centre.

12–2.30pm and 5–11pm Mon–Thurs; 12–11pm Fri; 12–3pm and 6.30–11pm Sat; 12–3pm and 7–10.30pm Sun.

Malt 'n' Hops

295 King Street, Fenton, Stoke on Trent SR4 3EJ
☎ *(01782) 313406*
Mr and Mrs Turner

Six beers permanently available from an ever-changing range (at least 15 per week) with the focus on small breweries.

A traditional pub with a homely atmosphere. Sandwiches only. On the main A50 road, one mile from Longton railway station.

12–3pm and 7–11pm.

Bungay

Green Dragon

29 Broad Street,
Bungay NR35 1EE
☎ *(01986) 892681*
William and Rob Pickard

Adnams Bitter plus the four beers in the Green Dragon range brewed and available on the premises.

The Green Dragon was purchased from Brent Walker in 1991 by William and Rob Pickard. The three-barrel brewery was built and the pub refurbished. Due to increased demand, a second brewery was then built and the capacity expanded to eight barrels. The Green Dragon is a popular pub with a friendly atmosphere. Bar food is available at lunchtime and evenings. Car park, garden, children's room.

MILD 3.4% ABV

CHAUCER ALE 3.7% ABV

BRIDGE STREET BITTER 4.5% ABV

DRAGON 5.5% ABV

11am–3pm and 5–11pm Mon–Thurs; 11am–11pm Fri–Sat; 12–3pm and 7–10.30pm Sun

Chequers Inn

23 Bridge Street,
Bungay NR35 1HD
☎ *(01986) 893579*
Mr and Mrs Godbold

Adnams Bitter is among those beers always available plus three guest beers from breweries such as Smiles, Hadrian, Cains, Burton Bridge, Morland, Thwaites, Dent, Fuller's, Burts, Daleside, Oakhill, Youngs, Hoskins & Oldfield and Exmoor.

A small sixteenth-century inn used by discerning drinkers. Bar food available at lunchtime (Monday to Friday only). Car park and garden. Children allowed. Situated down the hill just outside the town centre.

12–3pm and 5–11pm Mon–Thurs; all day Fri–Sat; 12–3pm and 7–10.30pm Sun.

Bury St Edmunds

Greene King

Westgate Brewery,
Westgate Street,
Bury St Edmunds IP33 1QT
☎ *(01284) 763222*
Visitors welcome by arrangement
Tied houses: 863

The history of brewing in Bury St Edmunds has been traced back to 1086, when ale brewers ("cerevisiarii") were mentioned as servants of Bury Abbey in the Domesday Book. Two hundred years after this, Abbot Ale was brewed in the monastery's own brewery with natural spring water drawn from its own well. Today water is still drawn from the same source and local barley is still used to make the same Abbot Ale. In 1799, at only 19 years of age, Benjamin Greene began to brew his own beer in Bury St Edmunds. Frederick King, a well established maltster, set up a rival brewery just down the road. Friendly competition developed until 1887, when the two breweries joined forces and Greene King was born.

GREENE KING XX DARK MILD 3.0% ABV
A full-bodied mild with malty overtones and a hint of chocolate.

GREENE KING IPA 3.6% ABV
Belies its gravity with its body and depth of flavour. Distinctively bitter with subtle, complex flavours that gradually reveal themselves leaving a fine clean finish.

RAYMENTS SPECIAL BITTER 4.0% ABV
A full, fruity flavour with smooth malty overtones.

ABBOT ALE 5.0% ABV
One of the great characters of the beer world. A complex beer, estery yet robustly bitter. Immense full-bodied flavour.

Plus a range of seasonal and occasional brews including:
KING'S CHAMPION (3.8% ABV)
THE SORCERER (4.5% ABV)
WINTER ALE (6.0% ABV)
MAD JUDGE and **BLACK BARON**.

CLARE

NETHERGATE BREWERY

11–13 High Street,
Clare CO10 8NY
☎ *(01787) 277244*
Visitors welcome. Tied houses: 2

The Nethergate Brewery was founded in 1986 and produces beers using totally traditional methods.

Beers available at: Bell Hotel, Market Hill, Clare, Sudbury, Suffolk *and* Cambridge Blue, 85 Gwydir Street, Cambridge.

NETHERGATE IPA 3.6% ABV
Light session beer.

UMBEL ALE 3.8% ABV
Brewed with coriander seeds to create an unusual herbal, spicy flavour.

NETHERGATE BITTER 4.0% ABV
Copper-coloured ale.

NETHERGATE GOLDEN GATE 4.5% ABV

OLD GROWLER 5% ABV
Dark and smooth porter ale.

UMBEL MAGNA 5.5% ABV
Also brewed with coriander.

FRAMSDEN

The Doberman

The Street, Framsden
Nr Stowmarket
☎ *(01473) 890461*
Sue Frankland

Adnams Bitter and Broadside always available and guests such as Felinfoel Double Dragon, Charles Wells Bombardier, Morland Old Speckled Hen, Smiles and Everard's brews.

A 400-year-old, traditional thatched and beamed Suffolk village pub. Bar food available. Car park, garden, accommodation. Children not allowed. Easy to find.

11.30am–2.30pm and 7–11pm Mon–Sat;
12–3pm and 7–10.30pm Sun.

IPSWICH

TOLLEMACHE & COBBOLD BREWERY

Cliff Road,
Ipswich IP3 0AZ
☎ *(01473) 231723*
Visitors welcome. Tied houses: 1

Thomas Cobbold built his first brewery at Harwich in 1723. However, problems with the water supply saw the business move to Cliff Quay in Ipswich in 1746. The merger with the Tollemaches finally took place in 1957 and the company remained in family hands until the late 1970s. After two changes of ownership in the 1980s, the brewery closed in 1989 and the brewing of the Suffolk ales was transferred to the Lion Brewery in Hartlepool. However, one year later, following a successful management buy-out, the Hon Peter Strutt, company chairman, raised the Tolly Cobbold flag above the Cliff Brewery once again. Today, the company is thriving and featured in Sir John Harvey-Jones's *Troubleshooter* television series. The brewery tap opened in 1992.

Beers available at: The Butt and Oyster, The Quay, Pin Mill, Chelmondiston, Suffolk *and* The Woolpack, 1 Tuddenham Road, Ipswich, Suffolk.

TOLLY MILD 3.2% ABV
A dark mild with a smooth distinctive malt flavour.

TOLLY BITTER 3.5% ABV
A session pint with a distinctive hop aroma and clean sharp taste.

TOLLY ORIGINAL BEST BITTER 3.8% ABV
A very full-bodied beer, well balanced.

COBBOLD'S IPA 4.2% ABV
A light golden best bitter with a hop nose character.

TOLLY'S OLD STRONG 5.0% ABV
Strong winter ale, noted for its full body and rich malty character.

TOLLYSHOOTER PREMIUM BITTER 5.0% ABV
A premium bitter with a rich ruby colour and a satisfying taste.

Also a range of bottled beers.

The Plough

2 Dog's Head Street,
Ipswich IP4 1AD
☎ *(01473) 288005*
Stuart Greaney

Marston's Bitter and Pedigree permanently available plus nine guest beers (100s per year) from breweries such as Black Sheep, Adnams, Titanic, Nethergate, Exmoor, Cotleigh, Morland, Shepherd Neame, Daleside, Burton Bridge, Bateman, Cains, Caledonian, Coachouse, Gale's and Jennings.

A traditional ale house with wooden floors. Bar food is available at lunchtime. Children allowed. Next to the old cattle market bus station.

11am–3pm and 5–11.30pm Mon–Thur; 11am–11pm Fri–Sat; 7–10.30pm Sun.

The Tap & Spile

76 St Helens Street,
Ipswich
☎ *(01473) 211270*

Eight beers always available (160 per year) from a wide range of ales offered by independent brewers from all parts of the United Kingdom.

A traditional alehouse. Bar food is served at lunchtime (except Sunday). Car park, garden and children's room. Close to Suffolk College and County Hall.

11am–3pm and 5–11pm Mon–Wed; 11am–11pm Thur–Sat; 12–3pm and 7–10.30pm Sun.

Kersey

The Bell

Kersey.
☎ *(01473) 823229*
Paul Denton

Three or four beers always available plus brews from a guest list including Shepherd Neame Spitfire, Fuller's London Pride, Adnams Bitter and Greene King Abbot.

Built in 1380, a timber-framed Tudor-style property with log fires and cobbles. Bar and restaurant food available at lunchtime and evenings. Car park, garden, private dining room. Children allowed. Signposted from Hadleigh.

11am–3pm and 6.30–11pm Mon–Sat; 12–3pm and 7–10.30pm Sun.

Lowestoft

The Green Jack Brewing Company

Oulton Broad Brewery,
Harbour Road Industrial Estate,
Oulton Broad, Lowestoft NR32 3LZ
☎ *(01502) 587905*
Visitors welcome. Tied houses: 1

Tim Dunford set up the Green Jack Brewing Company in Lowestoft in November 1993 on the site of the Forbes Brewery. The attached brewery bar has been refurbished.

Beers available at: Triangle Tavern, 29 St Peter's Street, Lowestoft, Suffolk.

GREEN JACK MOILD 3.0% ABV

GREEN JACK BITTER 3.5% ABV

SUMMER DREAM 4.0% ABV
Available May to August.

OLD THUNDER BOX 4.0% ABV
Available September to March.

BEST BITTER 4.5% ABV

GOLDEN SICKLE 5.0% ABV

NORFOLK WOLF PORTER 5.2% ABV

LURCHER 6.0% ABV

SANTA'S SACK 7.0% ABV
Christmas ale.

RIPPER 8.5% ABV

The Triangle Tavern

29 St Peter's Street
Lowestoft BR32 1QA
☎ *(01502) 582711*
Hayley Little

Green Jack Bitter, Best and Golden Sickle always available plus other Green Jack brews and three guests, one always from an East Anglian brewery, the others from smaller independent breweries. At least one Belgian beer always available on draught.

Owned by the Green Jack Brewing Company and overlooking the old market place, a two-bar pub. Rolls available at lunchtime. Parking nearby. Children allowed.

11am–11pm.

SOUTHWOLD

ADNAMS & CO.

Sole Bay Brewery,
Southwold IP18 6JW
☎ *(01502) 727200*

Trade visits welcome. Tied houses: 100

Ale has been brewed in Southwold for the past 650 years. In fact, on 6 December 1345 Johanna de Corby and 17 other "ale wives" of Southwold were charged by the manorial court with breaking the assize of ale. Undeterred, Johanna made regular court appearances over the next 20 years charged with selling ale in unmarked measures, at too high a price or of too poor a quality. Subsequently, business centred on The Swan, a medieval tavern and the most important inn in town. After Southwold was burnt to the ground by a fire in 1659, The Swan was rebuilt by John Rous. For most of the eighteenth century, The Swan was owned by the Thompson family. In 1818 it was bought by Thomas Bokenham, who made expensive alterations and built himself a grand house next door. Burdened by debt, Bokenham sold the brewhouse at the back of The Swan to William Crisp, a local maltster, who paid £350. Under Crisp's ownership, the Sole Bay Brewery became famous. He died in 1844 and it passed through a succession of owners until the arrival of George and Earnest Adnams, from Berkshire, in 1872. Adnams and Company was established on 22 March 1890. The directors bought pubs, rebuilt the brewery, constructed and enlarged hotels. Jack and Pierse Loftus arrived around the turn of the century and bought a stake in the company now burdened with debts. Pierse (PC) became MP for Lowestoft in 1932. RFB Coling and Edward Gaymer Parke did much to sustain the business as company secretaries. The former died in office aged 84, the latter retired in 1958 after 70 years' service to the company. A close-knit circle of families (the Sagins, Brabbens, Goffins and Says) all helped to sustain the brewery in the postwar years. Adnams survived the real ale depression of the 1960s and grew during the 1970s and 80s into the thriving operation of today. Among the present directors are members of the third and fourth generations of the Adnams family.

Beers available at: The Swan Hotel, Southwold, Suffolk *and* Lord Nelson, East Street, Southwold, Suffolk.

MILD 3.2% ABV
Traditional dark mild.

BITTER 3.7% ABV
Classic session bitter. Well-rounded with a distinctive, hoppy flavour.

OLD ALE 4.1% ABV
Rare, traditional winter warmer. Strong and dark with a rich malty flavour. Available October to March.

EXTRA 4.3% ABV
Late-hopped for extra taste.

BROADSIDE 4.7% ABV
Well-rounded, slightly bitter-sweet.

MAY DAY ALE 5.0% ABV
Light in colour, clean on the palate, with a lingering hop character.

BARLEY MOW 5.0% ABV
Strong harvest bitter, malty and full-bodied with a trace of nuttiness.

TALLY HO 7.0% ABV
Special quality beer brewed in December and matured in the cask.

Sudbury

Mauldons Brewery

7 Addison Road,
Chilton Industrial Estate,
Sudbury CO10 6YW
☎ *(01787) 311055*
Visitors welcome. Tied houses: None

Peter Mauldon, a former Watney's head brewer, set up this company in 1982. His family had their own local brewery in the late eighteenth century. The beer list changes frequently and is supplied to 150 free trade outlets in East Anglia and pubs further afield via wholesalers.

Beers available at: The Swan, The Street, Little Waldingfield, Nr Sudbury, Suffolk *and* Railway Tavern, 58 Station Road, Brightlingsea, Essex.

BEST BITTER 3.8% ABV
Well-balanced session beer with a hoppy bitterness and sweet malt.

ORIGINAL PORTER 3.8% ABV
A black beer with malt and roast malt flavours dominating.

MIDSUMMER GOLD 4.0% ABV
Light-coloured summer beer

EATANSWILL OLD XXXX 4.0% ABV
Uses the name used for Sudbury by Dickens in *Pickwick Papers*. A winter ale of deep red and brown hue, with well balanced fruit and malt plus a slight sweetness on the palate, ending in a pleasant roast bitterness.

SPECIAL BITTER 4.2% ABV
Hoppy, with a good bitter finish and some balancing malt.

SQUIRES BITTER 4.2% ABV
A best bitter with a good, malty aroma and a reasonably balanced flavour, which leans towards malt. Hops come through late and crisply into the aftertaste.

SUFFOLK PUNCH 4.8% ABV
A full bodied, strong bitter. The malt and fruit in the aroma are reflected in the taste and there is some hop character in the finish. Deep tawny-red in colour.

BLACK ADDER 5.3% ABV
Dark stout. Roast malt is strong in the aroma and taste, but malt, hop and bitterness provide an excellent balance and a lingering finish. Champion Beer of Britain 1991.

WHITE ADDER 5.3% ABV
Almost golden strong ale. A warming, fruity flavour dominates.

SUFFOLK COMFORT 6.6% ABV
A clean, hoppy nose leads to a malty flavour.

Walton

The Tap & Spile

303 High Street,
Walton
☎ *(01394) 282130*
Mr Wheeler

Eight beers always available, changed regularly but possibly including Nethergate and Greene King brews plus Woodforde's Wherry.

Old fashioned, friendly Suffolk town pub. Bar food available at lunchtime. Car park, garden, children's play area. Children over 14 allowed in bar.

11am–3pm and 5–11pm Mon–Thurs; 11am–11pm Fri–Sat; 11am–3pm and 7–10.30pm Sun.

Coldharbour

The Plough Inn

Coldharbour Lane,
Coldharbour,
Nr Dorking RH5 6HD
☎ *(01306) 711793*
Mr and Mrs Abberhart

Eight beers always available from Ringwood, Hall & Woodhouse, Adnams, Gibbs Mew and Bateman. Plus a guest beer each month including seasonal brews, milds, topical beers and special brews. Also farm cider.

A traditional family-run seventeenth-century pub. Allegedly the highest freehouse in south-east England. Bar and restaurant food is served at lunchtime and evenings. Car parking. Children allowed. Accommodation. Just over three miles south-west of Dorking.

11.30am–3pm and 6.30–11pm.

Englefield Green

The Beehive

34 Middle Hill,
Englefield Green,
Nr Egham TW20 0JQ
☎ *(01784) 431621*
Caren Middleton

Greene King Abbot, Gales HSB and Best permanently available plus four guest beers (50 per year) from breweries such as Adnams, Bateman, Everards, Hoskins & Oldfield, Kemptown, Nethergate, Oldbury, Orkney, Thwaites and Youngs. Beer festivals at May and August bank holidays.

A country pub now surrounded by expensive houses. Bar food is available at lunchtime and evenings. Car park and garden. Hard to find, but just off the A30 between Ferrari's and Royal Holloway College.

12–3pm and 5.30–11pm Mon–Fri; all day Sat and Sun.

Godalming

The Anchor Inn

110 Ockford Road,
Godalming GU7 1RG
☎ *(01483) 417085*
Mr and Mrs Jenkins

Hall & Woodhouse Tanglefoot, Hogs Back and Brakspear brews among those always available plus guests (60 per year) from Gales, Hop Back, Worldham, Ringwood, Titanic, Fuller's, Pilgrim, Wychwood and Greenwood.

A real ale pub with bar billiards and a good mix of clientele. Simple bar food available at lunchtime. Parking and beer garden. Situated on the edge of town on the main road.

12–3pm and 5.30–11pm.

Knaphill

The Garibaldi

136 High Street, Knaphill
☎ *(01483) 473374*
Mr Dennis

Four beers always available including Fuller's London Pride and Harvey's Best plus guests from Mole's and Gibbs Mew, also Hop Back Summer Lightning and others.

Two-bar local pub. Easy to find. Car park, garden. Accompanied children over 14 allowed.

11am–11pm Mon–Sat; 12–10.30pm Sun.

Reigate

Pilgrim Ales

The Old Brewery, West Street, Reigate RH2 9BL
☎ *(01737) 225785*
Visitors welcome by arrangement (open days on last Friday of each month).
Tied houses: 2

Pilgrim Ales was set up in Woldingham, Surrey, in January 1982 by David Roberts. The award-winning business moved to Reigate three years later and is now a ten-barrel brew-length operation.

Beers available at: William IV, Little Common Lane, Bletchingley, Surrey *and* The Ship Inn, High Street, Ripley, Surrey.

SURREY BITTER 3.7% ABV
Well-balanced session beer, light colour, fruity character.

PORTER 4.0% ABV
Rich and smooth, dark and full of character.

PROGRESS BEST BITTER 4.0% ABV
Rich and smooth ruby ale with a subtle hop aroma.

CRUSADER 4.9% ABV
Golden bitter, light and delicate, but strong. Available only in summer.

TALISMAN 5% ABV
Winter warmer, malty, roasty, with a hint of sweetness.

Plus a range of seasonal and occasional brews including:
AUTUMNAL (4.5% ABV)
EXCALIBUR (4.5% ABV)
SARACEN STOUT (4.5% ABV)
SPRING BOCK (5.2% ABV)
CONQUEROR (6.2% ABV)
GREAT CRUSADER (6.5% ABV) and
PUDDING (7.3% ABV).

Shackleford

The Shackleford Brewery

Cyder House Inn, Peperharow Lane, Shackleford, Godalming GU8 6AN
☎ *(01483) 810360*
Ted Gibbs

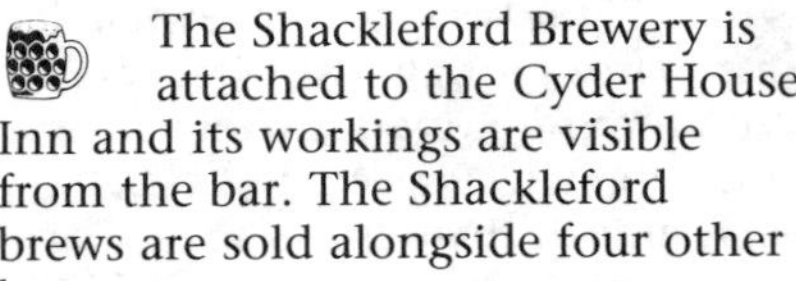
The Shackleford Brewery is attached to the Cyder House Inn and its workings are visible from the bar. The Shackleford brews are sold alongside four other beers.

The brewery was set up in 1992 and also supplies beer to the Thurlow Arms at Cranleigh. The Cyder House is a country pub in a beautiful location. Bar and restaurant food is available at lunchtime and evenings. Private function room available. Car park, garden. Children allowed.

PISTON BROKE 4.0% ABV

NORFOLK N' CHANCE 4.6% ABV

OLD SHACKLE 4.8% ABV
An occasional brew.

OVERDRAUGHT 4.8% ABV
A Christmas brew.

11am–3pm and 5.30–11pm Mon–Fri; 11am–11pm Sat; 12–10.30pm Sun.

Tongham

Hogs Back Brewery

Manor Farm, The Street, Tongham GU10 1DE
☎ *(01252) 783000*
Visitors welcome. Tied houses: None

Hogs Back Brewery was set up in 1992. It occupies five large restored farm buildings dating from 1768 and brews 12 different real ales to a traditional style and standard. The brewery has a busy off-licence and brewery fayre shop and regularly organises tours around the plant. Brewery merchandise is available and more than 400 bottled beers from Belgium plus 100 from England are on sale.

Beers available at: Prince of Wales, 184 Rectory Road, Farnborough, Hampshire *and* Nellie Dene's, Farnham Road, Elstead, Surrey.

DARK MILD 3.4% ABV
Smooth and easy to drink.

APB (A-PINTA-BITTER) 4.2% ABV
Tasty session bitter.

TEA (TRADITIONAL ENGLISH ALE) 4.2% ABV
Award-winning best bitter, well-balanced hops and malt.

BLACKWATER PORTER 4.4% ABV
Smooth and full flavoured.

BSA (BURMA STAR ALE) 4.5% ABV
Malty amber ale, lingering aftertaste.

HOP GARDEN GOLD 4.6% ABV
A well-hopped golden ale.

RIP SNORTER 5.0% ABV
Deep, red, rich malty and fruity.

YES (YOUR EVERY SUCCESS) 5.0% ABV
Well-hopped malt-wheat pale yellow ale.

OTT (OLD TONGHAM TASTY) 6.0% ABV
Strong dark winter brew.

BREWSTERS BUNDLE 7.5% ABV
Strong golden ale, well hopped.

SANTA'S WOBBLE 7.5% ABV
Very strong Christmas ale.

A-OVER-T (AROMAS OVER TONGHAM) 9.0% ABV
Rich and full flavoured.

WINDLESHAM

The Windmill

London Road, Windlesham, Surrey, GU20 6PJ
☎ (01276) 472281
Richard and Sandra Hailstone

Thirteen real ales available at any one time. Hop Back Summer Lightning, Adnams Broadside, Bishops Tipple permanently available plus guests (up to 700 per year) including brews from Ringwood Brewery, Hampshire Brewery, Archers, Greenwoods, Hogs Back, Pilgrim, Rebellion, Adnams, Gibbs Mew. Always willing to support micro breweries and will try any new brews. Three beer festivals each year, with 100 beers at each festival.

Small, friendly pub with two bars and a dining area. No pool tables. Food available. Car park. Large beer garden. Children allowed under parental control. Situated on the main A30.

11am–11pm

WRECCLESHAM

The Sandrock

Sandrock Hill Road, Farnham GU10 4NS
☎ *(01252) 715865*
Mr and Mrs Bayliff

Eight beers available. Batham, Enville and Brakspear brews always on offer plus guests (100 per year) from Holden's, Hampshire, Ballards, Hogs Back and Cheriton etc.

A small, no-frills pub, specialising in Midlands beers. CAMRA pub of the year. Bar food available at lunchtimes (except Sunday). Car park and garden. Children allowed. Along the bypass, left at roundabout onto the A325, left into School Hill, over the crossroads into Sandrock Hill Road.

All day every day.

Battle

The Squirrel Inn

North Trade Road,
Battle TN33 9LJ
☎ *(01424) 772717*
Mr and Mrs Wood

Harvey's ales and Fuller's London Pride permanently available plus several guest beers (200 per year) including Rother Valley Level Best and brews from Gales and Mansfield etc. New and seasonal beers ordered as and when available.

An eighteenth-century old drover's pub in beautiful Sussex countryside, surrounded by fields. Family-run freehouse. Unspoilt public bar with log fires. New restaurant (suitable for functions and weddings). Two large beer gardens, ample parking, purpose-built children's room. Families welcome. Located just outside Battle on the A271.

OPEN *11am–3pm and 5–11pm Mon–Fri; 11am–11pm Sat; 12–10.30pm Sun.*

Brighton

The Kemptown Brewery

The Hand in Hand,
33 Upper St James's Street,
Kemptown, Brighton BN2 1JN
☎ *(01273) 602521*

The brewery produces a range of seven ales which are on sale in The Hand in Hand.

The idea of building a brewery at The Hand in Hand followed a lively evening at the Great British Beer Festival in Leeds in 1988. Plans were drawn up after extracting many prototype versions jotted down on various beer mats and cigarette packets. Work commenced in December 1988 and the first brew was produced in November 1989. The Hand in Hand is probably the smallest brewpub in England, and the brewery is probably the smallest of the traditional tower breweries. The original Kemptown Brewery started operating around 1849 and ceased brewing in 1964. Bar food is available at lunchtime and evenings. Parking. Children not allowed.

BUDGET BITTER 3.5% ABV

BITTER 4.0% ABV

CREWSAVER 4.5% ABV

TIPPER'S TIPPLE 4.5% ABV

CELEBRATED STAGGERING ALE 5.0% ABV

STAGGERING IN THE DARK (SID) 5.2% ABV

OLD GRUMPY 6.0% ABV

11am–11pm Mon–Sat; 12–10.30pm Sun.

SKINNER'S ALES

The Evening Star,
55–56 Surrey Street,
Brighton BN1 3PB
☎ *(01273) 328931*
Peter Skinner and Rob Jones

Nine real ales always available, rotating constantly from a guest list running into thousands. Skinner's and Dark Star brews always available.

Skinner's Brewery was established in 1994 using a unique space-saving full-mash mini-brewing system. Production began in December 1994. In July 1995, Peter Skinner teamed up with brewer Rob Jones, who founded the Pitfield Brewery in 1981 and, more recently, the Brewery on Sea in Sussex. Together, they founded the Dark Star Brewing Company. The Evening Star is a specialist real ale house with wooden floors and church pews. It has sold more than 1,200 different beers since opening in 1992. Bar food is available at lunchtime. Children not allowed. Just 150 yards from railway station.

ALE TRAIL ROAST MILD 3.5% ABV

PALE ALE 3.7% ABV

42 4.2% ABV

OLD ALE 4.2% ABV

PENGUIN STOUT 4.2% ABV

OLD FAMILIAR 5.0% ABV

SUMMER HAZE 5.0% ABV

DARK STAR 5.0% ABV

CLIFF HANGER PORTER 5.5% ABV

MELTDOWN 6.0% ABV

PAVILION BEAST 6.0% ABV

12–11pm Mon–Sat;
12–10.30pm Sun.

Lion and Lobster

24 Sillwood Street,
Brighton BN1 2PS
☎ *(01273) 776961*
Jack Harding

Five guest beers (200 per year) which might include Hall & Woodhouse Tanglefoot, Morland Old Speckled Hen, Timothy Taylor Landlord, Harvey's Best, Spinnaker Buzz and Hyde's Anvil Bitter.

An Irish family-run pub with a great atmosphere. All ages welcome. Bar and restaurant food available at lunchtime and evenings. Parking and children's room. Located 200 yards from the seafront, in between the Bedford Hotel and Norfolk Hotel.

11am–11pm Mon–Sat;
12–3pm and 7–10.30pm Sun.

Exceat Bridge

Cuckmere Haven Brewery

*The Golden Galleon,
Exceat Bridge, Cuckmere Haven,
Seaford BN25 4AB*
☎ *(01323) 892247*
Stefano Diella

Cuckmere Haven Best etc. plus a range of guest beers (300 per year) including Greene King IPA, Shepherd Neame Bishop's Finger and Crouch Vale, Black Sheep, Ballards, Adnams and Timothy Taylor brews.

They have been brewing here since 1994 in very small five-barrel tanks. Planning permission for a pub extension will allow a move from an existing outbuilding into the pub. This should take place in early 1997. The pub is a prominent, fourteenth-century, black and white timbered building in the Cuckmere valley with beams and open fires in winter. Bar and restaurant food is available at lunchtime and evenings. Car park, garden, conservatory, no-smoking room. Accommodation. Children allowed, but not near the bar. Open all day at weekends in summer. Off the A259 on the River Cuckmere. Two miles from Seaford railway station.

BEST BITTER 4.1% ABV

SAXON KING STOUT 4.2% ABV

GENTLEMEN'S GOLD 4.5% ABV

GUVN'ER 4.7% ABV

11am–3pm and 5.30–11pm Mon–Sat; 11am–11pm Sun.

Frant

Abergavenny Arms

Frant Road, Frant
☎ *(01892) 750233*
Les Brackley

Eleven beers available including Rother Valley Level Best and Harvey's brews plus 400 guests per year including Exe Valley Devon Glory and many, many micro-brews.

Built in the 1430s, a large, two-bar country pub. The lounge bar was used as a courtroom in the eighteenth century, with cells in the cellar. Bar and restaurant food available at lunchtime and evenings. Car park, garden. Children allowed. Easy to find.

11am–3pm and 6–11pm Mon–Sat; 12–3pm and 7–10.30pm Sun.

Hove

Belchers Brewery

The Hedgehog and Hogshead
100 Goldstone Villas,
Hove BN3 3RX

☎ *(01273) 733660*

Seven Belchers brews are available at The Hedghog and Hogshead.

The brewery was started in 1990 by David Bruce, founder of the Firkin pub chain, and is currently owned and operated by Grosvenor Inns plc, who, along with D Bruce (director), are now expanding the brand into London and beyond. The Hedgehog and Hogshead is an upmarket traditional pub with the emphasis on own brews and quality food. Food available at lunchtime and evenings. Garden. Children not allowed. Five minutes from Brighton and seafront.

BELCHER'S ORIGINAL 3.8% ABV
Aromatic, hoppy quaffing ale.

BELCHER'S BEST BITTER 4.2% ABV
Balanced, slightly dry bitter.

OLD SLUG PORTER 4.2% ABV

BELCHER'S BOOTLEG 5.2% ABV
Full-bodied premium ale.

NEW BARBARIAN 5.2% ABV

HOGBOLTER 5.8% ABV

11am–11pm Mon–Sat;
12–10.30pm Sun.

Lewes

Harvey & Son

The Bridge Wharf Brewery,
6 Cliffe High Street,
Lewes BN7 2AH
☎ *(01273) 480209*
Visitors welcome, but there is a two-year waiting list. Tied houses: 37

This independent family concern was established in 1790 and operates from the Bridge Wharf Brewery on the banks of the River Ouse in Lewes. The brewery was re-built in 1881 and a major development in 1985 doubled the brewhouse capacity. Subsequent additional fermenting capacity has seen production rise to in excess of 30,000 barrels per year.

MILD ALE 3.0% ABV
Dark traditional mild, brewed all the year round. Well-balanced with a soft, slightly sweet palate.

SUSSEX PALE ALE 3.5% ABV
Originally brewed during the last war, when materials were strictly rationed. A well-balanced, well-hopped bitter.

SUSSEX BEST BITTER 4.0% ABV
A full, well-hopped bitter.

ARMADA ALE 4.5% ABV
A premium bitter, born from the bottled ale of the same name. Dry-hopped in the cask to produce a dry, bitter palate and a splendid aroma of hops.

Plus seasonal ales including:
KNOTS OF MAY LIGHT MILD (3.0% ABV)
SUSSEX XXXX OLD ALE (4.3% ABV)
1859 PORTER (4.8% ABV)
TOM PAINE (5.5% ABV)
CHRISTMAS ALE (8.1% ABV) and a range of bottled beers.

The Gardener's Arms

45 Cliffe High Street,
Lewes BN7 2AN
☎ *(01273) 474808*
Peter Skinner

Brews from Skinner's of Brighton and Dark Star Brewing Co. permanently available plus several guests (100s per year) from small independents such as Newale Brewing, Hogs Back, Reckless Eric etc.

Sister-pub of the Evening Star, Brighton. No juke box or games machines. Wooden floor, wooden tables and chairs. Bar food available at lunchtime. Parking. Opposite the Harvey's Brewery.

11am–3pm Mon–Wed; all day Thurs–Sat; usual Sun hours.

LITLINGTON

The Plough and Harrow

Litlington, Nr Alfriston BN26 5RE
☎ *(01323) 870631*
Roger Taylor

Hall & Woodhouse Badger Best and Tanglefoot permanently available plus four guests from a large list including Wadworth 6X, Charles Wells Bombardier and Eagle IPA, Fuller's London Pride and brews from Harveys and Buchanans.

A fifteenth-century freehouse with oak beams, two bars and a busy restaurant. Bar and restaurant food is available. Car park and garden. Children allowed in the restaurant. Three miles south of the A27, two miles from the nearest village of Alfriston.

11am–2.30pm and 6.30–11pm.

NORTHIAM

ROTHER VALLEY BREWING CO.

Gate Court, Northiam,
Rye TN31 6QT
☎ *(01797) 252922*
Visitors welcome. Tied houses: 1

The company was founded in 1992 and commenced brewing in August of that year on a farm in the Rother Valley. It is committed to brewing with raw materials sourced as locally as possible. All hops used are grown on the farm, a proportion of malt used is also grown on the farm and yeast is regularly propagated in the brewhouse from a pure culture. There are plans to sink a borehole for water to complete the entire sourcing of raw materials on site.

Beers available at: Cafe Moulin, The Mill, Station Road, Northiam, Rye, East Sussex *and* The Three Oaks, Butchers Lane, Nr Guestling, Hastings, East Sussex.

LEVEL BEST 4.0% ABV
A malty and hoppy beer with a pronounced long, dry finish.

OLD HEATHFIELD

The Star

Church Street,
Old Heathfield TN21 9AH
☎ *(01435) 863570*
Mr and Mrs Chappell

Harvey's brews and Fuller's London Pride always available plus a guest (50 per year) such as Harviestoun Ptarmigan, Hop Back Summer Lightning, Black Sheep Best; also Daleside Old Legover, Gravesend Shrimpers, NYBC Flying Herbert, Daleside Monkey Wrench and Burton Bridge Hearty Ale etc.

A freehouse built in 1348, licensed in 1388. Original beams and open fires. Famous gardens and views. Bar and restaurant food served at lunchtime and evenings. Car park and garden. Children allowed. At a dead end of a road to the rear of Old Heathfield church.

11.30am–3pm and 5.30–11pm.

ST LEONARDS ON SEA

The Dripping Spring

34 Tower Road,
St Leonards on Sea RN37 6JE
(01424) 434055
Mr and Mrs Gillitt

Arkells 3B and Fuller's London Pride plus at least one local beer from the Pett Brewing Co. Other guests (100 per year) from as far afield as possible, preferably four per cent and over.

A small two-bar public house with attractive courtyard to the rear. Bar food available at lunchtime. Car parking. Situated in a side street off the A21.

11am–3pm and 5–11pm Mon–Thurs; all day Fri–Sun.

TICEHURST

The Bull Inn

Dunster Mill Lane, Three Legged Cross, Nr Ticehurst TN5 7HH
☎ *(01580) 200586*
Mrs Josie Wilson-Moir

Seven beers available including Rother Valley Level Best, Morland Old Speckled Hen, King & Barnes Sussex and Harvey's brews plus hundreds of guests per year including brews from Adnams, Iceni etc.

Whealden Hall House was built between 1385 and 1425 in good walking country and has been a pub for 100 years. There are two bars with an adjoining restaurant. Food available at lunchtime and evenings (not Sunday and Monday evenings). Car park, garden, children's play area. Coming into Ticehurst from the north on the B2099, turn left beside corner house called Tollgate just before village.

11am–3pm and 6–11pm Mon–Sat; 12–3pm and 7–10.30pm Sun.

West Ashling

Richmond Arms

Mill Lane,
West Ashling
☎ *(01243) 575730*

Morland Old Speckled Hen, Timothy Taylor Landlord etc always available plus six or seven guest beers (60 per year) which may include Merriman's Old Fart, Uley Pigor Mortis and Crouch Vale Willie Warmer.

A friendly village local with two comfortably furnished bar areas, open fires, part wood-panelled walls. Bar and restaurant food is available at lunchtime and evenings. Car park, bar billiards, skittle alley, duck racing in nearby river (wooden ducks hanging on the wall in the bar), small terrace with picnic benches. Families and dogs welcome.

11am–3pm and 5.30–11pm Mon–Sat; 12–10.30pm Sun.

Yapton

The Maypole

Maypole Lane,
Yapton BN18 OPP
☎ *(01243) 551417*

Ringwood Best and a mild always available plus four guests (60 per year) such as Cotleigh Barn Owl Bitter, Oakhill Black Magic, B&T Black Bat, Brakspear Old Ale, Hook Norton Best, Jolly Boat and Plunder. A beer festival is held twice a year.

A pub built in 1760. Three bars, skittle alley and pool room. Bar and restaurant food available at lunchtime and evenings. Car park and garden. Children allowed in the restaurant. Hard to find, up a lane.

11am–2.30pm and 5.30–11pm

ARUNDEL

ARUNDEL BREWERY

Ford Airfield Estate,
Arundel BN18 0BE
☎ *(01903) 733111*
Visitors welcome. Tied houses: 1

Founded in 1992, the Arundel Brewery is the historic town's first brewery in more than 50 years, marking the rebirth of a local traditional which had once been the town's main provider of employment and local pride. The brewery is committed to traditional brewing, using only the finest English whole hops and malt. No additives, artificial flavourings or supplementary sugars are used. Arundel Brewery also produces a number of celebratory beers each year which have gained a popular following.

Beers available at: The Swan Hotel, 27 High Street, Arundel, West Sussex *and* George and Dragon, Burpham, Nr Arundel, West Sussex.

ARUNDEL BEST BITTER 4.0% ABV
Well-balanced bitter. Hoppy, with a fruity dry aftertaste.

ARUNDEL GOLD 4.2% ABV
Clean, refreshing golden bitter. Well hopped with a bittersweet edge.

ARUNDEL STRONGHOLD 5.0% ABV
A smooth full-flavoured premium bitter with a distinctive hoppy aroma and finish.

OLD KNUCKER 5.5% ABV
Classic dark ale with a rich fruity flavour and subtle lingering bitterness.

Plus seasonal brews including: **SUMMER DAZE** (4.7% ABV), **OLD CONSPIRATOR** (5.0% ABV), **ROMEO'S ROUSER** (5.3% ABV) and **OLD SCROOGE** (6.0% ABV).

ASHURST

The Fountain Inn

Ashurst, Nr Steyning BN44 3AP
☎ *(01403) 710219*
Maurice Caine

King & Barnes Festive permanently available plus a constantly changing guest list including Young's Special, Shepherd Neame Spitfire Ale and Fuller's London Pride.

An unspoilt sixteenth-century inn with low beams, a flagstone floor and large inglenook fireplace. No machines or music. Bar and restaurant food served at lunchtime and evenings (not Sunday pm). Large car park and garden. Children allowed in the restaurant. Located on the B2135 north of Steyning between Shoreham by the Sea and Horsham.

11am–2.30pm and 6–11pm Mon–Sat; 12–2.30pm and 7–10.30pm Sun.

SUSSEX (WEST)

Burpham

The George and Dragon

Burpham, Nr Arundel BN18 9RR
☎ *(01903) 883131*
James Rose

Arundel Best and Harvey's Best permanently available plus five guest beers (100 per year) from breweries such as Woodforde, Hop Back, Cotleigh, Harviestoun, Ash Vine etc.

Located in a small village two miles from Arundel off the main track, with some of the best views of the Arun valley. Excellent walking all around. Bar and restaurant food available (restaurant evenings and Sunday lunch only). Car park. Children over 12 allowed.

11am–2.30pm and 6–11pm Mon–Sat; 12–3pm and 7–10.30pm Sun.

Compton

The Coach and Horses

Compton, Nr Chichester PO18 9HA
☎ *(01705) 631228*
David Butler

Fuller's ESB always available plus five guest beers (100s per year) from breweries including Cains, Adnams, Hampshire, Hop Back, Timothy Taylor and Hook Norton.

Situated on the Sussex Downs, a coaching inn built in 1500 with exposed beams and a Victorian extension. Bar and restaurant food is available at lunchtime and evenings. Car parking, garden and skittle alley. Children allowed. Good walking. Take the signed road to Uppark House (B2146).

11am–2.30pm and 6–11pm Mon–Sat; 12–3pm and 7–10.30pm Sun.

Elsted Marsh

Elsted Inn

Elsted Marsh GU29 0JT
☎ *(01730) 813662*

All Ballard's brews permanently available plus Fuller's London Pride and a guest beer (52 per year) usually from Arundel, Cheriton, Worldham and Brewery on Sea breweries.

Formerly owned by Ballard's, a friendly, old-fashioned Victorian railway pub. Restored inside, with wooden shutters, wood floor, open fires. Very cosy in winter, very cool in summer. No canned music or juke box. Good bar and restaurant food available at lunchtime and evenings. Car park, garden, boules pitch. Children allowed in garden. Accommodation. Off the A272 between Midhurst and Petersfield, marked Elsted and Harting.

11am–3pm and 5.30–11pm Mon–Fri (6–11pm Sat); 12–3pm and 7–10.30pm Sun.

Fishbourne

The Bull's Head

99 Fishbourne Road, Fishbourne, Nr Chichester PO19 3JP
☎ *(01243) 785707*
Roger Jackson

Gales beers always available plus five guests (150 per year) from traditional family brewers from Adnams to Young's and small independents from Ash Vine to Yates. Repeat favourites include Yates Bitter, the Kelham Island range, Brewery on Sea brews, Butterknowle Conciliation Ale and Hop Back Summer Lightning.

A converted seventeenth-century farmhouse with a country atmosphere just one mile from the city centre. Bar and restaurant food available at lunchtime and evenings except Sunday. Car park, garden and children's room. On the A259.

11am–3pm and 5.30–11pm Mon–Fri; 11am–11pm Sat; 12–10.30pm Sun.

HALFWAY BRIDGE

Halfway Bridge Inn

Halfway Bridge,
Nr Petworth GU28 9BP
☎ *(01798) 861281*
Simon and James Hawkins

Cheriton Pots Ale and Gales HSB always available plus two guests (100 per year) changed each week often from Brewery on Sea, Hampshire or Arundel breweries. Also local cider.

Built in 1710 on the A272 halfway between Midhurst and Petworth, an authentic staging post on the Dover to Winchester road. Four rooms around a central serving area, inglenook fireplace. Bar and restaurant food at lunchtime and evenings. Car park, garden, no-smoking area, traditional games. Children over 10 allowed.

11–3pm and 6–11pm Mon–Sat; 12–3pm and 7–11pm Sun.

HAYWARDS HEATH

The Star

1 The Broadway,
Haywards Heath RH16 3AQ
☎ *(01444) 413267*
Philip Jordon

Up to 13 beers. Marston's Pedigree, Fuller's London Pride, Brakspear Bitter, Greene King Abbot Ale and Morland Old Speckled Hen permanently available plus several guests (78 per year) including Timothy Taylor Landlord, Archer's Old Cobleigh, Hook Norton Old Hooky, Exmoor Gold and Hop Back Summer Lightning.

A large cask ale house in the town centre. Bar food served at lunchtime and evenings. Car park and garden. Accommodation. Follow the one-way system.

11am–11pm Mon–Sat; normal hours Sun.

HORSHAM

KING & BARNES

The Horsham Brewery,
18 Bishopric,
Horsham RH12 1QP
☎ *(01403) 270470*
Visitors by arrangement, but a long waiting list. Tied houses: 57

In 1850, James King, great-great-grandfather of the present company chairman, came to Horsham to trade at the Maltings in Bishopric. He soon formed links with Satchells' at nearby North Parade Brewery, which had been brewing since about 1800. The two businesses joined forces in 1870, and the brewing operation was transferred to the Bishopric site.

James King acquired control of the company. His sons, Charles, Frederick and John took over after his death and formed a limited company in 1893. A new well was dug and many modernisations took place. The Barnes family had also been brewing in Horsham since around 1800 and the two families united in 1906. The brewery has survived bleak times for such small family businesses and there have been major redevelopments in the past 25 years. Much of the plant has been updated and replaced.

Beers available at: The Bear Inn, Market Square, Horsham, West Sussex *and* Shakespeare's Head, 1 Chatham Place, Brighton, East Sussex.

SUSSEX 3.5%

MILD ALE 3.5% ABV
Sweet dark mild.

BROADWOOD 4.2% ABV
Medium-strength, full-flavoured best bitter.

OLD ALE 4.5% ABV
Full-bodied strong mild.

FESTIVE 5.0% ABV
Full-flavoured premium bitter.

CHRISTMAS 6.5% ABV
Liquid Christmas pudding.

Plus a range of guest beers including:
WEALDSMAN (3.8% ABV)
WHEATMASH (4.3% ABV)
HARVEST ALE (4.5% ABV)
RYE BEER (4.5% ABV)
SPRING ALE (4.5% ABV) and
CORN BEER (6.5% ABV)

Also bottle-conditioned brews.

LANCING

THE BREWERY ON SEA

Unit 24, Winston Business Centre
Chartwell Road,
Lancing BN15 8TU
☎ *(01903) 851482*
Trade visitors only, by arrangement.
Tied houses: None

Brewing started in June 1993 and the weekly capacity is now about 55 barrels. New seasonal beers are added to the range whenever possible. The beers are distributed locally and on a national basis by wholesalers.

Beers available at: The Vine, 27–29 High Street, Tarring, West Worthing, West Sussex *and* The Quadrant, Queens Road, Brighton, West Sussex.

SPINNAKER MILD/LANCING SPECIAL DARK 3.5% ABV
Dark in colour, rich in flavour.

SPINNAKER BITTER 3.5% ABV
Traditional bitter, brewed to a very drinkable strength with no compromise on flavour. A light, clean tasting bitter.

SPINNAKER CLASSIC 4.0% ABV
The original beer from the Brewery on Sea. A medium strength beer with a balanced flavour gained from using a pure malt mash and the finest hops.

SPINNAKER BUZZ 4.5% ABV
Light in colour, primed with pure honey and dry hopped with Goldings hops. The honey ferments as the beer conditions to give a very aromatic flavour.

SPECIAL CREW 5.5% ABV
A full-bodied, full-strength bitter which gains colour and flavour from a mix of pale and crystal malt.

BLACK ROCK 5.5% ABV
A tasty, dark, strong beer.

SPINNAKER GINGER 5.5% ABV
A strong, fine, pale beer brewed with pure ginger.

RIPTIDE 6.5% ABV
Premium ale and very strong.

MIDHURST

The Crown Inn

Edinburgh Square,
Midhurst GU29 9NL
☎ *(01730) 813462*
Paul Stevens

Fuller's London Pride permanently available plus up to eight guest beers (150 per year). Favoured breweries include Cheriton, Hampshire, Ballard's, Hogs Back, Arundel, Otter, Adnams, Archers, Hop Back, Ash Vine, Shepherd Neame, Nethergate, Wye Valley, Woodfordes etc.

A sixteenth-century traditional freehouse hosting two annual beer festivals. Bar and restaurant food served at lunchtime and evenings. Parking, garden, function/games room. Children allowed in the restaurant. Accommodation. Behind and below the church in the old part of the town.

11am–11pm Mon–Sat.

OVING

THE GRIBBLE BREWERY

The Gribble Inn,
Oving, Nr Chichester PO20 6BP
☎ *(01243) 786893*
Anne and Ron May

Gribble Ale, Reg's Tipple, Plucking Pheasant, Pig's Ear and Hall & Woodhouse Badger Best available. Plus seasonal ales from the brewery.

The Gribble Inn's new brewery is now four years old, and true to brewing traditions, uses only the best quality hops and malts with no additives or extra sugars. The picturesque sixteenth-century inn is a traditional village pub serving food at lunchtime and evenings. Car park, garden, children's room, skittle alley.

HARVEST PALE 2.7%

GRIBBLE ALE 4.1% ABV

REG'S TIPPLE 5.0% ABV

PLUCKING PHEASANT 5.2% ABV

BLACK ADDER II 5.8% ABV

PIG'S EAR OLD ALE 6.0% ABV

WOBBLER 7.2% ABV

11am–2.30pm and 6–11pm Mon–Sat; 12–3pm and 7–10.30pm Sun.

SUSSEX (WEST)

STOUGHTON

The Hare and Hounds

Stoughton
☎ *(01705) 631433*

Adnams Broadside, Ringwood Best and Gale's HSB permanently available plus four guest beers (endless list) such as Hop Back Summer Lightning, Timothy Taylor Landlord, Fuller's ESB, Brakspear etc.

More than 300 years old, a flint-built pub nestling in folds of the Sussex Downs. Bar food available at lunchtime and evenings. Car park and garden. Children allowed. Signposted at Walberton off the B2146.

11am–3pm and 6–11pm Mon–Sat; 12–4pm and 7–10.30pm Sun.

WEST CHILTINGTON

The Five Bells

Smock Alley,
West Chiltington RH20 2QX
☎ *(01798) 812143*

Five beers always available from an ever-changing range. Favoured brewers include Ballards, Adnams, Bateman, Black Sheep, Brakspear, Bunces, Cheriton, Exmoor, Fuller's, Gale's, Greene King, Guernsey, Harveys, Hogs Back, Hook Norton, Jennings, King & Barnes, Mansfield, Morrells, Palmers, St Austell, Shepherd Neame, Smiles, Samuel Smith, Timothy Taylor and Young's.

An attractive Edwardian-style version of a Sussex farmhouse. Bar and restaurant food available lunchtime and evenings. Car park, conservatory and beer garden. Well-behaved children allowed. Ask for directions.

11am–3pm and 6–11pm.

Byker

The Cumberland Arms

Byker Buildings,
Byker NE6 1LD
☎ *(0191) 265 6151*

Five beers always available from a constantly changing range (250 per year) but including Hadrian Legion, Centurion and Gladiator, Marston's Pedigree and Fuller's London Pride.

An unchanged pub established in 1832 overlooking the Ouseburn Valley. Well known for its live music (traditional and rock). No food available. Parking, garden under development. Children allowed in the function room. Over Byker Bridge, then first right, second right, above farm.

12–11pm Mon–Sat;
12–10.30pm Sun.

The Tap & Spile

33 Shields Road,
Byker NE6 1DJ
☎ *(0191) 276 1440*
Peter Bland

Twelve beers always available from a constantly changing range (450 per year) with names such as Bateman's Valiant, Charles Wells Eagle and Black Sheep Bitter among them.

Beamed theme pub with open fires and friendly atmosphere. Bar food available at lunchtime and evenings. Car park. Children allowed. Easy to find.

12–11pm Mon–Sat;
12–10.30pm Sun.

Gosforth

Gosforth Hotel

High Street, Gosforth
☎ *(0191) 285 6617*
John Burtle

Marston's Pedigree is one of eight beers always available. Also guests including Bateman XB, Coach House Coachman's Best and Adnams and Burton Bridge brews.

Traditional Victorian ale house. Bar food available at lunchtime. Car park, accommodation. Children allowed.

11am–11pm Mon–Sat;
12–2.30pm and
7–10.30pm Sun.

Jesmond

Legendary Yorkshire Heroes

Archibold Terrace, Jesmond
☎ *(0191) 281 3010*
Colin Colquhoun

Nine beers always available from a rotating list including Black Sheep Bitter and brews from Jennings, Hadrian, Big Lamp and Thwaites.

A lively refurbished modern pub within an office complex. Bar food available on weekday lunchtimes. Four pool tables, big screen sports, live bands Thursday to Saturday. Children allowed at lunchtimes only.

11am–11pm Mon–Sat;
12–10.30pm Sun.

NEWCASTLE UPON TYNE

HADRIAN BREWERY

Unit 10, Hawick Crescent Industrial Estate, Newcastle upon Tyne NE6 5AS
☎ *(0191) 276 5302*
Visitors welcome. Tied houses: None

Hadrian Brewery was established as a five-barrel plant in 1987 and is a small independent brewery named after the Roman emperor, given his historical connections with the region. It moved premises in 1991 and has continued to expand since then. The beer names follow the Roman theme. It also brews specifically for the Tap & Spile pub chain.

Beers available at: Cooperage, 32 The Close, Quayside, Newcastle upon Tyne, Tyne and Wear *and* Tap & Spile, Shields Road, Byker, Tyne and Wear.

GLADIATOR BITTER 3.8% ABV
Well-balanced, delicately hopped session bitter.

LEGION ALE 4.2% ABV
Good malt flavour, balanced with a strong hop character.

CENTURION BEST BITTER 4.5% ABV
Pale, hoppy and very moreish.

EMPEROR ALE 5.0% ABV
Dark ruby red, old-fashioned style ale. Warming and well hopped.

The Tap & Spile

1 Nun Street, Newcastle upon Tyne
☎ *(0191) 232 0026*

Twelve beers always available from a constantly changing range (200 per year) with names such as Durham Canny Lad and Magus, Mordue Workie Ticket and Bateman Yellow Belly.

More than 100 years old, with a ground-floor and basement bar. Bar food available at lunchtime. Children allowed for meals. Live bands in the cellar. Two minutes from the railway station and Greys Monument.

11am–11pm Mon–Sat; 12–10.30pm Sun.

NORTH SHIELDS

MORDUE BREWERY

Unit 22c, Middle Engine Lane, West Chirton North Industrial Estate, North Shields NE29 8SF
☎ *(0191) 296 1879*
Visitors welcome.
Tied houses: None

The Mordue Brewery was first established in Wallsend in a nineteenth-century brewery, but it moved to its present site in April 1995. Run by Matthew and Gary Fawson, they supply wholesalers and local outlets.

Beers available at: Magnesia Bank, Campden Street, North Shields, Tyne and Wear *and* Ale Taste, Low Fell High Street, Low Fell, Gateshead, Tyne and Wear.

FIVE BRIDGE BITTER 3.8% ABV

GEORDIE PRIDE 4.2% ABV
Session ale.

WORKIE TICKET 4.5% ABV
Premium bitter.

RADGIE GADGIE 4.8% ABV
Strong ale.

The Porthole

11 New Quay,
North Shields NE29 6LQ
☎ *(0191) 257 6645*
Mike Morgan

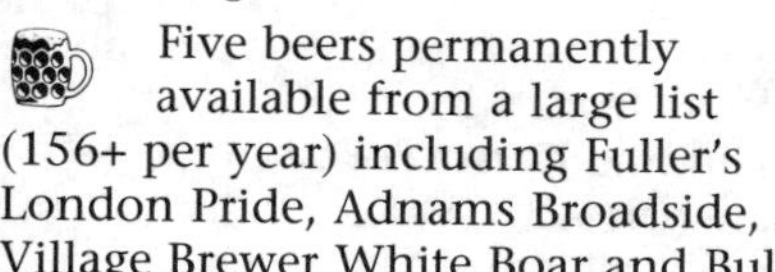

Five beers permanently available from a large list (156+ per year) including Fuller's London Pride, Adnams Broadside, Village Brewer White Boar and Bull Premium.

An old-fashioned friendly pub with a maritime theme on the banks of the Tyne. Bar food served at lunchtime and evenings. Car park. Children allowed. Near the North Shields ferry landing.

11am–11pm Mon–Sat;
12–10.30pm Sun.

The Tap & Spile

184 Tynemouth Road,
North Shields NE30 1EG
☎ *(0191) 257 2523*

Village Brewer White Boar and Black Sheep Special permanently available plus eight guest beers from a large list.

A real ale bar with a friendly atmosphere. Bar food served at lunchtime. Parking. Opposite the magistrates court in North Shields.

11.30am–11pm Mon–Sat;
12–3pm Sun.

SUNDERLAND

THE DARWIN BREWERY

University of Sunderland,
Chester Road,
Sunderland SR1 3SD
☎ *(0191) 515 2535*
No visitors. Tied houses: None

The Darwin Brewery is a half-barrel brew-length plant based on campus at the University of Sunderland. Established in July 1994, it has developed its product range making use of the extensive research and laboratory expertise of the university's scientific staff. The result is a range of superior quality cask ales using the finest ingredients blending traditional methods with modern advancements.

Beers available at: The Red Lion, Roker Avenue, Sunderland, Tyne and Wear.

EVOLUTION ALE 4.0% ABV
A full-bodied, traditional Wearside bitter, dark amber in colour with a fruity flavour and a clean bitter aftertaste.

SAINTS SINNER STRONG ALE 5.0% ABV
A rich and smooth strong dark ale with a subtle hop character and strong malt and roast flavour, culminating in a long-lasting roast aftertaste.

KILLER BEE 6.2% ABV
A gold-coloured ale with a strong hop flavour, balanced by the subtle sweetness of honey, that lingers in the aftertaste.

VAUX GROUP

The Brewery,
Sunderland SR1 3AN
☎ *(0191) 567 6277*
Visitors welcome. Tied houses: 826

Cuthbert Vaux founded C Vaux and Sons in 1837 and moved to the Castle Street Brewery in 1875. His sons, John Story Vaux and Edwin Vaux, took over in 1878 and the company developed and passed through the generations until it was one of the largest brewery businesses in the North of England. Major Cuthbert Vaux, John Story Vaux's son, spent time working at the Ny Carlsberg Brewery in Copenhagen and elsewhere in Europe and he helped the company to lead the way as demand for bottled beer grew. A limited company was formed in 1896 and, eventually, Vaux merged with the mighty North Eastern Breweries conglomerate. Associated Breweries was formed in 1927 and the company, which by now had expanded greatly, changed its name to Vaux and Associated Breweries in 1973. It became a plc in 1985. Vaux have always been proud of the central role they have played as one of the region's leading independent companies.

NORSEMAN 3.0% ABV

VAUX LIGHT 3.0% ABV

COOPER'S BITTER 3.6% ABV

LORIMERS BEST SCOTCH 3.6% ABV

VAUX BITTER 3.9% ABV

VAUX SAMSON 4.2% ABV

DOUBLE MAXIM 4.7% ABV

The Tap & Spile

Salem Street, Hendon,
Sunderland
☎ *(0191) 232 0026*
Janice Faulder

Nine beers always available from a list of 400+ including North Yorkshire Best, Bateman XB, Charles Wells Bombardier and Marston's Pedigree.

Traditional three-bar ale house with bare boards and exposed brickwork. Bar food available at lunchtime. Function room. Children allowed in eating area.

11am–11pm Mon–Sat;
12–3pm and 7–10.30pm Sun.

Alcester

The Bull's Head Brewery

The Three Tuns,
34 High Street, Alcester B49 5AB
☎ *(01789) 766550*
D Parker

From April 1996, the Bull's Head Brewery began production of four ales on site. In addition, six real ales are available through the week from breweries such as Hobsons, Goffs, Hardingtons, Wyre Piddle, Woods and Lichfield. Weekend beers include Everards Tiger, Hardington's Cupid, Hobsons Best, Woods Shropshire Lad, Fuller's London Pride, Lichfield Resurrection, North Yorkshire Dizzy Dick, Mildmay Old Horse Whip, Brains SA and Brandy Cask Brandysnapper.

The brewery was founded on a farm at Inkberrow, Hereford and Worcestershire, in December 1994 and moved to the rear of The Three Tuns in early 1995. It brews mostly for the pub itself. The Three Tuns is a sixteenth-century public house with open-plan bar, converted back from a wine bar. Beer festivals are held every three months. Occasional live music. Sandwiches only.

BULLHEAD LIGHT 4.5% ABV

GLOBE ALE

GENESIS

11am–11pm Mon–Sat;
12–10.30pm Sun.

Great Wolford

The Fox and Hounds

Great Wolford CV36 5NQ
☎ *(01608) 674220*
Mrs Seddon

Hook Norton Best and Shepherd Neame Spitfire always available plus hundreds of guests per year (up to five at any one time) including Wychwoods Best, Little Avenham Pickled Priest, Morland Old Speckled Hen and brews from Eldridge Pope, Smiles and Thwaites.

An atmospheric sixteenth-century pub with stone-flagged floors. Tudor fireplace and dining room. Bar food served at lunchtime and evenings. Car park, terrace. Accommodation. Children allowed in the dining room.

12–3pm and 7–11pm
(10.30pm Sun).

Shipston on Stour

Feldon Brewery

The Coach and Horses
16 New Street,
Shipston on Stour CV36 4EM
☎ *(01608) 661335*
Bob Payne

FBI from the brewery plus Hook Norton Best permanently available. Also three guests from long list including Hook Norton Haymaker, Wye Valley Brew 69, Dorothy Goodbody's Summertime Ale, Ash Vine Toxic Waste, Bateman XXXB and XB.

A 250-year-old village pub close to the Cotswolds serving bar and restaurant food at lunchtime and evenings. Car park, garden, accommodation. On the A3400 Birmingham to Oxford road, on the Oxford side of town.

FBI 4.4% ABV
Bitter.

11am–11pm (10.30pm Sun).

Brierley Hill

Daniel Batham & Son

Delph Brewery, Delph Road,
Brierley Hill DY5 2TN
☎ *(01384) 77229*
No visitors. Tied houses: 10

Small, award-winning brewery established in 1877 and now in its fifth generation of family ownership. Serving ten tied houses and 50 free trade outlets.

Beers available at: The Bull and Bladder (The Vine), 10 Delph Road, Brierley Hill, West Midlands *and* The Lamp, Lower High Street, Dudley, West Midlands.

MILD ALE 3.5% ABV
Fruity dark brown mild with a malty sweetness and roast malt finish.

BEST BITTER 4.3% ABV
Pale yellow, very fruity and lightly refreshing bitter. Initial sweetness progresses to a complex, dry hopping taste.

XXX 6.3% ABV
Winter ale.

The Bull and Bladder

10 Delph Road,
Brierley Hill DY5 2TN
☎ *(01384) 78293*
Mr Wood

Bathams Mild, Best and XXX always available.

Also known as The Vine, the brewery tap for Bathams, which is situated behind. A multi-roomed pub with open fires. Bar food available at lunchtime. Car park, garden, children's room.

12–11pm Mon–Sat;
12–4pm and 7–10.30pm Sun.

Coventry

Rainbow Inn and Brewery

73 Birmingham Road,
Allesley Village,
Coventry CV5 9GT
☎ *(01203) 402888*

Rainbow Piddlebrook Belcher's Wood, Firecracker and Sley Alle plus at least two guest beers.

Brewing started in October 1994 providing ale only for the pub and a few beer festivals. Production at the two-barrel plant takes place twice a week. An unpretentious pub in village location. Grade II-listed building dating from around 1650. Bar and restaurant food served at lunchtime and evenings. Parking, garden. Children allowed. Just off the main A45 at Allesley.

PIDDLEBROOK 3.8% ABV

BELCHER'S WOOD 4.2% ABV

SLEY ALLE 4.8% ABV

FIRE CRACKER 4.8% ABV

11am–11pm.

CRADLEY HEATH

The Waterfall

132 Waterfall Lane,
Cradley Heath B64 6RG
☎ *(0121) 561 3499*
Alan Davis

Nine beers always available including Bathams (local brewery) also Enville, Freeminer Stairway to Heaven, Hook Norton Old Hooky and Marston's Pedigree. Plus guests such as Oak Double Dagger, Titanic White Star, Wyre Piddle Piddle in the Wind, RCH Fiery Liz and Gibbs Mew Bishops Tipple.

A traditional Black Country pub. Bar food available at lunchtime and evenings. Car park, garden with waterfall, children's room. Also function room for skittle nights, quiz nights etc. Up the hill from the old Hill Station.

12–3pm and 5–11pm Mon–Thurs; all day Fri–Sun.

HALESOWEN

The Waggon and Horses

21 Stourbridge Road,
Halesowen B63 3TU
☎ *(0121) 602 2082*
Peter Rawson

Bathams Bitter, Enville Simpkiss and Enville Ale, Everards and Waggoners brews always available plus up to ten guests (800 per year) from far and wide.

A West Midlands Victorian boozer. Bar food is available at lunchtime. Car parking. Children allowed.

12–11pm Mon–Sat;
12–10.30pm Sun.

LOWER GORNAL

The Fountain Real Ale Bar

8 Temple Street,
Lower Gornal
☎ *(01384) 834888*
Alan Brookes

Hall & Woodhouse Tanglefoot, Blackbeard Stairway to Heaven, Everard's Tiger, Shepherd Neame Bishops Finger and Adnams Broadside permanently available plus four guest beers such as Kelham Island Pale Rider, Hop Back Summer Lightning, Berrow Topsy Turvy, Moorhouse Pendle Witches Brew, Fuller's ESB, RCH Pitchfork, etc. Festivals of ales held four times a year.

A real ale bar with a warm and pleasant atmosphere. Bar food served at lunchtime and evenings. Parking, garden and function room. Children allowed.

7–11pm Mon–Fri;
12–3pm and 7–11pm Sat;
12–3pm and 7–10.30pm Sun.

OLDBURY

The Waggon and Horses

Church Street, Oldbury
☎ *(0121) 552 5467*

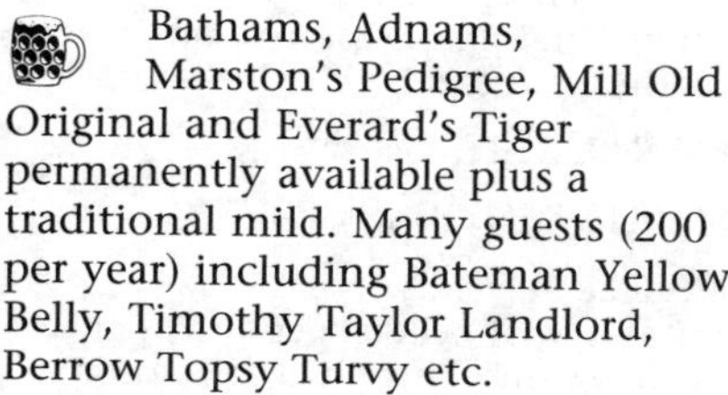

Bathams, Adnams, Marston's Pedigree, Mill Old Original and Everard's Tiger permanently available plus a traditional mild. Many guests (200 per year) including Bateman Yellow Belly, Timothy Taylor Landlord, Berrow Topsy Turvy etc.

A Victorian, grade-ll listed building with tiled walls, copper ceiling and original brewery windows. Bar food available at lunchtime and evenings. Car parking. Children allowed when eating. At the corner of Market Street and Church Street in Oldbury town centre, next to the library. The pub has no sign.

12–2.30pm (–3pm Fri); 5–11pm (6–11pm Sat, 7–10.30pm Sun).

SEDGLEY

SARAH HUGHES BREWERY

Beacon Hotel, 129 Bilston Street, Sedgley, Dudley DY3 1JE
☎ *(01902) 883380*
Visitors welcome.Tied houses: 1

Upnorton, Sedgley Surprise, M&V Mild and Dark Ruby Mild brewed and available on the premises.

The brewery reopened in 1988 after a 30-year absence to serve the Beacon and a few other outlets.

M&V MILD 3.3% ABV

UPNORTON 3.6% ABV
Best bitter.

SEDGLEY SURPRISE 5.0% ABV
Bitter.

DARK RUBY MILD 6.0% ABV

Phone for details.

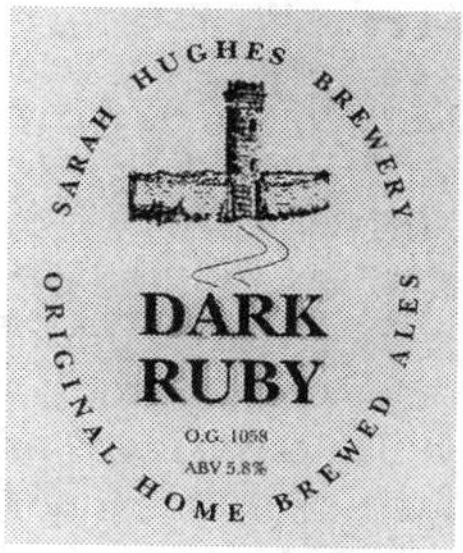

SHUSTOKE

CHURCH END BREWERY

The Griffin Inn,
Church Road,
Shustoke B46 2 LP
☎ *(01675) 481567*

At least six Church End brews plus Marston's Pedigree always available plus 200 guest beers per year.

A large country freehouse with oak beams and open fires set in large grounds. Bar food is available at lunchtime (except Sunday). Car park, garden. Children allowed in the conservatory and grounds. Take the B4114 from Coleshill.

GRAVEDIGGERS 3.8% ABV

WHAT THE FOX'S HAT 4.2% ABV

WHEAT A BIX 4.2% ABV

M-REG GTi 4.4% ABV

PEWS PORTER 4.5% ABV

OLD PAL 5.5% ABV

12–3pm and 7–11pm Mon–Sat; 12–2.30pm and 7–10.30pm Sun.

STOURBRIDGE

ENVILLE ALES

Enville Brewery,
Cox Green,
Stourbridge DY7 5LG
☎ *(01384) 873728*
Visitors welcome. Tied houses: None

The original brewery in Enville, at the Stanford Arms Hotel, ceased production in 1919. Until that time, workers on the Enville estate received tokens as part of their wages, which could be cashed in at the brewery for the appropriate amount of beer. The new brewery, a mile and a half from the original site, on a derelict farm at Cox Green, draws its water from the same source. Enville Ale represents about 80 per cent of the 40-barrels per week output. The original recipe dates back to 1850 and the proprietor's great-great-aunt in Cumbria. Mr Constantine-Cort also keeps bees, and several tonnes of honey goes into the beer production each year. The brewery now also grows its own barley at the farm.

Beers available at: The Cat Inn, Enville, Stourbridge, West Midlands *and* The Black Horse, 52 Delph Road, Brierley Hill, West Midlands.

ENVILLE MILD LOW GRAVITY 3.6% ABV

ENVILLE BITTER 3.8% ABV
Pale, using Challenger and Goldings hops. Dry hopped with Goldings.

SIMPKISS BITTER 3.8% ABV
An original Black Country bitter now produced at the Enville Brewery.

ENVILLE WHITE 4.0% ABV

ENVILLE MILD HIGH GRAVITY 4.0% ABV

ENVILLE ALE 4.5% ABV
A traditional beerkeeper's ale, pale yellow, fruity bitter, with an initial sweetness progressing to a complex dry hoppy taste.

GOTHIC ALE 5.2% ABV
A black beer traditionally referred to as dinner ale. Derived from pale ale, a specially produced black malt and a selection of specialised sugars.

The Robin Hood Inn

196 Collis Street Amblecote, Stourbridge. DY8 4EQ
☎ (01384) 822122

Bathams Bitter, Enville Ale, Marston's Pedigree, Morland Old Speckled Hen and Banks Mild permanently available plus three guests (120 per year) such as Timothy Taylor Landlord, Hall & Woodhouse Tanglefoot, Shepherd Neame Bishops Finger, Fuller's ESB, Exmoor Gold and Hook Norton Old Hooky.

A family-run business, cosy Black Country freehouse. Good beer garden. Non-smoking dining room. Bar and restaurant food available. Parking. Children allowed in the pub when eating. Accommodation.

12–3pm and 6–11pm Mon–Sat; 12–10.30pm Sun.

TIPTON

The Port 'n' Ale

178 Horseley Heath Road, Great Bridge, Tipton DY4 7DS
☎ (0121) 557 7249
Nigel Griffin

Blackbeard Stairway to Heaven and Bathams Best permanently available plus six guests (400 per year) including Big Lamp Old Genie, Daleside Monkey Wrench, Church End Vicar's Ruin, Tring Ridgeway Bitter, Eccleshall Premium, Spinnaker Black Rock, Hoskins & Oldfield Navigation Ale etc.

Bar, lounge, dining room and beer garden. Car park at rear. Bar and restaurant food served at lunchtime and Thursday to Saturday evenings. Children allowed in the restaurant. Just down the road from Dudley Port railway station.

12–3pm and 5–11.30pm Mon–Sat; 12–3pm and 7–10.30pm Sun.

WOLVERHAMPTON

WOLVERHAMPTON & DUDLEY BREWERIES

PO Box 26, Park Brewery, Bath Road, Wolverhampton WV1 4NY
☎ (01902) 711811
Visitors welcome. Tied houses: 1,000

Wolverhampton and Dudley Breweries was formed on 14 May 1890 from an amalgamation of three local businesses: Banks and Company (who has been brewing at Park Brewery since 1875), George Thompson and Sons from Dudley (maltsters since 1840, brewers since 1878) and Charles Colonel Smith's Fox Brewery in Wolverhampton. Edwin John Thompson became a manager of the new company and managing director in 1894. His great grandson David is managing director today. A number of breweries have been bought up over the past 100 years, most recently JW Cameron and Company Ltd in 1992. Banks's Brewery is firmly committed to a policy of controlled expansion into new areas and market dominance within its Black Country heartland.

HANSONS BITTER 3.3% ABV
HANSONS MILD 3.3% ABV
BANKS'S 3.5% ABV
BANKS'S BITTER 3.8% ABV
CAMERONS BEST SCOTCH 3.5% ABV
CAMERONS BITTER 3.6% ABV
CAMERONS STRONGARM 4.0% ABV
ZAMER LAGER 4.5% ABV

Plus a range of bottled beers.

WOODSETTON

HOLDEN'S BREWERY

Holden Brewery, George Street,
Woodsetton DY1 4LN
☎ *(01902) 880051*
Visitors welcome.
Tied houses: 20

Now in its fourth generation, this family-run Black Country brewery began as a brewpub in 1916. The Park Inn is now the brewery tap. Holden's brews for its 20 pubs and about another 60 free trade outlets. There is also a brewery shop.

Beers available at: The Bell Inn, Wombourne Road, Trysull, Wolverhampton, West Midlands *and* The Great Western, Sun Street, Wolverhampton, West Midlands.

HOLDEN'S STOUT 3.7% ABV

MILD 3.7% ABV
Medium-bodied dark red/brown mild. A blend of roast malt, hops and fruit dominated by maltiness throughout.

BITTER 3.9% ABV
Medium-bodied golden ale.

XB (OR LUCY B) 4.1% ABV
Sweet, slightly fuller version of the bitter, named after Lucy Blanche Holden.

SPECIAL BITTER 5.1% ABV
Sweet and malty, full-bodied amber ale with a pleasant bitterwseet aftertaste.

Corsham

The Two Pigs

38 Pickwick, Corsham SN13 0HY
☎ *(01249) 712515*
Mr Doyle

Bunces Pigswill among four beers always available plus three guests (200 per year) including Hop Back Summer Lightning, Foxley Barking Mad, Fuller's London Pride and Greene King Abbot Ale.

A traditional wood-panelled pub with stone floors. No food. Parking nearby. Covered courtyard, No children. Live blues music on Monday. On the A4 between Chippenham and Bath.

7–11pm Mon–Sat; 12–2.30pm and 7–10.30pm Sun.

Devizes

Wadworth & Co.

Northgate Brewery, Devizes SN10 1JW
☎ *(01380) 723361*
Visitors welcome (ring for details).
Tied houses: 221

Henry Wadworth built his classic red-brick Victorian tower brewery in 1885 and it still dominates Devizes marketplace today. The brewing process remains solidly traditional, because the company believes it delivers the best results. However, Wadworths continue to invest in the technological advances to improve the process control.

HENRY'S ORIGINAL IPA 3.8% ABV
Golden-brown beer with a good balance of flavours and a long-lasting aftertaste, becoming biscuity. A good session beer.

6X 4.3% ABV
Full-bodied and distinctive, mid-brown in colour, malty and fruity with balancing hop character.

FARMER'S GLORY 4.5% ABV
May be discontinued. A dark, hoppy and fruity beer with malt aroma and dryish, hoppy taste.

OLD TIMER 5.8% ABV
Rich, copper-brown beer with strong, fruity, malty aroma and full-bodied flavour.

Plus seasonal brews including:
VALENTINES (4.5% ABV)
EASTER ALE (4.5% ABV)
SUMMERSAULT (4.5% ABV) and
MALT & HOPS 1996 (4.5% ABV).

The British Lion

9 Estcourt Street, Devizes SN10 1LQ
☎ *(01380) 720665*
Michael Dearing

Coach House Lion's Pride (house bitter, 99p) permanently available plus two guests (100 per year) from Archers, Bunces, Foxley, Hop Back, Moles, Ash Vine, Bridgewater, Cottage, New Ale, Ringwood and Hampshire breweries. Also winter special.

A straightforward locals' community pub for all ages. On the main Swindon (A361) road, opposite The Green.

11am–11pm Mon–Sat; all day Sun.

DOWNTON

HOP BACK BREWERY

Units 22–24, Batten Road Ind Est.,
Downton, Nr Salisbury SP5 3HU
☎ *(01725) 510986*
Visitors welcome. Tied houses: 4

In 1986, John Gilbert and his wife Julie found the ideal venue to fulfil their ambitions – The Wyndham Arms on the outskirts of Salisbury. The space in the cellar and yard of the pub enabled John to commence brewing his own uniquely individual quality ales. The idea was simple: use only natural ingredients, no additives, and deliver real character and value for money. Within two years, the beers were achieving recognition at beer festivals around the country. Hop Back products were also going down well in the pubs around Salisbury and Southampton, where demand increased substantially. In October 1991, Hop Back Brewery Ltd. was formed to increase the scale of the brewing operations without sacrificing the quality. The company acquired the lease of a factory unit in Downton, between Salisbury and Southampton, where they designed a brewery to their own unique requirements.

Beers available at: The Swan, Enford, Wiltshire *and* The Wheatsheaf, Figheldean, Wiltshire.

MILD 3.2% ABV
A traditional dark mild. Made with the best Golding hops.

GFB 3.5% ABV
Refreshing, golden beer. Hoppy aroma and taste lead to a good dry finish.

HBS SPECIAL 4.0% ABV
A medium-strength bitter, slightly sweet with a good balance of malt and hops.

WILT ALTERNATIVE 4.0% ABV
A light-coloured, medium-strength beer.

ENTIRE STOUT 4.5% ABV
A rich dark stout with a strong roasted malt flavour and a long, smooth malty aftertaste.

SUMMER LIGHTNING 5.0% ABV
Straw-coloured beer with a fresh, hoppy aroma and a well rounded, malty flavour with an intense bitterness which leads to an excellent long, dry finish.

THUNDERSTORM 5.0% ABV
Cask-conditioned wheat beer. Brewed from equal amounts of pale barley malt and wheat malt, with a touch of coriander.

Ebbesbourne Wake

The Horseshoe Inn

Ebbesbourne Wake SP5 5JF
☎ *(01722) 780474*

Wadworth 6X, Ringwood Best and Adnams Broadside permanently available straight from the barrel, plus a guest (12 per year) perhaps from Bateman's, Poole, Felinfoel, Fuller's, Tisbury or Hop Back breweries.

A remote, old–fashioned unspoilt pub hung with old tools of a bygone age. Bar and restaurant food available lunchtime and evenings (except Monday). Car park, garden, accommodation. Children are allowed if eating. From Salisbury (A354), turn right to Bishopston, Broadchalke then on to Ebbesbourne Wake.

11.30am–3pm and 6.30–11pm.

Enford

The Swan

Longstreet, Enford, Nr Pewsey SN9 6DD
☎ *(01980) 670338*
Colin Edwards

Hop Back Special plus three guests (200 per year) including brews from Smiles, Fuller's, Ringwood and Shepherd Neame.

Old thatched and beamed pub with two bars and open fires. Bar food available at lunchtime and evenings. Car park, garden, children's room. Easy to find.

12–3pm and 7–11pm Mon–Sat; 12–4pm and 7–10.30pm Sun.

Figheldean

The Wheatsheaf

High Street, Figheldean, Nr Salisbury SP4 8JJ
☎ *(01980) 670357*

Hop Back brews always available plus a couple of guests (20 per year) including ales from Titanic, Eldridge Pope, Youngs, Exmoor, Mitchells, Hook Norton and Wychwood.

A single-bar pub with open fire and alcoves. Family room, garden. Bar food available lunchtime and evening (not Monday). Off the A345, north of Amesbury.

12–3pm and 7–11pm (closed Monday lunchtime).

Ford

The White Hart

Ford, Nr Chippenham SN14 8RP
☎ *(01249) 782213*
Chris Phillips

Twelve beers at any one time. Smiles Best, Marston's Pedigree, Wadworth 6X and Fuller's London Pride always. Four guests may include Hook Norton Best, Marston's Owd Roger, Shepherd Neame Spitfire, Black Sheep Best, Morland Old Speckled Hen and Uley brews.

Old coaching inn off the A420 on the edge of a river. One main bar, restaurant and buttery. Bar food available at lunchtime. Restaurant open at lunchtime and evenings. Car parks, river terrace, accommodation. Children allowed in the buttery.

11am–2.30pm and 5–11pm Mon–Sat; usual hours Sun.

Hamptworth

The Cuckoo Inn

Hamptworth Road, Hamptworth, Nr Salisbury SP5 2DU
☎ *(01794) 390302*
Ray Proudley

Wadworth 6X, Hall & Woodhouse Tanglefoot, Cheriton Pots Ale, Hop Back Summer Lightning and GFB, also Bunces permanently available plus three guest beers from a long list including brews from Tisbury, Juwards, Ringwood, Hampshire, Shepherd Neame and Cottage breweries.

A 300-year-old thatched pub in the New Forest. Bar food available at lunchtime and evenings. Car park, garden, play area, petanque area, children's room. Just off the A36 near Hamptworth golf course.

11.30am–2.30pm and 6–11pm Mon–Fri; 11.30am–11pm Sat; 12–3pm and 7–10.30pm Sun.

Lacock

The Rising Sun

32 Bowden Hill, Lacock, Nr Chippenham SN15 2PP
☎ *(01249) 730363*
Mr and Mrs Maxwell

Five beers always available including Moles Tap, Best, Landlord's Choice, Brew 97 and Black Rat. Guests include Crouch Vale Willie Warmer and Wadworth 6X.

A Cotswold stone pub with flagstone floors and open fires. Bar food available at lunchtime and evenings. Car park, garden. Children allowed. Turn into village, then go up Bowden Hill.

11am–3pm and 6–11pm Mon–Sat; 12–3pm and 7–10.30pm Sun.

Melksham

Moles Brewery

5 Merlin Way, Bowerhill, Melksham SN12 6TJ
☎ *(01225) 704734*
Visitors welcome. Tied houses: 14

Roger Catte set up a small brewery within a soft drinks group in 1982 and its rapid success and growth is attributed to the quality products and bright, breezy image.

Beers available at: The Rising Sun, Bowden Hill, Nr Chippenham, Wiltshire *and* The Duke, Melbourne Street, Bratton, Nr Westbury, Wiltshire.

MOLES TAP BITTER 3.5% ABV
Malty and dry with hoppy finish.

MOLES BEST BITTER 4.0% ABV
Well-balanced bitter with full body.

MOLES LANDLORD'S CHOICE 4.5% ABV
Deceptively dark bitter.

MOLES BREW '97 5.0% ABV
Rich malty flavour with fruit and hop.

MOLES XB 6.0% ABV
Seasonal. Wonderfully warming celebration ale.

NETHERAVON

BUNCES BREWERY

The Old Mill, Netheravon, Salisbury SP4 9QB
☎ *(01980) 670631*
Visitors welcome. Tied houses: None

The brewery is situated in a former electricity generating station built in 1914 and converted for brewing in 1984. The layout of the building allows the processed raw materials to be moved by gravity, as in the traditional tower brewery. Using an all-malt mash, current production is about 30 barrels a week, serving around 50 outlets and several wholesalers. Two years ago, the brewery was taken over by Danish master brewer Stig Anker Andersen. He continues brewing good quality English ales and has already added four new brews to the original range.

Beers available: Two Pigs, Corsham, Wiltshire *and* The Dog and Gun, Salisbury Road, Netheravon, Nr Salisbury, Wiltshire.

BENCHMARK 3.5% ABV
Bitter ale of remarkable character. The taste is malty, the aroma subtle and the very long finish is quite dry on the palate.

PIGSWILL 4.0% ABV
A full-bodied amber-coloured beer, not so bitter, but rich in hop aroma which gives the beer a delightful aftertaste.

BEST BITTER 4.1% ABV
The piquant aroma introduces a complex malty and bitter taste with a hint of fruit. Long, fresh, bitter aftertaste.

DANISH DYNAMITE 5.0% ABV
A light golden, dry, strong ale, slightly fruity with a well balanced hop flavour and bitterness.

OLD SMOKEY 5.0% ABV
A delightful, warming, dark winter ale, with a roasted malt taste and a hint of liquorice surrounding a developing bitter flavour.

Plus a range of seasonal brews including **SIGN OF SPRING** (4.6% ABV) **VICE BEER** (3.2% ABV), **GALE FORCE** (5.0% ABV) and **RUDOLPH** (5.0% ABV).

SALISBURY

GIBBS MEW

Anchor Brewery, Gigant Street, Salisbury SP1 2AR
☎ *(01722) 411911*
Visitors welcome by prior arrangement. Tied houses: 305

The Gibbs family started brewing in the eighteenth century at The Swan, in Haslemere. The business moved to the site of the Anchor Brewery in 1858. The present buildings were built in 1890 in the classic Victorian style. After the death of Bridger Gibbs, his sons formed a public company and amalgamated with Herbert Mew and Company in 1898. In 1960, Gibbs Mew became one of the first breweries to package beer in kegs but, in 1973, reintroduced real ale in the form of The Bishop's Tipple. The company has continued to expand over the past 20 years and exports to Europe, the USA and Canada.

SUPER MILD 3.0% ABV
Dark coloured, slighty chocolately mild ale.

WILTSHIRE TRADITIONAL BITTER 3.6% ABV
A cask-conditioned easy drinking medium coloured session beer.

WILTSHIRE SPECIAL BITTER 3.6% ABV
A well-balanced flavour.

OVERLORD 3.6% ABV
Cask-conditioned bitter in the traditional style, with a medium colour and clean taste.

SALISBURY BEST BITTER 4.0% ABV
Best bitter of traditional colour.

DEACON 5.0% ABV
Straw-coloured, cask-conditioned beer, with a light, clean, fresh hoppy flavour.

WAKE ALE 5.0% ABV
Very dark winter ale.

THE BISHOP'S TIPPLE 6.5% ABV
Strong ale with a style and character all of its own.

Plus a range of bottled beers.

The Village Freehouse

33 Wilton Road,
Salisbury SP2 7EF
☎ *(01722) 329707*

Hampshire King Alfred's, Oakhill Best Bitter, Timothy Taylor Landlord and Edmund Ironside Best permanently available plus a guest (160 per year) such as Cottage Southern Bitter, Golden Arrow, Worldham Old Dray Bitter and Summerskills Whistle Belly Vengeance.

A small, convivial street-corner pub. Bar snacks available lunchtime and evenings. Children allowed. Two minutes from Salisbury railway station.

11am–11pm Mon–Sat;
12–10.30pm Sun.

SWINDON

ARCHERS ALES

Station Industrial Estate,
London Street, Swindon SN1 5DY
☎ *(01793) 496789*
Trade visits only. Tied houses: 3

Archers was established in 1979 in the old Great Western Railway works and has expanded successfully to supply wholesalers and its three tied houses.

Beers available at: The Glue Pot, Emlyn Square, Swindon, Wiltshire *and* The Kemble Brewery Inn, 27 Fairview Street, Cheltenham, Gloucestershire.

VILLAGE BITTER 3.5% ABV
A dry, full-bodied, well-balanced beer.

BEST BITTER 4.0% ABV
Slightly sweeter and rounder than Village, with a fruity aroma and pronounced bitter finish.

BLACK JACK PORT 4.6% ABV
Winter beer.

GOLDEN BITTER 4.7% ABV
Full-bodied, hoppy, straw-coloured beer with an underlying fruity sweetness and a strong bitter finish.

ARCHERS SPECIAL BREW 5.5% ABV

ARKELL'S BREWERY

Kingsdown, Swindon SN2 6RU
☎ *(01793) 823026*
Visitors by invitation only.
Tied houses: 90

John Arkell, a farmer, brewed his first pint using barley from his own fields just over 150 years ago. Arkell's Brewery was duly established in 1843. Today, the company chairman and managing director are both members of the Arkell family.

Beers available at: The County Ground, 115 County Road, Swindon, Wiltshire *and* The Adam and Eve, 8 Townsend Street, Cheltenham, Gloucestershire.

2B 3.2% ABV
A well balanced, pale beer, slightly dry but full in flavour.

3B 4.0% ABV
Amber-coloured beer, full bodied, with a well balanced malt and hop flavour leaving a lingering dry finish.

KINGSDOWN ALE 5.0% ABV
A rich-coloured strong beer, with a distinct malt and hop flavour leaving a pleasant warming feeling in the mouth.

MASH TUN MILD 3.5% ABV
Seasonal beer. A fine dark, malty flavoured mild, lightly hopped with a creamy nutty after palate.

NOEL ALE 5.5% ABV
Seasonal beer. The golden pale colour disguises the full malty and hop flavour and leaves a clean dry aftertaste.

YEOMANRY BICENTENARY ALE 4.5% ABV
Seasonal beer. A delicate hop aroma and distinctive hop flavour due to the addition of whole hops in the cask.

SUMMER ALE 4.2% ABV
Seasonal beer. A light-coloured beer, with a taste of summer.

PETER'S PORTER 4.8% ABV
Autumn guest beer, strong and dark.

VICTORY BITTER 5.0% ABV
Occasional beer. Golden in colour, brewed using malted cereals and hops from many of the Allied countries in World War Two.

TISBURY

TISBURY BREWERY

Church Street,
Tisbury SP3 6NH
☎ *(01747) 870986*
Visitors welcome. Tied houses: None

Converted from a squalid village workhouse in 1868, Tisbury's first brewery was gutted by fire some 15 years later. The owner, Archibald Beckett, was undaunted by the disaster and soon the master maltster and local philanthropist had created a larger, more modern steam brewery on the site. Four years later, the brewery was bought by the eccentric FHS Styring, whose pet monkey acted as self-appointed beer taster until he fell into one of the vats and drowned. Despite this loss, the brewery continued to flourish and its drays, drawn by magnificent shire horses, delivered throughout the Nadder Valley and beyond. Today, Tisbury's aim is to become one of the best independent breweries, blending traditional skills and modern production techniques to produce a range of real ales known for their distinctive taste and consistent quality.

TISBURY BEST 3.8% ABV
A full-flavoured session bitter, with a rich burnt amber colour, delightful malt nose and a flavour that is both fruity and hoppy for a pleasant aftertaste.

ARCHIBALD BECKETT 4.3% ABV
A thirst-quenching premium bitter with a distinctive dark amber colour, unusual caramel bouquet and dry, fruity finish with lingering malt.

OLD WARDOUR 4.8% ABV
Named after nearby Wardour Castle, a full-bodied beer with an understated mahogany hue that balances a delicate, fruity sweetness with a subtle hop bite and dry, malty finish.

TROWBRIDGE

USHERS OF TROWBRIDGE

Directors House,
68 Fore Street,
Trowbridge BA14 8JF
☎ *(01225) 763171*
Visitors welcome. Write in advance.
Tied houses: 550

Thomas Usher established a small brewery at Back Street, Trowbridge in 1824. He brewed locally renowned ale which his wife, Hannah, sold from "The Tap" where the family also lived. The brewery grew and the couple retired in 1869 and their sons took over. Jacob Usher became the first chairman of the company after it was registered as Ushers Wiltshire Brewery Ltd in 1889. A family connection survived until 1941, when Thomas Usher, grandson of the founder, retired. Ushers merged with Watney Mann Ltd in 1964. Grand Metropolitan Ltd took over Watney Mann Ltd in 1972. In 1980, the regional company reverted back to the Ushers Brewery name. Courage took over the brewing interest until a management buy-out led by Roger North in 1991 saw Ushers re-established as an independent regional brewer. Since then, more than £2 million has been invested in the brewery's development.

USHERS BEST BITTER 3.8% ABV
A traditional session bitter. Bright and smooth with the full taste of hops and barley.

SPRING FEVER 4.0% ABV
An original ale crafted to reflect the freshness and frivolity of springtime. A unique light and subtle blend of oats and choicest Goldings hops.

SUMMER MADNESS 4.0% ABV
A light refreshing easy drinking ale with a distinctive fruity, floral, hoppy flavour with a slight tangy after-palate.

AUTUMN FRENZY 4.0% ABV
Smooth full-bodied ale mellowed with the addition of fragrant hops. It has a rich ruby red colour and is brewed with rye.

USHERS FOUNDERS ALE 4.5% ABV
Premium bitter with an enticing hop aroma and a hoppy and fruity finish.

1824 PARTICULAR 6.0% ABV
Strong winter ale with a full fruity palate combined with a pleasing floral hop character brewed with barley.

Barnsley

Barnsley Brewing

Elsecar Brewery, Elsecar Heritage Centre, Wath Road, Elsecar, Barnsley S74 8HJ
☎ *(01226) 741010*
Visitors welcome. Tied houses: None

Barnsley Bitter is recreated from a recipe using original yeast culture. No brewing adjuncts are used. It was first produced in March 1994.

Beers available at: Lundhill Tavern, Beech House Road, Hemingfield, Nr Barnsley, Yorkshire *and* Market Inn, 2 Wentwoth Road, Elsecar, Nr Barnsley, Yorkshire.

BARNSLEY BITTER 3.8% ABV
Dry, bitter, malty.

BLACKHEART STOUT 4.6% ABV
Rich, dark, full bodied.

Batley

Blackmoor Brewery

The Brewhouse, Unit 8, Healey Mill, Healey Lane, Batley WF17 5SH
☎ *(01924) 422400*
Visitors welcome. Tied houses: None

After three years of planning, the Blackmoor Brewery has been in production since December 1994, run by Graeme Marsh, Neil Ibbetson and Les Hadfield. There are plans for expansion.

Beers available at: The Royal Hotel, 111 High Street, Heckmondwike, Yorkshire and The Oaklands, Bradford Road, Batley, Yorkshire.

BLACKMOOR BITTER 3.6% ABV
Light session bitter.

BOG STANDARD BITTER 4.2% ABV
Full-bodied premium bitter.

EXHIBITIONISM ALE 4.4% ABV
Smooth golden fruity ale.

BANANA MADNESS 4.6% ABV
Award-winning fruit beer, very light and refreshing.

BATLEY SHAMPAYNE 4.8% ABV
Traditional brown ale.

DOA 5.0% ABV
Strong dark ale with malty aftertaste.

The Oaklands

Bradford Road, Batley WF17 5PS
☎ *(01924) 444181*

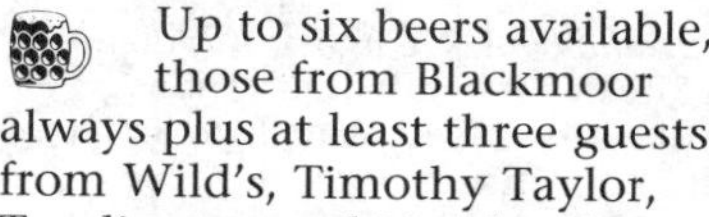

Up to six beers available, those from Blackmoor always plus at least three guests from Wild's, Timothy Taylor, Tomlinsons and Liverhead.

A busy circuit pub. Bar food available at lunchtime and evenings. Car park, garden. Children allowed up to 7pm.

12–3pm and 5–11pm; all day Friday and Saturday.

Beck Hole

Birch Hall Inn

Beck Hole, Goathland YO22 5LE
☎ *(01947) 896245*

Five beers always available including Black Sheep Mild. 200 guests per year may include York Stone Wall and Yorkshire Terrier, Marston's Pedigree, Daleside Country Stile, Shepherd Neame Spitfire, Blackawton Shepherd's Delight etc.

Tiny, traditional unspoilt pub with two bars dating from 1600s. CAMRA pub of the year. No juke box or games machines. Bar food available at lunchtime and evenings. Garden. Children allowed. Between Pickering and Whitby.

11am–11pm in summer; usual hours in winter.

BILTON

FRANKLIN'S BREWERY

Bilton Lane, Bilton,
Nr Harrogate HG1 4DH
☎ (01423) 322345
No visitors. Tied houses: None

Established in 1980 by Sean Franklin, a wine specialist, in an Elizabethan barn in this village near Harrogate.

Beers available at: George and Dragon, Main Street, Melmerby, Nr Ripon, Yorkshire *and* Castle Arms Inn, Snape, Bedale, Yorkshire.

BITTER 3.8% ABV

SUMMER BLOTTO 4.7% ABV

WINTER BLOTTO 4.7% ABV

DT'S 4.7% ABV

BRADFORD

The Castle Hotel

20 Grattan Road,
Bradford BD1 2LU
☎ *(01274) 393166*
James Duncan

Mansfield Riding and Riding Mild permanently available plus seven guest beers (200 per year) from brewers such as Goose Eye, Ridleys, Brains, Moorhouse, Marston's, Eldridge Pope, Jennings, Wadworth, Shepherd Neame and many more.

A pub built like a castle in 1898. Bar food is served at lunchtime from Monday to Thursday and until 7.30pm on Friday and Saturday. Parking at weekends and evenings. Children not allowed. Located in the city centre.

11.30am–11pm Mon–Sat; closed Sun.

The Corn Dolly

110 Bolton Road,
Bradford BD1 4DE
☎ *(01274) 720219*
Mr Duncan

Up to 12 beers available. Moorhouse's Bitter, Black Sheep and Black Bull always plus four guests (500 per year) from brewers including Fuller's, Charles Wells, Morrells, Wadworth and Goose Eye.

CAMRA Bradford Pub of the Year 1993 and 1994. Bar food is available at lunchtime. Car park and garden. Situated off Forster Square.

11.30am–11pm.

The Fighting Cock

21–23 Preston Street,
Bradford BD7 1JE
☎ *(01274) 726907*
Kevin Quill

At least ten beers on sale. Beers from Old Mill, Timothy Taylor and Black Sheep permanently available plus many guests (200 per year) from Greene King, Fuller's, Archers, Jennings and Ringwood etc.

A friendly back-to-basics original ale house. Bar food available at lunchtime. Go left on Thornton Road from the cinema in the city centre, then left again at the lights.

11am–11pm Mon–Sat; 11am–3pm and 7–10.30pm Sun.

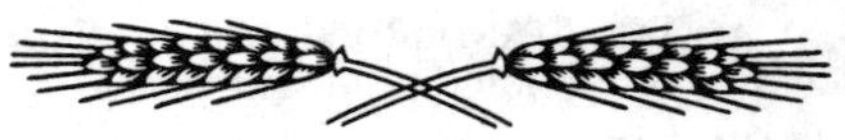

The Idle Cock

Bolton Road, Bradford BD2 4HT
☎ *(01274) 639491*
Jim Wright

Sam Smith's OBB, Black Sheep Special, Timothy Taylor Landlord and Vaux Samson permanently available plus several guests (130 per year) including Tomintoul Stag, Hop Back Summer Lightning, Fuller's London Pride, Daleside Old Legover, Joseph Holts etc.

A York stone pub with two separate bars, part wood, part flagstone floors, wooden bench seating. A proper no-frills ale house. Bar food is available. Parking and garden. Follow the "Idle" signs along Bolton Road for approximately two miles from the city centre.

11.30am–11pm Mon–Sat; 12–3pm and 7–10.30pm Sun.

BREARTON

The Malt Shovel

Brearton,
Nr Knaresborough HG3 3BX
☎ *(01423) 862929*
Mr Mitchell

Five beers always available including 100 guests per year. Favourites include Durham Canny Lad, Jennings Sneck Lifter, Old Mill Bitter, Black Sheep Bitter and Daleside brews.

A sixteenth-century village inn, beamed with open fires in winter. Bar food available at lunchtime and evenings. Car park, garden. Children allowed. Off the B6165.

12–3pm and 6.45–11pm Mon–Sat; 12–3pm and 7–10.30pm Sun.

CROPTON

CROPTON BREWERY

The New Inn, Cropton,
Nr Pickering YO18 8HH
☎ *(01751) 417310*

Cropton King Billy, Two Pints Best, Scoresby Stout and Special Strong Bitter always available plus guests.

Cropton Brewery was established in 1984 in the basement of the New Inn in this tiny moorland village. It owes its existence to the deep-seated local fear that, one day, the harsh moors winter weather would prevent the beer waggon from getting through. The brewery's reputation has since spread and, as demand exceeded capacity, a new purpose-built brewery was constructed in an adjacent quarry. Bar and restaurant food is served at lunchtime and evenings. Car park, garden, children's room, accommodation.

KING BILLY BITTER 3.6% ABV
TWO PINTS BEST BITTER 4.0% ABV
SCORESBY STOUT 4.2% ABV
SPECIAL STRONG BITTER 6.0% ABV

11.30am–3pm and 6–11pm; all day Sat.

DONCASTER

STOCKS BREWERY

The Hallcross Public House
33–34 Hallgate,
Doncaster DN1 3NL
☎ *(01302) 328213*

Five Stocks brews are produced and served on the premises.

The brewery was established in 1981 behind The Hallcross. It is owned and run by Cooplands, a Doncaster bakers, on the site of the first shop, which was opened in 1931 to sell homemade sweets. The pub is of traditional Victorian style with a beer garden. Bar food is served at lunchtime and evenings. Parking, children allowed.

BEST BITTER 3.9% ABV
Light hoppy ale brewed for the northern taste.

SELECT 4.7% ABV
Premium ale of smooth and slightly malty character.

ST LEGER PORTER 5.1% ABV
Award-winning, almost black, full-flavoured ale with deep fruit and roast malt flavours. A hoppy finish.

GOLDEN WHEAT 4.7% ABV

OLD HORIZONTAL 5.4% ABV
Strong ale with a distinctive nutty flavour, good body and excellent head retention, flavoured with a delicate blend of Fuggles and Goldings hops.

11am–11pm.

GUISBOROUGH

The Tap & Spile

11 Westgate,
Guisborough TS14 6BG
☎ *(01287) 632983*
Martin Slack and Mick Maslin

Tap & Spile Premium (brewed by Ushers of Trowbridge), always available plus seven guests (200 per year) which may include Hambleton ales and those from Hull Brewery, Cotleigh, Big Lamp, Durham and Butterknowle.

Plenty of olde-worlde charm, a beamed ceiling, no-smoking room, snug and beer garden. Bar food available at lunchtime. Parking. Children allowed. Situated on the main street in Guisborough.

11am–3pm and
5.30–11.30pm Mon–Weds;
11am–11pm Thurs–Sat;
12–3pm and 7–10.30pm Sun.

HARROGATE

ROOSTERS BREWERY

Unit 20,
Claro Court Business Centre,
Claro Road, Harrogate HG1 4BA
☎ (01423) 561861
Visitors welcome. Tied houses: None

Roosters Brewery is three years old and produces award-winning aromatic and individual brews.

Beers available at: The Maltings, Tanner's Moat, York, Yorkshire.

MAYFLOWER II 3.7% ABV
Pale straw yellow colour, a fraction lighter than the Yankee. Grapefruit and passion fruit aroma. Light citrus-grapefruit and passion fruit confirmed on the palate.

SPECIAL 3.9% ABV
Butterscotch and flowery nose. Light easy-drinking palate.

JAK'S 3.9% ABV
Aromatic. Rather like the Rooster's but lighter, with more of the lychees and less of the toffee.

YANKEE 4.3% ABV
Pale straw colour. Fresh soft malty nose, faint lychees. Soft palate.

ROOSTER'S 4.7% ABV
Light chestnut-brown colour. Malty-toffee-like aroma with lychees on top. Faint citrus note. Palate full with aroma confirmed. Medium bitterness. Aromatic finish that does not cloy.

HEBDEN BRIDGE

The Fox and Goose

9 Heptonstall Road,
Hebden Bridge HX7 6AZ
☎ *(01422) 842649*
Robin Starbuck

Goose Eye Bitter permanently available plus three guest beers (400 per year) including Exmoor Gold, Old Mill Bitter, Fuller's London Pride and Orkney Dark Island.

A small, friendly three-roomed pub with a wide variety of customers. Foreign bottled beers also stocked. Bar food is available at lunchtime and evenings. Garden. Children allowed. Off the A646.

11.30am–3pm and 7–11pm.

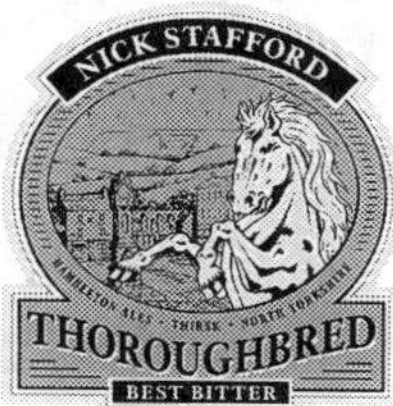

HOLME ON SWALE

HAMBLETON ALES

The Brewery,
Holme on Swale,
Nr Thirsk YO7 4JE
☎ *(01845) 567460*
Visitors welcome in small, pre-arranged groups. Tied houses: None

Hambleton Ales is a small brewery situated on the banks of the River Swale, a few miles west of Thirsk. Nick Stafford and his wife, Sally, began the business in March 1991, and it soon established itself locally in many pubs in James Herriot country and nationally, earning several awards. Brewing methods are very traditional using the finest malted barley from West Yorkshire and Northdown hops. The local water is perfect for producing a well flavoured, finely balanced and refreshing product. The brewery has grown rapidly, employing five local men and women. New premises have been constructed and will shortly receive new plant and machinery in order to continue the expansion programme.

Beers available at: Number Twenty 2, Coniscliffe Road, Darlington, Durham *and* The Nag's Head, Pickhill, Nr Thirsk, Yorkshire.

HAMBLETON BITTER 3.6% ABV
A 100 per cent malt mash giving a full flavour and mid-brown colour. Northdown hops produce a bitterness which is refreshing and moreish.

STALLION 4.2% ABV
This premium bitter has a distinctive malty character with a hint of nuttiness. A true Yorkshire bitter.

GOLDFIELD 4.2% ABV
Although the same alcoholic strength as Stallion, Goldfield is very different. Antique gold in colour and lighter in texture, not overly bitter with a good, clean aftertaste.

NIGHTMARE 5.0% ABV
This is an extra stout porter. Nightmare is not harsh or overly bitter. A smooth, massively flavoured creamy drink, best served on the warm side.

THOROUGHBRED 5.0% ABV
A pale ale from the finest Halcyon malt, well rounded in body, a dry finish and packed with the aroma of Northdown hops.

Plus ales for Village Brewer including:
WHITE BOAR (3.8% ABV)
BULL (4.0% ABV) and
OLD RABY (4.8% ABV).

HOLMFIRTH

The Farmer's Arms

Liphill Bank Road,
Holmfirth AD7 1LG
☎ *(01484) 683713*
Mr Gosling

Eight beers always available including Timothy Taylor Best and Black Sheep Bitter. Guests (350 per year) might include Kelham Island Pale Rider, Mitchell's Lancaster Bomber and Adnams brews.

An eighteenth-century pub. Bar food available. Parking nearby. Garden and function room. Accommodation. Children allowed. Off the A635.

6–11pm Mon–Fri; 12–11pm Sat; 12–10.30pm Sun.

HUDDERSFIELD

LINFIT BREWERY

Sair Inn, Lane Top, Linthwaite, Huddersfield HD7 5SG
☎ *(01484) 842370*

A dozen Linfit brews are produced and served in the Sair Inn.

An award-winning brewery that began production in 1982 for the Sair Inn and free trade. New plant installed in 1994 increased the capacity. The pub is a traditional nineteenth-century inn with four rooms, stone floors and open fires. Parking in road, children's room.

DARK MILD 3.0% ABV

SUMMER ALE 3.1% ABV

BITTER 3.7% ABV

SPECIAL 4.3% ABV

JANET STREET PORTER 4.5% ABV

AUTUMN GOLD 4.7% ABV

ENGLISH GUINEAS STOUT 5.3% ABV

OLD ELI 5.3% ABV

SPRINGBOK BIER 5.7% ABV

BRISTOL CREAM 5.8% ABV

LEADBOILER 6.6% ABV

ENOCH'S HAMMER 8.6% ABV

XMAS ALE 8.6% ABV

7.30–11pm Mon–Fri; 12–3pm and 7.30–11pm Sat–Sun and public holidays.

Old Court Brewery

The Old Court Brewhouse,
Queen Street, Huddersfield HD1 2SL
☎ *(01484) 454035*

Four Old Court brews produced and served on the premises.

The brewery is raised up from the lower floor and is visible from the public bar. This listed building was formerly the county court. Bar and restaurant food available at lunchtime and evenings (Monday to Saturday). Metered parking, garden.

COPPERS 3.4% ABV

M'LUD 3.5% ABV

1825 4.5% ABV

MAXIMUM SENTENCE 5.5% ABV

Ring for details.

Rat and Ratchet

40 Chapel Hill,
Huddersfield HD1 3EB
☎ *(01484) 516734*

Fourteen ales at all times. Three home brews plus Adnams Bitter, Bateman Mild, Mansfield Old Baily, Marston's Perigree, Timothy Taylor Landlord and several more.

The brewery opened at the Rat and Ratchet in December 1994. A popular pub with beer festivals and special events held regularly.

THE GREAT GNAWTHERN 4.0% ABV

THE GREAT ESCAPE 4.2% ABV

CRATCHET'S CHRISTMAS CRACKER 4.3% ABV

12–11pm.

Hull

The Hull Brewery

144–148 English Street,
Hull HU3 2BT
☎ *(01482) 586364*
Visitors permitted. Tied houses: None

The assets of the Hull Brewery were purchased by Dieter Ellwood in March 1994. He set up a micro-brewery employing only three people, one of whom is the brewer, Paul Hutchings. The brewery has continued to produce the Mild, Hull Bitter and Governor to their original recipes and has now added two more beers to the portfolio – Ellwood's Best Bitter and Amber Ale.

Beers available at: The Red Lion, Clarence Street, Hull *and* Ye Old Black Boy, High Street, Hull.

HULL BREWERY MILD 3.3% ABV
This full-flavoured dark mild with a malty aroma is traditionally served with a thick creamy head.

ELLWOOD'S BEST BITTER 3.8% ABV
An amber-coloured session best bitter with a malty taste and aroma. It has subtle hints of fruit and a refreshing bitter aftertaste.

HULL BREWERY BITTER 3.8% ABV
A dry-hopped, well-balanced easy drinking, golden session bitter with a smooth hoppy aftertaste.

GOVERNOR STRONG ALE 4.4% ABV
This ale was brewed to commemorate the anniversary of the outbreak of the English Civil War. A tawny golden-coloured premium bitter with a malty taste and a distinctive hop aroma, it is deceptively powerful.

AMBER ALE 4.0% ABV
An amber-coloured easy drinking beer, brewed using crystal malt with English and American hop varieties.

Plus special brews on a bi-monthly basis.

Springbank Tavern

29 Spring Bank,
Hull HU3 1AS
☎ *(01482) 581879*
Mr and Mrs O'Conner

Mansfield and Deacon Standard Bitter, Riding Bitter and Riding Mild permanently available plus up to ten (100 per year) guests including Ruddles, Woods and Old Hazy Cider. Emphasis on small breweries.

A one-room ale house with traditional games (darts and dominoes). Students and locals provide mixed clientele. Background music, but no jukebox. Bar food available 12–2pm and 5–7pm daily. Street parking, disabled facilities. Children allowed in the bar for meals. Just off the city centre.

11am–11pm Mon–Sat;
12–3pm and 7–10.30pm Sun.

Ye Olde Black Boy

150 High Street,
Hull HU1 1PS
☎ *(01482) 326516*
Barry Fenn

Hull Brewery Bitter permanently available plus nine guest beers (300 per year) from Hambleton, Rooster's, Old Mill, John Joules, Cropton, North Yorkshire, Hadrian, Bateman's and Steampacket breweries.

The first Tap and Spile charter house. The original building dates back to 1331. Traditional wood-panelled walls and floors. Upstairs bar open for food at lunchtimes and on Friday and Saturday evenings. Bar food available at lunchtime and evenings. Parking. Children allowed in the upstairs bar when having food. Situated on the Old High Street, next to the River Hull.

12–3pm and
7–11pm Mon–Thurs;
all day Fri–Sun.

Keighley

Commercial Brewing

Worth Brewery,
Worth Way,
Keighley BD21 5LP
☎ *(01535) 611914*
Visitors welcome. Tied houses: 1

The company was founded in a garage in 1992 and has hosted the Keighley Beer Festival in association with CAMRA. A brewery visitors' centre should now be complete. Bottled beer production is scheduled for 1997.

Beers available at: The Red Pig, Church Street, Keighley, Yorkshire *and* The Slaters Arms, Cragg Lane, Bradley, Nr Skipton, Yorkshire.

ALESMAN BITTER 3.7% ABV
Session bitter.

WORTH BITTER 4.5% ABV
Distinctive premium bitter.

WORTH PORTER 4.5% ABV

KNOBWILLTER 5.1% ABV
Wheat beer.

WORTH STOUT 4.2% ABV)

OLD TOSS 6.5% ABV
Rich, fruity, barley wine.

Plus a range of special brews.

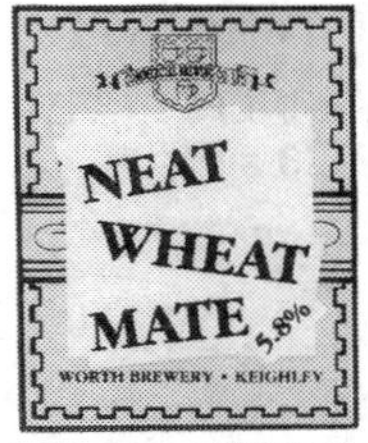

GOOSE EYE BREWERY

Ingrow Bridge, South Street, Keighley BD21 5AX
☎ *(01535) 605807*
Visitors welcome. Tied houses: None

Goose Eye Brewery was reopened after several years' closure in 1991, by the original owner, Mr B Eastell, and Jack Atkinson. Jack bought Mr Eastell's share of the business after two years and is now in partnership with his son, David.

Beers available at: Turkey Inn, Goose Eye, Oakworth, Nr Keighley, Yorkshire *and* Wuthering Heights, Main Street, Stanbury, Keighley, Yorkshire.

GOOSE EYE BITTER 3.8% ABV
Pale golden, additive free, traditionally brewed beer with a refreshing lingering taste of hops.

BRONTE 4.0% ABV
Similar to the bitter, but more hoppy and darker.

WHARFEDALE 4.5% ABV
Darker, richer, stronger bitter but still light on the palate with the taste of hops coming through.

POMMIES REVENGE 5.2% ABV
Extra strong, single-malt bitter. Very palatable without the heaviness of an old ale but the same effect.

THE OLD WHITE BEAR AND BREWERY

6 Keighley Road, Crosshills, Keighley BD20 7RN
☎ *(01535) 632115*

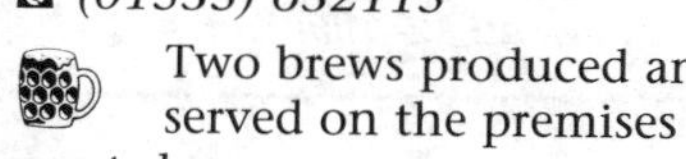

Two brews produced and served on the premises plus guests beers.

The owner ran the Goose Eye Brewery from 1978 to 1991 but wanted to produce a fuller beer using natural water and ingredients, so he started production in the old stables here in 1993. The pub was built in 1735 and retains its original beams. Bar and restaurant food is available at lunchtime and evenings. Car park, small garden. Children allowed if kept under control.

BITTER 3.9% ABV

BARNSEY BITTER 3.9% ABV

11.30am–3pm and 5–11pm Mon–Thurs (not Mon lunch); 11.30am–11pm Fri–Sat; 12–4pm and 7–10.30pm Sun.

KIRK HAMMERTON

MARSTON MOOR BREWERY

Crown House, Kirk Hammerton, York YO5 8DD
☎ *(01423) 330341*
Visitors welcome, by appointment. Tied houses: None

The company commenced brewing in 1983 and the fabrication and supply of brew plant and equipment to other small breweries has become an important part of the business.

Beers available at: The Wakefield Labour Exchange, 18 Vicarage Street, Wakefield, Yorkshire *and* The Beer Exchange, 121 Woodhouse Street, Leeds, Yorkshire.

CROMWELL BITTER 3.6% ABV
Superb, light, refreshing ale with a distinctive hop flavour.

BREWERS PRIDE 4.2% ABV
Full-bodied, smooth premium beer. Amber coloured with a well-balanced hop flavour.

MERRIE MAKER 4.5% ABV
A premium bitter with a typical Yorkshire taste, but with an untypical strength.

PORTER 4.2% ABV
Dark, ruby-coloured, full-bodied, stout-like ale. The use of roast barley contributes to the smooth, dry and extremely palatable finish.

BLACK TOM STOUT 4.5% ABV
One for special occasions, brewed intermittently during the winter. Robust, strong, black and proud.

BREWER'S DROOP 5.1% ABV
Award-winning powerful ale, but dangerously drinkable. This straw-coloured ale has a sweet but not cloying taste.

TROOPER 1050 5.1% ABV
Rustic coloured ale with its own rustic charms. Crisp, strong with a wonderful aroma.

KNARESBOROUGH

Blind Jack's

19 Market Place, Knaresborough HG8 5AL
☎ *(01423) 869148*
David Llewellyn

Six beers always available including Timothy Taylor Landlord and Hambleton White Boar plus guests (300 per year) including Hambleton Bitter, Daleside Legover, Crompton Two Pints, Elgood's Pageant, Tom Woods Bitter, Goose Eye and Morland brews.

A seventeenth-century listed building, beamed with wooden floors and lots of mirrors. Bar and restaurant food available at lunchtime and evenings. Parking nearby. Children allowed.

12–11pm Mon–Fri; 11.30am–11pm Sat; 12–10.30pm Sun.

LEEDS

The Duck and Drake

43 Kirkgate, Leeds LS2 7DR
☎ *(0113) 246 5806*
Mr and Mrs Morley

Timothy Taylor Landlord and Old Mill Bitter permanently available plus six guests (300 per year) from breweries including Jennings, Clarks, Exmoor, Roosters, Pioneer and Steam Packet. Also real cider.

A traditional ale house with wooden floors, coal fires, bare boards and live bands. Bar food is served at lunchtime. Get to Leeds market and ask.

All permitted hours.

The Eagle Tavern

North Street, Sheepscar, Leeds LS2 1AF
☎ *(0113) 245 7146*
Mr Moon

Timothy Taylor brews always available plus lots of local and distant guest beers (200 per year). Has sold more than 1,000 different beers. CAMRA Yorkshire Pub of the Year 1994.

An 1826 Georgian building close to the city centre. Bar food available at lunchtime. Parking. Ten minutes walk out of the city centre.

11.30am–3pm and 5.30–11pm Mon–Sat; 12–3pm Sun.

MALTON

MALTON BREWERY

Suddaby's Crown Hotel,
Wheelgate, Malton YO17 0HP
☎ *(01653) 697580*
G Woollons, C Parlett and N Suddaby

Malton Pale Ale, Double Chance, Pickwick's Porter, Nutbrown and Owd Bob available plus guests.

The Malton Brewery Company was formed in 1984 by Geoff Woollons, Colin Sykes and Bob Suddaby in the converted stables behind Suddaby's Crown Hotel. The first pint was pulled in February 1985. The pub is traditional in character, located in the town centre and popular with locals and visitors alike. No juke box but a dartboard, domino tables and TV showing the latest starting prices for the days horse racing meetings. Bar food available at lunchtime (except Sunday and Tuesday). Parking, children's room. Accommodation.

PALE ALE 3.2% ABV

DOUBLE CHANCE BITTER 3.8% ABV

PICKWICK'S PORTER 4.0% ABV

NUTBROWN 4.1% ABV

OWD BOB 5.9% ABV

Usual pub hours.

MASHAM

BLACK SHEEP BREWERY

Wellgarth, Masham,
Nr Ripon HG4 4EN
☎ (01765) 689227
Visitors welcome. Tied houses: None

The Black Sheep Brewery was set up in Masham by Paul Theakston, from the fifth generation of the famous brewing family. He left the family firm after the takeover by Scottish and Newcastle Breweries in 1989 and the brewhouse was built during 1992. The brewery now sells to more than 200 pubs as well as supplying larger pub groups, supermarkets and off-licences.

Beers available at: The Maltings, Tanner's Moat, York, Yorkshire *and* The Bruce Arms, Morton Row, Masham, Yorkshire.

BEST BITTER 3.8% ABV
A full-bodied session bitter. Light golden in colour and rounded in taste. A well-hopped bitter in the finest Masham tradition.

SPECIAL STRONG BITTER 4.4% ABV
Clean-drinking. Distinctly darker and stronger than the best bitter. Brewed with many generous handfuls of choicest Golding hops.

Plus **BLACK SHEEP ALE** (4.4% ABV) carefully brewed for the bottle.

MIDDLESBROUGH

NORTH YORKSHIRE BREWING CO.

80–84 North Ormesby Road, Middlesbrough TS4 2AG
☎ *(01642) 226224*
Visitors welcome. Tied houses: None

Established in March 1990, this purpose-built brewery produces a range of traditional beers using only traditional brewing methods and materials.

Beers available at: The Malt Shovel, 92 Corporation Road, Middlesbrough, Yorkshire *and* The Tap 'n' Barrel, 86 Newport Road, Middlesbrough, Yorkshire.

BEST BITTER 3.5–3.8% ABV
A clean tasting, well-hopped, pale, traditional bitter.

YORKSHIRE BROWN 3.8–4.0% ABV
A ruby-red northern-style brown ale, full-bodied and very slightly sweet.

YORKSHIRE PORTER 3.8–4.0% ABV
A medium-bodied porter, black in colour, a complex mix of tastes with roast barley and hops prominent.

FOOLS GOLD 4.2–4.6% ABV
A full-bodied, pale-coloured, well-hopped strong bitter. Originally brewed as a special, now a regular by popular demand.

FLYING HERBERT 4.5–5.0% ABV
A full-flavoured premium bitter, smooth and well balanced.

DIZZY DICK 7.6–8.2% ABV
A very full-bodied barley wine with a mellow taste, achieving an excellent balance on the palate

Also Scatterbrain Scrumpy and seasonal and occasional brews.

The Malt Shovel

92 Corporation Road, Middlesbrough TS1 2RR
☎ *(01642) 213213*
Martin Gilbert

Black Sheep Best Bitter and Special Strong Bitter always available plus many guest beers including a good selection from the smaller independents.

Live music and quiz nights. Food available at lunchtime. Parking, disabled toilets and children's area. Children not allowed in the bar.

11am–11pm Mon–Sat; 12–10.30pm Sun.

The Tap 'n' Barrel

86 Newport Road, Middlesbrough TS1 5JA
☎ *(01642) 219995*
Kevin and Joyce Johnson

Specialises in guest beers, of which up to 15 may be available. Examples include Fools Gold, Flying Herbert and Dizzy Dick from NYBC, Joules Crown, Big Lamp Bitter, Ward's Best, Norkies' Summer Ale, Marston's Pedigree, Charles Wells Bombardier, Yorkshire Porter, Timothy Taylor Landlord.

A traditional Victorian-style real ale pub converted from a shop with gas lighting, stone floors, beamed ceiling and a warm, friendly atmosphere. Close links with NYBC. Bar food available at lunchtime. Parking opposite. Children allowed at lunchtime. A function room with own bar upstairs. From the A19, follow the

A66 towards Middlesbrough, take the second exit and turn right. The pub is opposite Sainsbury's, near the bus station.

11am–11pm Mon–Sat; 12–3pm and 7–10.30pm Sun.

PICKERING

LASTINGHAM BREWERY

Unit 5, Westgate Carr Road,
Pickering YO18 8LX
☎ *(01751) 477628*
Visitors welcome. Tied houses: None

The company was established in June 1993 and quickly expanded to supply 50 accounts. The first tied house was sold in March 1995. The brewery won several business awards in 1994, one of which was from The Prince of Wales. This led to the commemorative brew, Royal Oui, which Prince Charles duly tried. The brewery is expanding to a ten-barrel plant to meet increased demand.

Beers available at: Birch Hall Inn, Beck Hole, Nr Goathland, Yorkshire *and* Blacksmith's Arms, Lastingham, Yorkshire.

CHURCH BITTER 3.7% ABV
Dry, hoppy session beer. Full bodied.

CURATE'S DOWNFALL 4.3% ABV
Balanced hop and malt taste. Very smooth, dry aftertaste.

CELTIC ALE 4.2% ABV
Full tasting fruity premium bitter with tangy resonance.

ROYAL OUI 4.5% ABV
Smooth, dry hop taste. Very fruity. Golden colour.

AMEN 5.4% ABV
Powerful old ale, roasted malt and dry fruit.

PONTEFRACT

TOMLINSON'S OLD CASTLE BREWERY

Unit 5, Britannia Works,
Skinner Lane,
Pontefract WF8 4HU
☎ *(01977) 780866*
Visitors welcome. Tied houses: None

When Tomlinson's Old Castle Brewery was established in 1993, it marked the return of brewing to Pontefract after a 60-year absence. The original Old Castle Brewery was established by Mr T Taylor prior to 1857. William Pickersgill acquired the brewery in about 1887 until it was purchased by Bentley's Yorkshire Breweries in 1932. The trade mark for the brewery was a broken bridge, the Latin for which, *pontus fractus*, gave Pontefract its name. The Liquorice Bush pub was owned by the original Old Castle Brewery and was then called the Central Hotel.

Beers available at: Tap & Spile, 28 Horsefair, Pontefract, Yorkshire *and* Liquorice Bush, 8 Market Place, Pontefract, Yorkshire.

SESSIONS 4.0% ABV
A pale light session beer, named after Sessions Yard, in Pontefract, where the old courts were held and the present court house still stands.

DOWN WITH IT 4.3% ABV
A full-bodied session beer with an all-malt flavour and a Golding hop aroma. Named after the cry of the townspeople who, after many years of war, were asked by Cromwell's Parliament what they wanted to do with the castle.

FRACTUS XB 4.5% ABV
A premium, dry, strong Scotch-style beer with an almost nutty brown ale flavour.

RICHARD'S DEFEAT 5.0% ABV
A deep ruby red old-style porter whose three malts and two hops give a rich deep roast and chocolate aroma and a full rich deep roast aftertaste. Named after Richard II, who died at Pontefract Castle after being overthrown and imprisoned by his cousin, Henry Bollingbroke, who owned the castle.

DECEITFUL ROSE 5.0% ABV
A light easygoing but deceitfully strong beer. A name for Pontefract Castle which, in the Wars of the Roses, was Lancastrian-owned.

HERMITAGE MILD 3.7% ABV
A fine malty dark mild, lightly hopped. Named after Adam de Laythorpe, the town's hermit, who lived underneath the present hospital.

THREE SIEGES 6.0% ABV
A strong winter ale. Pontefract Castle withstood three sieges by Oliver Cromwell.

DE LACY 4.6% ABV
A light easygoing beer with a smokey aftertaste. Named after the Norman de Lacy family who built the castle.

FEMME FATALE 4.5% ABV
A strong tasting, malty beer brewed by Tracy Tomlinson. Named after Catherine Howard, Henry VIII's fifth wife, who had an affair in Pontefract Castle.

Also many specials and one-off beers.

The Tap & Spile

28 Horsefair,
Pontefract WF8 1NX
Mr Coles

Tomlinson's Sessions and something from Cotleigh Brewery always available plus up to nine guest beers from everywhere.

Two beer festivals per year, usually in April and November. Situated opposite Pontefract bus station.

12–11pm Mon–Sat;
12–3pm and 7–10.30pm Sun.

POOL-IN-WHARFEDALE

The Hunter's Inn

Harrogate Road,
Pool -in-Wharfedale,
Nr Otley LS21 2PS
☎ *(0113) 284 1090*
Geoffrey Nunn

Daleside Bitter always available plus six guests (300 per year) including Rudgate Battleaxe, Charles Wells Eagle, Ryburn Best, Enville Ale, Daleside Old Legover, Shepherd Neame Bishop's Finger, Kelham Island Pale Rider, Black Sheep Bitter and Special, Moorhouse's Pendle Witches Brew, NYBC Toffee Apple, Butterknowle High Force, Nix Wincott THAT and Wychwood Dr Thirsty.

Pub with real ale, real fire and real characters, from bikers to businessmen. Families welcome. Bar food is available 12–5pm Mon–Fri. Car park, garden patio with tables and chairs, pool table, juke box, pub cats. Children are allowed but not encouraged too much (no play area). One mile from Pool-in-Wharfedale, on the Harrogate road. Seven miles from Harrogate.

All day, including Sun.

RIPON

One Eyed Rat

51 Allhallowgate,
Ripon HG4 1LQ
☎ *(01765) 607704*

Seven beers always available including Wadworth 6X and 80 guests per year including Exmoor Gold, Shepherd Neame Bishop's Finger and Daleside brews.

A simple ale house. No music, no food. Parking nearby. Garden. Children allowed in garden. Not far from the bus station.

12–2pm and 6–11pm Mon–Fri;
12–3pm and 6–11pm Sat;
12–3pm and 7–10.30pm Sun.

SELBY

SELBY BREWERY

131 Millgate,
Selby YO8 0LL
☎ *(01757) 702826*
No visitors. Tied houses: 1

An old family brewery which resumed production in 1972, now mostly involved in the wholesale market. Old Tom is brewed once a year, in November and is available while stocks last through its Brewery Tap off-licence.

OLD TOM 6.5% ABV

SCARBOROUGH

The Tap & Spile

94 Falsgrave Road,
Scarborough YO12 5AZ
☎ *(01723) 363837*
Brett Bennett

Big Lamp Bitter permanently available plus nine guests (250 per year) including brews from Bateman, Jennings, Old Mill, Steam Packet, Cropton and Whitby.

A lovely old coaching inn with low beams, old Yorkshire stone floor and no-smoking room. Bar food served at lunchtime. Car park, garden, children's room. Turn left out of the railway station, going towards the roundabout.

All day, every day.

SHEFFIELD

KELHAM ISLAND BREWERY

The Fat Cat,
23 Alma Street,
Sheffield S3 8SA
☎ *(0114) 278 2195*

Kelham Island brews plus Timothy Taylor Landlord, Marston's Pedigree and various guests.

The brewery was purpose-built in 1990 on land beside The Fat Cat. Equipment came from the Oxford Brewery and Bakehouse and the first brew was delivered by steam dray to the Sheffield Beer Festival in September 1990. This is the first independent brewey to open in Sheffield this century. Brews are produced according to German purity laws using only grains, water, hops and yeast. The brewery has won eight awards in the past 12 months. The olde-worlde pub has no music, no machines, real fires and ten real ales. It is situated in a back street near the city centre. Food served at lunchtime. Parking, garden, children's room.

FAT CAT PALE ALE 3.6% ABV

BITTER 3.8% ABV

GOLDEN EAGLE 4.2% ABV

WHEAT BEER 5.0% ABV

BETE NOIRE 5 5% ABV

12–3pm and 5.30–11pm Mon–Sat; 12–3pm and 7–10.30pm Sun.

WARD'S BREWERY

Ecclesall Road, Sheffield S11 8HZ
☎ *(0114) 275 5155*
Visitors welcome. Tied houses: 229

Ward's Brewery has its origins in the 1840s, when a partnership was formed between John Kirby and George Wright. These two began brewing at Sheaf Island Brewery in Sheffield and, with the additional capital of Septimus Henry Ward, the company has continued ever since. In 1972, Ward's Brewery merged with Vaux Breweries of Sunderland and, in 1979, Darley's of Thorne, another long-established family company, joined the group. The company is proud of its heritage and continues to brew high quality beers in the traditional manner.

VAUX MILD 3.2% ABV
A pleasant dark brown colour with a hint of red and a very malty aroma. A smooth beer with plenty of malt and chocolate flavours just touched by a hint of hops. The sweet malty aftertaste is rather short.

THORNE BEST BITTER 3.8% ABV
Light brown, almost ginger, in colour with a complex aroma which includes hops, malt and orchard fruit. A grainy mouthfeel with malt and crystal malt flavours underscored by hops. It has a sharp, dry, lasting finish.

WARD'S BEST BITTER 4.0% ABV
A pale golden-coloured beer with an intense malt aroma, touched by a hint of orchard fruit. A clean tasting beer with a grainy body and lots of malt flavour. Malt again dominates the finish with just a hint of hops.

WAGGLE DANCE 5.0% ABV
A delicate straw-coloured and unusual beer in which honey plays the main part. It is very obvious in the aroma and, with the malt, provides the main flavour. The finish is rather sweet and lasting.

VAUX EXTRA SPECIAL 5.0% ABV
An attractive golden colour with a malty, fruity aroma leading to a full smooth beer with bittersweet malt and crystal malt flavours underscored by hops. The finish is long and complex, malt is the main component.

Cask and Cutler

1 Henry Street, Infirmary Road, Sheffield S3 7EQ
☎ *(0114) 272 1487*

Hexhamshire Low Quarter Ale always available plus four guest beers (300 per year) from breweries such as Black Bull, Whim, Townes, Tomlinsons, Church End, Durham, Cottage, Newale and Wild's. No nationals. Also traditional cider.

A largely unspoilt, two-roomed street-corner local. Bar food available at lunchtime and evenings. Parking. Children allowed in the bar until 8pm. Situated 100 yards from Shalesmoor supertram stop. At the junction of the A61 and B6079, north of the city centre.

12–2pm and 5.30–11pm Mon–Thurs; 12–11pm Fri–Sat; normal hours Sun.

The Tap & Spile

48 Waingate, Sheffield S3 8LB
☎ *(0114) 272 6270*
K Fletcher

Tap & Spile Bitter and Premium always available plus six guest beers (200 per year) from independent brewers only.

A traditional ale house with two rooms. Traditional pub games (no pool), background music only. Folk music Wednesdays, quiz night Thursdays. Bar food available at lunchtime. Situated 100 yards from Sheffield canal basin, five minutes from the railway station.

11.30am–3pm and 5.30–11pm Mon–Fri; 11.30am–3pm and 7–11pm Sat; 7–10.30pm Sun.

SLAITHWAITE

WILD'S BREWERY

Unit 3E, Spa Field Industrial Estate, Slaithwaite, Huddersfield HD7 5BB
☎ *(01484) 841119*
Visitors welcome in organised parties, usually at one month's notice.
Tied houses: None

Wild's Brewery is a small traditional recently established company based in the Pennine mill village of Slaithwaite, producing a range of five award-winning real ales, brewed only with the finest ingredients and toughest quality controls.

Beers available at: Marsh Liberal Club, Glenfield, 31 New Hey Road, Marsh, Huddersfield, Yorkshire *and* Packhorse Hotel, Carr Lane, Slaithwaite, Nr Huddersfield, Yorkshire.

WILD SESSION 3.8% ABV
A thoroughly quaffable session beer.

WILD OATS 4.1% ABV
A truly smooth drink with a clear, orange hue.

WILD BLONDE 4.1% ABV
An award-winning lager lookalike, perfect for summer.

WILD REDHEAD 4.5% ABV
A full-bodied hoppy beer with a reddish tint.

WILD THING 5.0% ABV
An almost yellow coloured beer, rather too easy to drink for its strength.

Sowerby Bridge

Ryburn Brewery

Owenshaw Mill, Old Cawsey,
Sowerby Bridge HX6 2AJ
☎ *(01422) 835413*
Visitors welcome. Tied houses: 1

Founded in a former dye works in 1990, new plant and a move to larger premises became necessary in 1994. Ryburn supplies one tied house and 15 other outlets.

Beers available at: Griffin Inn, Stainland Road, Barkisland, Nr Halifax, Yorkshire *and* White Swan, Oldham Road, Ripponden, Sowerby Bridge, Yorkshire.

BEST MILD 3.3% ABV

BEST BITTER 3.8% ABV

RYDALE BITTER 4.4% ABV

OLD STONE TROFF BITTER 4.7% ABV

LUDDITE 5.0% ABV

STABBERS BITTER 5.2% ABV

COINERS 6.0% ABV

Starbeck

Daleside Brewery

Camwal Road, Starbeck,
Harrogate HG1 4PT
☎ *(01423) 880041*
No visitors. Tied houses: None

Daleside Brewery started life as the Big End Brewery in 1988, run by Bill Witty, a CAMRA stalwart. In 1991, Bill and his son Craig relocated and changed the company name. They now supply approximately 200 outlets.

Beers available at: Malt Shovel, Brearton, Nr Knaresborough, Yorkshire *and* One Eyed Rat, 81 Allhallowgate, Ripon, Yorkshire.

DALESIDE NIGHTJAR 3.7% ABV
Well-balanced medium-hopped bitter with some sweetness and a touch of fruitiness.

DALESIDE COUNTRY STILE 4.1% ABV
Medium-dark malty beer, nicely hopped with a sharp, crisp finish.

DALESIDE OLD ALE 4.1% ABV
Dark, medium-strength, malty bitter. Roasted malt is evident with some sweetness, with a small amount of hops.

MIDSUMMER DELIGHT 4.1% ABV
Very light bitter.

MONKEY WRENCH 5.5% ABV
Strong and dark with a deceptive smoothness. Malt dominates, slight sweetness.

Staveley

The Royal Oak

Main Street, Staveley,
Nr Knaresborough HG5 9LD
☎ *(01423) 340267*

Four beers always available including Viking (Rudgate) brews plus two guests (25 per year) from small independent breweries.

A typical country pub, cosy, friendly, with open fires and two bars. Bar and restaurant food available at lunchtime and evenings (not Sunday and Monday evenings). Car park, garden, children's play area.

12–3pm and
6–11pm Mon–Sat;
12–5pm and 7–10.30pm Sun.

Sutton upon Derwent

St Vincent Arms

Main Street,
Sutton upon Derwent
☎ *(01904) 608349*
Philip Hopwood

Fuller's Chiswick, London Pride and ESB and Timothy Taylor Landlord always available plus guests including Adnams Extra, Old Mill Bitter, Charles Wells Bombardier, Mansfield Old Baily and seasonal and special ales.

About 200 years old, with white-washed walls. Two bars, four rooms, open fires. Bar and restaurant food available at lunchtime and evenings. Car park, beer garden, no-smoking room. Children allowed. On main road through village.

11.30am–3pm and
6–11pm Mon–Sat;
12–3pm and 7–10.30pm Sun.

Tadcaster

Samuel Smith Old Brewery

The Old Brewery,
High Street,
Tadcaster LS24 9SB
☎ *(01937) 832225*
Visitors welcome

All Sam Smith's ales and stouts are brewed with well water and fermented in stone Yorkshire squares. The naturally-conditioned beer is produced in wooden casks.

Beers available at: The Angel and White Horse, Bridge Street, Tadcaster, Yorkshire *and* The Greyhound, Saxton, Nr Tadcaster, Yorkshire.

SAMUEL SMITH'S OLD BREWERY BITTER 4.0% ABV

SAMUEL SMITH'S MUSEUM ALE 5.0% ABV

SAMUEL SMITH'S CELEBRATED OATMEAL STOUT 5.0% ABV

SAMUEL SMITH'S FAMOUS TADDY PORTER 5.0% ABV.

Tockwith

Rudgate Brewery

2 Centre Park,
Marston Business Park,
Rudgate, Tockwith,
Nr York YO5 8QF
☎ *(01423) 358382*
Visitors welcome

Rudgate Brewery was founded in 1992 in an old armoury building on a disused airfield near York. The area has Viking connections, hence the names of the beers. This is a small traditional brewer of high-quality cask beers. All brews are full mash using Yorkshire malted barley, English whole hops and local water. Fermentation takes place in open square vessels using a Yorkshire strain of brewing yeast.

Beers available at: Royal Oak, North Street, Wetherby, Yorkshire *and* Royal Oak, Staveley, Boroughbridge, Yorkshire.

VIKING 3.8% ABV
Easy-drinking session bitter.

BATTLE AXE 4.2% ABV
A robust and smooth premium bitter.

THOR'S HAMMAR 5.5% ABV
Strong and distinctive pale ale. Seasonal brew.

PILLAGE PORTER 4.0% ABV
A rich, nutty, ruby brew. Seasonal.

MAY POLE 4.5% ABV
Popular Spring brew.

EASTER SPECIAL 5.0% ABV
An amber ale.

RUDOLF'S RUIN 6.0% ABV
A full-drinking Christmas classic.

WAKEFIELD

HB CLARK & CO.

Westgate Brewery,
Westgate, Wakefield WF2 9SW
☎ *(01924) 373328*
Visitors welcome. Tied houses: 4

Clark's beers were first produced in Wakefield in 1905 when the Kingswell and Horsfall families financed the operation. A year later, Henry Boon Clark took over the running of the company. It was wound up in 1912, but re-emerged a year later as HB Clark and Company. During the 1960s and 1970s, the company developed and began to expand into the wholesale sector. Norman Garthwaite served the company for 50 years as manager and then managing director, until his death in 1981. His sons, John and David Garthwaite, then acquired the majority shareholding. Further developments took place and a new purpose-built brewery opened in 1982. The company is now one of the largest independent wholesalers in the drinks industry.

CLARK'S TRADITIONAL BITTER 3.8% ABV
Amber-coloured. Smooth, hoppy and fruity.

CLARK'S FESTIVAL ALE 4.2% ABV
Straw-coloured brew. Well balanced with hops and fruit. Distinctive hoppy aroma, light crisp palate.

CLARK'S BURGLAR BILL 4.4% ABV
Full-bodied with a rich malty palate. Strong hop flavour and aroma.

CLARK'S RAMS REVENGE 4.8% ABV
Dark copper-coloured ale. Well balanced with its roast barley and malt. Smooth dry finish.

CLARK'S HAMMERHEAD 5.5% ABV
Full flavoured robust and strong ale. Rich and malty, it has a long dry finish that accentuates the flavour of its Yorkshire malt.

CLARK'S WINTER WARMER 6.4% ABV
Dark coloured ale. Distinctive roast malt flavour. A hint of sweetness which belies its strength. Available November to March.

CLARK'S T'OWD DREADNOUGHT 9.0% ABV
Very strong, surprisingly light coloured ale. Full and rich with malt. Also slightly sweet.

The Tap & Spile

77 Westgate End,
Wakefield WF2 9RL
☎ *(01924) 375887*

Tap & Spile Premium always available plus seven guest beers (100s per year) from all sorts of breweries such as Morland, Hambleton, Tomlinson, Bateman, Joules, Cropton, Daleside, Exmoor, Hardington etc.

A traditional ale house with flagstone floors and three areas, TV and bar games. Gas lighting, open fires. Bar food is served at lunchtime. Garden. Children not allowed.

12–11pm Mon–Sat;
12–10.30pm Sun.

WOMBWELL

Royal Oak Hotel

13 Burch Street, Wombwell
☎ *(01254) 883541*
Helen Jones

Five real ales available from a long list including Spinnaker Bitter and Bateman brews.

A 1920s-style town-centre pub. Bar food available at lunchtime and evenings. Car park, accommodation. Children allowed at restricted times.

11am–11pm Mon–Sat; 12–10.30pm Sun.

WORTLEY

WORTLEY BREWERY

Wortley Arms Hotel, Halifax Road, Wortley S30 4DB
☎ *(0114) 288 2245*

Wortley beers brewed and served on the premises plus a range of guests.

The brewery started up in December 1991 producing Earls Ale. It closed for six weeks in spring 1992 for refurbishment. The sixteenth-century coaching house inn has oak beams, wood panels and an open fire. Bar and restaurant food available at lunchtime and evenings. Car park, children's room, no-smoking room, accommodation.

BEST BITTER 3.6% ABV

EARLS ALE 4.2% ABV

COUNTESS ALE 5.8% ABV

12–2.30pm and 5.30–11pm Mon–Fri; 12–11pm Sat; 12–3pm and 7–10.30pm Sun.

YORK

YORK BREWERY CO.

12 Toft Green, Mickelgate, York YO1 1JT
☎ (01904) 621162
Visitors welcome. Tied houses: None

Established in June 1996, this claims to be the first brewery to open in York for 40 years (the last was JJ Hunts, which was taken over by Camerons and closed in 1956). Andrew Whalley, the brewer, formerly worked at the now-closed Lastingham Brewery.

Beers available at: Birch Hall Inn, Beck Hole, Goathland, Yorkshire.

STONE WALL 3.7% ABV

YORKSHIRE TERRIER 4.2% ABV

The Ackhorne

9 St Martins Lane, York YO1 1LN
☎ *(01904) 629820*
Tony Featherstone

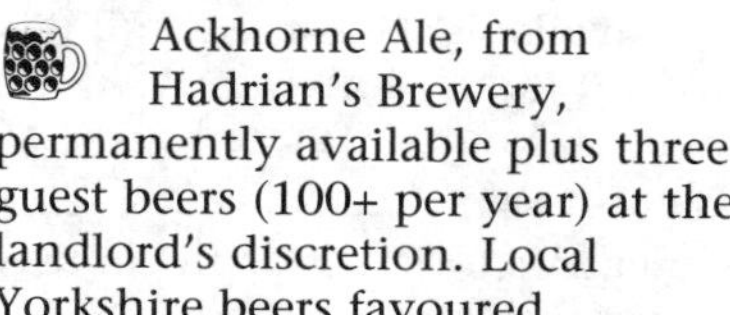

Ackhorne Ale, from Hadrian's Brewery, permanently available plus three guest beers (100+ per year) at the landlord's discretion. Local Yorkshire beers favoured.

Bar food is available at lunchtime except Sundays. Children are allowed in the pub at meal times. Located off Micklegate.

11.30am–3pm and 5.30–11pm.

The Maltings

Tanners Moat,
York YO1 1HU
☎ *(01904) 655387*
Maxine Collinge

Black Sheep Bitter always available plus six guests changing daily (700 per year). Too many to mention but with an emphasis on SIBA beers. Beer festivals twice a year. Also Belgian bottled beers, fruit wines and draught cider.

Small city-centre freehouse. CAMRA Yorkshire Pub of the Year 1994–95. Pub grub served at lunchtime. Situated on Lendal Bridge.

11am–11pm Mon–Sat; 12–10.30pm Sun.

Spread Eagle

98 Walmgate, York
☎ *(01904) 635868*
Michael Dandy

Seven or eight beers always available. Guests including Mansfield Riding Bitter and Old Baily and Timothy Taylor Landlord.

Popular Victorian-style freehouse. Bar and restaurant food available at lunchtime and evenings. Garden. Children allowed.

11am–11pm Mon–Sat; 12–10.30pm Sun.

The Tap & Spile

Monkgate, York
☎ *(01904) 656158*
Vicki Office

Eleven beers always available from a long list including Old Mill Bitter and brews from Marston Moor, Big Lamp and Ushers.

Traditional city centre ale house. Bar food available at lunchtime and evenings. Car park, garden. Children not allowed.

11.30am–11.30pm Mon–Sat; 12–10.30pm Sun.

ALLOA (CENTRAL)

MACLAY & Co.

Thistle Brewery, East Vennel, Alloa, Clackmanshire FK10 1ED
☎ *(01259) 726687*
No visitors. Tied houses: 33

The company was founded in 1830 by James Maclay and the present brewery was built in 1870. The business was bought by Frasers of Dunfermline in 1886 but still run by descendants of the founder until Evelyn Matthews and his family took over in 1992. Maclay still uses traditional brewing methods and direct-fired coppers, with the beers produced using only bore-hole water. Plant improvements are underway.

BROADSWORD 3.8% ABV
Light in colour, refreshing and very drinkable. Combines smooth, light fruity flavour with a zesty, flowery aroma.

KANE'S AMBER ALE 4.0% ABV
Light in colour with a delicious malty flavour and a clean, slightly hoppy flavour. Named after Dan Kane, a respected Edinburgh publican.

WALLACE IPA 4.5% ABV
Full-bodied, strong malt and a wonderful spring hop nose, with a clean, bitter finish.

OAT MALT STOUT 4.5% ABV
"The only oat malt stout in the world." Malted oats give this product a unique smooth, fruity flavour with a hint of chocolatey roast character. The recipe was granted a letters patent by Queen Victoria in 1895.

SCOTCH ALE 5.0% ABV
A robust traditional Scottish ale. Slight sweetness is balanced by subtle hopping, producing a full-bodied, satisfying, malty brew.

Plus limited-edition brews.

AYR (STRATHCLYDE)

Geordie's Byre

103 Main Street, Ayr KA8 88U
☎ *(01292) 264325*

Caledonian 80/– and Deuchars IPA permanently available plus three guest beers (450 per year) from Orkney (Skullsplitter) to Cornwall and Devon (Summerskill's Whistle Belly Vengeance).

A friendly freehouse managed by the owners. Decorated with memorabilia and Victoriana. No food available. CAMRA award 1995. Children not allowed. Located 50 yards from the police headquarters on King Street.

11am–11pm (midnight Thurs–Sat); 12.30–11pm Sun.

BONCHESTER BRIDGE (BORDERS)

Horse and Hound Hotel

Bonchester Bridge, Hawick TD9 8JN
☎ *(01450) 860645*
Mr and Mrs Tunnah

Maclay, Charles Wells and Border brews always available plus a guest beer (20 per year) from Longstone, Bateman, Jennings, Caledonian, Belhaven or Joseph Holt breweries.

This former coaching inn dating from 1704 offers comfortable accommodation. No–smoking areas. Bar and restaurant food is available at lunchtime and evenings. Car park. Children's certificate. Hawick is seven miles from Carter Bar on the England–Scotland border.

11.30am–2.30pm and 6–11pm.

BROUGHTON (BORDERS)

BROUGHTON ALES

Broughton, ML12 6HQ
☎ *(01899) 830345*
Visitors welcome. Tied houses: 1

Broughton Brewery was founded in 1980 by James Collins and David Younger, the latter from the seventh generation of the famous brewing family. Greenmantle Ale is named after the John Buchan book, written in 1920 and part of a trilogy that also includes *The Thirty-Nine Steps*. The author spent much of his childhood in the village. The brewery grew through the 1980s, supplying central and southern Scotland and outlets further afield, but problems subsequently arose and it fell into receivership in August 1995. A week later, Giles Litchfield of Whim Ales, Buxton, Derbyshire, bought the company and took over the business.

Beers available at: The Douglas Arms, 75 Friars Vennel, Dumfries, Dumfries and Galloway *and* The Spread Eagle, 5–6 Galloway Street, Dumfries, Dumfries and Galloway.

GREENMANTLE ALE 3.9% ABV
A delicate bitter-sweet ale with a fruity palate.

MERLIN'S ALE 4.2% ABV
A deep golden well-hopped ale.

SCOTTISH OATMEAL 4.2% ABV
Refreshing and nourishing with subtle oatmeal flavours.

OLD JOCK ALE 6.7% ABV
A robust well matured strong ale.

GHILLIE ALE 4.5% ABV
Rich copper-coloured ale. Full malty flavour with a distinctive, spicy hop flower aroma.

BROUGHTY FERRY (TAYSIDE)

Fisherman's Tavern

12 Fore Street, Broughty Ferry, Dundee DD5 2AD
☎ *(01382) 775941*
Mrs M Buntin

Belhaven 60/–, 80/– and St Andrew's Ale plus Maclay 80/– permanently available. Also three guest beers (600 per year) which include Traquair Bear Ale, Harviestoun Schiehallion, Buchan Gold, Belhaven Festival Gold and Sandy Hunter's, Maclay Wallace, plus beers from every corner of England and Wales. Also Belgian and German bottled beers.

A 300-year-old listed building, formerly a fisherman's cottage. Bar and restaurant food available at lunchtime and evenings. Parking, secluded walled garden. Children welcome. Accommodation. Situated by the lifeboat station at Broughty Ferry.

11am–midnight Mon–Sat; 12.30–midnight Sun.

CANONBIE (DUMFRIES & GALL)

The Riverside

Canonbie DG14 0UX
☎ *(013873) 71295/71512*
Mr and Mrs Phillips

Yates Bitter always available plus a guest (30 per year) from Adnams, Maclay, Caledonian or Fullers.

A civilised English-style country inn on the River Usk. Bar and restaurant food available at lunchtime and evenings. Car park and garden. Accommodation. Children allowed. 14 miles north from the M6 junction 44.

11am–2.30pm and 6.30–11pm.

CUPAR (FIFE)

The Drookit Dug

43 Bonnygate,
Cupar KY15 4BU
☎ *(01334) 55862*
Christopher Burke

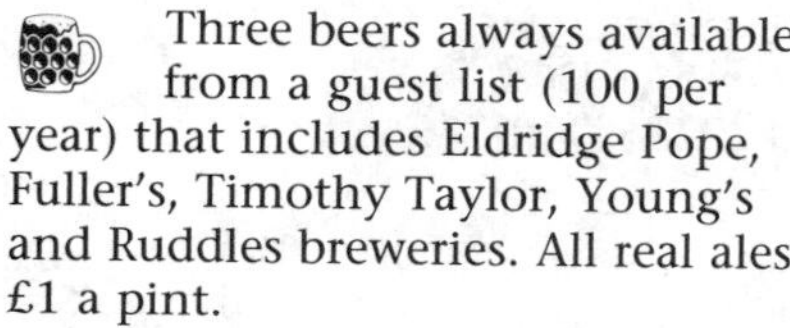

Three beers always available from a guest list (100 per year) that includes Eldridge Pope, Fuller's, Timothy Taylor, Young's and Ruddles breweries. All real ales £1 a pint.

A very traditional looking town-centre pub with wood-lined walls. Bar food is available at lunchtime. Children's room. Situated on the corner at the second set of traffic lights.

11am–midnight or 1am.

DOLLAR (CENTRAL)

HARVIESTOUN BREWERY

Devon Road, Dollar,
Central FK14 7LX
☎ *(01259) 742141*
Visitors welcome by arrangement.
Tied houses: None

The small brewery of Harviestoun lies at the foot of the Ochil Hills, beside the River Devon. It is housed in a 200-year-old stone building which was once a dairy. There were, at one time, at least two breweries in Dollar. One of these, at Brewers Knowe at the foot of Dollar Glen, had to pay a duty of 15 gallons of ale to the king whenever he passed by en route to Falkland Palace. Today, Harviestoun Ales are brewed using the same traditional methods as in those earlier days. Only the choicest natural ingredients are used and the brewing water is that which steeps down through the Ochil Hills. A new brew-plant was installed in 1991.

Beers available at: Tormaukin Hotel, Glendevon, Nr Dollar, Central *and* Guildford Arms, 1 West Register Street, Edinburgh, Lothian.

WAVERLEY 70/– 3.7% ABV
Chestnut-coloured session brew. Crisp and hoppy with a good balance of roast malt flavour and English Progress and Golding hops.

ORIGINAL 80/– 4.1% ABV
A best Scotch ale but with more emphasis on the hops than some. A good blend of Scottish Pale and Crystal malts with Fuggles and Golding hops.

MONTROSE ALE 4.2% ABV
Rich fruity beer, burgundy in colour and brewed from 100 per cent malted barley giving it a full body. Nicely balanced and packed with flavour.

PTARMIGAN 4.5% ABV
Blond in colour, having only a small amount of Crystal malt in the grist, which is mainly Scottish Pale and Wheat malts. Uses Bavarian Saaz hops.

SCHIEHALLION 4.8% ABV
Cask-conditioned lager beer. Lager malt and Hersbrucker Lager hops are fermented at a very low temperature with lager yeast then served "on the yeast" at cellar temperature without filtering or extra fizz. Refreshing continental-style beer.

OLD MANOR 5.0% ABV
Winter beer. A full-flavoured, rich ruby beer.

NOUVEAU APPROX 10.5% ABV.

DOLLAR (CENTRAL)

The King's Seat Inn

19 Bridge Street,
Dollar FK14 7DE
☎ *(01259) 742515*
Mr and Mrs McGuee

Seven beers always available from a constantly changing range (300 per year) to include Fuller's London Pride, Timothy Taylor Landlord, Orkney Dark Island, Eldridge Pope Thomas Hardy and others from Adnams, Caledonian, Jennings, Harviestoun, Burton Bridge and Greene King breweries.

A village inn on the main street serving families (with a children's certificate). Bar and restaurant food available at lunchtime and evenings. Parking. Accommodation. Dollar is on the main A91 road between Stirling and St Andrews.

11am–2.30pm and 5pm–midnight Mon–Sat; 12.30–2.30pm and 6.30–11pm Sun.

DUMFRIES (DUM & GALLOWAY)

Douglas Arms

Friars Vennel,
Dumfries DG1 2RQ
☎ *(01387) 256002*
Mr and Mrs Webb

Broughton Greenmantle and Old Jock, Jennings' Cumberland Ale and Ghillie Ale permanently available plus two guest beers (150 per year) to include Moorhouse's Pendle Witches Brew and Woodforde's Head Cracker.

An old-style pub with a coal fire. No food available. Situated in the town centre.

11am–11pm.

The New Bazaar

38 Whitesands,
Dumfries DG1 2RS
☎ *(01387) 268776*
Ian McConnell

Maclay Wallace IPA, McEwans 80/–, Belhaven St Andrews and Broughton Greenmantle Ale always available plus a guest (150 per year) from a list including Timothy Taylor Landlord, Ringwood Old Thumper, Gale's HSB, Greene King Abbot, Hop Back Summer Lightning, Orkney Dark Island, Bateman XXXB, Tomintoul Wild Cat, Moorhouse's Pendle Witches Brew and Coach House beers.

A traditional Victorian public house consisting of public bar, lounge and games room. The public bar has an old-fashioned gantry stocked with more than 200 malt and other whiskies. No food available. Car park, children's room. The pub is on the bank of the river.

11–midnight.

DUNBAR (LOTHIAN)

THE BELHAVEN BREWERY CO.

Spott Road,
Dunbar EH42 1RS
☎ *(01368) 862734*
No visitors. Tied houses: 66

The Belhaven Brewery can trace its direct ancestry back to 1719, and so claims to be the oldest surviving brewery in Scotland. In fact it is probable that a brewery has existed on the site since the Middle Ages. Belhaven ale was certainly supplied to the Franco-Scottish army garrisoned at Dunbar Castle in the 1550s and an advert in the London-based *Morning Chronicle* in 1837 shows that Belhaven Ales and Beers were available in London at that time. Records also suggest that the brews found favour at the Imperial Court of the Emperor of Austria. Although proud of this heritage tradition and roots, the company is constantly investing in new plant and development. In 1994, Belhaven was awarded the Overall Scottish Marketing Award for its performance in a highly competitive industry

BELHAVEN 60/– 2.9% ABV
Pronounced roast character with a smooth malty palate and subtle hop aroma. A deliciously drinkable mild ale with an appealing walnut brown colour.

BELHAVEN 70/– 3.5% ABV
Honey-coloured, nutty on the tongue with a light sweet finish.

SANDY HUNTER'S TRADITIONAL ALE 3.6% ABV
Celebrating the contribution of Sandy Hunter, chairman and head brewer of Belhaven for more than 35 years. The beer has a full malty and nutty palate with a distinctive hop nose and flavour.

BELHAVEN 80/– 4.2% ABV
A complex mix of grain and hop producing Belhaven's recognised malty and nutty flavour.

ST ANDREWS ALE 4.9% ABV
A well-balanced Scottish ale with a distinctive hop flavour and an intense dry after-palate.

BELHAVEN 90/– 8.0% ABV
A rich and powerful warming ale with a full-bodied palate.

EDINBURGH (LOTHIAN)

CALEDONIAN BREWERY

42 Skateford Road,
Edinburgh EH11 1PH
☎ *(0131) 341 2603*
Visitors welcome. Tied houses: none

The Caledonian Brewery was founded in 1869 and is Edinburgh's last remaining independent operation. It currently produces a range of 13 cask-conditioned ales using the finest natural ingredients and direct-fired open coppers to create the unique flavours. The brewery has just completed a significant investment programme with the rebuilding of the maltings and cellars which were destroyed by fire in June 1994. There are now ambitious plans for expansion.

60/– ALE 3.2% ABV

70/– ALE 3.5% ABV

MURRAY'S SUMMER ALE 3.6% ABV

DEUCHARS IPA 3.8% ABV

EDINBURGH REAL ALE 4.1% ABV

80/– ALE 4.1% ABV

PORTER 4.1% ABV

MURRAY'S HEAVY 4.3% ABV

125 4.5% ABV

CAMPBELL, HOPE & KING'S DOUBLE AMBER ALE 4.6% ABV

PHOENIX 4.6% ABV

MERMAN XXX 4.8% ABV

GOLDEN PROMISE 5.0% ABV

EDINBURGH STRONG ALE 6.4% ABV

Royal Ettrick Hotel

13 Ettrick Road,
Edinburgh EH10 5BJ
☎ *(0131) 228 6413*
Mrs EM Stuart

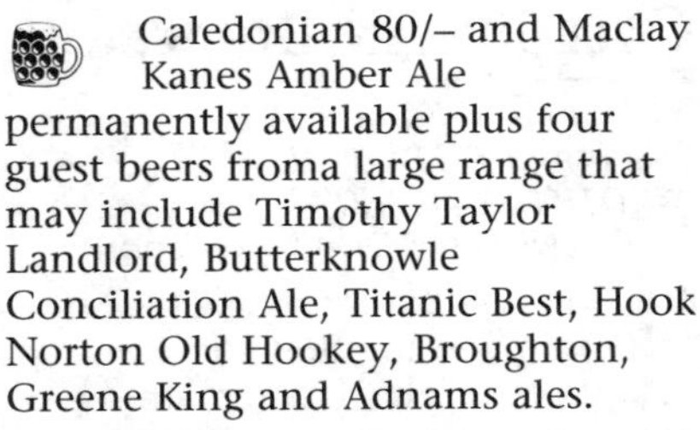

Caledonian 80/– and Maclay Kanes Amber Ale permanently available plus four guest beers froma large range that may include Timothy Taylor Landlord, Butterknowle Conciliation Ale, Titanic Best, Hook Norton Old Hookey, Broughton, Greene King and Adnams ales.

Part of a mansion and conservatory built in 1875 in the leafy suburbs. Bar and restaurant food available at lunchtime and evenings. Morning and afternoon teas also served. Car park, garden, banqueting and conference facilities. Weddings catered for. Children allowed. Accommodation.

11am–midnight Mon–Sat; 12.30–midnight Sun.

Southsider

3–5 West Richmond Street,
Edinburgh EH8 9EF
☎ *(0131) 667 2003*
Mr Hook

Four Maclay brews permanently available plus four guests including Old Bear Bitter, Border Rampart and Church End What the Fox's Hat. The emphasis is on smaller breweries and ales at 3.5–5 per cent. Also strong ale in winter.

A lounge and public bar, popular with locals and students. Bar food available at lunchtime. Car park in the city centre. Children allowed at lunchtime only.

11.30am–midnight.

The Bow Bar

80 West Bow,
Edinburgh EH1 2HH
☎ *(0131) 226 7667*
Bill Strachan

Caledonian ERA, Deuchars and 80/– plus Timothy Taylor Landlord always available. Also Caledonian 60/–, 70/– Golden Promise etc, plus Harviestoun, Broughton, Belhaven, Border, Jennings, Everards, Maclay, Orkney, Tomintoul, Hook Norton, Batemans, Mitchells and Black Sheep brews.

Take a step back in time to a genuine freehouse offering an unparalleled selection of real ales and malt whiskies. Bar food at lunchtime. Children not allowed.

11am–11.15pm.

The Cask and Barrel

115 Broughton Street,
Edinburgh EH1 3RZ
☎ *(0131) 556 3132*
Patrick Mitchell

Caledonian 80/– and Deuchars IPA among the brews permanently available plus five guest beers from breweries such as Hop Back, Harviestoun,

Mauldon's, Hambleton, Cotleigh, Coach House, Shepherd Neame and Larkins.

A large horseshoe bar with a wide range of customers. Bar food available at lunchtime. From the east end of Queen Street, turn left off York Place.

11am–midnight Sun–Wed;
11am–midnight Thurs–Sat.

The Guildford Arms

1 West Register Street,
Edinburgh EH2 2AA
☎ *(0131) 556 4312*
John Durnan

Caledonian 80/–, Deuchars IPA, Orkney Dark Island, Harviestoun Waverley 70/– and Schiehallion permanently available plus six guest beers (260+ per year) including Traquair Bear Ale and Festival Ale, plus a massive selection from all over England.

A beautiful Jacobean pub. Restaurant food available at lunchtime. At the east end of Princes Street, behind Burger King.

11am–1am Mon–Wed;
11am–midnight Thurs–Sat;
12.30–11pm Sun.

ELLON (GRAMPIAN)

ABERDEENSHIRE ALES

Mains of Inverbrie,
Drumwhindle,
Ellon AB41 8PX
☎ *01358 761457*
Visitors welcome by appointment only.
Tied houses: None

The brewery is situated 18 miles north of Aberdeen on a 400-acre farm, in a tastefully converted steading. Production of Buchan Gold started in May 1995 and it is brewed in a hand-made copper. The copper and fermentation vessels are good, old-fashioned Yorkshire squares. The copper was made by Forsyth and Sons, of Rothes, who make most of the copper kettles for the whisky industry. Buchan Gold pump clips have the Buchan coat of arms on.

Beers available at: New Inn Hotel, Ellon, Grampian *and* The Grill Bar, Aberdeen, Grampian.

BUCHAN GOLD 4.0% ABV
An earthy hop aroma with citrus fruit (grapefruit, damson). Rich firm malty palate. The finish starts bitter-sweet and becomes dry with strong malt hops and a hint of vanilla.

GLASGOW (STRATHCLYDE)

HEATHER ALE

736 Dumbarton Road,
Glasgow G11 6RD
☎ *(0141) 339 3479*
Visitors welcome. Tied houses: None

Fraoch Ale was re-introduced in 1992 as part of a crusade to revive a traditional indigenous craft ale whose roots can be traced back to the Isle of Rum in about 2000BC. The Picts were known to drink heather ale around 325BC and it survived as a recipe through the Middle Ages. The Act of Union of 1707 prevented brewers from using any ingredients other than hops and malt. As hops could not be grown in Scotland, heather ale all but vanished, except in the Highlands and Western Isles. The brew produced today is based on an original Gaelic recipe given to Bruce Williams in the Glasgow Homebrew Shop in 1986. In 1993, Bruce reached agreement with Maclay and Co at the Thistle Brewery in Alloa to allow him to produce Fraoch Ale during the heather season. A stronger (5.0% ABV) version is available in bottles throughout the year.

Beers available at: Brewery Tap, 1055 Sauchiehall Street, Glasgow, Strathclyde *and* Bannermans, 212 Cowgate, Edinburgh, Lothian.

FRAOCH 4.0% ABV
From the Gaelic word for "heather". A floral peaty aroma, full malt character, spicy herbal flavour, dry wine-like finish. Brewed with heather flowers in place of hops between July and November.

Also available throughout the year in bottles.

Athena Greek Taverna

780 Pollokshaws Road,
Strathbungo, Glasgow G42 2AE
☎ *(0141) 424 0858*
Nicholas Geordiades

Six beers always available from a list of 200 guests that may include Otter Bright and beers from Roosters, Yates, Belhaven, Caledonian and Shardlow breweries.

A cafe-style bar and adjacent Greek Cypriot restaurant serving Greek and European food. Children allowed. Situated beside Queen's Park railway station, not far from Shawlands Cross.

11am–2.30pm and 5–11pm Mon–Sat; closed Sun.

Tennents Bar

191 Byres Road,
Hillhead, Glasgow G12
☎ *(0141) 339 0649*
Alison O'Conner

Twelve beers permanently available from a guest list (100 per year) that may include Fuller's London Pride, Morland Old Speckled Hen and Marston's Pedigree.

A large public bar with a friendly atmosphere and no music. Bar and restaurant food is available at lunchtime and evenings. A refurbishment has just taken place. The bar is adjacent to Glasgow University and Hillhead subway.

11am–11pm Mon–Thurs; 11am–midnight Fri–Sat; 12.30–11.30pm Sun.

The Three Judges

141 Dumbarton Road,
Partick Cross,
Glasgow G11 6PR
☎ *(0141) 337 3055*
Helen McCarroll

Maclay 80/–, Broadsword and Wallace IPA always available plus five guest beers (250 per year) from independent and micro-breweries, old and new.

A lively West End pub. Bar food is available at lunchtime and evenings. Parking. Near Kelvin Hall underground.

11am–11pm Sun–Thurs; 11am–midnight Fri–Sat.

INNERLEITHEN (BORDERS)

TRAQUAIR HOUSE BREWERY

Traquair House, Innerleithen, Peeblesshire EH44 6PW
☎ *(01896) 830323*
Visitors welcome. Tied houses: none

A brewery was already operating when Mary, Queen of Scots, visited Traquair in 1566. In 1739 a 200-gallon copper was installed in the brewhouse which lies beneath the chapel. But the brewery fell into disuse, perhaps as a mark of repect to the passing of the Stuarts, until Peter Maxwell Stuart, the 20th laird, rediscovered the old mash tun, open coolers and wooden stirring paddles in perfect condition and recommenced brewing in 1965. Brewing at Traquair is still a very traditional craft, and this claims to be the only brewery in Britain which continues to ferment its total production in oak.

Beers available at: Guildford Arms, 1 West Register Street, Edinburgh, Lothian *and* Traquair Arms Hotel, Traquair Road, Innerleithen, Borders.

BEAR ALE 5.0% ABV

TRAQUAIR HOUSE ALE 7.2% ABV
A rich dark ale fermented in oak, with hints of chocolate and burnt pineapple.

TRAQUAIR JACOBITE ALE 8.0% ABV
Spiced with coriander, a limited edition to mark the 250th anniversary of the Jacobite Rebellion.

KETTLEBRIDGE (FIFE)

Kettlebridge Inn

9 Cupar Road, Kettlebridge
☎ *(01337) 830232*
James Alkman

Five beers always available at this award-winning pub from a list that runs into hundreds.

A traditional village coaching inn in Fife golfing country on the A92 road to St Andrews. Open fires, lounge bar and restaurant. Bar and restaurant food available at lunchtime and evenings. Street parking, garden. Children allowed in restaurant only.

12–2.30pm and 5–11pm Mon–Fri; 12–midnight Sat; 12–11pm Sun.

KINROSS (TAYSIDE)

The Muirs Inn

49 The Muirs, Kinross
☎ *(01577) 862270*
Mr Philip and Mr Westwood

Orkney Dark Island and Belhaven 80/– always available plus up to six guest beers (100 per year) perhaps from the Harviestoun or Border breweries. Also Scottish wines and whiskies.

A traditional Scottish country inn. Bar and restaurant food available at lunchtime and evenings. Car park and garden. Children allowed. Accommodation. M90 junction 6, then follow signs for the A922. At the T-junction, the inn is diagonally opposite to the right.

11am–2.30pm and 5–11pm Mon–Fri; all day Sat–Sun.

KIRKCALDY (FIFE)

FYFE BREWING CO.

Harbour Bar,
469 High Street,
Kirkcaldy KY1 2SN
☎ *(01592) 264270*

Auld Alliance brewed and available in the Harbour Bar plus guest beers from Belhaven and elsewhere.

The brewery is located in an old sailworks behind and above the pub. Auld Alliance was launched in May 1995 and there are plans for at least one other brew to follow. The plant size is for two and a half barrels, with a ten-barrel per week restriction. The Harbour Bar is a traditional ale house. Snacks are available at lunchtime and evenings. Parking. Children not allowed.

AULD ALLIANCE 4.0% ABV

11am–2.30pm and 5–midnight Mon–Thurs; 11am–midnight Fri–Sat; 12.30–midnight Sun.

LINLITHGOW (LOTHIAN)

The Four Marys

65 High Street,
Linlithgow EH49 7ED
☎ *(01506) 842171*
Mr Scott

Belhaven 80/– always available plus nine guest beers (400 per year) that may include Harviestoun Ptarmigan, Tomintoul Ginger Tom, Butterknowle Conciliation Ale, Cotleigh Harrier, Dent Bitter, Greene King IPA, Bateman Mild, RCH PG Steam and Caledonian ales.

A traditional pub with antique furniture and stone walls. The bar has masses of mementoes of Mary Queen of Scots, who was born at Linlithgow Palace. Bar food available at lunchtime and evenings (except Sunday evening). Parking. Children allowed. Opposite the entrance to Linlithgow Palace.

12–2.30pm and 5–11pm Sun–Fri; 12–11.30pm Sat.

ORKNEY

THE ORKNEY BREWERY

Quoyloo, Sandwick,
Orkney Islands KW16 3LT
☎*(01856) 841802*
Visitors welcome. Tied houses: None

Roger White started The Orkney Brewery in April 1988. A civil engineer, having worked abroad, he bought an old school in Orkney and decided to try something different. With no previous experience, he went south for some tuition. His intention was to supply keg ales on the island, but requests came from further afield for cask ale, and Roger duly obliged. Within a year demand had grown to the point where a brewer was employed to help him to cope. He initially produced Raven Ale. By

the winter of 1989, having found a wife and partner, Irene, they developed Skullsplitter as a winter warmer. Another brewer was employed in 1991 and Dark Island was added to the range. Dragonhead Stout followed the next year. The brewery now employs eight people and distributes throughout the UK and to Canada. Roger, a teetotaller, has his eye on markets in Scandinavia and Europe. The 25-barrel brewery can produce up to 150 barrels a week.

RAVEN ALE 3.8% ABV
A rounded ale with a fruitiness that suggests a higher gravity.

THE RED MACGREGOR 4.0% ABV
A simple session beer.

DRAGONHEAD STOUT 4.0% ABV
Smooth with a roasted aftertaste.

DARK ISLAND 4.6% ABV
A rich wine-coloured ale with a good hop and malt balance.

SKULLSPLITTER 8.5% ABV
Satiny smooth in the mouth and deceptively light.

PITLOCHRY (TAYSIDE)

MOULIN BREWERY

Moulin Hotel,
11–13 Kirkmichael Road,
Pitlochry PH1 5EH
(01796) 472196

Three brews produced and available on the premises.

The brewery and visitor centre opened in 1995 in the old coach house adjacent to the popular 300-year-old village coaching inn, which enjoys log fires and low ceilings. Bar and restaurant food served at lunchtime and evenings. Car park, garden, accommodation. Children allowed in the restaurant.

BRAVEHEART 4.0% ABV
Light and smooth.

ALE OF ATHOLL 4.5% ABV
Ruby, malty.

OLD REMEDIAL 5.2% ABV
Strong with a good body.

11am–11pm Mon–Fri.

RUTHVEN (GRAMPIAN)

BORVE BREW HOUSE

Ruthven, Huntley,
Aberdeenshire AB54 4SR
☎ *(01466) 760343*

Three Borve brews are produced and available on the premises.

The Borve Brew House is a former school house converted into a small brewery. It relocated to Ruthven, a hamlet in the foothills of the Grampian mountains, in 1988, having originated at Borve, on the Isle of Lewis, in 1983. The beer is available bottled or on draught. No food available. Car park. Children not allowed.

BORVE ALE 3.92% ABV

UNION STREET 200 4.8% ABV

TALL SHIPS IPA 4.9% ABV

11am–3pm Mon–Thurs;
11am–11.45pm Fri–Sat;
12.30–11pm Sun.

SAUCHIE (CENTRAL)

MANSFIELD ARMS

7 Main Street, Sauchie,
Nr Alloa, Clackmanshire,
Central FK10 3JR
☎ *(01259) 722020*
John Gibson

Three beers brewed and sold on the premises.

The Mansfield Arms was named CAMRA Scottish Pub of the Year in 1993 and started brewing in May 1994. Located just north of Alloa, the four-barrel brewhouse was built from spare parts and discarded equipment and now produces cask ales very much in the English tradition. Food is available in the bar until 9pm. Car park, garden. Children allowed.

DEVON ORIGINAL 3.8% ABV

DEVON THICK BLACK 4.1% ABV

DEVON PRIDE 4.6% ABV

11am–midnight.

STONEHAVEN (GRAMPIAN)

The Marine Hotel

9–10 Shorehead,
Stonehaven AB3 2JY
☎ *(01569) 762155*
Mr and Mrs Duncan

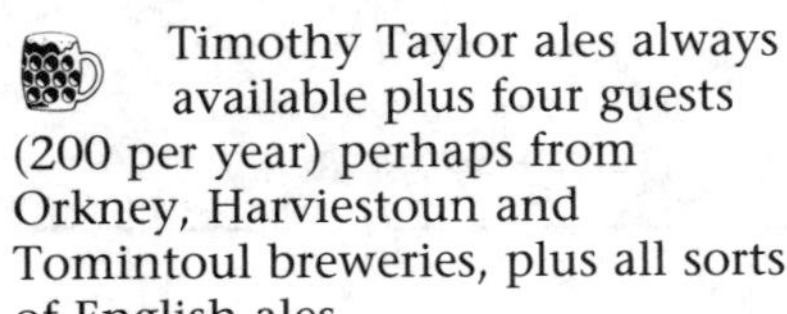

Timothy Taylor ales always available plus four guests (200 per year) perhaps from Orkney, Harviestoun and Tomintoul breweries, plus all sorts of English ales.

The pub overlooks the harbour and has a large bar with a juke box and pool table. Bar and restaurant food is served at lunchtime and evenings. Local seafood. Parking. Follow the signs to the harbour.

11am–midnight.

TOMINTOUL (GRAMPIAN)

TOMINTOUL BREWERY

Mill of Auchriachan,
Tomintoul, Ballindalloch,
Banffshire, Grampian AB37 9EQ
☎ *(01807) 580333*
Visitors welcome by appointment.
Tied houses: None

Tomintoul Brewery began production in November 1993 in a converted water mill just outside Tomintoul, which is among the highest villages in the Highlands. This is the only brewery in the Highlands and the beers are available by direct delivery throughout Britain.

Beers available at: Glen Avon Hotel, 1 The Square, Tomintoul, Grampian *and* Station Bar, 7/8 Broomfield Square, Tomintoul, Grampian.

TOMINTOUL CAILLIE 3.6% ABV
Pale, hoppy session beer, clean crisp and moreish

TOMINTOUL STAG 4.1% ABV
Distinctive dark, malty bitter, rounded and welcoming.

TOMINTOUL 80/- 4.2% ABV
Traditional Scottish style.

TOMINTOUL PORTER 4.6% ABV
Classic porter with distinctive bite.

TOMINTOUL WILD CAT 5.1% ABV
Full-bodied, deep amber, premium ale, complex and flavoursome.

HIGHLAND HAMMER 7.3% ABV
Strong but balanced, with long nutty finish. Brewed in winter.

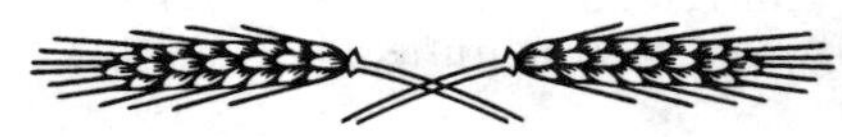

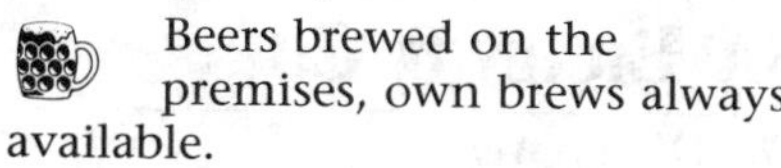

Uplawmoor (Strathclyde)

Lugton Inn

1 Lochlibo Road,
Uplawmoor, Glasgow G78 4AA
☎ *(01505) 850267*
Christopher Lynas

Beers brewed on the premises, own brews always available.

An old coaching inn in a village location near Glasgow with open fires and copper wedge wire floor. Bar and restaurant food served at lunchtime and evenings. Car park, garden, children's room, accommodation. Children allowed.

LUGTON BLACK 3.4% ABV
Old-fashioned, Scottish session beer

LUGTON BEST 3.7% ABV

LUGTON GOLD 4.1% ABV
A lager-type beer, made from citrus fruits and all New Zealand hops, so can be classified as "organic".

JOHN BARLEYCORN GOLD 4.2% ABV
Originally brewed for Burns' birthday using four types of barley, one hop and honey.

BRAVE HEART 4.5% ABV

BLACK HIGHLANDER 4.6% ABV

OPEN *11am–11pm.*

Nr Aberystwyth (Dyfed)

The Halfway Inn

Devil's Bridge Road,
Pisgah, Aberystwyth,
Dyfed SY23 4NE
☎ *(01970) 880631*

Felinfoel Double Dragon among those beers always available plus two guest beers (30 per year) including Wadworth 6X, Bateman XXX, Hook Norton Old Hookey, Shepherd Neame Spitfire, Fuller's London Pride and Ringwood Old Thumper.

A traditional olde-worlde hostelry 700 feet up with magnificent views of the Cambrian mountains. Bar and restaurant food is available at lunchtime and evenings. Car park and garden. Children allowed. Accommodation. Halfway along the A4120 Aberystwyth to Devil's Bridge road. Note, this is not the Pisgah near Cardigan.

11.30am–2.30pm and 6.30–11pm Mon–Sat;
12–3pm and 7–10.30pm Sun.

Blaenavon (Gwent)

Cambrian Inn

Cambrian Row, Llanover Road,
Blaenavon, Gwent NP4 9HR
☎ *(01495) 790327*
J and P Morgans

Blaenavon Pride and Glory and Brains brews permanently available plus a guest (50 per year) such as Morland Old Speckled Hen or another beer from a small or local brewery.

A typical Welsh mining village pub. Darts, pool, cards etc. No food. Street parking opposite the pub. Children not allowed.

6–11pm Mon–Thurs;
12–11pm Fri–Sat;
12–3pm and 7–10.30pm Sun.

Cardiff (South Glamorgan)

SA Brain & Co.

The Old Brewery,
49 St Mary Street, Cardiff,
South Glamorgan CF1 1SP
☎ *(01222) 399022*
Visitors welcome. Tied houses: 72

The Old Brewery was established in the heart of Cardiff in 1713 and, in 1882, it was purchased by Samuel Arthur Brain and his uncle, Joseph Benjamin Brain. Once under family control, the company flourished and, over the past century, has grown into the largest independent brewery in Wales. Still under family ownership, the company brews its distinctive, cask-conditioned beers at the original Old Brewery site, which is now dedicated solely to the production of traditional ales. All of the Brains brands are available through the company's own tied estate in Cardiff and South Wales and in free trade outlets. Brains beers are now available from wholesalers across Britain.

DARK 3.5% ABV
A medium-gravity, lightly-hopped dark beer. Exceptionally smooth drinking, less sweet than most mild ales. Traditionally served with a creamy head.

BITTER 3.7% ABV
A distinctive, medium-gravity well-hopped bitter with a characteristic golden-amber colour.

SA BEST BITTER 4.2% ABV
A full, well-hopped but easy drinking bitter.

CILFYNYDD (MID-GLAMORGAN)

RECKLESS ERIC'S BREWING

Unit 4, Albion Industrial Estate, Cilfynydd, Nr Pontypridd, Mid-Glamorgan CF37 4NX
☎ *(01443) 409229*
Visitors welcome. Tied houses: None

A small brewery opened in 1993 and now supplying more than 50 free trade outlets.

RETRIBUTION 3.4% ABV

RENOWN 4.0% ABV

RESTORATION 4.3% ABV

RECKED 'EM 5.2% ABV

REJOICE 6.0% ABV

CLYTHA (GWENT)

Clytha Arms

Clytha, Gwent NP7 9BW
☎ *(01873) 840206*
Mr and Mrs Canning

Hook Norton Best is among those beers permanently available plus three guests (360 per year) from breweries such as Freeminers, Felinfoel, RCH, Wye Valley, Jennings, Fullers, Harviestoun, Exmoor and Adnams. A mild is always available.

A large old dower house with restaurant and traditional bar. Bar and restaurant food available at lunchtime and evenings. Car park, garden, accommodation. Children allowed. Located on the old Abergavenny to Raglan road.

6–11pm Mon; 11.30am–3pm and 6–11pm Tues–Fri and Sun; all day Sat.

DREENHILL (DYFED)

The Denant Mill Inn

Dale Road, Dreenhill, Haverfordwest, Dyfed SA62 3TS
☎ *(01437) 766569*
Mr and Mrs Davis

At least three beers always available from a guest list including Hop Back Summer Lightning, Exmoor Gold, Otter Ale, Timothy Taylor Landlord, Cotleigh Tawny and Bateman brews.

A converted sixteenth-century water-driven corn mill with an inside waterwheel. Bar and restaurant food available at lunchtime and evenings. Car park, garden and children's room. Camping site nearby. Children allowed. The Dreenhill sign is just under three miles from Haverfordwest, along the Dale Road (B4327). Take the first left after the sign, to the bottom of the valley.

12–3pm and 6–11pm Mon–Sat; normal hours Sun.

HAVERFORDWEST (DYFED)

King's Arms Hotel

23 Dew Street,
Haverfordwest, Dyfed
☎ *(01437) 763726*
Chris Hudd

Six beers are always available from a list of approximately 150 brews per year.

An old, beamed and flagstoned pub in the town, just past the library. Street parking, function room. No children.

11am–3pm and 6–11pm Mon–Sat; 12–3pm and 7–10.30pm Sun.

GILWERN (GWENT)

Bridgend Inn

Main Road, Gilwern, Gwent
☎ *(01873) 830939*
Mrs PD James

Felinfoel Double Dragon and three other real ales always available. Guests include Fuller's London Pride and ESB, also Wadworth 6X and IPA.

Canal-side olde-worlde pub. Bar and restaurant food available at lunchtime and evenings. Car park, patio garden. Children allowed for meals.

12–2pm and 7–11pm Mon–Thurs; 12–11pm Fri–Sat; 12–10.30pm Sun.

GLAN-Y-LLYN (MID-GLAM)

Fagins Ale and Chop House

Cardiff Road, Glan-y-Llyn,
Mid-Glamorgan
☎ *(0122) 811800*
Jeff Butler

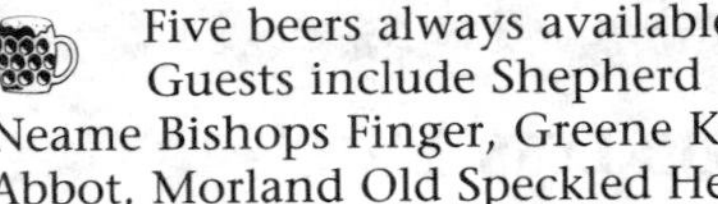

Five beers always available. Guests include Shepherd Neame Bishops Finger, Greene King Abbot, Morland Old Speckled Hen and many more.

A converted terraced house in Mid-Glamorgan. CAMRA pub of the year. Bar and restaurant food available at lunchtime and evenings. Function room. Children allowed.

12–11pm Mon–Sat; 12–10.30pm Sun.

LLANELLI (DYFED)

CROWN BUCKLEY

Gilbert Street, Llanelli,
Dyfed SA15 3PP
☎ *(01443) 225453*
Visitors welcome. Tied houses: 70

Crown Buckley brings together two great names in Welsh brewing. Buckley's Brewery claims to be the oldest brewery in the Principality, tracing its roots back to the sixteenth century. The present company took shape in Llanelli in 1767 under the ownership of Henry Child. Crown Brewery was founded in the South Wales valleys in 1919. The two companies combined in January 1989 and a management buy-out in 1993 saw Crown Buckley revert to independent Welsh ownership.

Beers available at: Thomas Arms Hotel, Thomas Street, Llanelli, Dyfed *and* The Olde Inn, 6 Swansea Road, Penllegaer, Swansea, West Glamorgan.

BUCKLEYS DARK MILD 3.4% ABV
A full-bodied mild with a pronounced roast malt association, which develops into a characteristic aftertaste.

BRENIN 3.4% ABV
A rich, golden brew, with a distinctive nutty, sherry-like flavour which produces a lingering aftertaste.

CROWN PALE ALE 3.4% ABV
A light refreshing drink with subtle hop characteristics.

BUCKLEYS BEST BITTER 3.7% ABV
A well-balanced bitter with nutty overtones.

SPECIAL BEST BITTER 3.7% ABV
A mellow bitter with a rich finish, a rounded, mature hop palate and ripe fruit notes.

REVEREND JAMES BITTER 4.5% ABV
Full bodied and warming, rich in palate, spicy and aromatic, with a deep satisfying aftertaste.

FELINFOEL BREWERY

The Brewery, Farmers Row,
Felinfoel, Llanelli,
Dyfed SA14 8LB
☎ *(01554) 776657*
Visitors welcome by prior arrangement.
Tied houses: 82

Felinfoel is a small village near Llanelli. The brewery was built in 1878 and its beers were distributed throughout the old Welsh counties of Carmarthenshire, Cardiganshire and Pembrokeshire. Inns and hotels were purchased and the company pioneered canned beer production during the 1930s. The brewery remains an independent family concern and the present managing director represents its fifth generation. The brewery exports to Canada, the United States, Europe and Japan.

TRADITIONAL BITTER 3.2% ABV

TRADITIONAL DARK 3.2% ABV

DOUBLE DRAGON 4.2% ABV
A full-bodied premium Welsh ale, malty and subtly hopped with a rich colour and smooth balanced character.

MYNYDD Y GARREG (DYFED)

The Prince of Wales

Heol Meinciau,
Mynydd y Garreg,
Dyfed SA17 4RP
☎ *(01554) 890522*
Richard Pickett

Six beers permanently available from a guest list that includes brews from Ash Vine, Dorothy Goodbody, Bull Mastiff, Black Sheep, Wadworth and Camerons. Phone ahead for details of beers on tap.

A 200-year-old cottage pub with a collection of cinema memorabilia and bric-a-brac. Bar and restaurant food is available at lunchtime and evenings. Car park and garden. Take the Mynydd y Garreg turn from the Cydweli bypass. Then just over a mile on the right.

OPEN *Seasonal – please phone to check.*

PENALLT (GWENT)

The Boat Inn

Lone Lane, Penallt,
Nr Monmouth, Gwent NP5 4AJ
☎ *(01600) 712615*
Stephen Rowlands

Wadworth 6X and Oakhill Bitter are always available straight from the barrel plus six guests, some from a rolling rota of about ten regulars, others for the first time.

A small riverside inn on the England-Wales border built into the hillside with stone floors and simple decor. Jazz /blues and rock/folk nights twice weekly. Very cosy with no juke box or games machines. Bar food available at lunchtime and evenings. Car park on the other side of the river, terraced garden with ponds, streams and waterfalls. Children allowed. The car park is in Redbrook (Gloucestershire) on the A466, next to a football field. Follow the footpath over an old railway bridge, across the Wye.

11am–3pm and 6–11pm Mon–Sat; 12–3pm and 7–10.30pm Sun.

RHAYADER (POWYS)

The Cornhill Inn

West Street, Rhayader,
Powys LD6 5AB
☎ *(01597) 810869*
Barbara Fraser

Marston's Pedigree and Wye Valley Hereford Bitter permanently available plus two guests (100 per year) which may include Hop Back Summer Lightning, Titanic brews, Dent T'owd Tup, Ringwood 49er, Wye Valley Brew 97, NYBC Fools Gold and Moorhouse's Pendle Witches Brew.

A sixteenth-century freehouse with olde-worlde charm, low beams and open fires. Bar food available at lunchtime and evenings. Parking. Children allowed. Accommodation. Situated on the road to Elan Valley.

11am–3pm and 7–11pm.

TALYBONT-ON-USK (POWYS)

The Star Inn

Talybont-on-Usk,
Nr Brecon, Powys LD3 7YX
☎ *(01874) 676635*
Mrs Coakham

A constantly changing range of 12 beers including Felinfoel Double Dragon and brews from Freeminer's, Bullmastiff, Wadworth and Crown Buckley.

A riverside and canalside site with lovely garden. Bar and restaurant food is available at lunchtime and evenings. Parking, garden, live music on Wednesdays. Children allowed. Accommodation. Less than a mile off the A40 between Brecon and Abergavenny (Brecon six miles, Abergavenny 14 miles).

11am–11pm in summer; otherwise closed 3–6pm.

LISBURN (CO ANTRIM)

HILDEN BREWERY

Hilden House,
Grand Street,
Hilden, Lisburn BT27 4TY
☎ *(01846) 663863*
Visitors welcome 11am–3pm daily.
Tied houses: 1

Hilden Brewery is a small business established in 1981 by Ann and Seamus Scullion. The brewery is located in a cobbled courtyard adjacent to the Scullion's attractive Georgian house.

Beers available at: Denvers Hotel, Downpatrick, Co Antrim *and* Hillside Restaurant and Bar, 21–23 Main Street, Hillsborough, Co Antrim.

HILDEN ALE 4.0% ABV
A dry, well–hopped beer.

SPECIAL RESERVE 4.2% ABV
A darker, smoother beer.

Plus occasional beers brewed and sold throughout the year.

ST HELIER (JERSEY)

THE JERSEY BREWERY

57 Ann Street,
St Helier, Jersey JE1 1BZ
☎ *(01534) 31561*
Visitors welcome. Tied houses: 50

The brewery was built in 1857 and became The Ann Street Brewery in 1905. During the occupation of World War Two, the brewery was used to produce beer for the German forces. It was renamed as The Jersey Brewery in 1994 to emphasise the point that the brewery is the last remaining major brewery in Jersey. Cask ales were relaunched in 1990 after a 30-year absence.

Beers available at: Seymour Inn, Grouville, Jersey *and* Moulin de Lecq, St Ouens Street, Greve de Lecq, Jersey.

OLD JERSEY ALE 3.6% ABV
A dark session beer with a chocolate malty taste and pleasant hop aromas.

ANN'S TREAT 5.2% ABV
An amber, tawny–coloured ale with fruity flavours and hoppy nose.

WINTER ALE 7.0% ABV
A dark, roasted malt flavoured seasonal ale with sweet undertones and a hoppy aftertaste.

THE TIPSY TOAD TOWNHOUSE

57–59 New Street,
St Helier, Jersey
☎ *(01534) 615000*
Colin Manning

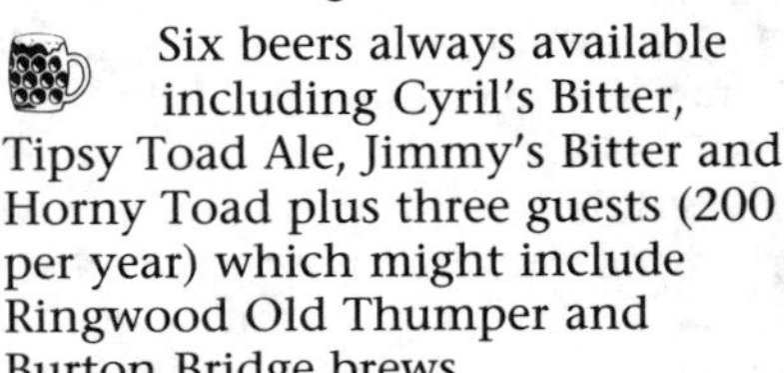

Six beers always available including Cyril's Bitter, Tipsy Toad Ale, Jimmy's Bitter and Horny Toad plus three guests (200 per year) which might include Ringwood Old Thumper and Burton Bridge brews.

Brewpub in a converted warehouse with three function rooms for live music etc. CAMRA pub of the year. Bar and restaurant food available at lunchtime and evenings. Parking nearby. Children allowed.

CYRIL'S BITTER 3.7% ABV

TIPSY TOAD ALE 3.8% ABV

JIMMY'S BITTER 4.2% ABV

HORNY TOAD 5.0% ABV

11.30am–11pm Mon–Sat;
11am–1pm and
4.30–11pm Sun.

ST PETER PORT (GUERNSEY)

THE GUERNSEY BREWERY

South Esplanade, St Peter Port,
Guernsey GY1 1BJ
☎ *(01481) 720143*
Visitors welcome by arrangement.
Tied houses: 30

The Guernsey Brewery was first established in 1845, when the site comprised two adjoining houses and a garden. In October 1845, John Le Patourel, a St Peter Port merchant, began expanding the business and the brewery really opened in 1856 under the name of the London Brewery. The present company was born in 1895, when Messrs BAP Schreiber and Thomas Skurray leased the property. Skurray had links with Morland and Co, in Abingdon, Oxon, which was where the company was registered until a change in the income tax laws in 1920. In 1923, the plant was expanded and survived the German occupation and changes in the pattern of trade. The Guernsey Brewrey is still a small company today, producing fewer than 10,000 barrels of beer a year.

Beers available at: Thomas de La Rue, The Pollet, St Peter Port, Guernsey *and* La Couture Inn, La Couture, St Peter Port, Guernsey.

BRAYE 3.8% ABV
A traditional mild ale.

SUNBEAM 4.2% ABV
A traditional draught bitter held in high esteem.

Plus various bottled and occasional brews.

RW Randall

Vauxlaurens Brewery,
St Julians Avenue, St Peter Port,
Guernsey GY1Q 3JG
☎ *(01481) 720134*
Visitors welcome each Thursday in summer and by arrangement.
Tied houses: 20

There is another Randall's brewery in Jersey, although these days there is no direct link between the two. Robert Randall arrived in Jersey in 1823, aged 12. He began work there and in 1847 bought the Clare Street Brewery. In 1868 he decided to expand into Guernsey and bought the Vauxlaurens site, which had been a brewery since 1821, from Joseph Gullick. Eventually this became the family's sole interest and their connections with Jersey ended during the 1930s. The family's future in the Vauxlaurens Brewery now lies in the hands of Ben Randall, who was born in 1969 and has been learning the trade with Harvey's in Lewes, Sussex. The company were pioneers in the production of low alcohol bitter. Randall's LA, launched in 1988, was among the first into production.

Beers available at: Hotel de Havelet, St Peter Port, Guernsey *and* The Yacht Inn, St Peter Port, Guernsey.

RANDALL'S MILD 3.6% ABV

RANDALL'S BITTER 5.0% ABV

Plus various bottled brews.

The Drunken Duck

The Charroterie,
St Peter Port,
Guernsey GY1 1EL
☎ *(01481) 725045*
Christian Weetman

The only freehouse to bring guest beers into Guernsey. A Ringwood brew permanently available plus two guest beers (80 per year to include Hop Back Summer Lightning and Wheat Beer, Morland's Old Speckled Hen, Hadrian Centurian and Shepherd Neame Spitfire.

A small friendly pub for young and old. Live music each week. Light snacks available at lunchtime. Parking from 5pm. Garden, children's room and bar billiards.

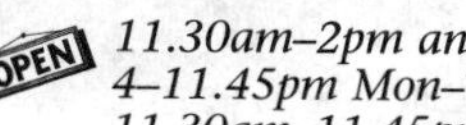

11.30am–2pm and 4–11.45pm Mon–Thurs; 11.30am–11.45pm Fri–Sat.

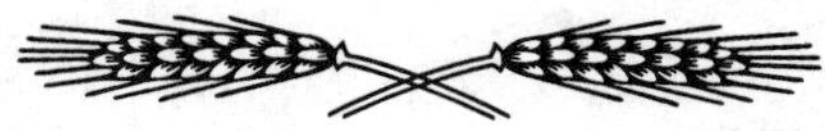

ST PETER'S VILLAGE (JERSEY)

THE TIPSY TOAD BREWERY

The Star,
La Grande Route de St Pierre,
St Peter's Village,
Jersey JE3 7AA
☎ *(01534) 482608*
Tours and tastings every day

Tipsy Toad Ale, Jimmy's Bitter, Horny Toad and Star Drooper always available plus guests.

Jersey's first brewpub is situated in renovated and restored Victorian premises. The result is a cosy pub with a family atmosphere. The brewing process can be observed through a wall of windows. Bar food is available at lunchtime and evenings. Family room and conservatory, outdoor children's play area. Baby-changing facilities and disabled toilets. There is now a sister pub in St Helier.

TIPSY TOAD ALE 3.8% ABV

JIMMY'S BITTER 4.2% ABV

HORNY TOAD 5.0% ABV

STAR DROOPER 6.0% ABV

10am–11.30pm.

BRADDAN

BUSHY'S BREWERY

Mount Murray Brewery,
Castletown Road,
Braddan IM4 1JE
☎ *(01624) 661244*
Visitors welcome. Tied houses: 5

Bushy's Brewery was started as a brewpub by Martin Brunnschweiler in 1986 and moved to larger premises as a self-contained brewery in 1990 with a ten-barrel Robert Morten plant, which came from the Brighton Brewery in Sussex. The Isle of Man has its own beer purity laws dating back to 1874, ensuring that the products are free from chemical additives. The TT Pilsner is the island's first brewed lager, especially produced for the TT Races in June. The brewery currently supplies 25 outlets on the island and regularly sends ales across to England.

BUSHY'S DARK MILD 3.5% ABV

BUSHY'S BEST BITTER 3.8% ABV

BUSHY'S TT PILSNER BEER 4.2% ABV

OLD BUSHY TAIL 4.5% ABV

PISTON BREW 4.5% ABV
Seasonal.

LOVELY JUBBELY 5.8% ABV
Winter ale.

READERS' RECOMMENDATIONS

Research for the next edition of the guide is already under way and, to ensure that it will be as comprehensive and up-to-date as possible, we should be grateful for your help.

We hope you will agree that every pub included this year is in the book on merit, but ownership and operation can change both for better and worse. Equally, there are bound to be hidden gems that have so far escaped our attentions and that really ought to be included next time around.

So, if what you discover does not live up to expectations, or if you know of another pub that we cannot afford to be without, please let us know. Either fill in the forms below or send your views on a separate piece of paper to:

The Editor, The Guest Beer Guide,
Foulsham, Bennetts Close, Slough, Berkshire SL1 5AP.

Please let us know if you would like additional forms. Every reply will be entered into a draw for one of five free copies of next year's guide. Thank you very much for your help.

Pub name: ______________________ Already in the guide? Yes ❑ No ❑

Address: ______________________

____

Comments: ______________________

____

____

____

Your name: ______________________

Your address: ______________________

____

______________________ Tel: ______________________

Pub name: ______________________ Already in the guide? Yes ❑ No ❑

Address: ______________________

____

Comments: ______________________

____

____

____

Your name: ______________________

Your address ______________________

____

______________________ Tel: ______________________

Pub name: ______ Already in the guide? Yes ❑ No ❑

Address: ______

Comments: ______

Your name: ______

Your address: ______

Tel: ______

Pub name: ______ Already in the guide? Yes ❑ No ❑

Address: ______

Comments: ______

Your name: ______

Your address ______

Tel: ______

Pub name: ______ Already in the guide? Yes ❑ No ❑

Address: ______

Comments: ______

Your name: ______

Your address ______

Tel: ______

QUESTIONNAIRE

Pub name: ________ Already in the guide? Yes ❑ No ❑

Address: ________

Comments:________

Your name:________

Your address: ________

Tel: ________

Pub name: ________ Already in the guide? Yes ❑ No ❑

Address: ________

Comments:________

Your name:________

Your address ________

Tel: ________

Pub name: ________ Already in the guide? Yes ❑ No ❑

Address: ________

Comments:________

Your name:________

Your address ________

Tel: ________